Lean Architecture for Agile Software Development

James Coplien
Gertrud Bjørnvig

A John Wiley and Sons, Ltd, Publication

A catalogue record for this book is available from the British Library.

ISBN 978-0-470-68420-7

Typeset in 11/13 Palatino by Laserwords Private Limited, Chennai, India.
Printed in Great Britain by TJ International, Padstow, Cornwall

Dedication

To Trygve Mikkjel Heyerdahl Reenskaug, also a grandfather

Publisher's Acknowledgments

Some of the people who helped bring this book to market include the following:

Editorial and Production
VP Consumer and Technology Publishing Director: Michelle Leete
Associate Director – Book Content Management: Martin Tribe
Associate Publisher: Chris Webb
Executive Commissioning Editor: Birgit Gruber
Assistant Editor: Colleen Goldring
Publishing Assistant: Ellie Scott
Project Editor: Juliet Booker
Content Editor: Nicole Burnett
Copy Editor: Richard Walshe

Marketing:
Senior Marketing Manager: Louise Breinholt
Marketing Executive: Kate Batchelor

Composition Services:
Compositor: Laserwords Private Limited, Chennai, India
Proof Reader: Alex Grey
Indexer: Annette Musker

Contents

About the Authors

Gertrud Bjørnvig is an agile requirements expert with over 20 years' experience in system development. She is a co-founder of the Danish Agile User Group and is a partner in Scrum Training Institute.

Jim Coplien is a software industry pioneer in object-oriented design, architecture patterns, and agile software development. He has authored several books on software design and agile software development, and is a partner in the Scrum Training Institute.

Preface

What my grandfather did was create options. He worked hard to allow my father to have a better education than he did, and in turn my father did the same.

Danny Hillis, quoted in *The Clock of the Long Now***, p. 152.**

Harry Grinnell, who was co-author James Coplien's grandfather, was a life-long postal worker, but many of his life's accomplishments can be found in his avocations. His father was an alcoholic and his mother a long-suffering religious woman. Grandpa Harry dropped out of school after eighth year to take a job in a coal yard to put food on the table after much of the family budget had gone to support his father's habit. Harry would go on to take up a job as a postal worker in 1925 at the age of 19, and married Jim's grandmother the next year. He faced the changes of the Great Depression, of two world wars, and of great economic and social change.

You're probably wondering why an Agile book starts with a story about Grandpa Harry. It's because his avocation as a master craftsman in woodworking together with his common-sense approach to life offer a fitting metaphor for the Agile and Lean styles of development. This is a book about common sense. Of course, one person's common sense is another one's revelation. If you are just learning about Agile and Lean, or are familiar only with their pop versions, you may find new insights here. Even if you know about Agile and Lean and are familiar with architecture, you're likely to learn from this book about how the two ideas can work and play together.

As a postal employee, Grandpa Harry of course worked to assure that the post office met its business objectives. He worked in the days when the U.S. postal service was still nationalized; the competition of UPS and DHL didn't threaten postal business until late in his career. Therefore, the focus of his work wasn't as much on business results and profit as it was on quality and individual customer service. Grandpa Harry was a rural mail carrier who delivered to rural Wisconsin farmers, one mailbox at a time, six days a week, come rain or shine. It wasn't unusual for him to encounter a half-meter of snow, or snow drifts two meters high on his daily rounds. Flooded creek valleys might isolate a farm, but that could be no obstacle. He delivered mail in his rugged four-wheel drive Willys Jeep that he bought as an Army surplus bargain after World War II. He outfitted it with a snowplow in the winter, often plowing his way to customers' mailboxes.

There are many good parallels between Grandpa Harry's approach to life and the ideals of Lean and Agile today. You need close contact with your customer and have to earn the trust of your customer for Agile to work. It's not about us-and-them as typified by contracts and negotiation; such was not part of Grandpa Harry's job, and it's not the job of a modern software craftsperson in an Agile setting. The focus is on the end user. In Grandpa Harry's case, that end user was the child receiving a birthday card from a relative thousands of miles away, or a soldier in Viet Nam receiving a care package from home after it being entrusted to the United States Postal Service for dispatching to its destination, or the flurry of warm greetings around the Christmas holidays. The business entity in the middle – in Grandpa Harry's case, the U.S. Postal Service, and in our case, our *customers* – tend to become transparent in the light of the *end users'* interests. Customers care about the software CD as a means for profit; end users have a stake in those products' use cases to ensure some measure of day-to-day support of their workflow.

To say this is neither to deny customers a place, nor to infer that our employers' interests should be sacrificed to those of our ultimate clientele. A well-considered system keeps evolving so *everybody* wins. What Grandpa Harry worked for was called the postal *system*: it was really a system, characterized by systems thinking and a concern for the whole. So, yes, the end user was paramount, but the system understood that a good post office working environment and happy postal workers were an important means to the end of user satisfaction. Postal workers were treated fairly in work conditions and pay; exceptions were so unusual that they made the news. In the same sense, the Agile environment is attentive to the needs of the programmer, the analyst, the usability engineer, the manager, and the funders. Tools such as architectural articulation, good requirements management, and lean minimalism improve the quality of life for the production side too. That is important because it supports the business goals. It is imperative because, on a human scale, it is a scandal to sacrifice development staff comfort to end user comfort.

Life in Grandpa Harry's time was maybe simpler than it is today, but many of the concepts of Lean and Agile are simple ideas that hearken back to that era. Just because things are simple doesn't mean they are simplistic. The modern philosopher Thomas Moore asks us to "live simply, but be complicated" (Moore 2001, p. 9). He notes that when Thoreau went to Walden Pond, his thoughts became richer and more complicated the simpler his environment became. To work at this level is to begin to experience the kinds of generative processes we find in nature. Great things can arise from the interactions of a few simple principles. The key, of course, is to find those simple principles.

Grandpa Harry was not much one for convention. He was a doer, but thinking backed his doing. In this book, we'll certainly relate practices and techniques from 15 years of positive experiences together with software partners worldwide. But don't take our word for it. This is as much a book about thinking as about doing, much as the Agile tradition (and the Agile Manifesto itself (Beck et al 2001)) is largely about doing, and the Lean concepts from the Toyota tradition relate more to planning and thinking (Liker 2004, ff. 237). These notions of thinking are among the lost practices of Agile. Agile perhaps lost this focus on thinking and product in its eagerness to shed the process-heavy focus of the methodology-polluted age of the 1980s.

Grandpa Harry's life is also a reminder that we should value timeless domain knowledge. Extreme Programming (XP) started out in part by consciously trying to do exactly the opposite of what conventional wisdom recommended, and in part by limiting itself to small-scale software development. Over time, we have come full circle, and many of the old practices are being restored, even in the halls and canon of Agiledom. System testing is now "in," as is up-front architecture – even in XP (Beck 1999, p. 113, 2005, p. 28). We're starting to recover insights from past generations of system development that perhaps we didn't even appreciate at the time; if we did, we've forgotten. Many of these "old" ideas such as architecture and planning, and even some of the newer ideas such as use cases that have fallen into disfavor, deserve a second look. We find many of these ideas re-surfacing under different names anyhow in today's Agile world: architecture reappears as metaphor, and use cases reappear as the collections of user story cards and supplementary constraint and testing cards that go with them (Cohn 2004), or as the requirement structuring we find in story maps (Patton 2009).

The domain knowledge in this book goes beyond standing on our tiptoes to standing on the shoulders of giants. We have let our minds be sharpened by people who have earned broad respect in the industry – and double that amount of respect from us – from Larry Constantine and David Parnas to Jeff Sutherland and Alistair Cockburn. We also draw on our own experience in software development going back to our first hobby programs in the 1960s, and our software careers going back to the early 1970s (Coplien) and 1980s (Bjørnvig). We draw lightly on Coplien's more recent book together with Neil Harrison, *Organizational Patterns of Agile Software Development* (Coplien and Harrison 2004), which stands on ten years of careful research into software development organizations worldwide. Its findings stand as the foundations of the Agile discipline, having been the inspiration for stand-up meetings in the popular Scrum product management framework (Sutherland 2003, 2007), and of much of the structural component of XP (Fraser et al 2003). Whereas the previous book focused on the organizational with an eye to the technical, this one focuses on the technical with an eye to the organizational. Nerds: enjoy!

As long as we have you thinking, we want you thinking about issues of lasting significance to your work, your enterprise, and the world we as software craftsmen and craftswomen serve. If we offer a technique, it's because we think it's important enough that you'd notice the difference in the outcome of projects that use it and those that don't. We won't recommend exactly what incantation of words you should use in a user story. We won't bore you with whether to draw class diagrams bottom-up or top-down nor, in fact, whether to draw diagrams at all. We won't try to indoctrinate you with programming language arguments – since the choice of programming language has rarely been found to matter in any broadly significant way. As we know from Agile and Lean thinking, people and values matter most, and bring us to ideals such as *caring*. The byline on the book's cover, *Software as if people mattered*, is a free re-translation of the title of Larry Constantine's keynote that Coplien invited him to give at OOPSLA in 1996. People are ultimately the focus of all software, and it's time that we show enough evidence to convict us of honoring that focus. We will dare use the phrase "common sense," as uncommon as its practice is. We try to emphasize things that matter – concrete things, nonetheless.

There is a subtext to this book for which Grandpa Harry is a symbol: valuing timelessness. In our software journey the past 40 years we have noticed an ever-deepening erosion of concern for the long game in software. This book is about returning to the long game. However, this may be a sobering concern as much for society in general as it is for our relatively myopic view of software. To help drive home this perspective we've taken inspiration from the extended broadside *The Clock of the Long Now* (Brand 1999), which is inspired in no small part by software greats including Mitchell Kapoor and Daniel Hillis. The manuscript is sprinkled with small outtakes from the book, such as this one:

> What we can do is convert the design of software from brittle to resilient, from heedlessly headlong to responsible, and from time corrupted to time embracing. (Brand 1999, p. 86)

These outtakes are short departures from the book's (hopefully practical) focus on architecture and design that raise the principles to levels of social relevance. They are brief interludes to inspire discussions around dinner and reflection during a walk in the woods. We offer them neither to preach at you nor to frighten you, but to help contextualize the humble software-focused theses of this book in a bigger picture.

We've worked with quite a few great men and women to develop and refine the ideas in this book. It has been an honor sparring with Trygve Reenskaug about his DCI (Data, Context and Interaction) architecture, learning much from him and occasionally scoring an insight. We have also traded many notes with Richard Öberg, whose Qi4j ideas echo many aspects of DCI, and it has been fun as we've built on each other's work.

We've also built on the work of many people who started coding up DCI examples after a presentation at JaOO in 2008: Serge Beaumont at Xebia (Python), Ceasario Ramos (who thoroughly explored the Java space), Jesper Rugård Jensen (ditto), Lars Vonk (in Groovy), David Byers (also in Python), Anders Narwath (JavaScript), Unmesh Joshi (AspectJ), Bill Venners (Scala, of course), and Christian Horsdal Gammelgaard of Mjølner (C#/.Net). Many examples in this book build on Steen Lehmann's exploration of DCI in Ruby. We, and the entire computing community, should be ever grateful to all of these folks.

We appreciate all the good folks who've devoted some of their hours to reading and reflecting on our early manuscripts. Trygve, again, offered many useful suggestions and his ideas on the manuscript itself have helped us clarify and sharpen the exposition of DCI. It goes without saying that the many hours we spent with Trygve discussing DCI, even apart from any focus on this book, were memorable times. Trygve stands almost as a silent co-author of this book, and we are ever indebted to him and to his wife Bjørg for many hours of stimulating discussion. Thanks, Trygve!

We are also indebted to Rebecca Wirfs-Brock for good discussions about use cases, for clarifying the historical context behind them, for confirming many of our hunches, and for straightening out others.

We owe special thanks to Lars Fogtmann Sønderskov for a detailed review of an early version of the manuscript. His considerable experience in Lean challenged our own thinking and pushed us to review and re-think some topics in the book. Brett Schuchert, who was a treasured reviewer for *Advanced C++* 20 years ago, again treated us to a tough scouring of the manuscript. Thanks, Brett! Thanks also to our other official reviewer, the renowned software architect Philippe Kruchten, who helped us make some valuable connections to other broadly related work. Atzmon Hen-tov not only found many small mistakes but also helped us frame the big picture, and his comments clearly brought years of hard-won insights from his long journey as a software architect. Thanks to the many other reviewers who scoured the manuscript and helped us to polish it: Roy Ben Hayun, Dennis L DeBruler, Dave Byers, Viktor Grgic, Neil Harrison, Bojan Jovičić, Urvashi Kaul, Steen Lehmann, Dennis Mancl, Simon Michael, Sandra Raffle Carrico, Jeppe Kilberg Møller, Rune Funch Søltoft, Mikko

Suonio, and Lena Nikolaev. Many ideas came up in discussions at the Agile Architecture course in Käpylä, Finland, in October 2008: Aleksi Ahtiainen, Aki Kolehmainen, Heimo Laukkanen, Mika Leivo, Ari Tikka, and Tomi Tuominen all contributed mightily. Thanks, too, to James Noble, Peter Bunus, and John McGregor for their evaluations of the book proposal in its formative days and for their encouragement and feedback.

A big thanks to Paul Mitchell Design, Ltd., for a great job working with us on the book cover design. Claire Spinks took on the unenviable job of copy editing and helped us polish up the manuscript. And, of course, many thanks to Birgit Gruber, our editor, and to Ellie Scott, who oversaw much of the editorial hand-holding during the book's formative years.

Thanks to Magnus Palmgård of Tobo, Sweden for providing a lovely venue for several months of thoughtful reflection and writing.

We appreciate the pioneers who have gone before us and who have influenced the way we look at the world and how we keep learning about it. Phillip Fuhrer lent useful insights on problem definition. We had thoughtful E-mail conversations with Larry Constantine, and it was a pleasure to again interact with him and gain insight on coupling and cohesion from a historical context. Some of his timeless ideas on coupling, cohesion, and even Conway's Law (which he named) are coming back into vogue. Nathanael Schärli, Stéphane Ducasse, Oscar Nierstrasz, Andrew Black, Roel Wuyts and others laid the foundations for traits. Trygve Reenskaug, Jeff Sutherland, Alistair Cockburn, Jerry Weinberg, and hundreds of others have all led us here. So, of course, has Grandpa Harry.

Introduction

We are changing the Earth more rapidly than we are understanding it.
– Peter Vitousek et al. quoted in *The Clock of the Long Now*, p. 9.

A proper book isn't just a collection of facts or even of practices: it reflects a cause and a mission. In the preface we couched this book in a broad context of social responsibility. Just as the motivation section (goal in context, summary, or whatever else you call it) in a use case helps the analyst understand requirements scenarios, this chapter might shed light on the ones that follow. It describes our philosophy behind the book and the way we present the ideas to you. If you're tempted to jump to a whirlwind tour of the book's contents, you might proceed to Chapter 2. However, philosophy is as important as the techniques themselves in a Lean and Agile world. We suggest you read through the introduction at least once, and tuck it away in your memory as background material for the other chapters that will support your day-to-day work.

1.1   The Touchstones: Lean and Agile

Lean and Agile are among the most endearing buzzwords in software today, capturing the imagination of management and nerds alike. Popular management books of the 1990s (Womack et al 1991) coined the term *Lean* for the management culture popularized by the Japanese auto industry, and which can be traced back to Toyota where it is called The Toyota Way. In vernacular English, *minimal* is an obvious synonym for *Lean*, but to link lean to minimalism alone is misleading.

Lean's primary focus is the enterprise value stream. Lean grabs the consumer world and pulls it through the value stream to the beginnings of development, so that every subsequent activity adds value. Waste in production reduces value; constant improvement increases value. In Western cultures managers often interpret Lean in terms of its production practices: just-in-time, end-to-end continuous flow, and reduction of inventory. But its real heart is The Lean Secret: an "all hands on deck" mentality that permeates every employee, every manager, every supplier, and every partner. Whereas the Agile manifesto emphasizes customers, Lean emphasizes stakeholders – with everybody in sight being a stakeholder.

Lean architecture and Agile feature development aren't about working harder. They're not about working "smarter" in the academic or traditional computer science senses of the word "smart." They are much more about focus and discipline, supported by common-sense arguments that require no university degree or formal training. This focus and discipline shines through in the roots of Lean management and in many of the Agile values.

We can bring that management and development style to software development. In this book, we bring it to software architecture in particular. Architecture is the big-picture view of the system, keeping in mind that the best big pictures need not be grainy. We don't feel a need to nail down a scientific definition of the term; there are too many credible definitions to pick just one. For what it's worth, the IEEE defines it this way:

> . . . The fundamental organization of a system embodied in its components, their relationships to each other, and to the environment and the principles guiding its design and evolution. (IEEE1471 2007)

Grady Booch gives us this simple definition:

> Architecture represents the significant design decisions that shape a system, where *significant* is measured by cost of change. (Booch 2006)

That isn't too bad. But more generally, we define architecture as the *form* of a system, where the word *form* has a special meaning that we'll explore a bit later. For now, think of it as relating to the first three components of the IEEE definition. No matter how we care to define it, software architecture should support the enterprise value stream even to the extent that the source code itself should reflect the end user mental model of the world. We will deliver code just in time instead of stockpiling software library warehouses ahead of time. We strive towards the practice of continuous flow.

Each of these practices is a keystone of Lean. But at the heart of Lean architecture is the team: the "all hands on deck" mentality that everyone is in some small part an architect, and that everyone has a crucial role to play in good project beginnings. We want the domain experts (sometimes called the architects) present as the architecture takes shape, of course. However, the customer, the developer, the testers, and the managers should also be fully present at those beginnings.

This may sound wasteful and may create a picture of chaotic beginnings. However, one of the great paradoxes of Lean is that such intensity at the beginning of a project, with heavy iteration and rework in design, actually reduces overall life cycle cost and improves product quality. Apply those principles to software, and you have a lightweight up-front architecture. *Lightweight* means that we reduce the waste incurred by rework (from inadequate planning), unused artifacts (such as comprehensive documentation and speculative code), and wait states (as can be caused by the review life cycle of architecture and design documents, or by handoffs between functional teams).

Software folks form a tribe of sorts (Nani 2006) that holds many beliefs, among them that architecture is *hard*. The perception comes in part from architecture's need for diverse talents working together, compounded by the apparently paradoxical need to find the basic form of something that is essentially complex. Even more important, people confuse "takes a long time" with "hard." That belief in turn derives from our belief in specialization, which becomes the source of handoffs: the source of the delays that accumulate into long intervals that makes architecture look hard. We tend to gauge our individual uncertainty and limited experience in assessing the difficulty of design, and we come up short, feeling awkward and small rather than collaborative and powerful. Architecture requires a finesse and balance that dodges most silver bullets. Much of that finesse comes with the Lean Secret: the takes-a-long-time part of *hard* becomes softer when you unite specialists together in one room: *everybody, all together, from early on*. We choose to view *that* as hard because, well, that's how it's always been, and perhaps because we believe in individuals first and interactions second.

Neither Lean nor Agile alone make architecture look easy. However, architecture needn't be intrinsically hard. Lean and Agile together illuminate architecture's value. Lean brings careful up-front planning and "everybody, all together, from early on" to the table, and Agile teaches or reminds us about feedback. Together they illuminate architecture's value: Lean, for how architecture can reduce waste, inconsistency, and irregular development; and Agile, for how end user engagement and feedback can drive down long-term cost. Putting up a new barn is hard, too. As Grandpa Harry used to say, many hands make light work, and a 19th-century American farm neighborhood could raise a new barn in a couple of days. So can a cross-functional team greatly compress the time, and therefore the apparent difficulty, of creating a solid software architecture.

Another key Lean principle is to focus on long-term results (Liker 2004, pp. 71–84). Lean architecture is about doing what's important *now* that will keep you in the game for the long term. It is nonetheless important to contrast the Lean approach with traditional approaches such as "investing for the future." Traditional software architecture reflects an investment model. It capitalizes on heavyweight artifacts in software inventory and directs cash flow into activities that are difficult to place in the customer value stream. An industry survey of projects with ostensibly high failure rates (as noted in Glass (2006), which posits that the results of the Standish survey may be rooted in characteristically dysfunctional projects) found that 70% of the software they build is never used (Standish Group 1995).

Lean architecture carefully slices the design space to deliver exactly the artifacts that can support downstream development in the long term. It avoids wasteful coding that can better be written just after demand for it appears and just before it generates revenues in the market. From the programmer's perspective, it provides a way to capture crucial design concepts and decisions that must be remembered throughout feature production. These decisions are captured in code that is delivered as part of the product, not as extraneous baggage that becomes irrelevant over time.

With such Lean foundations in place, a project can better support Agile principles and aspire to Agile ideals. If you have all hands on deck, you depend more on people and interactions than on processes and tools. If you have a value stream that drives you without too many intervening tools and processes, you have customer engagement. If we reflect the end user mental model in the code, we are more likely to have working software. And if the code captures the form of the domain in an uncluttered way, we can confidently make the changes that make the code serve end user wants and needs.

This book is about a Lean approach to domain architecture that lays a foundation for Agile software change. The planning values of Lean do not conflict with the inspect-and-adapt principles of Agile: allocated to the proper development activities, each supports the other in the broader framework of development. We'll revisit that contrast in a little while (Section 1.4), but first, let's investigate each of Lean Architecture and Agile Production in more detail.

1.2   Lean Architecture and Agile Feature Development

The Agile Manifesto (Beck et al 2001) defines the principles that underlie the Agile vision, and the Toyota Way (Liker 2004) defines the Lean vision. This book offers a vision of architecture in an organization that embraces these two sets of ideals. The Lean perspective focuses on how we develop the overall system form by drawing on experience and domain knowledge. The Agile perspective focuses on how that informed form helps us respond to change, and sometimes even to plan for it. How does that vision differ from the classic, heavyweight architectural practices that dominated object-oriented development in the 1980s? We summarize the differences in Table 1-1.

Table 1-1 What is Lean Architecture?

Lean Architecture	Classic Software Architecture
Defers engineering	Includes engineering
Gives the craftsman "wiggle room" for change	Tries to limit large changes as "dangerous" (fear change?)
Defers implementation (delivers lightweight APIs and descriptions of relationships)	Includes much implementation (platforms, libraries) or none at all (documentation only)
Lightweight documentation	Documentation-focused, to describe the implementation or compensate for its absence
People	Tools and notations
Collective planning and cooperation	Specialized planning and control
End user mental model	Technical coupling and cohesion

- Classic software architecture tends to embrace engineering concerns too strongly and too early. Agile architecture is about form, and while a system must obey the same laws that apply to engineering when dealing with form, we let form follow proven experience instead of being driven by supposedly scientific engineering rationales. Those will come soon enough.

- This in turn implies that the everyday developers should use their experience to tailor the system form as new requirements emerge and as they grow in understanding. Neither Agile nor Lean gives coders wholesale license to ravage the system form, but both honor the value of adaptation. Classic architecture tends to be fearful of large changes, so it focuses on incremental changes only to existing artifacts: adding a new derived class is not a transformation of form (architecture), but of structure (implementation). In our combined Lean/Agile approach, we reduce risk by capturing domain architecture, or basic system form, in a low-overhead way. Furthermore, the architecture encourages *new* forms in those parts of the system that are likely to change the most. Because these forms aren't pre-filled with premature structure, they provide less impedance to change than traditional approaches. This is another argument for a true architecture of the forms of domain knowledge and function rather than an architecture based on structure.

- Classic software architecture sometimes rushes into implementation to force code reuse to happen or standards to prevail. Lean architecture also adopts the perspective that standards are valuable, but again: at the level of form, protocols, and APIs, rather than their implementation.

- Some classic approaches to software architecture too often depend on, or at least produce, volumes of documentation at high cost. The documentation either describes "reusable" platforms in excruciating detail or compensates for the lack of a clarifying implementation. Architects often throw such documentation over the wall into developers' cubicles, where it less often used than not. Agile emphasizes communication, and sometimes written documentation is the right medium. However, we will strive to document only the stuff that really matters, and we'll communicate many decisions in code. That kills two birds with one stone. The rest of the time, it's about getting everybody involved face-to-face.

- Classic architectures too often focus on methods, rules, tools, formalisms, and notations. Use them if you must. But we won't talk much about those in this book. Instead, we'll talk about valuing individuals and their domain expertise, and valuing the end-user experience and their mental models that unfold during analysis.

- Both Lean and classic architecture focus on long-term results, but they differ in how planning is valued. Even worse than heavy planning is a prescription to follow the plan. Lean focuses on what's important now, whenever "now" is – whether that is hitting the target for next week's delivery or doing long-term planning. It isn't only to eliminate waste by avoiding what is *never* important (dead code and unread documents), but has a subtler timeliness. Architecture isn't an excuse to defer work; on the contrary, it should be a motivation to embrace implementation as soon as decisions are made. We make decisions and produce artifacts at the most responsible times.

As we describe it in this book, Lean architecture provides a firm foundation for the ongoing business of a software enterprise: providing timely features to end users.

1.3   Agile Production

If your design is lean, it produces an architecture that can help you be more Agile. By Agile, we mean the values held up by the Agile Manifesto:

We are uncovering better ways of developing software by doing it and helping others do it. Through this work we have come to value:

Individuals and interactions over processes and tools

Working software over comprehensive documentation

Customer collaboration over contract negotiation

Responding to change over following a plan

That is, while there is value in the items on the right, we value the items on the left more. (Beck et al 2001)

1.3.1   Agile Builds on Lean

Just as with the "all hands on deck" approach of Lean, Agile development also embraces close person-to-person contact, particularly with the clients. Unlike the tendencies of Lean, or much of today's software architecture, our vision of Agile production plans for change. Lean architecture provides a context, a vocabulary, and productive constraints that make change easier and perhaps a little bit more failure-proof. It makes explicit a value stream along which stakeholder changes can propagate without being lost. We can respond to market whims. And we love market whims – because that's how we provide satisfaction and keep the enterprise profitable.

Agile production not only builds on a Lean domain architecture, but it stays Lean with its focus on code – working software. The code is the design. No, *really*. The code is the best way to capture the end user mental models in a form suitable to the shaping and problem solving that occur during design. We of course also need other design representations that close the feedback loop to the end user and other stakeholders for whom code is an unsuitable medium, so lightweight documentation may be in order – we'll introduce that topic in Section 1.6.4. We take this concept beyond platitudes, always striving to capture the end-user model of program execution in the code.

Classic architectures focus on what doesn't change, believing that foundations based on domain knowledge reduce the cost of change. Agile understands that nothing lasts forever, and it instead focuses explicitly on what is likely to change. Here we balance the two approaches, giving neither one the upper hand.

Lean also builds on concepts that most people hold to be fundamental to Agile. The Lean notion of value streams starting with end users recalls individual and interactions as well as customer focus. The Lean notion of reduced waste goes hand-in-hand with Agile's view of documentation. It is not about Lean versus Agile and neither about building Lean on top of Agile nor Agile on top of Lean. Each one is a valuable perspective into the kind of systems thinking necessary to repeatedly deliver timely products with quality.

1.3.2   The Scope of Agile Systems

Electronically accelerated market economies have swept the world for good reasons. They are grass-roots driven (by customers and entrepreneurs), swiftly adaptive, and highly rewarding.
The Clock of the Long Now, p. 25.

Software architects who were raised in the practices and experience of software architecture of the 1970s and 1980s will find much comfort in the Lean parts of this book, but may find themselves in new territory as they move into the concepts of Agile production. Architecture has long focused on stability while Agile focuses on change. Agile folks can learn from the experience of previous generations of software architecture in how they *plan* for change. As we present a new generation of architectural ideas in this book, we respond to change more directly, teasing out the form even of those parts of software we usually hold to be dynamic. We'll employ use cases to distill the stable backbones of system behavior from dozens or hundreds of variations. We go further to tease out the common rhythms of system behavior into the roles that are the basic concepts we use to describe it and the connections between them.

Grandpa Harry used to say that necessity is the mother of invention, so need and user *expectation* are perhaps the mother and father of change. People expect software to be able to change at lightening speed in modern markets. On the web, in financial services and trading, and in many other market segments, the time constants are on the order of hours or days. The users themselves interact with the software on time scales driven by interactive menus and screens rather than by daily batch runs. Instead of being able to stack the program input on punched cards ahead of time, decisions about the next text input or the next menu selection are made seconds or even milliseconds before the program must respond to them.

Agile software development is well suited to such environments because of its accommodation for change. Agile is less well suited to environments where feedback is either of little value (such as the development of a protocol based on a fully formal specification and development process) or is difficult to get (such as from software that is so far embedded in other systems that it has no obvious interaction with individuals). Libraries and platforms often fall into this category: how do you create short feedback loops that can steer their design? Sometimes a system is so constrained by its environment that prospects for change are small, and Agile approaches may not help much.

Lean likewise shines in some areas better than others. It's overkill for simple products. While Lean can deal with *complicated* products, it needs innovation from Agile to deal with *complex* products where we take *complicated* and *complex* in Snowden's (Snowden 2009) terms. Complicated systems can rely on fact-based management and can handle known unknowns, but only with expert diagnosis. Complex systems have unknown unknowns, and there is no predictable path from the current state to a better state (though such paths can be rationalized in retrospect). There are no right answers, but patterns emerge over time. Most of the organizational patterns cited in this book relate to complex problems. Even in dealing with complex systems, Agile can draw on Lean techniques to establish the boundary conditions necessary for progress.

The good news is that most systems have both a Lean component and an Agile component. For example, embedded or deeply layered system software can benefit from domain experience and the kind of thorough analysis characteristic of Lean, while other software components that interact with people can benefit from Agile.

Below the realm of Lean and Agile lie *simple* systems, which are largely knowable and predictable, so we can succeed even if our efforts fall short of both Lean and Agile. On the other end are *chaotic* system problems such as dealing with a mass system outage. There, even patterns are difficult to find. It is important to act quickly and to just find something that works rather than seeking the right answer. Chaotic systems are outside the scope of our work here.

1.3.3 Agile and DCI

If we can directly capture key end-user mental models in the code, it radically increases the chances the code will work. The fulfillment of this dream has long eluded the object-oriented programming community, but the recent work on the Data, Context and Interaction (DCI) architecture, featured in Chapter 9, brings this dream much closer to reality than we have ever realized. And by "work" we don't mean that it passes tests or that the green bar comes up: we mean that it does what the user *expects* it to do.[1] The key is the architectural link between the end user mental model and the code itself.

1.4 The Book in a Very Small Nutshell

We'll provide a bit meatier overview in Chapter 2, but here is the one-page (and a bit more) summary of the technical goodies in the book, for you nerds reading the introduction:

- System architecture should reflect the end users' mental model of their world. This model has two parts. The first part relates to the user's thought process when viewing the screen, and to what the system *is*: its *form*. The second part relates to what end users *do* – interacting with the system – and how the system should respond to user input. This is the system *functionality*. We work with users to elicit and develop these models and to capture them in code as early as possible. Coupling and cohesion (Stevens, Myers, and Constantine 1974) follow from these as a secondary effect.

- To explore both form and function requires up-front engagement of all stakeholders, and early exploration of their insights. Deferring interactions with stakeholders, or deferring decisions beyond the responsible moment slows progress, raises cost, and increases frustration. A team acts like a team from the start.

- Programming languages help us to concretely express form in the code. For example, abstract base classes can concretely express domain models. Development teams can build such models in about one Scrum Sprint: a couple of weeks to a month. Design-by-contract, used well, gets us closer to running code even faster. Going beyond this expression of *form* with too much *structure* (such as class implementation) is not Lean, slows things down, and leads to rework.

- We can express complex system functionality in use cases. Lightweight, incrementally constructed use cases help the project to quickly capture and iterate models of interaction between the end user (actor) and the system, and to structure the relationships between scenarios.

---

[1] What users really *expect* has been destroyed by the legacy of the past 40 years of software deployment. It's really hard to find out what they actually *need*, and what they *want* too often reflects short-term end-user thinking. Our goal is to avoid the rule of least surprise: we don't want end users to feel unproductive, or to feel that the system implementers didn't understand their needs, or to feel that system implementers feel that they are stupid. Much of this discussion is beyond the scope of this book, though we will touch on it from time to time.

By making requirement dependencies explicit, use cases avoid dependency management and communication problems that are common in complex Agile projects. Simpler documents like User Narratives are still good enough to capture simple functional requirements.

- We can translate use case scenarios into algorithms, just in time, as new scenarios enter the business process. We encode these algorithms directly as *role methods*. We will introduce *roles* (implemented as role classes or *traits*) as a new formalism that captures the behavioral essence of a system in the same way that classes capture the essence of domain structure. Algorithms that come from use cases are more or less directly readable from the role methods. Their form follows function. This has profound implications for code comprehension, testability, and formal analysis. At the same time, we create or update classes in the domain model to support the new functionality. These classes stay fairly dumb, with the end-user scenario information separated into the role classes.

- We use a recent adaptation of traits to glue together role classes with the domain classes. When a use case scenario is enacted at run time, the system maps the use case actors into the objects that will support the scenario (through the appropriate role interface), and the scenario runs.

Got your attention? It gets even better. Read on.

1.5 Lean and Agile: Contrasting and Complementary

You should now have a basic idea of where we're heading. Let's more carefully consider Agile and Lean, and their relationships to each other and to the topic of software design.

One unsung strength of Agile is that it is more focused on the ongoing sustenance of a project than just its beginnings. The waterfall stereotype is patterned around greenfield development. It doesn't easily accommodate the constraints of any embedded base to which the new software must fit, nor does it explicitly provide for future changes in requirements, nor does it project what happens after the first delivery. But Agile sometimes doesn't focus enough on the beginnings, on the long deliberation that supports long-term profitability, or on enabling standards. Both Lean and Agile are eager to remove defects as they arise. Too many stereotypes of Lean and Agile ignore both the synergies and potential conflicts between Lean and Agile. Let's explore this overlap a bit.

Architects use notations to capture their vision of an ideal system at the beginning of the life cycle, but these documents and visions quickly become out-of-date and become increasingly irrelevant over time. If we constantly refresh the architecture in cyclic development, and if we express the architecture in living code, then we'll be working with an Agile spirit. Yes, we'll talk about architectural beginnings, but the right way to view software development is that everything after the first successful compilation is maintenance.

Lean is often cited as a foundation of Agile, or as a cousin of Agile, or today as a foundation of some Agile technique and tomorrow not. There is much confusion and curiosity about such questions in software today. Scrum inventor Jeff Sutherland refers to Lean and Scrum as separate and complementary developments that both arose from observations about complex adaptive systems (Sutherland 2008). Indeed, in some places Lean principles and Agile principles tug in different directions. The Toyota Way is based explicitly on standardization (Liker 2004, chapter 12); Scrum says always to inspect and adapt. The Toyota Way is based on long deliberation and thought, with rapid deployment only *after* a decision has been reached (Liker 2004, chapter 19); most Agile practice is based on rapid *decisions* (Table 1-2).

Table 1-2   Contrast between Lean and Agile.

Lean	Agile
Thinking and doing	Doing
Inspect-plan-do	Do-inspect-adapt
Feed-forward and feedback (design for change and respond to change)	Feedback (react to change)
High throughput	Low latency
Planning and responding	Reacting
Focus on Process	Focus on People
Teams (working as a unit)	Individuals (and interactions)
Complicated systems	Complex systems
Embrace standards	Inspect and adapt
Rework in design adds value, in making is waste	Minimize up-front work of any kind and rework code to get quality
Bring decisions forward (Decision Structure Matrices)	Defer decisions (to the last responsible moment)

Some of the disconnect between Agile and Lean comes not from their foundations but from common misunderstanding and from everyday pragmatics. Many people believe that Scrum insists that there be no specialists on the team; however, Lean treasures both seeing the whole as well as specialization:

> [W]hen Toyota selects one person out of hundreds of job applicants after searching for many months, it is sending a message – the capabilities and characteristics of individuals matter. The years spent carefully grooming each individual to develop depth of technical knowledge, a broad range of skills, and a second-nature understanding of Toyota's philosophy speaks to the importance of the individual in Toyota's system. (Liker 2004, p. 186)

Scrum insists on cross-functional team, but itself says nothing about specialization. The specialization myth arises in part from the XP legacy that discourages specialization and code ownership, and in part from the Scrum practice that no one use their specialization as an excuse to avoid other kind of work during a Sprint (Østergaard 2008).

If we were to look at Lean and Agile through a coarse lens, we'd discover that Agile is about *doing* and that Lean is about *thinking* (about continuous process improvement) *and* doing. A little bit of thought can avoid a lot of doing, and in particular *re*-doing. Ballard (2000) points out that a little rework and thought in design adds value by reducing product turn-around time and cost, while rework during making is waste (Section 3.1.2). System-level-factoring entails a bit of both, but regarding architecture only as an emergent view of the system substantially slows the decision process. Software isn't soft, and architectures aren't very malleable once developers start filling in the general *form* with the *structure* of running code. Lean architecture moves beyond structure to form. Good form is Lean, and that helps the system be Agile.

Lean is about complicated things; Agile is about complexity. Lean principles support predictable, repeatable processes, such as automobile manufacturing. Software is hardly predictable, and is almost always a creative – one might say artistic – endeavor (Snowden and Boone 2007). Agile is the art of the possible, and of expecting the unexpected.

This book tells how to craft a Lean architecture that goes hand-in-glove with Agile development. Think of Lean techniques, or a Lean architecture, as a filter that prevents problems from finding a way into your development stream. Keeping those problems out avoids rework.

Lean principles lie at the heart of architectures behind Agile projects. Agile is about embracing change, and it's hard to reshape a system if there is too much clutter. Standards can reduce decision time and can reduce work and rework. Grandpa Harry used to say that a stitch in time saves nine; so up-front thinking can empower decision makers to implement decisions lightening-fast with confidence and authority. Lean architecture should be rooted in the thought processes of good domain analysis, in the specialization of deeply knowledgeable domain experts, and once in a while on de facto, community, or international standards.

1.5.1   The Lean Secret

The human side of Lean comes down to this rule of thumb:

Everybody, All together, Early On

Using other words, we also call this "all hands on deck." Why is this a "secret"? Because it seems that teams that call themselves Agile either don't know it or embrace it only in part. Too often, the "lazy" side of Lean shines through (avoiding excess work) while teams set aside elements of social discipline and process. Keeping the "everybody" part secret lets us get by with talking to the customer, which has some stature associated with it, while diminishing focus on other stakeholders like maintenance, investors, sales, and the business. Keeping the "early on" part a secret makes it possible to defer decisions – and to decide to defer a decision is itself a decision with consequences. Yet all three of these elements are crucial to the human foundations of Lean. We'll explore the Lean Secret in more depth in Chapter 3.

1.6   Lost Practices

> *We speak . . . about the events of decades now, not centuries. One advantage of that, perhaps, is that the acceleration of history now makes us all historians.*
> **The Clock of the Long Now, p. 16.**

As we distilled our experience into the beginnings of this book, both of us started to feel a bit uncomfortable and even a little guilty about being old folks in an industry we had always seen fueled by the energy of the young, the new, and the restless. As people from the patterns, Lean and object communities started interacting more with the new Agile community, however, we found that we were in good company. Agile might be the first major software movement that has come about as a broad-based mature set of disciplines.

Nonetheless, as Agile rolled out into the industry the ties back to experience were often lost. That Scrum strived to remain agnostic with respect to software didn't help, so crucial software practices necessary to Scrum's success were too easily forgotten. In this book we go back to the fundamental notions that are often lost in modern interpretation or in the practice of XP or Scrum. These include system and software architecture, requirements dependency management, foundations for usability, documentation, and others.

1.6.1   Architecture

Electronically accelerated market economies have swept the world for good reasons. They are grass-roots driven (by customers and entrepreneurs), swiftly adaptive, and highly rewarding. But among the things they reward, as McKenna points out, is short-sightedness.
The Clock of the Long Now, p. 25.

A project must be strong to embrace change. Architecture not only helps give a project the firmness necessary to stand up to change, but also supports the crucial Agile value of communication. Jeff Sutherland has said that he never has, and never would, run a software Scrum without software architecture (Coplien and Sutherland 2009). We build for change.

We know that ignoring architecture in the long term increases long-term cost. Traditional architecture is heavily front-loaded and increases cost in the short term, but more importantly, pushes out the schedule. This is often the case because the architecture invests too much in the actual structure of implementation instead of sticking with form. A structure-free up-front architecture, constructed as pure form, can be built in days or weeks, and can lay the foundation for a system lifetime of savings. Part of the speedup comes from the elimination of wait states that comes from all-hands-on-deck, and part comes from favoring lightweight form over massive structure.

1.6.2   Handling Dependencies between Requirements

To make software work, the development team must know what other software and features lay the foundation for the work at hand. Few Agile approaches speak about the subtleties of customer engagement and end-user engagement. Without these insights, software developers are starved for the guidance they need while advising product management about product rollout. Such failures lead to customer surprises, especially when rapidly iterating new functionality into the customer stream.

Stakeholder engagement (Chapter 3) is a key consideration in requirements management. While both Scrum and XP encourage tight coupling to the customer, the word "end user" doesn't appear often enough, and the practices overlook far too many details of these business relation-ships. That's where the subtle details of requirements show up – in the dependencies between them.

1.6.3   Foundations for Usability

The Agile Manifesto speaks about working software, but nothing about usable software. The origins of Agile can be traced back to object orientation, which originally concerned itself with capturing the end-user model in the code. Trygve Reenskaug's Model-View-Controller (MVC) architecture makes this concern clear and provides us a framework to achieve usability goals. In this book we build heavily on Trygve's work, both in the classic way that MVC brings end user mental models together with the system models, and on his DCI work, which helps users enact system functionality.

1.6.4   Documentation

Suppose we wanted to improve the quality of decisions that have long-term consequences. What would make decision makers feel accountable to posterity as well as to their present constituents? What would shift the terms of debate from the immediate consequences of the delayed consequences, where the real impact is? It might help to have the debate put on the record in a way that invites serious review.
The Clock of the Long Now, p. 98.

Documentation gets a bad rap. Methodologists too often miss the point that documentation has two important functions: to *communicate* perspectives and decisions, and to *remember* perspectives and decisions. Alistair Cock-burn draws a similar dichotomy between documentation that serves as a *reminder* for people who were there when the documented discussions took place, and as a *tutorial* for those who weren't (Cockburn 2007, pp. 23–24). Much of the Agile mindset misses this dichotomy and casts aspersions on any kind of documentation. Nonetheless, the Agile manifesto contrasts the waste of documentation with the production of working code: where code can communicate or remember decisions, redundant documentation may be a waste.

The Agile manifesto fails to explicitly communicate key foundations that lie beneath its own well-known principles and values. It is change that guides the Agile process; nowhere does the Manifesto mention learning or experience. It tends to cast human interaction in the framework of code development, as contrasted with processes and tools, rather than in the framework of community-building or professional growth. Documentation has a role there.

We should distinguish the act of writing a document from the long-term maintenance of a document. A whiteboard diagram, a CRC card, and a diagram on the back of a napkin are all design documents, but they are documents that we rarely archive or return to over time. Such documentation is crucial to Agile development: Alistair Cockburn characterizes two people creating an artifact on a whiteboard as the most effective form of common engineering communication (Figure 1-1).

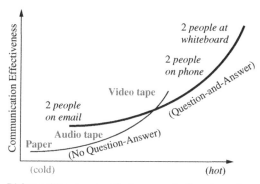

Figure 1-1   Forms of communication documentation. From Cockburn (2007, p. 125).

It is exactly this kind of communication, supplemented with the artifact that brings people together, that supports the kind of dynamics we want on an Agile team. From this perspective, documentation is fundamental to any Agile approach. There is nothing in the Manifesto that contradicts this: it cautions only against our striving for *comprehensive* documentation, and against a value system that places the documentation that serves the team ahead of the artifacts that support end-user services.

In the 1980s, too many serious software development projects were characterized by heavyweight write-only documentation. Lean architecture replaces the heavyweight notations of the 1980s with lightweight but expressive code. There in fact isn't much new or Agile in this: such was also the spirit of literate programming. Lean architecture has a place for lightweight documentation both for communication and for team memory. Experience repeatedly shows that documentation is more crucial in a geographically distributed development than when the team is collocated, and even Agile champions such as Martin Fowler agree (Fowler 2006).

Code Does Not Stand Alone

In general, "the code is the design" is a good rule of thumb. But it is neither a law nor a proven principle. Much of the crowd that advocates Agile today first advocated such ideas as members of the pattern discipline. Patterns were created out of an understanding that code sometimes does not stand alone. Even in the widely accepted Gang of Four book, we find that "it's clear that code won't reveal everything about how a system will work." (Gamma et al 2005, p. 23) We go to the code for *what* and *how*, but only the authors or their documentation tell us *why*. We'll talk a lot about *why* in this book.

Documentation can provide broad context that is difficult to see in a local chunk of code. Perhaps the best documentation is that which is automatically generated from the code through so-called reverse engineering tools. They can provide a helicopter view of a concrete landscape with a minimum of interpretation and filtering. That honors the perspective that the code is the design while rising above the code to higher-level views. The right volume of more intelligently generated high-level documentation can be even more valuable. Just following the code is a bit like following a path through the woods at night. Good documentation is a roadmap that provides *context*. More advanced roadmaps can even tell me *why* I should take a certain direction ("there are nettles on this path in July; take the other path instead," or, "we use stored procedures here instead of putting the traversals in the business logic because the traversal is simple, but changes frequently"). Different constituencies might need different roadmaps ("the architecture allows customer service to change route lookups without engaging the programming staff"). As Grandpa Harry said, one size does not fit all. Using code as a map suits programmers well, but other constituencies may need different sizes of maps.

Documentation can also be a springboard for discussion and action in much the same way that a culture's literature provides a backdrop for reflection. This is particularly true of the kinds of domain models we'll develop in Chapter 5. To take all documentation as formal, literal instruction is to undermine its highest value. Grandfatherly quotes on this topic abound, from Dwight D. Eisenhower's: "[P]lans are useless but planning is indispensable" to the old military saw: "Trust the terrain, not the map." There is a story (whether true or not) about a group of Spanish soldiers who became lost in the Pyrenees and who were desperately seeking a path to civilization to secure their survival. One of the group found a ratty old map in his luggage and the group squinted at the faded document to find a way out. They eventually reached a town, inspired by the life-saving document. Only later did they find that the map depicted a distant region in the French Alps. It's not so much what the map says about the terrain: it's what people read into the map. Again: "Trust the terrain, not the map." Updating the maps is good, too – but that means choosing map technology that avoids both technical and cultural barriers to currency. Document the important, timeless concepts so that change is less likely to invalidate them. In areas of rapid change, create code that needs minimal decoding; that's one goal of DCI.

Capturing the "Why"

As David Byers urged us as we were formulating ideas in the early days of this book, the *why* of software is an important memory that deserves to be preserved. Philippe Kruchten underscores this perspective in his IEEE Software article (Kruchten, Capilla and Dueñas 2009). Though we can efficiently communicate the *why* in oral communication with feedback, it is the most difficult to write down. Alistair Cockburn notes that we need cultural *reminders* that capture valuable decisions. Human transmission of the ideas, practices, and memes of development is still the most important, so we still value domain experts and patterns like Alistair's DAY CARE (Coplien and Harrison 2004, pp. 88–91): to place a treasured expert in charge of the novices so the rest of the team can proceed with work. Jeff Sutherland tells that at PatientKeeper, the architects gave a chalk talk about the system architecture – a talk that is kept in the company's video library and which is a cornerstone of team training. The written media are just another way to record and present *why*: a way that supports indexing, convenient real-time random access, and which becomes a normative cultural artifact that can contribute to Lean's goal of consistency.

It takes work to write things down, but the long-term payoff is usually worth it. The authors of *The Clock of the Long Now* argue why long-term documentation might be a good idea:

> One very contemporary reason is to make the world safe for rapid change. A conspicuously durable library gives assurance: *Fear not. Everything that might need to be remembered is being collected ... we're always free to mine the past for good ideas.* (Brandt 1995, p. 94)

This first chapter is our own attempt to explain the *why* of Lean architecture and Agile software development. We know it is a bit long, and we've explored many ways to cut it down, but decided that what remains here is important.

1.6.5   Common Sense, Thinking, and Caring

Finally, this book is about simple things: code, common sense, thinking, and caring. Code is the ever-present artifact at the core of the Agile development team. Properly done, it is an effigy of the end-user conceptual model. It constantly reminds the programmer of end-user needs and dreams, even when the customer isn't around. In the end, it all comes down to code, and that's because code is the vehicle that brings quality of life to end users.

Common sense hides deeply within us. Thinking and caring are equally simple concepts, though they require the effort of human will to carry out.

Will takes courage and discipline, and that makes simple things look hard. That in turns implies that simple things aren't simplistic. As we said in the Preface, we try to find the fewest simple things that together can solve complex problems.

As the intelligent designer in the middle, we sometimes must wrestle with the entire spectrum of complexity. But we should all the while strive to deliver a product that is pure. It's like good cooking: a good cook combines a few pure, high quality ingredients into a dish with rich and complex flavor. The chef combines the dishes with carefully chosen wines in a menu du jour whose tastes and ingredients are consistent and that complement each other. That's a lot better than trying to balance dozens of ingredients to achieve something even palatable, or throwing together ingredients that are just good enough. Such food is enough for survival, but we can reach beyond surviving to thriving.

Like a cook, a programmer applies lean, critical thinking. Keep the set of ingredients small. Plan so you at least know what ingredients you'll need for the meals you envision. That doesn't necessarily mean shopping for all the ingredients far in advance; in fact, you end up with stale-tasting food if you do that. Software is the same way, and Lean thinking in particular focuses on designing both the meal and the process to avoid waste. It places us in a strategic posture, a posture from which we can better be *responsive* when the need arises. Maybe Agile is more about *reacting* while Lean is about *responding*. It's a little like the difference between fast food and preparing a meal for guests. Both have a place in life, and both have analogues in software development. But they are *not* the same thing. And it's important to distinguish between them. Barry Boehm speaks of a panel that he was asked to join to evaluate why software caused rockets to crash. Their conclusion? "Responding to change over following a plan" (Boehm 2009).

Much of this book is about techniques that help you manage the overall form – the culinary menus, if you will – so you can create software that offers the services that your end users expect from you. It's about lining things up at just the right time to eliminate waste, to reduce fallow inventory, and to sustain the system perspectives that keep your work consistent.

Last, we do all of this with an attitude of caring, caring about the human being at the other end. Most of you will be thinking "customer" after reading that provocation. Yes, we care about our customers and accord them their proper place. We may think about end users even more. Agile depends on trust. True trust is reciprocal, and we expect the same respect and sense of satisfaction on the part of developers as on the part of end users and customers. Nerds, lest we forget, we care even about those nasty old managers. Envision a team that extends beyond the Scrum team, in an all-inclusive community of trust.

That trust in hand, we'll be able to put powerful tools in place. The Lean Secret is the foundation: everybody, all together, from early on. Having such a proverbial round table lightens the load on heavyweight written communication and formal decision processes. That's where productivity and team velocity come from. That's how we reduce misunderstandings that underlie what are commonly called "requirements failures." That's how we embrace change when it happens. Many of these tools have been lost in the Agile rush to *do*. We want to restore more of a Lean perspective of *think and do*, of strategy together with tactics, and of thoughtfully responding instead of always just reacting.

1.7   What this Book is *Not* About

This is not a design method. Agile software development shouldn't get caught in the trap of offering recipes. We as authors can't presume upon your way of working. We would find it strange if the method your company is using made it difficult to adopt any of the ideas of this book; it's those ideas we consider important, not the processes in which they are embedded.

While we pay attention to the current industry mindshare in certain fad areas, it is a matter of discussing how the fundamentals fit the fads rather than deriving our practices from the fads. For example, we believe that documentation is usually important, though the amount of documentation suitable to a project depends on its size, longevity, and distribution. This brings us around to the current business imperatives behind multi-site development, which tend to require more support from written media than in a geographically collocated project. We address the documentation problem by shifting from high-overhead artifacts such as comprehensive UML documents[2] to zero-overhead documentation such as APIs that become part of the deliverable, or through enough low-overhead artifacts to fit needs for supplemental team memory and communication.

The book also talks a lot about the need to view software as a way to deliver a service, and the fact that it is a product is only a means to that end. The word "service" appears frequently in the book. It is by coincidence only that the same word figures prominently in Service-Oriented Architecture (SOA), but we're making no conscious attempt to make this a SOA-friendly book, and we don't claim to represent the SOA perspective on what constitutes a service. If you're a SOA person, what we can say is: if the shoe fits, wear it. We have no problem with happy coincidences.

---

[2] That they are comprehensive isn't UML's fault by the way. UML is just a tool, and it can be used tastefully or wastefully.

We don't talk about some of the thorny architectural issues in this book such as concurrency, distribution, and security. We know they're important, but we feel there are no universal answers that we can recommend with confidence. The spectra of solutions in these areas are the topics of whole books and libraries relevant to each. Most of the advice you'll find there won't contradict anything that we say here.

The same is true for performance. We avoid the performance issue in part because of Knuth's Law: Premature optimization is the root of all evil. Most performance issues are best addressed by applying Pareto's law of economics to software: 80% of the stuff happens in 20% of the places. Find the hot spots and tune. The other reason we don't go into the art of real-time performance is partly because so much of the art is un-teachable, and partly because it depends a great deal on specific domain knowledge. There exist volumes of literature on performance-tuning databases, and there are decades of real-time systems knowledge waiting to be mined. That's another book. The book by Noble and Weir (Noble and Weir 2000) offers one set of solutions that apply when memory and processor cycles are scarce.

Though we are concerned with the programmer's role in producing usable, habitable, humane software, the book doesn't focus explicitly on interaction design or screen design. There are plenty of good resources on that; there are far too many to name here, but representative books include Graham (2003) for practical web interface design, (Raskin 2000) for practical application of interaction design theory, and Olesen (1998) for mechanics. We instead focus on the architectural issues that support good end-user conceptualization: these are crucial issues of software and system design.

1.8   Agile, Lean – Oh, Yeah, and Scrum and Methodologies and Such

If any buzzwords loom even larger than Agile on the Agile landscape itself, they are *Scrum* and *XP*. We figured that we'd lose credibility with you if we didn't say something wise about them. And maybe those of you who are practicing Scrum confuse Lean with Scrum or, worse, confuse Agile with Scrum. Scrum is a great synthesis of the ideas of Lean and Agile, but it is both more and less than either alone. Perhaps some clarification is in order. This section is our contribution to those needs.

This book is about a Lean approach to architecture, and about using that approach to support the Agile principles. Our inspirations for Lean come through many paths, including Scrum, but all of them trace back to basics of the Lean philosophies that emerged in Japanese industry over the past century (Liker 2004): just-in-time, people and teamwork, continuous improvement, reduction of waste, and continuous built-in quality. We drive deeper than the techno-pop culture use of the term *Lean* that focuses on the technique alone, but we show the path to the kind of human engagement that could, and should, excite and drive your team.

When we said that this book would build on a Lean approach to architecture to support Agile principles, most of you would have thought that by *Agile* we meant "fast" or maybe "flexible." *Agile* is a buzzword that has taken on a life of its own. Admittedly, even speed and flexibility reflect a bit of its core meaning. However, in this book we mean the word in the broader sense of the Agile Manifesto (Beck et al 2001). Speed and flexibility may be results of Agile, but that's not what it *is*. The common laws behind every principle of the Manifesto are *self-organization* and *feedback*.

Scrum is an Agile framework for the management side of development. Its focus is to optimize return on investment by always producing the most important things first. It reduces rework through short cycles and improved human communication between stakeholders, using self-organization to eliminate wait states. Scrum encourages a balance of power in development roles that supports the developers with the business information they need to get their job done while working to remove impediments that block their progress.

This is not a Scrum book, and you probably don't need Scrum to make sense of the material in this book or to apply all or part of this book to your project. Because the techniques in this book derive from the Agile values, and because Scrum practices share many of the same foundations, the two complement each other well.

In theory, Scrum is agnostic with respect to the kind of business that uses it, and pretends to know nothing about software development. However, most interest in Scrum today comes from software development organizations. This book captures key practices such as software architecture and requirements-driven testing that are crucial to the success of software Scrum projects (Coplien and Sutherland 2009).

Agile approaches, including Scrum, are based on three basic principles:

1. Trust
2. Communication
3. Self-organization

Each of these values has its place throughout requirements acquisition and architecture. While these values tend to touch concerns we commonly associate with management, and architecture touches concerns we commonly associate with programmers, there are huge gray areas in between. These areas include customer engagement and problem definition. We take up those issues, respectively, in Chapter 3 and Chapter 4. Those in hand, we'll be ready to move toward code that captures both what the system is and what the system does. But first, we'll give you a whirlwind tour of the book in Chapter 2.

1.9 History and Such

> *Like a tree, civilization stands on its past.*
> *The Clock of the Long Now*, p. 126.

"Lean production" came into the English language vernacular in a 1991 book by Womack, Jones, and Roos (Womack et al 1991). The book presented manufacturing models of what automobile manufacturer Toyota had been doing for decades. "Lean production" might better be called the Toyota Production System (TPS).

The Toyota Way has its roots in Sakichi Toyoda, a carpenter who went into the loom business in the late 1800s. Toyoda was influenced by the writings of Samuel Smiles, who chronicled the passion of great inventors and the virtue of attentive, caring production and empirical management (Smiles 1860). Toyoda formed Toyoda Automatic Loom Works in 1926. It used steam-powered looms that would shut down when a thread broke, so it could be repaired and the piece of cloth could thereby be rescued instead of becoming waste. These looms generated the fortune that would launch Toyota Motor Corporation in 1930 at the hand of his son, Kiirchiro Toyoda.

In the post-war reconstruction, Toyoda took note of inefficiencies in Ford in the U.S. Drawing on some of Ford's original ideas which had been misread or badly implemented by his namesake company, with a nod to Taylor's empirical methods and Deming's statistical process control (SPC), the new Toyota president Eiji Toyoda gave the Toyota Production System many of the concepts that we associate with Lean today: single-piece continuous flow, low inventory, and just-in-time delivery. Deming's Plan-Do-Act cycle would become a foundation of *kaizen*: continuous, relentless process improvement.

Toyota refined and grew its manufacturing approaches. In about 1951 Toyota added the practices of Total Productive Maintenance (TPM) to the Toyota Way. Associated with the spotless Toyota service garages and the silhouettes that ensure that every tool is returned to its proper place, TPM is perhaps a better metaphor for the ongoing software life cycle than TPS is – though TPS is a great foundation for system architecture (Liker 2004, pp. 16–25).

Some Lean concepts appeared in recognized software practice as early as the 1970s. *Everybody, all together, from early on* is a time-honored technique. One early (1970s), broadly practiced instance of this idea is Joint Application Design, or JAD (Davidson 1999). JAD was a bit heavyweight, since it involved all the stakeholders, from the top management and the clients to the seminar secretary, for weeks of meetings. While it probably didn't admit enough about emergent requirements (its goal was a specification), its concept of broad stakeholder engagement is noteworthy. Letting everybody be heard, even during design, is a lost practice of great software design.

In the early 1990s Jeff Sutherland would become intrigued by a Harvard Business Review article, again about Japanese companies, called *The New New Product Development Game*, authored by Hirotaka Takeuchi and Ikujiro Nonaka (Takeuchi and Nonaka 1986). Its tenets, together with ideas from iterative development and time boxing, and some practices inspired by an early draft of the Borland study published in Dr. Dobbs Journal (Coplien and Erickson 1994), led to the birth of Scrum.

Lately, Lean has made more inroads into the software world from the manufacturing world. The excellent work of Mary and Tom Poppendieck (e.g., Poppendieck and Poppendieck 2006) features many elements of the Toyota Production System, though it tends to focus less on up-front decisions and value streams than historic Lean practice does.

Agile Production in a Nutshell

This is the big-picture chapter, the get-started-quick chapter. It's for those readers who make it only through the first pages of most books they pick up in spite of best intentions to struggle through to the end. We got you this far. Hold on for eight pages as we describe six basic activities of Lean Architecture and Agile software development.

These activities are neither waterfall phases nor steps; however, each one provides a focus for what a team member is doing at any given time. The ensuing chapters are:

- Chapter 3: Stakeholder Engagement
- Chapter 4: Problem Definition
- Chapter 5: What the System *Is*, Part I: Lean Architecture
- Chapter 6: What the System *Is*, Part II: Coding It Up
- Chapter 7: System Functionality
- Coding it up: Chapter 8: Basic assembly, and Chapter 9: The DCI Architecture

Here's the skinny on what's to come.

2.1 Engage the Stakeholders

What is a "stakeholder"? Team members, system engineers, architects, and testers all have a stake in creating sound system form. There may be many more: use your imagination. People appreciate being invited to the party early. And remember the Lean Secret: *everybody, all together, from early on.*

Identify the people and systems that care that this system even exists, what it does, or how it does it. Remember that you are building a system. A system (Weinberg again) is a collection of parts, none of which is interesting if separated from the others. Snowden defines it as "a network that has coherence." (Snowden 2009) When you are building a system, you need a system view – and in the system view, everything matters.

In the following chapters, we'll often divide the system roughly in two. As shown in Figure 2-1, one part is what the system *is*; the other part is what the system *does*. (We will use variations of this figure several times throughout the book to illustrate the lean architecture principles.) The what-the-system-*is* part relates to what is commonly called the architecture or platform: the part that reflects the stable structures of the business over time. Our key stakeholders for that part of the system are domain experts, system architects, and the wise gray-haired people of the business. The what-the-system-*does* part relates to the end user's view of the services provided by the system: the tasks the system carries out for users and the way those tasks are structured. The end user, user experience folk, interface designers, and requirements folks are the key stakeholders in this part of the system. Of course, this system dichotomy isn't black and white, and even if it were, most people have insights that can inform both of these areas.

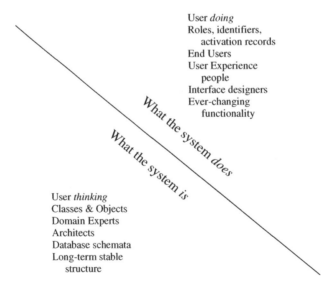

Figure 2-1   What the system *is*, and what the system *does*.

While we must acknowledge emergence in design and system development, a little planning can avoid much waste. Grandpa Harry used to quote George Bernard Shaw in saying that good fences make good neighbors – and Grandpa Harry knew that Shaw was cynical in that observation, much preferring that there be no fences at all.

By all means, don't fence off your customer: customer engagement is one of the strongest of Agile principles. But it doesn't mean dragging the customer or end user into your workplace and interrogating them, or keeping them on hand to clarify important perceptions on a moment's notice. It means getting to know them. As a rural postal carrier, Grandpa Harry got to know his clients over time by being attentive to the upkeep of their farms and by noticing the kind of mail they received. He would recall Yogi Berra's quip: You can observe a lot just by watching. That's how it should be with customers: to understand their world-model and to reflect it in our design. In fact, this goes to the original foundations of object-oriented programming: the goal of Simula (the first object-oriented programming language, created in 1965 and fitted with object-oriented features in 1967) was to reflect the end user world model in the system design. That key principle has been lost in decades of methodology and programming language obfuscation, and we aim to help you restore it here.

2.2 Define the Problem

Grandpa Harry used to say that if you didn't know where you were going, any road would get you there. Get the group together to write a short, crisp problem definition. We like Jerry Weinberg's definition of *problem*: the difference between the current state and a desired state. Write down this compass heading in a sentence or two. If the group collectively owns a notion of what problem they are solving, then they can own the notion of *done* when you're done. So we start with a one- or two-sentence problem definition.

Do this early in the project. A problem definition is a better compass than the first release's feature set, or the map of a domain which is yet unexplored. Don't wait until you've engaged every last stakeholder: great projects start with a visionary and vision rather than a market analysis. The important market analysis will come soon enough. Again, remember: *everybody, all together, from early on.*

Without a problem definition, it's hard to know when you're done. Sure, you can tick off some list of tasks that you may actually have completed and which were initially designed to bridge the gap between the current and desired state, but that doesn't mean that you're done. Emergent requirements cause the landscape to shift during development, and even the best-planned path may not lead you to the best-conceived destination.

For the same reasons, be sure to check both your destination and your current compass heading in mid-journey. Revisit your problem definition once in a while to make sure it's current.

2.3   Focusing on What the System *Is*: The Foundations of Form

> *How do [ecological systems] manage change, and how do they absorb and incorporate shocks? The answer appears to lie in the relationship between components in a system that have different change rates and different scales of size.*
>
> **The Clock of the Long Now, p. 34.**

As is true for a house, software architecture just *is*: what the system does is what we make of it, tying building blocks together with the activities of business life. A house is not a tea party, but a good architecture can make a tea party more enjoyable, convenient, and even beautiful. Such is the dance between architecture and function in software – like the dance of a tightrope walker on the rope and balconies of a humble but beautifully sturdy setting.

Every system has two designs, i.e., reflects two kinds of intents: the design of its functionality – what it *does* – and the design of its form – what it *is*. At the beginning of a project you need to focus on both. This double-edged focus applies not only to good beginnings but is at the heart of long-term product health: the form, to establish a firm foundation for change, and the functionality to support end-user services.

Grandpa Harry was an ardent woodsman, and we'd sometimes find ourselves miles from nowhere in the wilderness. He used to say: Trust the terrain, not the map. The terrain is the part that some methodologies call architecture. We can call it Lean architecture. It is what the system *is* – as contrasted with what the system *does*, which we'll talk about later.

We'll introduce an architectural strategy that lays a foundation of abstract base classes early in the project. That establishes the basic *form* the system will take on over its lifetime. The *structure* of the system follows the form. It's not that form follows function, but function and form weave together into a real structure that we call member data and methods.[1] And when we do come to structure, we'll focus on the *objects* rather than classes (Figure 2-2). Classes are more of a nerd thing; objects relate to the end user and to the business. The initial base classes we'll put in place are placeholders for objects of many different classes – the fact that they are abstract classes distances us from the class specifics. Yes, we'll come to classes soon enough, and there's some cool stuff there. But objects should dominate the design thought process.

---

[1] Architectural critic Witold Rybczynski notes that in building architecture, form doesn't follow function: it follows *failure* (Rybczynski 1987). Contemporary design is embracing this perspective more and more. See Petroski (1992).

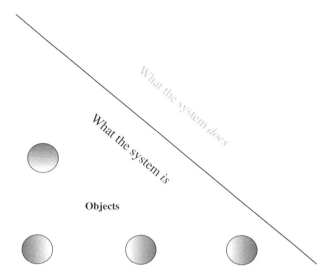

Figure 2-2 Focusing on what the system *is*: its *form*.

The end user mental model is one sound foundation for architecture, and domain knowledge helps us think critically and soberly about user models in light of longstanding experience. Think of domain expertise as a broadening of user expertise into the realms of all stakeholders taken together. Expert developers learn over time what the fundamental building blocks of a given system should be.

Of course, in real development we work on the problem definition, architecture, and use cases in parallel. From a conceptual perspective, architecture and its articulation give us vocabulary and solid foundations for use case implementation later on. So, guess what: *everybody, all together, from early on* rules again. So can up-front on architecture be Agile? Yes: even XP admits the need for architecture (Beck 1999, p. 113). We do architecture:

1. To capture stakeholders' perspectives that affect design;
2. To embrace change and to reduce the cost of solving problems;
3. To create a shared vision across the team and the stakeholders;
4. To smooth the decision-making process.

Software architecture disciplines from the 1980s delivered a truckload of artifacts that preceded the first line of code – artifacts never seen by the end user. That isn't Lean. Lean architecture very carefully slices the system to express the essence of system form in source code. While the interface is the program (Raskin 2000), the code is the design (Reeves 2005) – and architecture helps us see it from a perspective that's often invisible in the source code. We deliver a thin shell of declarative, compilable code: domain class interfaces as source code contracts, boilerplate, a domain dictionary and a bit of documentation.

We'll talk in Section 5.1 about the value of making decisions about form early in the project. Deferring these decisions reduces timely feedback that comes in the form of emergent requirements as we strive to realize the system form. It also leaves more time to add structure to the system in an uninformed way – structure that will have to be redone when we take the time to consider proper form. Good form up front reduces cost in the long term.

2.4   Focusing on What the System *Does*: The System Lifeblood

The architecture in place, we have a firm foundation where we can stand and respond to change. Most changes are new or revised end-user services. It is these services, where the action is, that are at the heart of system design. To belabor the metaphor with building architecture: whereas buildings change over decades and centuries (Brandt 1995), computers enact tasks at human time scales, and this animation is key to their role in life. It's important to collect and frequently refresh insights about the end user's connection to these system services.

We capture the end user's *mental model* of these services as the *roles* or *actors* they envision interacting inside the program (or in a real-world system controlled by the program), and by the interactions between these roles. Such modeling is a foundation of good interface design (Raskin 2000) and is the original foundation of the object paradigm (Reenskaug, Wold, and Lehne 1995; Laurel 1993).

Use cases capture roles and their interactions well. They are not only a good tool to elicit, explore, refine, and capture end user world models (*if* used in a user-centered, incremental way) but also serve to organize requirements by their functional grouping, mutual dependency, and priority ordering.

A sound architecture provides a context in which the user scenarios can unfold. These scenarios have two parts: the pure business logic, and the domain logic that supports the scenario. Most architectural approaches would have us do the "platform" code up front. We establish the form up front, but we wait to fill in the structure of the domain logic until we know more about the feature. And architecture lubricates the value stream: when the feature comes along, we don't have to create the form from scratch. It's already there.

So we start with Grandpa Harry's saw again: you can observe a lot just by watching. We observe our users and become sensitive to their

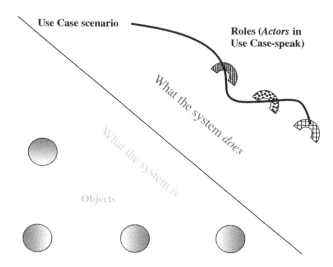

Figure 2-3 Focusing on what the system *does*.

needs, so our software improves their business. User experience folks capture business models, task flows, and end-user cognitive models; screen designers build prototypes; but the programmer is continuously engaged, collecting insights to be used during the coding sprint. Testers pay close heed to what the system is supposed to do. The programmer also keeps an eye on all the code that has to work together with the new stuff, so the current base and neighboring software systems also come into analysis.

This is an exploration activity but, in the spirit of Scrum, we always want to focus on delivering something at the end of every work cycle. The artifacts that we deliver include:

1. Screen Designs, so the program not only works, but is usable;
2. Input to the Domain Model, to scope the domain;
3. Use cases, to organize the timing of responsible decisions.

2.5 Design and Code

Grandpa Harry not only built two houses for himself and worked on countless others, but was also a pretty good cabinetmaker. He was acquainted both with structure in the large and in the small. When it came down to construction, he'd say: Measure twice, cut once. And as life went on, he re-designed parts of the house, built new furniture, changed a bedroom into a library, and made countless other changes.

It all comes down to code, and taking your design into code will flush out issues that help you see the big picture more clearly. By this time, many emergent requirements have been flushed out, and implementation can often move swiftly ahead. Developers lead the effort to produce code for the desired end-user services. With respect to process, we don't distinguish between code in the "architecture part" part and the "use case part" at this point. We code up what it takes to deliver business value. The stakeholders should be at hand to clarify needs. And this is where the testers turn use cases into tests and run them.

The main activities at this point are:

1. Turn the use case scenarios into algorithms and craft the roles that will be the home for the code that reflects end-user understanding of system scenarios. This is one of the most exciting parts of the book, as it builds on the recently developed DCI (Data, Context and Interaction) architecture from Trygve Reenskaug. This is code that you can inspect, analyze, and test more easily than under a simple object-oriented approach.

2. Write system tests.

3. Tailor the domain class interfaces to the new algorithms.

4. Code up the algorithms in the role code and the support logic in the domain code, re-factoring along the way.

5. Run the newly written system tests against the new code.

The output is running, tested, and documented code and tests. The functional code in the DCI architecture – what the system *does* – has the curious property of being readable with respect to requirement concerns. We have an updated domain architecture – what the system *is* – to support the new functionality.

2.6   Countdown: 3, 2, 1 . . .

There, you have it: everything your mother should have taught you about Lean software architecture and how it supports Agile development. We'll tell you a lot more about our perspectives on these ideas in the coming pages. Don't be a slave to what we tell you but let our perspectives challenge and inspire your thinking. We think that you'll stumble onto new ways of seeing many of these things.

Stakeholder Engagement

"Individuals and interactions over processes and tools," and "Customer collaboration over contract negotiation" comprise half of the values of the Agile Manifesto. These values are no less suitable to architecture than to any other facet of Agile development, and they lie at the heart of this chapter. Perhaps we hear much about the other two principles of *working software and embracing change* because they're closer to the programmer, and because popular Agile is a programmers' movement. Maybe half of software development is about nerd stuff happening at the whiteboard and about typing at the keyboard. But the other half is about people and relationships. There are few software team activities where this becomes more obvious than during architecture formulation.

This chapter is about the people in a software development effort, the roles they play, and a little bit about the processes that guide them. To summarize the chapter, everyone is in some small part an architect, and everyone has a crucial role to play in good project beginnings. We'll maybe have some surprising things to say about customers and architects, too.

3.1 The Value Stream

Software people work together to build products such as programs and documentation, each one of which adds value to the end user. They also build internal artifacts and go through internal processes that individually have value. The question is: who has responsibility for timely product delivery to the customer? In today's software management it is typically a Product Manager or Project Manager. Such managers do often intervene or "swoop into development" on an emergency basis to push a product to delivery. That violates the Lean principle of evening out flow. Here come stress, overtime, and cutting corners on the process to make the end date. Instead, we want a manager who owns the entire process of production and who can be accountable to the customer for timely delivery. If an enterprise consistently doesn't deliver, it should be viewed as an end-to-end process problem. This end-to-end process, its people, and its processes are called the *value stream.*

Lean production organizes around value streams instead of production steps. This organization structure has repercussions for the role structure of the organization. Instead of emphasizing the managers for each of the stovepipes, or of highlighting individual areas of specialization, we look at the whole. This may strike you as a bit odd if you're from a typical Western software company. We'll try to make this more real and concrete over the next few pages. Scrum, in fact, is based on exactly these principles, with cross-functional teams, and a role called the ScrumMaster who owns the end-to-end process. Alistair Cockburn's organizational pattern HOLISTIC DIVERSITY (Coplien and Harrison 2004, pp. 142–144) also talks about the benefits of cross-functional teams.

3.1.1 End Users and Other Stakeholders as Value Stream Anchors

Going back to that saw, "Customer collaboration over contract negotiation" brings to mind another human-centered artifact of development: *requirements*, or whatever term one chooses to ascribe to them. Though the values of the Manifesto don't mention end users, Agile practices tend to focus on the informally communicated needs of users, commonly called user stories. Now you've picked up a book about architecture – one that even dares to use the word *requirements* – and perhaps you're afraid that all of that will go away.

No, don't worry: in fact, we're going to pursue the Agile perspective even further. We'll venture beyond just the paying customer to the even more-important end user, who is often a different person than the customer. Our main value stream stops there.

In fact, many different stakeholders derive value from your product. We feed multiple, hopefully complementary value streams: one each for end users, customers, employees, stockholders, and each of the other potential stakeholders in the business. We can understand some of these stakeholding relationships in terms of raw economics: both customers and end users can benefit from low incremental cost and fast incremental time to market. End users are stakeholders who, apart from the economics, want a well-tailored solution to *their* problem, including ease of use. The solution and the economics to make it feasible are part of the end-user value proposition. Both Lean and Agile help us out here. Lean teaches us that the value stream is important, and that every activity and every artifact should contribute to end-user value. Agile's "customer collaboration" lets the value stream reach the deepest recesses of the software development process so user needs are explicit and visible to the vendor community.

There are important stakeholders outside your market as well. Your company benefits from a high return on investment (ROI), which comes from low cost and good sales. While good sales come from meeting market stakeholders' needs, low costs relate to how vendors meet internal needs. Designers, coders and testers have more fulfilling jobs if they feel they are contributing to the value stream: reducing time to market by shortening the development interval, and reducing cost by reducing frustrating rework. We can reduce rework by carefully watching and listening to our customers and to the market on one hand, but to history and standards on the other. So both Lean and Agile can help on the vendor side, too.

3.1.2 Architecture in the Value Stream

The main goal of Lean is to create a value stream, every one of whose activities adds value to the end user. Architecture too often is viewed as an awkward cost rather than as something that provides end-user value. Where does architecture fit in the value stream? Again, the interplay of Lean and Agile adds end-user value:

- *Time*: A good architecture shortens the time between understanding user needs and delivering a solution. It does this by eliminating rework and by providing a de-facto standard framework based on the end user domain model.

- *Function*: Unlike traditional architecture which deals almost exclusively with domain structure, the Agile production side of this book embraces the deep form of function and gives it first class standing in the architecture. This focus improves the likelihood that we will deliver what the customer expects.

- *Cost*: A Lean process results in cost savings that can be passed on to the user. These cost savings come from reducing the distance between the end user world model and the code structure and from reduced waste, including just-in-time feature production. We can also avoid rework with enough up-front deliberation, built on history and experience, that we can generalize our overall approach and the basic system form without the clutter of premature implementation.

Lean adds yet more to the value stream with a vision that helps keep the system consistent. A good architecture is a de-facto standard that helps system parts fit together. Agile keeps the links in the value stream consistent with each other through "individuals and interactions over processes and tools." The feedback in Agile supports Lean's goal of consistency, while Lean's trimmed and fit processes make Agile change more flexible. Together, all of these contribute to reduced time and cost. [Coplien et al 1998]

Architecture is not just a band-aid that Agile projects apply to technical debt or to prepare for upcoming massive changes. By then, it's too late. Architecture is an ongoing discipline with a substantial up-front planning component. Done right, the up-front planning can go quickly. Done right, the planning can provide the thinking tools that make incremental feature development as inexpensive as it can be. Architecture is the framework for, and result of, such thinking.

Along with eliminating waste and smoothing out flow, overall consistency completes the three fundamental goals of Lean. To a software team that means making the product consistent with end user needs. That implies a many-way consistency between end user mental models, end user actions, use cases, the code, its architecture, tests, the human interface – everything, everyone, everywhere. If everyone is communicating at just the right time we can avoid inconsistent actions that lead to waste and irregular production. And it's hard to schedule the "right time" in advance because the future is full of surprises. You could wait until you were done coding and testing to engage the sales people, but maybe they want to develop an advertising campaign that they can launch right when you're done. You could wait until you're done coding to make friends with the testers, but engaging them early smoothes later communication and builds the environment of team trust that is crucial to success. Lean offers a powerful answer to these problems: the Lean Secret.

3.1.3   The Lean Secret

To make Lean work requires a carefully coordinated and synchronized team that is focused on end user value and on continuously improving that value. The key to success in both Lean and Agile is the Lean Secret: *Everybody, all together, from early on.* This "secret" is what makes the human side of Lean work.

The roots of Lean go back to just-in-time delivery concepts developed by Kiichiro Toyoda in Toyota's predecessor company in the early twentieth century. The system became defunct after the war, and was revamped by an engineer in charge of final car assembly in Toyota at the time, Taiichi Ohno. He based the key Lean tenets on reduced waste, on consistency and order, and on maintaining a smooth process flow without bunching or jerkiness (Liker 2004, Chapter 2). Honda operated the same way (Takeuchi and Nonaka 1986, p. 6):

> Like a rugby team, the core project members at Honda stay intact from beginning to end and are responsible for combining all of the phases.

The first step is to avoid waste: taking care to make the best use of materials and to not produce anything unless it adds value to the client. The second step is to reduce inconsistencies by making sure that everything fits together and that everyone is on the same page. The third step is to smooth out flow in the process, reducing internal inventory and wait states in the process.

Parts of the Agile world embody Lean principles in different measures. Too many Agile rules of thumb have roots in a naive cause-and-effect approach to Lean principles. They might reason as follows: to reduce waste, reduce what you build; to reduce what you build, remove the thing furthest from the client: the internal documentation. To reduce inconsistencies, defer any decision that could establish an inconsistency, and introduce tight feedback loops to keep any single thread of progress from wandering too far from the shared path. To smooth out flow, keep the work units small. To reduce the work of making decisions, defer or ignore them.

While some of these practices (such as small work units) are squarely in the center of Lean practice, others are overly brute-force attempts that can benefit from exactly the kind of systems thinking that Lean offers. Ballard (2000) has developed a model of Lean production based on a few simple concepts:

- Rework in production creates waste. However, design without rework is wasted time. If design rework is a consequence of a newly learned requirement, it saves even more expensive rework that would arise in production. Rework in design creates value.
- You can increase the benefits of such rework in design, and avoid rework in production, by engaging all stakeholders together (a cross-functional team) as early as possible.
- Make decisions at the responsible moment – that moment after which the foregone decision has a bearing on how subsequent decisions are made, or would have been made. Note that "[k]nowledge of the lead times required for realizing design alternatives is necessary in order to determine last responsible moments" (Ballard 2000). Therefore, line up dependencies early to optimize the decision-making process: front-load the process with design planning. There is rarely any

difference between the first responsible moment and the last responsible moment: it's just *the responsible moment*. Not to decide is to decide; not to decide is a decision that has consequences. No matter what you do, or don't do, it has consequences. Maybe rework is caused by work done before or after the responsible moment.[1]

In addition to these principles, Ballard adds that batch sizes should be small and that production should use feedback loops carrying even incomplete information.

This combination of teamwork, iteration, and up-front planning is part of Lean's secret – more insights that are too often lost in the Agile world. Agile often fails to value up-front design or celebrate value-adding rework in design. Too many Agilists confuse the sin of following a plan with planning itself. In Scrum, the Product Owner does ongoing up-front planning, and the team and Product Owner together order the Product Backlog decisions to optimize revenue and to reduce cost – very much like a Lean decision structure matrix (Austin et al 1999). In addition, the team does design at the beginning of each Sprint and may do task sequencing before starting to work. However, few Agile practices bring mature domain design knowledge forward in a way that reduces the cost and effort of later design decisions, or that simply makes them unnecessary.

Much of the challenging part of design lies in partitioning a system into modules and collections of related APIs. That is exactly the problem that up-front architecture addresses. While popular Agile culture holds out hope that such partitioning and groupings can easily be re-factored into shape, few contemporary re-factoring approaches rise to the occasion. Most re-factoring approaches are designed to work within one of these partitioned subsystems or within a class hierarchy that reflects such a grouping of APIs: they don't deal with the more complex problem of moving an API from one neighborhood to another. That's hard work.

Architecture doesn't eliminate this hard work but can greatly reduce the need for it. Contrary to being hard, architecture can actually make it easier to deal with change. When the world shifts and technology, law or business cause wrinkles in a domain, you either have to start over (which isn't always a bad idea) or do the hard work of restructuring the software. And that *is* hard work. *Agile* doesn't mean *easy*, and it offers no promises: only a set of values that focused, dedicated team members can employ as they face a new situation every day. Architecture takes work, too, and requires foresight (obviously), courage, and commitment – commitment that may be too much for timid developers. But it becomes hard work only because we choose to view it that way, and becomes futile work only because we do it in the absence of Lean principles, or because we are too

---

[1] Thanks to Lars Fogtmann Sønderskov.

used to instant gratification. Facing change without architectural support is even harder work. Short-term responsiveness is important, too, and that's the Agile side of this book. There is no contradiction in saying that Lean investment and Agile responsiveness go hand in hand.

That's the technical side of the story. There is also an organizational side to Lean and Agile, which usually dominates the industry buzz around the buzzwords. Lean strives to eliminate waste, which goes by the Japanese word *muda* (無駄) in the Toyota Way. There are many causes of waste, including discovering mistakes later rather than sooner, overproduction, and waiting. If one person has to wait and is idle until a supplier delivers needed information or materials, it is a wasted opportunity to move things quickly along the value stream. For Lean architecture and Agile production to work, we must engage the right stakeholders and ensure that the process keeps them on the same page, optimizing value to the end user.

3.2 The Key Stakeholders

We identify five major stakeholder areas:

- end users,
- the business,
- customers,
- domain experts, and
- developers.

You might be tempted to partition these roles by process phases. However, Agile's emphasis on feedback and Lean's emphasis on consistency suggests another organization: that these roles are more fully present in every development phase than you find in most software organizations. We focus on the value stream as a whole rather than on the individual stovepipes.

This doesn't mean that everyone must attend every meeting, and it doesn't mean that you should force your end users or businesspeople to write code. It does mean breaking down the traditional organizational walls that hamper communication between these roles, particularly at those times of crucial design decisions.

A good development organization is organized around roles that have a solid place in the lean value stream. In the Organizational Patterns book (Producer Roles, Coplien and Harrison 2004, pp. 182–183) we discussed producer roles, supporting roles, and deadbeat roles. You might think that your organization has no deadbeat roles – until you map out your value stream.

We probably miss some of your favorite roles in our discussion here. We discuss the roles that have distinguished contributions to the value stream, and a few of the key roles that help lubricate the value stream. For example, user experience people open doors to the end user role. The roles here should be interpreted broadly: so, for example, "developer" covers designers, coders, and testers; "domain expert" may cover your notion of architect, system engineer, and maybe business analyst or internal consultant; "business" includes sales and marketing and perhaps key management roles; and so forth.

Since this is a book on architecture you might expect more conscious focus on a role called "architect." A true software architect is one who is a domain expert, who knows how to apply the domain expertise to the design of a particular system, and who materially participates in implementation (ARCHITECT CONTROLS PRODUCT (Coplien and Harrison 2004, pp. 239–240) and ARCHITECT ALSO IMPLEMENTS (Coplien and Harrison 2004, pp. 254–256)). Such an architect can be a valuable asset. We still avoid that term in this book for three key reasons. First, having a role named "architect" suggests that the people filling that role are the ones responsible for architecture, when in fact a much broader constituency drives system design. Second, the word often raises a vision of someone who is too far removed from the feedback loop of day-to-day coding to be effective. This drives to a key point of Agile software development, and can be traced back to the Software Pattern discipline and to Christopher Alexander's notion of the architecture as "master builder" rather than "artistic genius." The term itself has dubious historic value. As the best-selling architecture critic Witold Rybczynksi writes in his book *The Most Beautiful House in the World*,

> ... But who is an architect? For centuries, the difference between master masons, journeymen builders, joiners, dilettantes, gifted amateurs, and architects has been ill defined. The great Renaissance buildings, for example, were designed by a variety of non-architects. Brunelleschi was trained as a goldsmith; Michelangelo as a sculptor, Leonardo da Vinci as a painter, and Alberti as a lawyer; only Bramante, who was also a painter, had formally studied building. These men are termed architects because, among other things, they created architecture – a tautology that explains nothing. (Rybczynski 1989, p. 9)

Third, most valuable contributions of good architects are captured in the other roles mentioned above: domain experts, the business, and developers.

It is crucial to also have a coordination function, a point person for the architectural work. There is at least anecdotal evidence that this is the main job of titled software architects today (Coplien and Devos 2000). While the architect usually wears this mantle there are many ways to achieve the same goal, from self-organization to titled positions. Keep coordination in mind, but we will not raise it to the stature of a role here. Many roles can rise to the coordination task on demand.

We don't separate out system engineering as a separate role. It isn't because we find systems engineering boring or useless; it's more that few people know what it is any more, and those that do don't need much advice. For the purposes of this book, systems engineers can be viewed as domain experts (which are too commonly called architects) who can translate architectural idealism into stark reality, or as requirements engineers who are part of the end user camp. Done right, an architect's job looks like great architecture; a coder's work looks like great craftsmanship; and a system engineer's job looks like magic.

Let's explore the roles.

3.2.1 End Users

End users anchor the value stream. The buck stops there. Their stake in your system is that it does what they *expect* it to. By "expect" we don't mean a casual wish, but a *tacit* expectation that goes beyond conscious assumptions to models that lie partly in the user unconscious. Most customers can express their wants; some can justify their needs; and *when using your product* they can all tell you whether it does what they *expect* it to. Most software requirements techniques (and some architecture techniques) start by asking users what they *want* or *need* the system to do, rather than focusing on what they *expect* it to do. Too many projects collect lists of potential features, driven by the business view of what the customer is willing to pay for (in other words, what the customer *wants*). Just having a description of a feature alone doesn't tell us much about *how* it will be used or *why* he or she will use it (we'll talk more about the *why* question in Section 7.3).

We learned a lesson in user expectations from a client of ours. The client builds noise analysis systems for everything from automobiles to vacuum cleaners. One thing we learned is that their clients for vacuum cleaners insist that a good vacuum cleaner make a substantial amount of noise when on the high setting. For the German market, this is a low roar; for other markets, it is a high whine. The goal isn't to minimize noise, even though it's possible to make vacuum cleaners very quiet without reducing their effectiveness.

Our goal, therefore, is usually to meet user *expectations*. There must be a compelling business reason behind any other goal – for example, to break out of a familiar computer interaction paradigm into new designs that either distinguish us in the market or which make radical enough improvements in the end user experience that they are willing to change their expectations. In that case, we have raised their expectations. But even there, the focus is on expectations; initial end user expectations are only *wants* that dissolve in the light of the new interaction paradigm.

One way to uncover expectations is to start a conversation with user stories and proceed to goal-driven use cases that include scenarios and user motivations for the functionality. User stories help end users think in a concrete way, and if we feed back our understanding of their expectations, we can gain foresight into how they will react if the system were deployed according to *our* understanding. If we do that job well we can build a system that technically meets end user needs.

Once you've gotten the conversation started, make it concrete quickly. One thing Dani Weinberg teaches people, inspired from her experience with training dogs, is that dogs learn well from timely feedback. They have difficulty associating delayed feedback with the associated behavior so they are at best bewildered by your untimely praise or criticism. If you can turn around a feature quickly at low cost to deliver to the end user for a test drive, you can concretely calibrate your interpretation of their expectations. Prototypes can be a good vehicle to elicit the same feedback at lower cost and in shorter time.

One problem with requirements is that they never anticipate all the scenarios that the user will conceive. So we need to go deeper than scenarios and explore the end user's perception of the system *form*. This is called the *end user cognitive model*, and it has everything to do with architecture. And it closely relates to what the user *expects* from a system. We'll explore the mechanics of user stories and use cases more in Chapter 7, but here we'll help set the context for those practices.

Psyching Out the End Users

Use cases capture user/system interactions that end users can anticipate. If end users can anticipate every interaction for every possible data value and input, then the specification is complete. It also makes it unnecessary to build the system because we've delineated every possible input and every possible answer, and we could just look up the answer in the spec instead of running the program. Of course, that is a bit absurd. Good software systems have value because they can, to some degree, handle the unanticipated. For example, let's say that my word processor supports tables, text paragraphs, and figures. One requirements scenario captures the user/system interactions to move a table within the document. I can describe the possible scenarios: moving a table from one page to another; moving the table to a point *within* a paragraph; moving the table just *between* two existing paragraphs; or even moving a table within another table. The possibilities are endless.

Instead of depending on an exhaustive compilation of requirements scenarios alone we instead turn to something that matters even more: the end user's cognitive model. Users carry models in their head of the internals of the program they are using. They trust that the program "knows" about tables, paragraphs, and figures. The end user trusts the programmer to have paid attention to the need for white space between the table and any adjoining paragraphs. These elements of the end user mental model, while quite static, are useful for reasoning about most possible use case scenarios.

If the program doesn't have an internal representation of a text paragraph, of a table and of a figure, then the program must work hard to present the illusion that it does. Otherwise, the program will endlessly surprise the end user. This is true even for scenarios that the end user might not have anticipated while helping the team compile requirements. Another way of talking about user expectations is to note that, unless we are designing video games, the end user rarely finds surprises to be pleasant. Therefore, it is crucial that the system architecture reflect the end user cognitive model. That helps us design the system so it not only meets end users anticipated wants and needs, but so it is also resilient when asked to support an un-anticipated but reasonable scenario.

If we capture this model well, the system and its initial code will handle most reasonable scenarios as they arise. Users will of course invent or stumble onto scenarios that the system doesn't yet handle quite right – perhaps, for example, creating a table within the table of contents. As programmers we then need to extend the system to support the new variation on an existing use case. But the system *form* is unlikely to fundamentally change. Such business domains models remain relatively stable over time.

Feature testing and validation explore the match between the system *behavior* and end-user expectations. System tests, usability testing, and an attentive ear during end-user demos all help. But when we are laying out the product architecture we want the end user's *cognitive* model of the system. Because the architecture reflects that model, the end user is a stakeholder in the architecture. In fact, the original goal of object-orientation was that the code should capture the end user mental model (we'll speak more to this in Section 5.3 and Section 8.1). Eliciting that model is an important part of architecture – in fact, is the key component of an Agile architecture.

Programmers can have a hard time separating themselves from their engineering world enough to grasp the end user perspective, and it can be difficult for end users to objectively introspect about what their internal world models really are. This is where user experience people bring value: they are often the key to the stake held by the end user. User experience people are also trained to recommend interfaces and approaches that, while natural to end users and their mental models and behaviors, look crazy to a programmer. (If you don't believe us, just read Raskin's book on interaction design (Raskin 2000)). Among their common tools are prototypes (often just on paper) to explore the requirements space. Most of this stuff isn't rocket science! And you may be doing much of it already.

Don't Forget Behavior

Yes, of course we still collect use cases, even if they handle only the most common needs and even if they can't be exhaustively enumerated. Software ultimately is a service, not a product, and use case scenarios help us keep that fact in focus. The more use cases, the better? Well yes, but moderation is a key virtue here. A team of five to ten people can absorb about 15 use cases in an annual release, where each use case has a list of scenarios that grows in number and detail as the business plan requires and as requirements emerge. A single product can juggle about 240 use cases at once (Cockburn 2008). It's easy to go too deep into requirements too early, because end users may behave differently when faced with a delivered system than they envision in the abstract. To gather detailed requirements about ever-changing behaviors is waste, so that's not Lean.

It's important to strike a balance between domain modeling (Chapter 5) and behavior modeling (Chapter 7). Behavior has form too (as in the phrase "form follows function"), is part of the end user mental model, and should be captured in the architecture. In the long term, the domain structure tends to be more stable than the behaviors we capture in use case scenarios, and its forms are the cornerstones of a good architecture. Object-oriented design techniques traditionally have been satisfactory at capturing the domain model but really bad at capturing the behavioral models.

There's another good reason to capture use cases: testers are also stake-holders in the system's quality and they need something to exercise the system behavior. In fact, one good way to drive system design is to gather the domain structure and the system behaviors in parallel and to let both drive the design. This is called behavior-driven development (BDD, North 2006). Note that this means that the end user, the developer, the tester and the user experience specialist should be engaged together from very early in the project. It's just the Lean Secret again.

Focusing more on form than on function will help drive you in a direction that supports what users *expect*. Do that well, and you'll easily be able to provide what they say that they *want* and *need*.

The End User Landscape

Many systems have multiple end users and potentially multiple value streams. Think of a banking system. Simple exercises in object-oriented design courses often present account classes as the typical design building blocks and account-holders as the typical users. Yet bank tellers are also end users of a bank computer system. So are actuaries: the folks who look at the details of financial transactions inside the bank. So are the loan officers and the investment staff inside the bank. Does the concept of "account" suit them all?

Identifying such end user communities is crucial to a sound architecture. Different user communities have different domain models. Derivatives and commodities are potential domain entities to the investor, but not to the teller nor to the loan officer. Mortgages are domain entities to the loan folks but not the investment people. Yet somehow banks seem to run with a single common underlying domain model. What is it? In most complex financial system, the basic building blocks are financial transactions: those become the "data model." From the user interface, different end users have the illusion that the system comprises accounts and loans and pork bellies. We'll find in Chapter 9 that accounts really fall into a middle ground called Contexts: stateless collections of related behavior that behave like domain objects but which are richer in functionality and closer to the end user than many domain objects are. The Agile world has started to recognize the need for such user community differentiation, and that realization is making a comeback in tools like Concept Maps (Patton 2009) – though use cases have supported such notions all along.

Much of the rest of this book is about learning to identify these layers and to create an architecture that will allow the most common changes over time to be encapsulated or handled locally. Object-oriented architecture isn't just a matter of "underline the nouns in the requirements document" any more. Before a project can build a resilient architecture, its people must know enough about the end user communities and their many mental models that they can form the system around long-term stable concepts of the business.

3.2.2   The Business

End users are system stakeholders who ultimately want the software to provide a service to them. The business has a stake in providing that service to support its ROI and survival. It has a stake in the well-being of its employees who create those services. The business pays the employees wages, salary and/or bonuses, and that usually implies making money from the software. Good software businesses usually have a stake in growing their customer base and giving good return to investors – which means that the enterprise will seek a diversity of end users or customers to support in the market. We usually think of business stake-holding as lying with line management, sales and marketing, or with the Product Owner in Scrum.

If the business can serve more customers, it both grows its stake in its customer base and likely increases revenues. Good revenues are one way to be able to pay employees well; another is to reduce costs. Architecture is a means to hold down long-term development costs and to accelerate the rate of revenue generation.

The business itself provides key inputs to the architectural effort that can hold down cost. One of the most important business decisions is the project scope. The business owns decisions about product scope. Nonetheless, these must be informed decisions. Scoping has to balance the expectations of all customers and users against financial objectives. For example: should the scope be the union of the entire market's expectations, or should the business focus on the 20% of the market where 80% of the revenues lie? But scope also has to look to the supply side. For example, the product scope can't take development into an area that depends on technology that won't yet be mature in the product's lifetime (are we building electric cars? Business forecast software that uses artificial intelligence?) Such insights come from domain experts and developers.

Just who is "the business"? The board of directors, executive management, business management, marketing, and sales are all key roles in this broad view of the business. Again, you probably don't need all of these people at all meetings. But if you are discussing scope, or the what-the-system-does part of the architecture, invite selected representatives of these areas to the table.

The business may also hold down costs by making a buy-versus-build decision. Such decisions of course have broad and lasting influence on the architecture. Such decisions should be informed by customers and end users, who desire selected standards, and by domain experts who can advise the business on the feasibility of integrating third-party software. And don't forget the developers, who actually have to do the work of integrating that software, and the testers, who have the burden of testing a system that contains a potential "black box."

A Special Note for Managers

The Scrum framework is a risk-reduction framework, or a framework to optimize ROI, with no role named *manager*. The ScrumMaster has many of the characteristics of a good servant-leader manager, and the Product Owner has the business savvy and the command-style attributes of a good Product Manager while lacking all of that role's control-style attributes. Scrum's roles come directly from the Chief Engineer and workers in Lean: the Product Owner and ScrumMaster reflect a splitting of the Chief Engineer role in two. Most of the entries for *manager* as indexed in some Agile books are about how managers resist and challenge XP (Auer and Miller 2002; Cohn 2010), while others thoughtfully talk about manager rights and responsibilities (Jeffries, Anderson and Hendrickson 2001). What place do managers have in Lean architecture and Agile deployment?

Remember that two keystones of Agile are self-organization and feedback. For your team to be successful, you as a manager should use the influence and power of your position to help make that happen. One of the most important jobs of line management is to remove impediments that frustrate the team or that slow the team's progress. A line manager's attitude can make or break the esprit de corps of a team. That is worth more than any methodology or tool.

A good way to think about managers in an Agile context is as members of a team whose product is the organization (Greening 2010). As such, managers aren't preoccupied with the production process for the enterprise product; instead, they influence that process by putting the right organization in place. Good organizations support effective communication through group autonomy, collocation, and group functions. Further, there are close links between the architecture and organizational structure as commonly acknowledged in Conway's Law ((Conway 1968) – see also Section 5.2.2). While teams may locally be self-organizing, the higher-level organizational structure is often in the hands of the managers. That makes managers de facto über-architects: a responsibility not to be taken lightly.

While developers should set their horizons on end users who care about the product, managers can focus on customers. This helps free the development team from "pure business" issues that require the experience, insight, and responsibility that is more typically lodged with managers than with developers. Because most software these days is sold as a commodity, customers are more concerned with revenue streams and delivery dates than the actual product itself. That means that they may be more interested in the process than the product (as we discuss further in the following section). Managers are a good entry point for these concerns – much better than the development team. The organizational structure is also the cradle of the development process that emerges from it; see for example Swieringa and Wierdsma (1992) and Coplien and Harrison (2004, pp. 309–311).

All that said, don't forget: everybody, all together, from early on.

3.2.3   Customers

Customer is an almost emotive term. To not sign up to be customer-driven or to strive for customer satisfaction is to be a heathen and to be "not a team player." If we look beyond the mythical associations of the terms we find that it's useful to separate the customer role from the end user role. Simply put: end users relate to products and services, while customers relate more to the development process.

. . . As Contrasted with End Users

Customers and end users are interesting links in the value stream. We find the term "customer" featured both in the Agile Manifesto and in much of the original Scrum vocabulary. Yet the Agile Manifesto says nothing about the end user, and we don't find either role formally in today's Scrum framework!

Customer and end users are very different stakeholders. Of the two, the end users' stake is relatively simple by comparison. They seek service from the software you are developing; you create that value for them. The end-user value to the development organization is that they are usually the source of revenues that ultimately feed your team members. It's a good deal for end users if your software supports services that increase their quality of life.

The customer is essentially a middleman. In general terms, customers are not consumers of the service that your software provides; they treat your software as a commodity that passes through their systems the same way that gold in a Japanese martini passes through the digestive system of its consumer. It may come out the other end in different packaging, but it is still the same product. When engaging such customers, consider their stake in opportunistically developing products for which there are yet no end users. While all stakeholders want to reduce risk, customers in this position are particularly averse to risk. They are much more interested in delivery times and in your development costs (because those become their costs) than they are in functionality. *Therefore, the customer has a larger stake in your development process than in the service that your software provides.* You may be engaging customers more in the area of process improvement than in development enactment. It is important to accord such activities a place in your enterprise using retrospectives – and here, retrospective means a serious activity that encompasses business scope and issues of trust. What passes for a retrospective in the three-hour "check-ups" at the end-of-sprint is inadequate. See (Kerth 2001) for more on retrospectives.

Customers have at least one other key stake-holding relationship to the architecture, and that relates to the market segments that they serve. In general, the more customers the merrier: customers are a path to markets and therefore to revenue (value) streams. However, different customers often represent different constituencies and bring their own power of negotiation or market leverage to the negotiating table. If customers want to distinguish themselves from their competition, they will want their own configuration of your product. As Grandpa Harry used to say, one size does not fit all. Such configurations may extend beyond simple algorithms to variations on the system form: its architecture. A good architecture can be a tool that helps the Business cater to the needs of individual customers and market segments by supporting plug-and-play substitution of system modules. You can best understand how to manage change if you understand what doesn't change. In other words, you want to constructively constrain change and the sites of system variation. The stable part and changing part of the system are the yin and yang of its architecture.

Of course, many combinations of customer and end user are possible. They are sometimes one and the same. Sometimes you have the luxury of working directly with end users, achieving the ultimate Agile goal of short feedback loops that minimize requirements misunderstandings.

It is common that a Scrum team delivers to another software team developing code in which its own code is embedded. These projects are challenging to run in an Agile way. It is rare that such a team has or even can have meaningful discussions with end users. If your software has repercussions for end users (and what software doesn't?), then your own customer is likely to introduce delay that makes it difficult to receive timely customer feedback before starting your next Sprint. Testing, and, in general, most notions of "done," become difficult. *In these situations it is much better to extend the scope of "done" to include such customers and to effectively enlarge the scope of development to engage the party as a development partner rather than as a customer.*

Sometimes you have customers who yet have no end users because they are striving to develop a market, trying to develop a service that they hope will sell. In an Agile context, be wary of the possibility that your customer will look to you as a vendor to be the source of the requirements! Take such opportunities gladly and work with your end-user constituency to shape their expectations together.

Other times you yourself are both the developer and the end user, such as might occur when developing tools that support the development team. That's great! We encourage you to continue the discipline of separating your customer role from your developer role. Dave Byers relates:

Because in the developer role you're trying to get away with doing as little as possible, but in the customer/user role you want as much done as possible. Separate the two and it's possible to find a decent balance. Don't separate them and chances are you'll drift too far to one or the other. (Byers 2008a)

Indeed, the possibilities are endless. Use common sense, guided but not constrained by Agile and Lean principles.

"Customers" in the Value Stream

Sometimes our "customers" are just politically or organizationally separate entities on the production side of the value stream. If you build framework software and sell it to a company that embeds it in their product, then there are no real end users of your product in your customer. Your end users are on the other side of your customer – and that can cause a break in the value stream.

If you are in this situation, look carefully at the interfaces between the organizations and look for waste, delay, inconsistency, or boom-and-bust production cycles. If you find such problems, then Lean has some answers for you. (If you don't find such problems, then that's great! Like Grandpa Harry said: If it ain't broke don't fix it.)

Lean's main answer to these problems is to integrate both parties more fully into a single value stream. Remove obstacles to feedback between the teams. Leverage standards as a supplement to communication, and as a way of reducing changes in dependencies.

Remember that the same principle applies if you are taking software from another vendor and embedding it in your project. Try to close the gap. Toyota did this when they found they needed a new battery for their hybrid car. They didn't have the expertise to build one in-house and couldn't find one from any supplier. They solved the problem by partnering with Matsushita to jointly design a battery uniquely suited to the design of the Prius (Liker 2004, pp. 208–209).

3.2.4   Domain Experts

> *You need the space of continuity to have the confidence not to be afraid of revolution.*
>
> **Freeman Dyson, quoted in *The Clock of the Long Now*, p. 162.**

Domain experts are usually the grey-haired folks in the organization who know stuff. Domain experts are often the most direct and most explicit source of insight and advice on how to structure a new system. Most new systems in a domain look – from the perspective of form – much like previous systems in the same domain.

It's important to understand that everyone in an organization is probably an expert on something; otherwise, they wouldn't be there. Software development is rarely a matter of having enough muscle to get the job done, but rather of having the right skill sets present. It's about having diversity of skill sets, not just that one can overtake the market with Java muscle.

On the other hand, the folks commonly *called* domain experts have a special role in architecture. *Over the years they have integrated the perspectives of multiple end user communities and other stakeholders into the forms that underlie the best systems.* From the perspective of Agile and of engaging the people who use your software, these are crucial insights.

Such knowledge is a priceless asset. Consider the alternative. With no knowledge of the best long-term structure of the system, designers would have to start with first principles – end user domain models at best, but more likely use cases – and try to derive the objects from those. It becomes more difficult if the team must deal with use cases from several different kinds of end users (e.g., both Savings Account Holders and actuaries for a bank), and becomes even more difficult if the scope covers multiple clients or customers. The knowledge of the form suitable to such a complex landscape assimilates over years or decades, not over sprints or months. If you have your domain experts handy, they can relate the forms that they have already integrated, and in any case can point out areas that have been particularly challenging in the past.

Domain expert engagement is to architecture as end user engagement is to feature development. You should find that end users and domain experts are your most treasured contacts in a Lean and Agile project. It is difficult to establish good working relationships with both of these roles (with end users because of organizational boundaries and with domain experts because of their scarcity), but make the extra effort. It's worth it.

No Ivory Tower Architects

Domain experts often bear the title of Architect. In the Organizational Patterns book (Coplien and Harrison 2004) we find patterns such as Architect Controls Product and Architect Also Implements, which employ the title "architect" exactly in this sense. Both patterns suggest that architectural principles and domain expertise are embodied in the title.

Today, we prefer the term "domain expert" more and more and the term "architect" less and less. The reason? In practice, "architect" isn't a very distinguishing title. Interaction designers and coders have as much or more influence on the overall form of the system – its architecture – as titled architects do. In an Agile framework we value everybody's contribution to the architecture, and to have a titled "architect" can actually disempower other stakeholders with deep insights. Differentiating the role of "domain expert'' along the lines of expertise and experience, instead of along the lines of contribution to product foundations, better captures the stake-holding relationships.

One important role of traditional, titled architects is to coordinate development activities, focusing on late analysis and early design activities in particular. Domain experts often don't do that. In fact, titled architects are often not the great minds of design that we sometimes hold them to be, but are more like primary contractors in the construction field (Coplien and Devos 2000). Every organization should attend to this function as needed: whether it falls into the realm of the architect, a line manager, the ScrumMaster, or technical lead. A leader can lead and a coordinator can coordinate without disrupting self-organization, and the best ones actually sew the seeds of self-organization. Such self-organization is crucial to Agile execution.

Experts in Both Problem and Solution Domains

Don't forget solution domain experts! It's easy to get too caught up in value stream thinking that is preoccupied with tracing all business decisions to the end user as stakeholder. The business itself is also a stakeholder, attending to ROI. It is perhaps easiest to forget that developers are stakeholders, too. Of course, developers support ROI with their contribution to the value stream, and because that's the source of their income, they're stakeholders in the architecture. If we look at developers from a more human perspective, we realize that enterprises exist to provide not only products and services to the market but also employment to the community. We support developer-stakeholders, our solution domain experts, with work aids that not only make them more effective, but which make work life more enjoyable. More importantly, we want to tap their insights about how to improve the enterprise, the product, and its architecture.

Innovation in the solution domain goes hand-in-hand with long-term experience of solution domain experts. For example, a good object-oriented expert can tell you both where object orientation will give you benefits and where it won't. (In fact, a good rule of thumb is to trust someone as an expert only if they are good at telling a balanced story. An advocate is not always an expert, and an expert is not always an advocate.) You need good dialog on the team between the innovators (which can be any role on the team) and the solution domain experts.

Keep your architecture team (well, your *team*) balanced so that both problem domain experts and solution domain experts have an equal say. One problem with stovepipe development is that needed dialog between these two perspectives too easily becomes a conflict, because the first mover often over-constrains the other. It is often a problem for a business to be driven too much by technological innovation, but it is even more problematic to be driven by the MBAs. To read a depressing case study about how this imbalance can go wrong, read Richard Gabriel's post-mortem of Lisp innovator Lucid (Gabriel 1998, pp. 175–230).

Of course, we know many classic criteria must be met for an architecture team, or any team, to succeed. Kruchten writes about success factors for architecture-focused teams in (Kruchten 1999). He emphasizes the need for leadership on these teams. He also notes, very importantly, that the architecture team is a team among other teams: not a group of elitist appointees, or imminent retirees, but a small, vibrant, committed group whose schedule is tied to that of other teams. He warns against confusing a tool with the architecture (individuals and interactions over processes and tools). And of course, he recognizes the need to communicate, communicate, communicate.

Everybody, all together, from early on.

3.2.5 Developers and Testers

Developers are where the rubber meets the road. Their main job in architecture is often to rein in the grand visions of the business and architects with grounded domain expertise, both from the business and solution domains. As in Scrum, the developers should own the development estimates – after all, they're the ones who will do the actual work of implementing. As we mentioned before, it's even better if the architects also implement (ARCHITECT ALSO IMPLEMENTS, Coplien and Harrison 2004, pp. 254–256) – or, turning it the other way in terms of this book's terminology, if at least some of the developers also have deep domain expertise.

We use the collective term *developer* in this chapter instead of the individual task labels of *designer*, *coder*, and *maintainer*. To separate these roles is to encourage handoffs that challenge the Lean principles because organizations too often implement these separate roles in separate people. Such distinction can breed a lack of commitment or, worse, can lead to low morale, especially in the people filling the last two roles. Designers should bear the responsibility of implementing their plans, and coders should bear the responsibility for the business values of their creations. We fold these perspectives into the developer role. Developers may or may not develop documentation themselves, but they certainly have a strong stake in the documentation of the code they write (see MERCENARY ANALYST, Coplien and Harrison 2004, pp. 92–95).

Developers are the prime oracles of technical feasibility. They are the primary solution domain experts. They should be *active* experts. For the tough questions, opinion alone isn't well informed enough to make long-term business or architecture decisions; it's important to gather empirical insights. This is another Lean principle, which in Japanese is called *genchi genbutsu* (現地現物): go look and see for yourself. Developers can help by building prototypes that compare and contrast architectural alternatives that are up for discussion. At PatientKeeper in Massachusetts, the Scrum Product Owners might spend months building prototypes and workflow models to refine their understanding of the design space. Developers are taxed to support them with prototyping tools so they can build and deliver working prototypes as requirements oracles.

Remember that developers are the primary channels of interaction between teams. If you believe Conway's Law, which says that the team structure mirrors the architecture, then you can probably believe that the interaction between parts of your architecture will be only as effective as the interactions between the team members representing those parts of the architecture. As you frame out the form of your system, make sure that the stakeholders for the parts – at the level of the coders – negotiate the interfaces through which they will interact. Much of this negotiation will of course involve domain experts.

Developers and testers should be friends. While every serious system needs some acceptance or system testers who write double-blind tests, you should have ongoing testing support during development. You even need that at the system level. For such testing, the testers need to know requirements at least as well as the developers, so they're likely to be invited to a lot of the same meetings as developers. Everybody, all together, from early on.

Even though developers and testers should be friends, at least some of them should play a game of "hide and seek." The developer and tester can have a friendly meeting with the businesspeople to agree on the requirements, and then they go their separate ways. The tester codes up tests for the new feature while the developer implements the feature in the current architecture. The developers strive to implement the feature exactly as they come to understand it, going back to the business for clarification if necessary. The testers strive to test the feature as they understand it, also asking for clarification when they need it. After one or two days of work, they come together to see if their perspectives meet up. Grandpa Harry used to say that two heads are better than one. Start by having two sharp thinkers develop their interpretation independently; this doubles the opportunity to discover latent misunderstandings. That's the "hiding" part of hide-and-seek. Working independently avoids groupthink, and avoids one personality overpowering the other with arguments that things must be thus-and-so (Janis 1971). Then, having "found" each other, reason together (again, with the business if necessary) to clarify mismatches. Not only does this approach increase the chance of uncovering requirements problems, but it is also a weak form of pipelining, or parallelism, that shortens feedback cycles. This is effectively what Behavior-Driven Development (BDD) does (North 2006; Chelimsky et al 2010).

As for testers, there's an old saw that *architecture defines your test points*. Testers have a stake in the architecture that it be testable. Hardware designers have become good at something called DFT, or "design for testability" (Wu and Wen 2006). Most software people haven't come quite that far, but some software testers have more insights and instincts in this area than most of the rest of us do. Use testers' insight to create architectural APIs that support your test program. For example, having a well-delineated GUI API makes it feasible to drive the program with an ersatz GUI that can simulate end users (e.g., by re-playing interactions from real field applications). Such an API can be one foundation for automated system testing. The decision to create this interface, and where to place it, is an architectural one, though testing needs drive it.

Last but certainly not least are usability testers. Usability testing comes rather early in development, after use cases have been firmed up *but before coding begins*. The architecture in most Agile systems is driven by the end user's mental model, so if you wait to test your interface until after you've completed your architecture and filled it out with running code, you may have a mountain of rework to do. Here, in particular, is where the *early on* of the Lean Secret is crucial. You can support user experience testing with prototypes or with simple hard-copy mock-ups of the anticipated screen designs. Usability testing can validate whether the team has captured the end user mental models properly: a crucial test of the architecture. We talk a little bit more about usability testing in Section 7.8.

3.3   Process Elements of Stakeholder Engagement

Your longstanding development process is in place, and you're wondering what an Agile process should look like. Organizations usually conceive their development processes as following one (or both) of two patterns. The first alternative is to exhaustively cover the stages of development and their sequencing. The second is to enumerate the roles and to specify each one's tasks. A total ordering of tasks can over-constrain self-organization, and a task organization alone can become arbitrary if it's detached from the value chain. A generic framework like RUP (Rational Unified Process) that tries to delineate all the roles in general has difficulty mapping onto domain-specific roles and processes, and it's also difficult to map these roles onto the value stream.

In this book, we discuss only the most basic notions of software process as they relate to Lean architecture and Agile production. This is a book about architecture and implementation. You might ask: Where does architecture start and end? To answer that, we need to answer: What is architecture? Architecture isn't a sub-process, but a product of a process – a process called design. Design is the act of solving a problem. Viewed broadly, and a bit tongue-in-cheek, we might say that there are only four processes in software development: analysis (understanding the need); design (solving the problem); verification (usually, testing); and delivery (which may include engineering, installation, shipping and deployment). This means that the time scope of architecture is broad – a long now.

A pithy but adjustable problem statement (Chapter 4) makes a great project compass. To do a good job analyzing an extensive, complex market takes time. Getting everyone in the same room shortens feedback loops. If you can't get the stakeholders in the same room, minimize the number of communication hops between them (see the pattern RESPONSIBILITIES ENGAGE in Coplien and Harrison 2004, pp. 209–211). We care more about how roles connect to the value stream (everyone focused on the product as the goal) than to their place in the process (e.g., to have marketing people focus on feeding analysts who feed architects who feed designers who feed developers who feed testers) or to how their responsibilities fit together into a comprehensive set of tasks (as in RUP).

You can find the stakeholders: the end users, the business, customers, domain experts, and developers in just about every enterprise that builds something for someone else. Some traditional software development processes translate well to an Agile and Lean world, but others merit special attention. So, with a light touch this section offers some rules of thumb on the process.

3.3.1 Getting Started

The vision and problem statement come very early in development – often even before you have customers. Once the vision is in place, use your marketing people to extract knowledge from the market, and your domain experts to extract knowledge from the business world and technology sector. This knowledge can prepare both the business and the development community to shape their understanding of the domain and to start to understand the architectural forms.

If this is a new project, consider the organizational patterns that tie together the structures of your domain, your market, and the geographic distribution of your development team. (Here, "geographic distribution" includes separations as small as one building away or more than 50 meters distant. Don't underestimate the power of space!) In particular, CONWAY'S LAW (Coplien and Harrison 2004, pp. 192–193) and the related patterns ORGANIZATION FOLLOWS LOCATION (Coplien and Harrison 2004, pp. 194–196) and ORGANIZATION FOLLOWS MARKET (Coplien and Harrison

2004, pp. 197–198) are major considerations in organizing your teams. We'll cover Conway's Law more in Section 5.2.

We have heard several conference talks on software architecture that start with a claim such as, "To get started on architecture, first get your requirements in hand." It is true that we need to understand end user requirements if we are to deliver value to them; we dedicate Chapter 7, Chapter 8, and Chapter 9 to that topic. But the foundations of system structure lie elsewhere. The other side of the same modeling coin is domain expertise. Think of domain expertise as a broadening of the end user mental model into the realms of all stakeholders taken together. Expert developers learn over time what the fundamental building blocks of a given system should be. This is where customer concerns – as opposed to end user concerns – weigh most heavily. Other stakeholders hold important perspectives that are radically different from those of the end user. For example, Checking Account Holders think that banking software comprises a ledger that mirrors the entries in their own checkbooks. However, a bank auditor chooses to view that account as a process over an audit trail in a transaction log. Both of these are real; which of these wins out as the systems foundation is a function of many Agile concerns, particularly ease of use, and frequency and type of changes to system functionality.

Those models balance enough generality to accommodate a wide variety of business scenarios with enough concreteness to provide a shared vocabulary for all stakeholders. Such care for the end user perspective on architecture, combined with its concreteness, take us from the problem definition one step closer to a delivered system. Of course, in real development we work on the problem definition, architecture, and use cases in parallel; however, from a conceptual perspective, architecture and its articulation provides a vocabulary and foundation for the later concerns with what the system does. So, guess what: *everybody, all together, from early on* rules yet again.

If this is a new project, start small. Great projects grow from small projects that work. Have your developers work with analysts to explore the domain through prototyping. Once you have a vision of where you're headed, put together one or two teams to frame out the architecture and to demonstrate rudimentary functionality. Here, *team* means three to seven people. Aim for an early success and for a firm foundation that will support the product throughout its lifetime. The primary consideration should be on supporting change in the long term, being particularly attentive to creating effective feedback loops. If you can respond to change, you can improve the value stream. The second consideration is to build your process around the value stream. Strong domain knowledge, and its articulation in an architectural framework, is one of the best things you can do to support change and to draw attention to the value stream.

3.3.2 Customer Engagement

Your thoughts will soon turn to delivering features. We'll emphasize a previous point again: focus on user expectations rather than just wants or *your* perception of their needs. User experience people are experts in extracting (and anticipating) user expectations. And a good need elicitation process may change expectations – on both sides of the table.

It is usually important to study end users and even customers in their native habitat. Don't bring them into your office, but go to theirs. It doesn't matter whether your office has all the touches of the best interior decorator in town, or whether it's just a nerd's paradise – it just can't replace the client's home base as an environment to gain domain knowledge and to learn about the context in which requirements arise.

To say this goes against the popular practice of on-site customer. Recent studies have found that on-site customers can in fact compound the requirements process by creating problems of trust (Martin, Biddle, and Noble 2004; Martin 2004). On top of that is the more obvious problem of missing key contextual cues that arise in the environment. Our colleague Diana Velasco tells of a site visit where the client was describing the process they used but failed to mention the sticky notes posted around the border of the computer screen. By watching how they actually worked, Diana also discovered heavy dependence on a "crib sheet" notebook that everyone kept as a guide to navigating the screen command structures. These are crucial components of the developer world and are crucial to system architecture. They are best discovered by having the architects spend time in the end user environment – another powerful form of Lean's principle of *genchi genbutsu*, or "go look and see for yourself."

Beyer and Holtzblatt's book *Contextual Design* (Beyer and Holtzblatt 1998) offers a wealth of techniques for exploring and capturing end-user mental models. Be selective in the tools you adopt from this and other sources. Use these tools on site visits to garner insight both for architecture and use cases.

As described in Section 3.2.1, you want to actively elicit feedback from end users through short development cycles or by using prototypes and models during analysis. A good feedback cycle has the appearance of causing problems. It will cause emergent and latent requirements to surface. That means rework: the value of prototypes is that they push this rework back into analysis, where it has more value because it potentially lowers the long-term cost. And most important, good end user engagement *changes end user expectations*. Good feedback loops that are grounded in reality give customers the opportunity to reflect on what they're asking for. If your customer changes their expectations in the process, you've both learned something. Embracing change doesn't just mean reacting to it: it means providing the catalysts that accelerate it, and then responding appropriately. Respond with thought to expectations rather than reacting in blind servitude to need.

3.4   The Network of Stakeholders: Trimming Wasted Time

Now that we have covered the roles, we come to the heart of the matter. There is nothing particularly Lean or Agile about the roles themselves. What is important is how they work together. Here we come back to the Lean Secret: everybody, all together, from early on.

3.4.1   Stovepipe Versus Swarm

Old-style software development is patterned after the industrial assembly-line models of the Henry Ford era. In a simple, old-fashioned assembly line, workers interact directly only with the people in the adjacent station on the line. Worse yet, they may not even interact with the people, but may focus exclusively on the artifact and on their task of reshaping it or attaching something to it that adds value to the product. In manufacturing one can push this independence all the way back into the design process, because even designers can count on the laws of physics holding for the parts they design and how they will fit together and hold up in deployment. The development process is divided up into stovepipes: independent spheres of influence lined up side-by-side to create a product piecemeal.

Software has no equivalent to the laws of physics. Alistair Cockburn likens software construction to group poetry writing. It requires many different talents, ranging from knowledge of the business domain to good programming skills to keen insights into ergonomics and interaction design. What's worse, these skill sets can't easily be separated into process steps that can be done one at a time. And even worse, most of these skill sets drive some aspect of the basic system *form*: its *architecture*. If you follow that chain of dependencies, we arrive to the conclusion that we need everybody, all together, from early on.

Table 3-1 summarizes stakeholder relationships discussed earlier in this chapter. If we had drawn such a diagram for a manufacturing assembly line, each role might have a direct dependency only on the one immediately preceding it in the process. But in software, there are essential, ongoing design decision dependencies that imply an almost fully connected network of interactions between roles.

Many software organizations handle these dependencies more or less one at a time as the need arises. One role might perceive the need to interact

Table 3-1   Stakeholder relationships.

	End User	The Business	Customers	Domain Experts	Developers and Testers
End User		Feature priorities, scope	Purchase convenience	Product/ feature feasibility	Quality and proper functionality
The Business	Feasibility	Create standards	Process requirements	Feasibility	Source of revenue
Customers	A market	Products and services	Create standards	Compliance with standards	Source of revenue
Domain Experts	Range of product variation	Workplace well-being	Need for standards	Domain synergies and conflicts	Constraints on technology
Developers and Testers	Requirement Ccarification	Workplace well-being	Advice on delivery process	Guidance, APIs, *poka-yoke*	Clarification of how existing code works

Read down the columns to see what the roles contribute to the value stream; rows indicate the roles to whom the value is provided.

with another and, believing in individuals and interactions over processes and tools, will do a good deed for the day by initiating a communication. There may be many more feedback links to reach the person in the value stream who can deal with the problem. Furthermore, the handoffs waste time and can at best optimize only locally. If the architect is sitting at his or her desk writing the Big Architecture Document, and if he or she needs the insight of the interaction designer before proceeding, too often the information request must go "through channels."

Such interactions often draw many non-producer roles into the process, and that puts the architects into a wait state. If the architect is waiting, so are the GUI designers, the coders, the customers, and the end users. In the very best case, the answer will come back to the architect in days or weeks and is still a useful piece of information that hasn't been invalidated by changes in the market, standards, technology, or development team staffing. More typically, the response raises as many questions as it provides answers (knowing the interaction designer's recommendation, do we need to ask the coder if we can implement it?). Unfortunately, in most cases the architect assumes premises or makes guesses simply because it would take too much time to clarify the details. And that means that when the Big Architecture Document reaches the interaction designer and coder, there will be much wailing and gnashing of teeth – and another big cycle of rework and waste (Figure 3-1).

So by trying to do the right thing in an assembly-line organization, an architect will cause delay. By failing to do the right thing but instead taking all the decisions upon himself or herself, the architect incurs even more delay. This is why architecture development takes months or years in linearly organized complex projects. (These are called "NASA-type phased program planning (PPP) systems" in (Takeuchi and Nonaka 1986).) *It isn't that architecture is so much work; it's that everybody spends so much time waiting while E-mails sit languishing in in-boxes, while architects write architecture documents, or unread memos sit awaiting review* (Figure 3-1).

A good team that develops relationships between the roles – relationships that correspond to the dependencies between stakeholders – can trim the architecture effort from months down to days or weeks.

Organize more like an insect swarm rather than as stovepipes. We're writing this chapter from the middle of the Swedish Northwoods. Yesterday we took a walk in the forest and passed several anthills. The largest one was more than a meter high and more than two meters in diameter, and every millimeter of its surface was alive with scurrying ants. We couldn't find a single project manager among them, nor a single process description. And we didn't see anyone in an architectural wait state.

If you're using Scrum, try to fit your architecture exercise into a single Sprint. Who is the architecture team (Kruchten 1999)? It's the cross-functional Scrum team. If you're in a multi-team Scrum project, you'll need input from multiple teams.

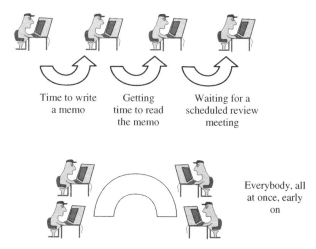

Time to write   Getting   Waiting for a
a memo   time to read   scheduled review
the memo   meeting

Everybody, all
at once, early
on

Figure 3-1   Stovepipe versus swarm.

Your team members should be collocated so they can respond to questions in seconds rather than hours, days, or weeks. What does "team" mean here? It comprises at least those roles described in this chapter. Too often, Agile initiatives limit Agile principles and practices to developers, perhaps with a token on-site customer thrown in. Scrutinizing roles and their stake-holding relationships more carefully shows that things are more complicated than that.

3.4.2   The First Thing You Build

Even in a game that rewards distrust, time teaches the players the value of cooperation, however guarded they may be.
The Clock of the Long Now, p. 123.

Brad Appleton is an old colleague of mine from the Pattern Community and is a long-time respected person of influence at Motorola. His E-mail byline has consistently said for years: "The first thing you build is trust."

Jerry Weinberg tells a story of a company where a highly placed, powerful manager issued an urgent request for new computing equipment. The requirements were a little bit sketchy, but he did insist that "the cabinets had to be blue." His subordinates, and purchasing, and others, scurried around trying to decode this supposedly mysterious message. "Blue! Does he mean to buy from 'big Blue' (IBM)?" "Does he mean that he wants it the same color as the other equipment? But some of it isn't blue!" Someone finally got the nerve to ask him (whether it was actually before or after the equipment arrived, I don't remember) and he said, "No, blue is my wife's favorite color, and she thought that the new computers should be blue."

One exercise in Lean is called "ask five times." If someone makes an unclear or unexpected claim, ask him or her about it. More often than not you'll get another unexpected claim. Within about five exchanges you'll come to the core of it. Why didn't anyone ask the executive why he wanted blue? It was perhaps out of fear of being an idiot for not knowing the answer. Or perhaps it was out of fear of potentially embarrassing the boss in public. There wasn't enough trust in the organization to clarify the requirements.

Jerry talks about egoless development teams – a commonly misunderstood phrase that simply means that you put your personal stake in perspective so you can defer to the team's stake as a whole. We've all heard the saw: "There are no stupid questions here," but we are not always good at following it. We should be. An Agile team is a team of trust that can ask such questions openly.

3.4.3   Keep the Team Together

As stakeholders, team members have expectations, too. In addition to their value stream expectations, they come to expect certain abilities, reactions, and ways of working from each other. That includes the team's focus on kaizen, or continuous improvement. Such exchanges should be informal matters of habit rather than formalisms of a rigorous process. That means that these expectations must be cultivated as tacit knowledge, and that takes patience and time.

To support the team in the ever-ongoing learning of how to improve, keep the team together over time. If you re-assemble teams for every new product or on a periodic business cycle, each reorganization will take every restructured team into the well-known struggle of forming, storming, and norming before reaching a performing stage (Tuckman 1965). That's waste. Get rid of it.

Teamwork happens on the scale of milliseconds. Just watch a football team. Or, better yet, watch a software team engaged in a design meeting. It's exactly this kind of feedback that can reduce architecture efforts from months to days by displacing formal communication channels and forums with real people in real time. If a team is not co-located, you lose these feedback loops. To sustain team effectiveness, keep the team together in space. A multi-site team can work but will have difficulty sustaining the same pace as a collocated team, everything else being equal. Martin Fowler writes (Fowler 2006) that multi-site development requires more written documentation and, in general, more formal communication styles, than co-located teams do.

There are many variations of Conway's Law that provide guidance for organizing teams. The primary organizing principle is that the team structure should reflect the architecture. However, even that is difficult, because architectures themselves have crosscutting concerns. In the DCI architecture (Chapter 9), the structure of roles and their interactions cuts across the structure of the domain objects. And beyond this simple part of Conway's Law, you also want the organizational structure to align with your market structure. You also want it to align with the physical distribution of people. You also want it to align with the structure of the business. Figuring out exactly how to structure a team means balancing the tradeoffs that emphasize different ones of these organizations. We'll cover this more intricate form of Conway's Law in more detail in Section 5.2.

For completeness, one organizational structure that we know does not work is to isolate all the architects in their own team.

No matter how you organize it's important to keep the boundaries between the teams thin. Any work on the architecture must cut across organizational boundaries.

3.5   No Quick Fixes, but Some Hope

Today's software products are complex, and are often developed by a multinational work force. We live in a global economy, and multi-site development is a common strategy to grow the organization. It's hard to do "everybody, all together, from early on" in a multi-site organization. The simple solution is for each location to work as an independent enterprise. That is possible only if the parts are adequately de-coupled.

We revisit organizational concerns again in Section 5.2 and elsewhere in upcoming chapters to deepen our appreciation of the complex relationships between teams and their code. While this book is perhaps enough to get you started, other sources add deeper insight to organizational issues. The book *Organizational Patterns of Agile Software Development* (Coplien and Harrison 2004) describes how to balance approaches such as ORGANIZATION FOLLOWS MARKET, ORGANIZATION FOLLOWS LOCATION, and CONWAY'S LAW. These patterns at first seem contradictory and, in reality, it's a challenge to make all three alignments co-exist. Dozens or perhaps hundreds of organizations have found how to keep their stakeholders content with a suitable balance of these patterns.

You probably feel that it's daunting, or that it's hard. Many organizations have gone before you and risen to the challenge. You're Agile. We trust you. You'll figure it out.

Problem Definition

Architecture is one product of an activity called design, and there is no design without a *problem*. A problem definition is an explicit, written statement of a problem: the gap between the current state and the desired state.

Before we lay out the route to our destination, we have to know where we're going. More often than not, when we ask software developers what problem their product solves, the discussion goes something like this:

What problem are you solving?

"We're trying to become more object-oriented."

No, that's a solution to some problem, not a problem. What problem are you solving?

"Oh, we're using object orientation so we get better reuse."

No: reuse is itself a solution to some problem. What problem are you solving?

"Well, the last project was too costly and we're trying to reduce our costs."

How many alternatives did you consider?

"Well, none. Everyone else is using objects, so we decided to take a low-risk path."

If you recognize your organization in this reasoning, you're hardly alone.

Grandpa Harry always had a sense of purpose when he set out to build something. Whether it was serious (a house for his family), generous (a small railway station for Jim's model railroad set), or whimsical (carving a small wooden puzzle or toy) it was always *purposeful*. Your projects should probably be purposeful, too. A good problem definition can help point the way.

Many of the principles of problem definition apply in many other microcosms of design. Problems are closely related to goals in use cases and, in general, are closely linked to requirements. Keep this in mind when reading Chapter 7 in particular. However, also remember that problem definitions aren't a club that you can use to beat other project members into submission, and don't go looking for problem definitions under every rock. Most problems are a matter of everyday conversation and feedback. Related concepts such as goals and objectives also have their own specific place in your planning (Section 4.6).

4.1   What's Agile about Problem Definitions?

Agile is about working software. Software provides a service that solves some problem, and it *works* only if it solves that problem.

A good problem definition can be a catalyst for self-organization. The Agile notion of "self-organization" means neither "no organization" nor total lack of structure. Systems in nature that self-organize are called *autopoeietic systems*. They usually organize around some simple law or set of laws or ideas, and always include a notion of reflection or at least of self-reference. Nothing outside of a cell organizes a cell; its structures take the molecules and energy in its environment to build and sustain the overall cell organization that in turn gives rise to these structures (Wikipedia 2009). Problem definitions can provide the catalyst, or seed crystal, that can cause a team to organize and figuratively crystallize its thoughts into a consistent whole.

4.2   What's Lean about Problem Definitions?

The deepest foundations of Lean feature a continuous process of innovation that increases value to the end user, and decreases or eliminates everything else. A good problem definition brings focus to the entire team – an outward focus that is broader than the local problems of their cubicle or work group and that ultimately supersedes any local focus.

Even though a problem definition draws the team's focus beyond its own proverbial navel, it is still within the scope of the system that gives the team its reason for being. Much of Lean is about systems thinking, and a properly leveled problem definition can take the team beyond its preoccupation with the solution to more clearly be able to understand the problem in context. We'll talk more about the contextual framing of problems in Chapter 7, but for now we'll focus more basic notions of good problem definitions.

To a casual observer, problem definitions look like waste. It is time spent away from the keyboard, and our Western upbringing tells us that we are avoiding work or being unproductive when "just talking." But Lean is full of paradoxes like this (Liker 2004, pp. 8–9). Sometimes the best thing you can do is to idle your equipment and stop making parts; sometimes it is better to avoid computers and IT and to resort to manual processes, just because people are a more flexible resource.

Perhaps the most obvious tie from problem definitions to Lean is their foundation for consistency. Lean asks us to reduce tensions and inconsistencies in a system. A problem statement at least articulates a consistent objective. Too often projects suffer from the simple problem that its members are not all solving the same problem. A well-written problem statement offers a consistent vision of direction. As such, it can be a powerful team tool or management tool.

A problem definition forms near the beginning of a project and may evolve over time. You should view it as an up-front investment – not investment in a reusable artifact, but an investment in your people and your customers. Lean is based on "a culture of stopping or slowing down to get quality right the first time to enhance productivity in the long run" (Liker 2004, p. 38). Reworking ideas early in the process helps you avoid the more costly reworking of code later in the process. This fits with Boehm's software engineering findings that a bug discovered in a requirements review costs you 70 times less to fix than one discovered in the field (Boehm 1976). Problem definition is one of your first chances to get it right. It takes time, but time taken here is potentially a lot of time saved later. As Grandpa Harry used to say: A stitch in time saves nine.

We won't make any pretense that you'll always get it right the first time. Lean is also about continuous process improvement, about turning every coder into an architectural innovator. It's about challenging the expectations of your end user and customer, lifting them to new levels of awareness about their own wants and needs. That means that you'll be chasing a moving target. But we almost always do, anyhow, and good process improvement coupled with Agile principles can help the target settle down more quickly. And as for moving targets – well, we embrace change. We'll discuss this more below.

The Lean literature is full of techniques to support problem definition, such as asking "Why?" five times every time you encounter a problem; the goal is to drive to the root cause (Liker 2004, p. 252–254). Lean is designed for *complicated* systems, whose problems often can be isolated to a "root cause." Software systems are not only complicated: they are *complex*. Though you can track a system effect back to set of causes you can't always chart a path from cause to effect. We compensate for this with the Agile principle of frequent feedback. In any case, a good problem definition removes one large degree of uncertainty from development. It won't remove your team from the ship in the storm, but it will at least help ensure that they are on a chartered ship.

4.3   Good and Bad Problem Definitions

A good problem definition has these characteristics:

1. It is written down and shared.
2. It is a difference between the current state and some desired state of the organization or business.
3. Its achievement is measurable, usually at some mutually understood point in time.
4. It is short: one or two sentences in clear, simple, natural language.
5. It is internally consistent: that is, it does not set up an over-constrained problem.

Though problem definitions are short and can be developed in a short period of time, their importance far outweighs their size. As with many artifacts in Agile, it isn't so much the artifact itself that is important as the process for creating it. Good problem definitions nonetheless share a few key properties that help focus that process. We'll take a little time here exploring good problem definitions and some of the ways that problem definition can get off-track.

Here are some examples of good problem definitions:

To be able to sell a picture transfer application that will work with 90% of the phones on the market.

This is a pretty good problem definition. It is measurable. It defines the problem as "being able to sell," which is a business proposition, rather than "designing and building." The latter is a more constrained *solution*; as stated, it points more directly at the *problem*.

Here is another one:

All television signal transmissions will be converted to FCC standard digital format by 1 January 2009.

The result is measurable (provided that the FCC standard is well-defined), and we are even told when we should apply the measurement to evaluate success. If we ask *Why?* we might be told that the law requires us to meet this conversion timetable. We might have written another problem statement that viewed the impending law itself as a problem and might have worked with our lobbyist to delay the enforcement of the law, at least for us. But *that* would be a different problem, and it would show up as a different problem definition.

Let's look at some bad examples. Consider this one:

We need to become object-oriented.

We actually heard this one a lot from our clients in the 1980s. Why is it not a good problem definition? Because it's not at all apparent that there is even a problem: a difference between the current state and a desired state. This is a *solution*, not a *problem*! We can get a hint that this is not a good problem definition by asking *Why?* five times. In fact, if we do that, one of the answers may point the direction to a good problem definition.

Here is another one:

To be the best we can be at delivering on time.

What's the problem with this one? The result isn't measurable (a short-coming of the preceding one as well). The problem will never be solved, almost by design.

Here is yet a third one:

We need to increase productivity 40% while cutting costs 40%.

This is more like a requirement list than a problem statement. First, it is really two problems, not one. Second, it may be a solution in disguise. Ask *why* we need to hit these targets. Third, it may set up an over-constrained problem if productivity and cost are linked.

Here is a subtle one:

We want the most user-friendly time entry system in the industry.

The main (but not only) challenge with this one is that it is not testable.

Sometimes asking *Why?* five times can lead you from a poor problem definition to a good one. Consider this one as a starting point:

Our quality sucks.

Well, O.K., there must be something more we can say. We ask *Why?* The answer comes back ''Because users report a lot of bugs.'' We could even make that into a problem statement:

Users report more bugs per release than our competition does.

Why? we ask, anticipating that the discussion will take a turn into testing. "Because users complain that they go all the way through our ordering and payment screens before they find that an item is out-of-stock." Aha. Maybe we are missing some scenarios in our use cases and we need to go back and ask for more user stories from the end users. Maybe our problem statement ends up being:

The system does not properly handle end-user orders for out-of-stock items.

That's a problem definition that the team can get its teeth into.

No matter what your title or organizational level, and no matter why you are creating a problem definition, it always pays to ask *Why?* five times. Get beyond the symptoms to the problem, and take ownership of the problem by articulating it yourself.

4.4 Problems and Solutions

If you think that *problem* is to *solution* like *cause* is to *effect*, you're probably in for some surprises during design. The relationship between problem and solution is rich and complex. Broad experience with methods has shown that, in fact, you can't start with a problem definition and methodically elaborate it into a solution.[1]

There are two simple facts to remember when administering your problems and solutions. The first one is that the mapping from problems to solutions is many-to-many. Consider a house that has a room with poor light. Furthermore, there are rooms in the house with poor summer ventilation. A single solution – a window in the dark room – might be enough to solve both problems. Grandpa Harry always loved it when he could kill two birds with one stone. However, you should also be aware that four or five seemingly unrelated solutions might be required to solve what you perceive as a single problem. Some problems, like world hunger or world peace, seem to defy any mapping at all. The problem that you face in software design has intrinsic complexity in the same family of problems as world peace and world hunger: they're called *wicked problems*. The comparison is a perhaps a bit dramatic, but it is a formally apt comparison. There are no proven escapes from this difficulty except constant attentiveness and adjustment. It's just enough to keep one humble. But such adjustment is also what Agile is all about.

---

[1] Cross (1984) is a good source on this topic.

4.5   The Process Around Problem Definitions

Your initial problem definitions might take a bit of work.

Much of Agile – and Scrum in particular – is based on a fact of life called emergent requirements. Grandpa Harry used to say that the best laid plans of mice and men often go astray. You can't master plan a project and expect to follow the plan. Agile folks know that. However, most Agile folks think that means only that we discover new problems along the way. It isn't just that we discover new problems: the act of design actually creates new problems. More to the point, the act of design sometimes changes the very nature of the problem we have set out to solve. We must revisit the problem definition to refresh it now and then.

4.5.1   Value the Hunt Over the Prize

The underlying Agile value here is people and communication. There is an old French saying: "The hunt is more valuable than the prize." It is much more important that the team is in dialogue, discussing the problem identity, than that the final problem definition is perfect. Any given definition is potentially ephemeral, anyhow, and the value comes from dialogue. Problem definition expert Phil Fuhrer says it well (2008):

> Just the effort of trying to crystallize the client's needs into a statement that speaks to the designers is worthwhile even if the output is not finalized. It is about communication.
>
> A good or great problem definition is harder to characterize. I would say that a good problem definition is one that leads to a successful project. It must fit project's product and process. Most of the problem with problem defining is that it is hard to align the defining effort with the project's process culture. Project managers often like to manage clear-cut deliverables and tend to rush the chartering, scoping, and other get-started tasks.
>
> Measuring how well it captures the critical success factors of the client or how well it focuses the design effort is itself a problem. The four considerations (function, form, economy, and time) are helpful but I have seen problem definition efforts get hung up on them.
>
> Having said that I would say that a great problem definition opens up possibilities and identifies and addresses overly constrained problems.

It is still crucial to drive toward a single, simple, closed-form problem definition; otherwise, you end up with analysis paralysis. Phil mentions another key concern: over-constrained problems. It's easy to define a problem that is impossible to solve, such as is often the case with space/time tradeoffs, cost/schedule tradeoffs, build/buy tradeoffs – in fact, just about all design decisions are tradeoffs and therefore open up the opportunity for conflict between desiderata. Great design is finding just the right solution that lets you have your cake and eat it too, but competent design is realizing when the business just won't allow such magic, owning up to that realization, and making hard decisions based on the consequences of that realization.

4.5.2   Problem Ownership

Jerry Weinberg is articulate on the topic of problem ownership. It is a simple concept but is commonly misconstrued. The question should arise: *Who owns the problem?* The answer should always respect the people with the power to solve the problem.

It's common in life that one person formulates a problem and hands it over to someone else to solve. You ask your secretary to get rid of a salesman. Your boss asks you to cut your budget by 15%. The customer asks you to fix a bug. While these situations will persist in the real world, it's better if the person who owns (or who will own) the problem writes the problem definition. Otherwise, problem statements become a way for one person to wield power over another, and that constrains the self-organization and feedback that make Agile work.

As a stopgap measure, anyone can receive a "request to fix something" that originated somewhere along the lines of power in the organization, re-write it as a good problem definition, and feed it back to the requestor. Such feedback ensures that you are solving the right problem, that you together understand what the solution criteria are (they are measurable), and that the problem doesn't have a built-in trap that will lead to failure. That is a way to use problem definitions responsively.

In a true Agile organization, the team strives to expand the scope of problem ownership so that the problem definition opens up possibilities rather than focusing on how to allocate blame. This means that those responsible for solving the problem have a part in defining the problem. Problem statements shouldn't be a way for one person to wield power over another, but should help channel the energy of the organization in a consistent direction. A problem definition has more power if used proactively than if used reactively. It won't always work out that way, but keep striving to expand the scope of problem ownership. Keep it simple, fast, and light.

An Example of Problem Ownership: Scrum

In Scrum, the Product Owner owns the problem of sustaining the ROI vision and meeting ROI targets. The Team supports the Product Owner in solving this problem by delivering product in the order specified by the Product Owner. The Team owns the problem of converting Product Backlog Items (PBIs, or requirements) into product, and the Product Owner supports the team with enabling specifications and ongoing clarification of requirements. The ScrumMaster owns the problem of improving the culture and the process, and supports the Team by working impediments that prevent them from solving their problems. The ScrumMaster owns a list of problems called the *impediment list*, one of the main artifacts supporting process improvement in Scrum. Taking away someone else's problem ownership (e.g. by taking over their problem) is disempowering and de-motivating.

4.5.3 Creeping Featurism

Though problem definitions evolve, it is important to avoid slippery slopes and creeping featurism. There is always a tradeoff between being able to take on new problems and being able to hold to your commitments for solving the ones already on the table. All kinds of red flags should go up when a latent requirement, emergent requirement, or other surprise substitutes something new for something you are working on. Scrum nicely solves this by giving the team the option of tackling the newly formulated problem or rejecting it, on the basis of keeping a time-boxed commitment to what the customer expects. If the business can't live with the team's decision, then the new problem becomes a business crisis suitable for discussion at the business level. Lean views such a crisis as a positive thing that draws the team onward and upward. It is usually important to convene a ceremony of the pertinent size and scope when the problem definition shifts; see the organizational patterns Take No Small Slips (Coplien and Harrison 2004, pp. 54–55) and Recommitment Meeting (Coplien and Harrison 2004, pp. 60–61).

4.6   Problem Definitions, Goals, Charters, Visions, and Objectives

Agile is full of casual terminology for this issue of what-direction-are-we-going. We urge teams to distinguish between the following named concepts.

An *objective* is a waypoint that we must achieve to succeed. To not achieve an agreed objective is a call for reflection and process improvement. In Scrum, the collective contents of a Sprint backlog form an objective for the Sprint. A problem definition is most often a form of objective. We can compare objectives to other important concepts that draw us forward.

A *vision* is a broad, inspiring portrait of a world that our system can help to create. It might relate to broad convenience that results from adopting our product; it might relate to increased profits for the company; it might relate to growing market share.

A *goal* is the desired endpoint in the best of all possible worlds. In use cases, the goal is what the main success scenario achieves. If we have a telephone use case named "Call up a friend," the goal is to talk to the party we are calling. Sometimes we don't achieve that goal – because our friend is busy, or because the system is overloaded, or because we forget the phone number in the middle of dialing. Yet all these scenarios are part of the "Call up a friend" use case and each works *toward* the same goal. Grandpa Harry always had the goal of completing his mail delivery route by 3:30 in the afternoon. Sometimes he made that goal, and sometimes he didn't. That he sometimes didn't make that goal doesn't mean that he was a failure.

A *Sprint goal* in Scrum is usually more closely tied to "Done" than in the broader use of the term *goal*, so a Sprint goal is really an objective most of the time. Therefore, a Sprint goal can conveniently be described as a problem definition. We've seen a lot of confusion around this term in Scrum, so you should be sure that everyone means the same thing when invoking this term.

A *charter* is a document that describes ongoing group work practice. A charter usually comes from a chartering organization to a chartered organization, though the chartered organization can have a say in the charter's content. Charters very easily challenge Agile foundations. I recently looked at a charter document template created by a well-known facilitator; the boilerplate itself was over 15 pages long. That's not Lean. Furthermore, the us-and-them notion of charter-er and charter-ee breaks down the notion of *team* that is crucial to effective communication in Agile approaches such as Scrum.

4.7   Documentation?

When a manager comes to me, I don't ask him, 'What's the problem?' I say, 'Tell me the story.' That way I find out what the problem really is.

Grocery store chain owner Avram Goldberg, quoted in *The Clock of the Long Now*, p. 129.

It's a good idea to circulate your problem definition broadly in written form. The work of producing a tangible problem definition provides focus for the team and can bring together what is initially just a group of people and provide a seed for team dynamics. But remember that the main value isn't in the document and that it's not Lean to produce something unnecessarily large. A statement of one or two sentences is ideal, and a page is too long.

There is something strangely powerful about documenting problem definitions on paper. Don't bury them as a field on some methodological form deep in some database. We'd discourage you even from using E-mail as the primary distribution mechanism. Try printing your problem definitions on small pieces of paper (small is beautiful, and emphasizes the non-methodological tone of a good problem definition) and hand them out to all the stakeholders. Have all the stakeholders autograph a copy on a major project. Make it fun, not a death march. Use problem statements to open up possibilities.

Software problem definitions, written or not, live in an oral culture. They may be written as stories, or as one- or two-sentence distillation of stories, but they almost always have stories behind them. Celebrate these stories in the oral culture and share them around the virtual campfire. Stories can range in formality from user stories to use cases to war stories from a client or an old project.

What the System *Is*, Part 1: Lean Architecture

Starting anew with a clean slate has been one of the most harmful ideas in history.
The Clock of the Long Now, p. 74.

Grandpa Harry had a riding lawnmower that he owned for about a decade. He took very good care of the machine, keeping it well oiled and in good repair. He knew every inch of that machine: each bearing, each belt, each linkage, and each engine part.

However, the lawnmower broke down after many years of loving use. The manufacturer had long ceased to stock parts for the old machine. We went down to the local repair shop where a couple of Grandpa Harry's contemporaries had been repairing small motors for years. Bill greeted us as we worked our way to his desk in the middle of the shop. The place was a mess: lawnmower carcasses, disembodied parts and fragments scattered everywhere. A casual visitor could see neither rhyme nor reason to the arrangement of parts in that shop; indeed, other than in Bill's memory, there probably was none.

But, yes, they had the part, and Bill worked his way gradually toward the treasure, moving obstacles large and small along the way. He came back to Grandpa Harry, part in hand, and sent us on our merry way after we paid a token fee for the almost-antique piece of gadgetry. Bill must have had a map of that entire mess in his head. Perhaps his frequent rummaging kept the map current, but only he and his partner knew the whereabouts of things.

It's a complex task to find our way around the old junkyard that we call our code base. Maybe the simplest way to maintain software is to create it from scratch every time instead of trying to patch the existing code. A program is only a delivery vehicle: the real end deliverable is a service, not a product. The service changes over time and the fact that we have a product – the code – is a liability. Code is not Lean.

Like it or not, most code becomes an investment, and it's usually unreasonable to recreate significant works of software from scratch every time we need a change. There must be some order to the artifacts that we create so we can find our way around in them. If we are a team of one, working on a simple, single application, then we can treat our software like Bill treated his repair shop. We can claim to know it all. If we work on large complex systems, we need some order to be able to find what we need when we need it. Furthermore, the order should stay more or less the same over time: if it changes every few days, then the order doesn't really help us.

In this chapter we will help you create a Lean domain architecture for your system. Such an architecture can support Agile software development much better than a traditional, heavyweight architecture can. The inputs to this architecture include well-informed experience of domain experts as well as end-user mental models. The process starts with simple partitioning and then proceeds to selecting a design style (paradigm) and coding it up. We'll take a short interlude into fine points of object-oriented design to provide a foundation for the what-the-system-does work coming up in Chapter 7 through Chapter 9. The output is code and system documentation. We will create class interfaces, annotated with pre-conditions and post-conditions, supported by a domain dictionary and a short domain document for each business area.

Before we get into the real work of architecture, we're going to cover important foundations that will make the work easier. This is an Agile book, and we'd rather give you a fishing pole than a fish. Sections 5.2 and 5.3 are fishing-pole stuff, and the remainder of the chapter talks more about technique.

5.1   Some Surprises about Architecture

Architecture is one of those terms that has as many meanings as there are people who use the term. The term came into software through Fred Brooks while at IBM, who one day in the 1960s asked Jerry Weinberg whether he thought that what architects did was a suitable metaphor for what we do in software, and Jerry agreed (Weinberg 1999). An early-published use of the term can be found in Buxton and Randell (1969). Even in the field of urban design and building architecture, the title of "architect" has taken on a disproportionate sense of power and mastery (Rybczynski 1989, p. 9; see Section 3.2). In this book we heed time-honored principles of architecture that may be a little bit different than you find in your culture or organization, and we want to avoid misunderstandings. So here are a few clarifications, drawn largely from the classic notion of the term *architecture*:

- *Architecture is more about form than structure. Form* is the essence of structure. Think of form as being the essential shape or arrangement of a thing without regard to what it is made of, and of structure as the reification of a form. In this chapter we strive toward an architecture, which, though concretely expressed in code, communicates form without the clutter of structure. If we capture the form (including its associations and attributes) without expanding into full structure (for example, methods and data members), we stay Lean. That leads to an architecture that can scale and evolve better than one cluttered with the structure of premature implementation.

- *Architecture is more about compression than abstraction.* Abstraction is "the process of considering something independently of its associations, attributes, or concrete accompaniments" (NOAD 2007). In architecture we want to consider system entities together *with* their associations and attributes! But we want to keep the architectural expression compact. We keep the architectural expression small by appealing to standards and the domain knowledge shared by the team. In the same sense that poetry is not abstract, but compressed, so is architecture: every word means something more than its common dictionary definition.

- *Much architecture is not about solving user problems.* Users care about the function of software more than its form, just as you care more about getting a good meal and night's sleep in a hotel than you do about its architecture. You care that the hotel supports the *activities* of eating and sleeping. There is an indirect link between form and function, because form arises over long periods of time as systems learn how to support what we want to do. Hotels have evolved to a form different from that of houses or churches, each according to its function. But the day-to-day end user focuses on function rather than architecture. Traditionally, it is function and not form that is in the value stream. This has led many schools of software architecture to make the mistake of driving architecture with requirements.

  A good system form gives the vendor enough flexibility to respond to new end user expectations within a given problem space. Much software architecture has evolved to the point where we focus on properties that we believe to reduce cost in the long term, such as coupling and cohesion, without much regard for function. By going beyond coupling and cohesion to the end user world model, Lean architecture brings architecture squarely back into the value stream.

- *Architecture has both a static and dynamic component.* In this chapter we'll focus on that part of architecture that changes little over time. This relatively static form comes from the domain structure. It is like the form of a great ballroom that over its lifetime will witness many balls and many dancers. We'll return to the dancers in Chapter 7, but for now we'll focus on building the environment suitable to whatever dance your system is bound to perform.

- *Architecture is everybody's job.* The job of architecture is too important to be left to the architect alone. In an Agile world based on stakeholder engagement and feedback, we invite everyone to the party. Doing so reduces waste, reduces the intervals that come with those review meetings that are scheduled weeks in advance, and develops buy-in across the enterprise for the system design. This isn't to say that architecture can be done by just anybody; we'll insist that the team collectively have many of the talents of traditional architects, and then some. But we also face the stark reality that it's becoming increasingly difficult to find the ideal single person to master plan the system. Instead, we recognize that together we know more than any one of us.

- *Architecture need not be hard!* Architecture has a tradition of taking a long time. It also has roots in project *fear* of *failure.* We also tend to have a misplaced belief that something can have great value only if it is hard to achieve. It needn't be that way. Lean eliminates the kind of wait states that draw out a few days or weeks of real architecture work over months of elapsed time. By involving the whole team in architecture, we not only reduce wait states, but also reduce the fear that comes from believing that architecture is something that somebody in power does to the coders. Yes, like all design and programming, it's good honest work and should be taken seriously – but if it feels like drudgery, you're probably doing it wrong.

5.1.1 What's Lean about This?

We started writing this book to relate useful architectural practices for an Agile project, as we felt that nature had left a vacuum to be filled. The more we put our thoughts to words, the more that we discovered that good Agile architectural practice might best be expressed in terms of Lean principles. In retrospect, that shouldn't have been a surprise. Lean in fact has little or nothing to do with automobiles and everything to do with product, with value, and with the people in the design, production and maintenance processes. Much of what passes for Agile in Scrum these days in fact comes directly from Lean (in particular, from the paper by Takeuchi and Nonaka (Takeuchi and Nonaka 1986)).

Deliberation and "Pull"

Lean is based on "a culture of stopping or slowing down to get quality right the first time to enhance productivity in the long run" (Liker 2004, p. 38). Architecture comes from early and ongoing deliberation about the overall form of a system, and it comes out of patience that can put aside pressure to attend to the squeaky wheel. Analogous to the quote from Liker, the goal is long-term productivity. Investing in architecture now lays a foundation for more productive work over the long term.

Getting quality right the first time is a goal to shoot for, not an objective that defines success and failure. To set an absolute definition of quality and to gauge success by whether we met that foreordained number or mandate is to presume more control over the future than is humanly possible. We embrace the changes that arise from latent requirements, emergent requirements, and just stupid surprises, because that's the real world. However, every moment we strive to do the best we can, given the information at hand, knowing that the future will bring us more information.

The Lean notion of quality makes more sense when we think of the value stream, and of the notion of "pull" versus "push." Pushing is like an act of distancing one's self from the rest of the system; pulling is a way of bringing the system closer. The end user "pulls" the product through the value stream from its raw materials to the delivered product. The human-centric ideas of the next section have their roots in the Lean principle of "pull."

Failure-Proof Constraints or *Poka-Yoke*

Grandpa Harry sometimes applied his woodworking skills to cabinet making. If he had a lot of duplicate cabinet doors or drawers to build, he would sometimes build a "jig" to guide the cutting or assembly of the parts. His cabinets were still hand-made craftsmanship, but he made tools to help him in the tedious repetitive tasks of assembly. It was a good way to avoid the kind of stupid mistakes one can make when undertaking tedious, repetitive tasks. What he was doing was a simple form of the Lean concept of *poka-yoke* – the idea of using a guide or jig that makes it almost impossible to put together an assembly incorrectly. It means "fail-proof" in Japanese. (They originally used the Japanese for "idiot-proof" but political correctness won out.)

Software architecture is a perfect reflection of the Lean concept of *poka-yoke*. It guides the engineer (in the case of software, the feature programmer) to write code that "fits" with the rest of the system. *Poka-yoke* is not a punishing constraint but a guide and help.

Poka-yoke is a good fit for Agile development. As team members work together during an iteration, it is possible for one developer to check in even a rough implementation of some feature while others work on other features, even within the same integration. Architectural firewalls protect the overall system form – a form that reflects longstanding experience and systems thinking. The structure remains more stable, which means less rework.

The Lean Mantras of Conservation, Consistency, and Focus

Good software architecture embodies several more Lean principles. As mentioned above, it reduces rework. It provides an overall consistent system view: to reduce inconsistency is a central theme in Lean. It helps keep the team focused on the feature and its value during feature development by removing most of the need to worry about system form, and that keeps development flowing in the heat of change. But most directly, software architecture reflects an investment economy. Lean believes in short-term loss for long-term gain. Here "investment" is a better term than "loss."

5.1.2   What's Agile about Architecture?

It's All About Individuals and Interactions

Agile is all about "individuals and interactions over processes and tools." So, in fact, is architecture! We ask people in our seminars, "Why do we do architecture?" The answer usually relates to coupling and cohesion (Stevens, Myers, and Constantine 1974; Yourdon and Constantine 1975) and other classic measures of good architecture. Why do we strive for those? Does our software run better if its modules have better cohesion and if they are better decoupled? In fact, one can argue that a good architecture slows the code down by adding layers of APIs and levels of indirection.

No, we value architecture for the sake of what it portends for individuals and interactions. Grandpa Harry used to quote the old saw that "birds of a feather flock together," so individuals group according to their domain expertise, or at least according to their domain responsibilities. Each of these little groups should have its own software artifact that it can manage and evolve with minimal interference from the outside – that means minimal coordination with other little groups who each have their own artifacts. If we divide up the artifacts according to the domain expertise we find in these groups of individuals, we provide each team more autonomy in the long term. That allows each team to be more responsive ("responding to change over following a plan"). This is called Conway's Law (Conway 1968). We support Conway's Law by delivering just enough architecture to shape the organizational structure.

It's not just about the individuals on the team and their interactions. Architectural concepts extend all the way to the end user. Jef Raskin tells us: the interface is the program (Raskin 2000). More precisely, the concepts in the end user's head extend all the way into the code. If these structures are the same, it closes the feedback loop of understanding between end user and programmer. This isomorphism is the key to the _direct manipulation metaphor_ developed in the early days of Smalltalk: that end users directly manipulate the software objects in the program, objects that should reflect the end user mental model. No amount of interface sugarcoating can hide the deep structures of code. Just try using your favorite word processor to place a picture exactly where you want it in the middle of the paragraph. The underlying program structure wins out in spite of the best efforts of interface designers and user intuition.

The organizational structure reflects the architecture; the architecture reflects the form of the domain; and the domain has its roots in the mental models of end users and other stakeholders. Architecture is the explicit artifact that aligns these views.

Past Excesses

Software architecture has a history of excesses that in part spurred the reaction called Agile. Software architecture of the 1980s was famous for producing reams of documentation that no one read. The CASE tools of the 1980s were particularly notorious for their ability to produce documentation even faster than human beings could – again, documentation that was often write-only.

But Agile is about "working software over comprehensive documentation." We will strive for an architecture delivered as APIs and code rather than duplicating that information in documents. While the interface is the program, the code is the design. One of the heaviest costs of software development is the so-called "discovery cost:" knowing where to find the code for a particular business area, or trying to find the source of a fault. Comprehensive documentation of the system organization is one way to do it. But if the code is well organized, we can let the code speak for itself instead. Code has formal properties that elude most documentation (for example, type conformance of interfaces) that make it even more valuable as a design document. Yes, there will be some documentation, too, but we'll keep it Lean. After all, the Agile Manifesto doesn't say to "eliminate documentation," and Lean just admonishes us to make sure that the documentation feeds the value stream.

In the past, architecture not only produced an impressive mountain of artifacts but also took an inordinate amount of time. We have a client who takes 6 months to take a new requirement into production, and much of that time is architecture work. If you look closely, much of the time is spent in writing and reviewing documents. One team member lamented that "many of the things we write down simply because they are true." That is waste. With everybody, all together, from early on, we eliminate these delays. It isn't unreasonable to compress these six months down to one or two weeks if communication between team members is great.

Dispelling a Couple of Agile Myths

> *Desire always misreads fate.*
> *The Clock of the Long Now*, p. 115.

The Agile world is full of practices that are reactions to these past excesses. Sometimes, these are over-reactions that go too far. Here we briefly look at two common failure modes in Agile projects.

The first belief is that you can always re-factor your way to a better architecture. While this is true in small degree, particularly for very small projects, it becomes increasingly difficult with the scale of the system and size of the organization. Time hardens the interfaces and the entire system slowly hardens. It is like stirring a batch of cement: eventually, it sets, and you can't stir it any more.[1]

Re-factoring shows up as a practice in its own right, done for the sake of clean code (Martin 2009) and as a key practice of Test-Driven Development (TDD) (Beck 2002). In its original form, TDD was a design technique for programmers based on unit-test-first.[2] It grew out of distaste for big up-front architecture, and proposed to displace such practices with incremental architecture evolution. It claimed that it would improve the coupling and cohesion metrics. It would be a fortuitous result if cleaned-up feature development would not only generate near-term revenues, but could reduce long-term cost as well. However, empirical studies don't bear these hopes out. A 2008 IEEE Software article, while reporting the

---

[1] Thanks to Ian Graham for this delightful image.
[2] Actually, the historic progression started with an article by Kent Beck (Beck 1994) that described how Smalltalk had suffered because it lacked a testing culture, and the article proposed how to solve the problem with a test framework. That framework evolved into the form it took in an joint article with Eric Gamma in 1998, which today we know as jUnit (Beck and Gamma 1998). Test-first was part of XP in 1999 (Beck 1999), and TDD techniques matured by 2002 (Beck 2002).

local benefits of re-factored code, found that their research results didn't support TDD's coupling and cohesion claims (Janzen and Saledian 2008). Research by Siniaalto and Abrahamsson concludes not only that there is no architectural benefit, but also that TDD may cause the architecture to deteriorate (Siniaalto and Abrahamsson 2007a, 2007b).

The supposed link from re-factoring to architecture arises from a belief that form follows function. That may be true, but only over the aggregation of hundreds or thousands of functions over the system lifetime. This link also presumes that re-factoring's scope is broad enough to straighten out system-level relationships. However, re-factoring is almost always a local activity, whereas architecture is a global concern. There is a serious mismatch between the two.

A second common belief of Agile is that we should do things at the last responsible moment (Cohn 2004, p. xv). It's a bit of a problematic formulation because one never knows exactly when the magic moment has slipped past. It might be better said that we shouldn't make decisions irresponsibly early – or late. If you have enough information to get started, then get started. Trying to solve the problem will cause emergent requirements to surface a lot faster than if you just wait for them to walk up and introduce themselves, or to come to you in a dream, or to appear while working on an unrelated feature. Use the pattern GET ON WITH IT (Coplien and Harrison 2004, p. 38): start as soon as you have enough insight to set an initial direction.

What makes a decision irresponsible? We get in trouble when we don't have enough insight to support the decision. Postponing decisions increases the time for learning to take place and for requirements to emerge, and that is the argument for deferral. But a deferred decision entails more than the passage of time: we aren't just sitting in the sun waiting for things to happen, but are doing work and committing to structure in the code. Letting time go by as we create structure in the mean time, without conscious attentiveness to form, leads to undisciplined form. We may learn something as we work on the code, forging our way a bit into the dark, but we have also left a trail of poorly informed work that may have to be unwound and re-done. Therefore, we must balance between an approach where we unearth and act on fundamental knowledge early, and one where we allow knowledge to emerge from compounded local, shortsighted actions.

The fundamental form of a business often repeats itself in system after system. This constancy means that we know much of it at the beginning of every project. To defer the decision of what essential domain form to lay as the system's foundation is irresponsible because it has a high chance of creating waste. Therefore, we embrace domain knowledge – stuff that we truly know about the business – at the beginning of product construction.

5.2   The First Design Step: Partitioning

Grandpa Harry always said that you put your pants on one leg at a time. As human beings, we are psychologically wired with a feature called a locus of attention that is closely tied to the notion of consciousness: we have exactly one of these and, at some level, we can focus on only one thing at a time. Our first inclination as human beings dealing with complexity is to divide and conquer.

There's an old saw that a complex system has many architectures. There's a lot of truth to that. If you think of the old-fashioned top-down approach to system design, it worked well for simple systems. Top-down design viewed a system as providing some function, where we can use the term "function" almost in the mathematical sense. A program was to take an input, transform it, and produce an output. Maybe it did this many times, once for each of thousands of punch cards provided to it as input in what was called batch processing. The function could be broken down into sub-functions, and those functions into smaller functions, and so forth.

Another way to think about complexity is in terms of *classification* rather than partitioning. Classification is a technique we use to partition items into distinct sets. There are of course many forms of classification. Think of classifying the items in the room where you are sitting right now: By color? By size? By use? By age? There are many different classification schemes you could use. The same is true with software. The problem is that though one classification scheme may seem best, many more are at least partly right. We know a story of some helpful painters who painted the living room of a couple who are friends of ours out in Glostrup while they were away on vacation. When they came back, their thousands of books had been neatly put back on the shelves – nicely sorted by color instead of their original ordering as they would have been in a library.

Top-down design breaks down for complex systems because a complex system has many "tops."[3] People don't use today's interactive, Agile systems in batch mode: their keystrokes and mouse clicks come in seemingly random order. End users juggle between "tops" in a session with the program. Picasso was said to do his oil paintings in an analogous way, jumping from one area of the picture to another rather than dwelling first on one part and then on another. (When doing our early work in the 1980s with the multi-window workstation called the **blit**[4] in Bell Laboratories, we found that one of the main uses of multiple windows was to maintain simultaneous views of these multiple "tops.") A good program presents many tops clearly, and a good architecture expresses them elegantly.

[3] Thanks to Dennis DeBruler for this insight.
[4] "Blit" does *not* stand for Bell Labs Intelligent Terminal.

Lean architecture consciously organizes a system according to multiple meaningful "tops." Let's investigate some of the important "tops" of software, and further investigate ways to use them to partition a system.

5.2.1   The First Partition: Domain Form Versus Behavioral Form

The Agile Manifesto contrasts responding to change with following a plan. A timeless goal of software engineering has been to separate code that changes frequently from code that is stable. For most software, that dividing line is the same as that between what the system *is* (that is relatively stable) and what the system *does* (that changes as customer expectations change and grow). In some sense, those are two different "tops" of the system. Most software architectures exhibit this split in one form or another. For example, client/server systems often load up the client with most of the "does" code and the server with the "is" code. As another example, UML divides models into static views (like class diagrams) and dynamic views (such as interaction diagrams). Our first step towards an Agile architecture is therefore:

Technique 1

Focus on the essence of the system form (what the system is) without being unduly influenced by the functionality that the system provides (what the system does).

There is no explicit design activity where we separate the what-the-system-does part from the what-the-system-is part. Rather, there are two parallel, cooperating development streams for these two forms. Work on the what-the-system-is component often precedes the what-the-system-does component, because you often have a development team in place before you have enough behavioral requirements to enable design and development. Of course, it happens the other way around, too: a customer arrives on your doorstep and asks for some new software service, and you already have a start on your what-the-system-does requirements.

This partitioning owes its roots to much history, including the basic way that computers work (the Von Neumann computational model), the way we are raised in the Western world (to believe in a dichotomy between form and function), and all the programming languages and tools that precipitate from those two foundations.

We can actually state a more general rule of thumb for architecture:

Technique 2

Separate the components of your architecture according to their differing rates of change.

This same principle applies to the architecture of houses. The stone foundation may change very slowly, whereas internal walls may come and go at a historically faster pace, and the floor covering may change even faster. Look for these "shear layers" in your architecture and separate the modules at the fault line between them.

5.2.2   The Second Partitioning: Conway's Law

Given this architectural context we can now actually get to work. As mentioned earlier, we have two design processes going on. One of them focuses on what-the-system-is, and another on what-the-system-does. We'll focus more on the latter in Chapter 7; here, we'll focus on what-the-system-is.

This second partitioning is both one of the least formal and most important steps of system architecture. Stated broadly and simply, it is:

Technique 3

Focus on the form of what the system is, partitioning it so that each part can be managed as autonomously as possible.

This recommendation is a consequence of Conway's Law (Conway 1968; Allen and Henn 2006). It seems to be a law of software systems that the form of the product looks a lot like the form of the organization that built it. It's not clear which is cause or which is effect in general, but the organization structure usually precedes design, so the organizational structure usually drives the architecture. This isn't a good thing or a bad thing; it just *is*, kind of like the law of gravity. And this technique doesn't exclude looking at what the system *does*; it's just that we'll come back to that later.

These partitions are sometimes called *subsystems*. This partitioning doesn't look very important to the nerds because of its low-tech and intuitive nature. In fact, it is a largely administrative partitioning and has only incidental ties to the business structure (although the administrative and business structures often align for reasons of history or convenience, which is a good thing when you can get it). Such partitioning is nonetheless crucial to the success of the enterprise in accordance with Lean and Agile principles. It minimizes how much information must pass back and forth between locations. It supports more effective interaction between team members, because they share mutual interests, and can talk across a table instead of across the Internet. (Yeah, it's fun to talk across the Internet but, believe it or not, face-to-face communication is usually more effective.)

Autonomy goes hand-in-hand with an important principle of the Agile Manifesto: responding to change. We want to organize our software so that common changes in the market and elsewhere in the "real world" can each be dealt with as a local change, inside one of the subsystems. Subsystems are a gross form of modularity. So when we talk about autonomy in the long term, think of it in terms of change.

Technique 4

The dominant consideration in supporting team autonomy is the locality with which common changes are handled.

Notice that we don't tell you to partition using objects, or modules, or rules, or database relations, or any specific methodology. The partitioning criteria should follow history, standards and convention, experience and common sense. How do you know if it's right? Think of the teams that will work on the software, and do the partitioning in a way that allows each team to work as independently as possible. (See also "Testing the architecture," Section 6.1.6.)

Remember, too, that architecture is mainly about people, and an Agile perspective helps bring that fact into focus. Think a bit about how your customers and even end users expect your system to be organized from a business perspective. Use their vocabulary whenever it makes sense and organize in a way that supports shared communication and understanding. For large systems, this initial activity of partitioning probably won't go very deep into the end user's cognitive model of their business and workflow; that is a more prominent concern of *structuring*, which we will address in Section 5.3.

A time-honored software engineering measure of success is that each subsystem be as cohesive as possible, and be as de-coupled as possible from the other subsystems. Coupling and cohesion are defined in terms of the amount of work it takes to change something (Stevens, Myers and Constantine 1974). Tight coupling between two subsystems isn't a serious problem if neither subsystem changes much. The challenges arise from change, so you should always be thinking dynamically when choosing a partitioning.

Of course we'll get to code (very soon) and we'll have to decide on an implementation technique (objects, or modules, or rules, or database relations, etc.) An Agile approach should honor these four rules of thumb:

1. We use design paradigms (object-oriented, modular, rule-based, databases) to best support the autonomy of teams in the long term and to reflect the end-user mental model of the system.

2. A complex system might use several paradigms.

3. The paradigm we use is ideally subordinate to, and supports, the partitioning based on autonomy of teams in the long term and the end-user mental model.

4. The object paradigm was consciously designed to meet these goals and it will usually drive the dominant partitioning.

The key notion here is #3: Strive to let the human issues drive the partitioning with an eye to the technological issues such as coupling and cohesion, depth of inheritance hierarchies, the Laws of Demeter (Lieberherr 1996), and so forth. It is sometimes too easy for nerds to get caught up in their educational degrees, their religious zeal for a design technique, or in a misplaced trust in the formalism of a type system or "formally" designed language.

Technique 5

Let the human considerations drive the partitioning, with software engineering concerns secondary.

Sometimes you are given an over-constrained problem (see Chapter 4) like "come up with software for a high-quality, automatic exposure camera that is compact, lightweight, easy to use, 30% cheaper than existing single-lens reflex cameras and which is written in Java." The Java stipulation will certainly influence your system partitioning. While not an ideal situation, it's a common one. In Agile software development we inspect and adapt. Don't look too hard for a fixed set of rules and guidelines; rather, follow experience and the deeper principles of design, balancing things as best as you can to optimize the value stream.

That's partitioning in a nutshell. Let's dig deeper into principles related to partitioning – principles that can help you reason about particularly complex systems.

5.2.3   The Real Complexity of Partitioning

If you are building a simple product, it is easy to partition the system based on the rule of thumb of long-term team autonomy. Again, simple implies "not complex," and complexity is proportional to the number of distinct, meaningful "tops" of the system. We can talk about these tops from a purely technological perspective, but that's not interesting. The technical perspective deals with only part of what is a much larger complex system. The organizational structure is also part of that system. If the two major reasons for architecture are to support the organizational structure and the end-user mental model, then we should pay careful attention to those.

Let's say that a company called ElectroCard produces printed circuit-card layouts for clients' electronic circuits. These circuits typically require three to twenty circuit cards to implement. ElectroCard software is to be an Agile application that has a GUI through which an ElectroCard engineer can guide the circuit card construction. The founder of the corporation has hit upon a fantastic opportunity. He has found a group in Hangzhou, China that knows how to group logic gates into packages available in commercial integrated circuits (chips), and how best to put chips together on a card to minimize the number of connections between cards. (This is called *chip placement* or just *placement* in the industry.) And the founder has found a group in New Jersey that has expertise in algorithms that automatically route the connections between chips on a board. (This is called *routing* in the industry.) Both groups have practical knowledge in human-assisted algorithms using a GUI. The question is: what are the major organizational components of the architecture?

If the founder wants to optimize group autonomy in the long term, then there should be one architectural component for placement and another for routing. Each would have its own GUI, its own notion of card and its own notion of chip. You might object and say that it's obvious that there should be a common GUI and common libraries for common components. However, that design doesn't optimize group autonomy in the long term given the current groups. It might reduce code duplication, and therefore reduce rework in the long term, but it would require tight coordination between groups to be successful. Is it worth it? There might be a tradeoff between group autonomy and code duplication! That's a *business* decision.

It wouldn't be unreasonable for the founder to ask the teams to create an architecture organized around the two functions of placement and routing. But let's step back a bit and look at the broader landscape of design.

This is in fact a complex problem – one with many more "tops" than just placement and routing. Emphasizing a particular top optimizes a specific business goal, so the selection of tops becomes a business question.

5.2.4 Dimensions of Complexity

Let's start with a simple case. Assume that you're in the same business as ElectroCard, but that your development team is collocated, you have one customer. What does your architecture look like?

Instead of focusing on how to divide work by geographic location (since you have only one), you create an architecture that will allow an individual, or a small group of individuals working together, to focus on one architectural component at a time with as much long-term autonomy as possible. What bits do you group together? As described above, you let the partitioning follow history, standards and convention, experience, and common sense.

Subject matter experts notice repeated patterns that recur over time in system after system. These patterns tend to follow recognized birds-of-a-feather areas. We call these areas *domains*. Domains commonly (but not always) reflect the end-user mental model of the domain. In some whimsical sense, domains are the mythological foundation of a given business that one finds rooted in culture or society.

5.2.5 Domains: A Particularly Interesting Partitioning

> *Reinventing beats inventing nearly every time.*
> **The Clock of the Long Now**, p. 75.

A domain is a business area of focus, interest, study, and/or specialization. It is an area for which a body of knowledge exists. Sometimes this is just a tacit body of knowledge, but it is nonetheless a body of knowledge. All other things aside, domains are the primary "tops" of a system.

What might the domains be in our circuit card application? The human-guided nature of the product suggests that there is a domain for interactively editing circuits. The chips themselves form a domain: chips have functionality, size, power ratings and configurations of connections that constitute a body of knowledge relevant to the product. Both routing and placement are traditional domains in electronic design automation. It is likely that we can find someone with training, experience, or special knowledge in *each* of these bodies of knowledge. We might even find small groups of such people, birds of a feather, who share such expertise in a small company. The most knowledgeable of them we call *subject matter experts* or *domain experts,* and their area of knowledge is their domain.

Domain knowledge is one of the most distinguishing factors supporting sound design decisions. Domain knowledge is a distillation of experience garnered from past systems, competitors' and partners' systems, and in general from being in touch with the area of discourse. Codified domains capture design decisions about years of tradeoffs between multiple stakeholders, including multiple communities of end users. These tradeoffs become refined over time to minimize the long-term cost of change. Therefore, if we want to give each group as much long-term autonomy as possible over its software, we form the organizational structure around the domain structure, and we organize the architecture accordingly. That's a key part of Conway's Law. The *Organizational Patterns* book (Coplien and Harrison 2004) describes this as a key pattern of software development organization.

So we add this to our list of techniques:

Technique 6

Be attentive to domain partitioning. In particular, don't split a domain across geographic locations or across architectural units.

What makes domains particularly interesting is that they commonly designate sets of closely related product variants grouped together in a *product line*. A product line closely corresponds to what most people would recognize as software reuse. A base set of software is common to several separately delivered variants. The source code in the base is large relative to the changes necessary for a given variant. Parameterization, selective use of derived classes with small snippets of custom code (using design patterns such as TEMPLATE METHOD (Gamma et al 2005)), or even conditional compilation constructs (such as `#ifdef` in C++) can be used to configure individual variants.

Think about Conway's Law again. If domains encapsulate product variants, then their structure corresponds either to the business structure or to the structure of some market. Just on basic management principles, you *want* your organizational structure to reflect the structure of the business. If we structure organizations around domains, then by Conway's Law we have aligned the business structure, the organizational structure, and the architecture! That leads us to another tip:

> **Technique 7**
>
> Be attentive to the opportunity to use product lines and use this insight to bolster support for domain partitioning where possible.

Families are collections of closely related architectural structures, often related by variations that are small relative to what they have in common. Family members often show up in the code as generics or templates that are used to generate multiple instances, or as a collection of derived classes that make small refinements on a common base class. We'll discuss these constructs more in Section 5.3.

5.2.6   Back to Dimensions of Complexity

We encountered two organizational patterns above. The first is called CONWAY'S LAW, which suggests that the code structure reflect the organizational structure. If all members of a development team are collocated then product development has all the freedom it needs to put together the best organization. The Lean Secret is based on getting everybody together, but geographic distribution constrains our ability to do that. (As we'll see later, even when you do the "best" for a collocated team doesn't necessarily mean that the team or architecture are "ideal," because most products have built-in over-constrained problems.) If team members are geographically separated it limits the organization's ability to mix and match individuals to teams. True team dynamics are found in true teams, and a true team is a collocated group of seven plus or minus two people working together under a common goal. In the end, CONWAY'S LAW says that you should evolve organizational structure and software structure together, but other patterns also constrain team formation.

In another pattern we found that the organizational structure followed geographic locations: one in New Jersey and one in China. That pattern is ORGANIZATION FOLLOWS LOCATION (Coplien and Harrison 2004, p. 194). That constrains the composition of true teams, since members of an ideal team are all drawn from the same location. If we want to give each group as much autonomy over its architectural units as possible in the long term, then we create architectural units that map onto the locations. Note that these two organizational structures, and the resulting architectures, are potentially in conflict. This is what we mean about complexity arising from multiple "tops:" there is no single reasonable top-down (hierarchical) partitioning that could satisfy both organizations. This is a form of over-constrained problem.

There is at least one more "top" that can reveal itself when selling products into complex markets, and that is the structure of the market itself. ElectroCard has a special client in France that wants a French language interface. In theory, the software representing each chip in the design needs to know how to display its signal names in French; the overall command structure for partitioning and placement should also be in French. Now we have a French product. Ideally, just from a practical perspective, we would have a team dedicated to that product. Maybe even more ideally, the team would be located in France, preferably in one of the Rhine wine regions. This is yet another organizational pattern: ORGANIZATION FOLLOWS MARKET (Coplien and Harrison 2004, p. 197).

Each of these patterns has the power to shape the organization and, therefore, the architecture. Yet we also want cross-functional teams that bring together the talents and insights necessary to keep moving forward. What, then, is the guiding light to a good architecture?

Consider Table 5-1. Assume that unless otherwise constrained by another staffing policy, we try to create cross-functional teams. The chart looks at consequences of multi-site development and how they relate to specific architectural choices. To build a single, "clean" organization, and expect optimal results, is unrealistic.

In the end, let the principles and common sense be your guides. You should strive to encapsulate change, so look at typical or common changes and count how many architectural boundaries each one would have to cross, particularly at the module level. That is the same as the number of teams that would have to coordinate with each other to make the change. Don't forget to count teams that work on the feature logic outside of the domain code. If that number is worrisome for a common class of changes, then seek another partitioning that encapsulates change better.

How many coordination relationships like this can you have before you start to worry? All interactions that do not take place face-to-face are more costly than face-to-face interactions. Even if there is a single coordination between mutually remote locations, it is a potential architectural stumbling block. Practical coupling and cohesion are functions not only of the properties of the code, but also of how the code maps onto programming teams for maintenance. This leads to the surprising conclusion that, except at the mechanical level, coupling and cohesion are subjective. You can't find them from the code alone, but need to include extrinsic organizational and market perspectives as well.

Remember that if you have the freedom to staff teams (including teams at different locations) however you want, much of this complexity vanishes. Organizational freedom removes many of the constraints that arise when trying to align the organization, the domains, and the markets into a single architectural structure. There is no single formula. Again: it's all about the principles of long-term local autonomy, and of common sense.

Table 5-1   Organizational (and therefore architectural) drivers.

Primary Architectural Structure	Pattern	Positive Consequence	Liability
Modules organized by business domain	Each location is staffed around a business domain	Good independence for general development	Special interests (target markets) may suffer
	Each location is staffed to support some market	Very few – chances for coordination within a location are random	General development requires heavy coordination across locations
Modules organized around markets	Each location is staffed around a business domain	Very few – chances for coordination within a location are random	Common development requires heavy coordination across locations
	Each location is staffed to support some market	Great responsiveness for local markets	General development requires heavy coordination
Modules organized by solution domain (programming language, etc.)	Each location is staffed around a solution domain	Reduces need to duplicate tools across location	Just about everything else
	Each location is staffed to support some market	Very few – chances for coordination within a location are random	Just about everything else

One common solution is to organize the architecture primarily by business domain knowledge (remember Technique 6), and to build teams around domain knowledge as well – no matter where they are located. This leads to an organization where most of the coordination is localized within individual domains, and the team members can coordinate with each other within the same location and time zone. In addition to these primary partitions, there can be additional partitions for each market that requires special focus. Those partitions are likely to have less than ideal coupling to the domain-based partitions, but crosscutting techniques like AOP (Aspect-Oriented Programming) (Ramnivas 2003) can help on the technical side. In any case, these points of interference can architecturally be made explicit as APIs.

Another benefit of this ideal organization is that geographically isolated staff can work on the market-specific partitions for their region. You can form groups around these market concerns and their realization in the architecture. Such groups are commonly located close to markets that align with geography. For example, a team could be placed in Japan to do the localization for the Japanese market. That not only meets the architectural objectives but also makes it easier to engage the key stakeholders for that architectural concern: the targeted end users for that market.

Figure 5-1 is a stylized example of how you might map the architecture onto an existing organization. It looks ahead to the next step: dividing the subsystems into modules according to domains. There are development teams in North and South America, as well as in Japan. The domains are divided among the American teams subject to the rule that no domain has strong coupling to more than one location. In South America two different teams work on Domain Module 2. This isn't ideal because it requires coordination between the two South American teams. However, because of the Lean Secret and because the teams are collocated we can quickly bring together the right people to address any coordination issues that arise in Domain Module 2.

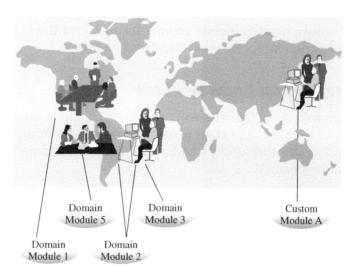

Figure 5-1 A typical organization-to-architecture mapping.

5.2.7   Architecture and Culture

Later in this chapter we'll cover mental models, domain dictionaries, and programming language. Each of these can be viewed as a trapping of culture. Each programming language has its own culture. Each company is unique in its culture. Each nation and locale obviously has its own culture.

One reason for the Lean approach of *everybody, all together, from early on* is to develop understanding across these boundaries. We don't say this out of any pretense that it will be a foundation of world peace (though every little bit helps). The cold, stark business reality is that it affects project success.

Different cultures not only have different words for business concepts, but may also have different views of what constitutes a given business. While writing this book we had many arguments about what a Savings Account and a Checking Account were: a concept familiar to most Americans (at least to most Americans over 30) but relatively foreign in the Nordic countries.

Some of these differences go deep into value systems. For example, there is an architectural pattern FRESH WORK BEFORE STALE (Hanmer 2007) whose essence is that a busy telecommunications system should give preference to the most recent requests for service over those that were in line first, if there isn't enough capacity to handle all requests. The pattern came from North American telecom architecture. A European might cry (and several have): That violates *fairness*!

If you work in a multinational market or have a multinational work force – or even a multiethnic work force – be attentive to these differences. The organizational pattern DIVERSE GROUPS (Coplien and Harrison 2004, p. 135–136) values heterogeneous groups for many of the same reasons that Lean and Scrum advocate cross-functional teams.

5.2.8   Wrap-Up on Conway's Law

It isn't enough to just say that one will optimize ROI and to quickly make a choice based on that: it's important to understand the dynamics of product evolution and to use that understanding to drive the architectural form. *That's* embracing change!

5.3   The Second Design Step: Selecting a Design Style

Attention, nerds! We're finally past all that people stuff and we're going to start using the kind of vocabulary that you might have expected from an architecture book, or a book on Agile development – which can perhaps whimsically be portrayed as the nerds' revenge. This section is about selecting the right design technique and about using it to identify the right modules. By "design technique" we mean design or programming paradigm: object-oriented, procedural, generic and generative programming, databases, and the like.

Most nerds will think of this activity as selecting a technology. However, object-orientation isn't really a technology, nor are most of the other design approaches discussed here or in the broader literature. (For a suitable definition of technology, these things _are_ technology. Alan Kay says that we use the term "technology" for anything that was invented since we were born, and Danny Hillis says that we use it for "the stuff that doesn't really work yet" (Brand 1999, p. 16)). Perhaps more in the spirit of classical architecture we use the term "design style" instead. In computer-ese we use the term _paradigm_. A computing paradigm is a set of rules and tools that relate to patterning or modeling. To select a design style is to select a paradigm.

From an Agile perspective in particular, much of design and architecture is about communication and, in part, the expressiveness of the code. The code should be able to capture and express the mental model of the end user and other stakeholders such as domain experts. The nice thing about paradigms is that we have programming languages whose syntax and semantics express their organizing power, and we can seek the right set of semantics to fit stakeholder concepts. That means choosing the right programming language feature and, sometimes, the right programming language or other "technology." We choose the design style that best fits the situation.

Almost every software paradigm has two important features. First, each one is a way to group related items by commonality. Our minds are good at noticing patterns of commonality among things in our environment, and software paradigms cater to that instinct and its place in language. What is in your hands? A book. It happens to be a particular book with a particular ISBN and a particular history, made of a particular set of atoms unlike any other book in the world. But for the sake of communication we call it "a book," going into the differentiating characteristics when in a discourse about more than one of them. Architecture is both about these commonalities and the way in which items can vary. Paradigms are configurations of recurring commonalities and variations, and they serve us well to describe architectures.

Second, most paradigms encapsulate frequent changes. This is true even for the procedural paradigm, which gets a bad rap for coupling and cohesion. On old UNIX® systems, the `sort(3)` library function actually comprised three algorithms. It selected the proper internal variant according to properties of the data it was given. The maintainer of `sort` might have added a fourth, but because the `sort` function encapsulated it, we wouldn't have noticed. That keeps the overall form – the architecture – stable even under a substantial change. An Agile approach to architecture responds to change by encapsulating it. So, in summary, paradigms group items by commonality, and shape modules that encapsulate classes of frequent changes.

5.3.1 Contrasting Structuring with Partitioning

A naïve view of structuring is as the next step of breaking down subsystems into smaller parts. To a degree that is true. We said that a good subsystem partitioning makes change easier by localizing common changes. The same is true at the structuring level. A paradigm helps us break down subsystems into modules according to rules of organization and grouping based on commonality. If any one of the major common kinds of change arises in a modular system, then ideally all of the work to accommodate that change can take place within a single module. A system has many modules, each one of which accommodates a common class of change or growth in requirements. This is, in fact, Parnas' original definition of the term module: that it hides a "design secret" that can be changed internally without instigating a ripple effect across the rest of the code (Parnas 1978). Change is how we generate new revenues; if we can keep the cost of change low, we increase our profitability. Localizing change lowers cost and makes programming more fun.

Also, as is true for subsystems, we can use coupling and cohesion as a rule of thumb for how well the module structure is serving us. As with subsystems, this must be a dynamic model that considers how well the system handles change – that is, what fraction of changes can be handled locally.

However, there are important differences between the gross partitioning into subsystems and the finer partitioning into modules that go beyond difference in scale. Subsystems are largely administrative, while modules have a necessary relationship to business semantics. *Modules are the most direct expression of the end user's mental model of the entities in their business world.*

Most of the time, change within a module doesn't mean that we throw the whole module away and replace it with another one. In fact, major parts of good modules stay constant over time. So each module is a mixture of stuff that changes a lot, and stuff that stays the same a lot. There can be many loci of change in a system – i.e., many modules – at multiple levels of granularity.

At the very top level of the system, the what-the-system-does software structure changes much more often than the what-the-system-is structure. That is our top level of classification, or partitioning (Technique 1). At the next level we partition according to our intuition and experience of how subsystems will map onto birds of a feather. It is a rather unsophisticated process, and though we analyzed it formally from a business perspective in Section 5.2, it most often follows intuition and domain insight. It is taking the things in our business world and just putting them in baskets, creating new baskets as needed. It is simple classification with no transformation. Partitioning is largely an act of analysis; the only design in partitioning comes from the decision of what classification scheme to use. But there are elements of design here, too, since we are forging boundaries that will last into the implementation. Almost by definition, whatever affects the implementation (the solution) entails design. As a practical issue analysis can never be clinically separated from design. Just as a building architect knows his or her building materials, a software architect knows the strengths and weaknesses of the programming languages and environments that lay ahead.

Structuring refines these partitions according to some design style, or, in other words, according to some paradigm. Within each partition we analyze what aspects change frequently and what aspects are more stable over time. Consider our ElectroCard example, where we have made *placement* to be one of the domains. The placement group in China may find that the algorithms have a rhythm that remains constant over time, except for one set of algorithms that are sensitive to the hardware technology being used (they support several different chip packaging technologies including dual in-line pin chips (DIP chips), surface mount components, discrete components, and others). In each of these cases, we start with the result of a business classification and end with an additional level of separation between stable parts and changing parts.

Structuring moves from *what* is in the business to *how* we will structure it in the product. We are now beyond analysis alone and firmly in design. Domain experts have a key role, since much of their experience relates to how such structuring was done in the past. Using the principle of "yesterday's weather," the design we have used in the past is often as good or better than what we can come up with now. (Grandpa Harry used to say that it was more reliable to predict that today's weather would continue tomorrow than it was to read the weather forecast in the newspaper.) We are still in contact with the end users so we can choose a paradigm that expresses the domain in a way that even they might find natural. We have the businesspeople on the team because issues of scope inevitably arise. Customers may want to configure certain domains for inclusion or exclusion from the product for specific markets. Programmers will soon find ways to express these forms in the code, so solution domain expertise becomes crucial at this point.

5.3.2 The Fundamentals of Style: Commonality and Variation

> *Is time long or is it wide?*
> **Laurie Anderson quoted in *The Clock of the Long Now*, p. 107.**

The structuring tasks in design build on the deepest building blocks of human cognition: being able to distinguish what is common from what changes.

To a domain analysis person or someone working on software families, commonality is something that exists *at any point in time* across software modules, and we use the term *invariant* to describe similarities across modules, and *variation* to describe how they differ. Simple object-oriented design is a good example: a base class captures what is common to all the modules (all the derived classes) and we capture the changes in the derived classes themselves. We can create a derived class object by "changing" the structure of a base class object according to the modifications explicit in the derived class. (Here, by *derived class*, we mean its source code – the part that contains only the delta from the base class. That's how most object-oriented programming languages express such differences.) The Lean angle on this is that we should plan how much variation of each type to tolerate in a system over its lifetime.

However, to an Agilist, change is something that happens to a given artifact (such as object structure) *over time*. To be common over time is to (tend to) be *stable* over time. We use the terms *evolution, change in version*, or sometimes just *change* to describe the differences over time. Again, strangely enough, we can use the same example as before: in a style of object-oriented programming called programming by difference, Bertrand Meyer points out that you can evolve programs over time largely through subclassing (Meyer 1994, ch. 14).

In the end, it doesn't matter: change is change, and we have programming languages and other tools that raise the expression of change to the level of objects and classes that encourage and enable us to use everyday business vocabulary instead of computer-ese. We can call a SavingsAccount a SavingsAccount, and we can find it in the code. We can talk about the differences between SavingsAccounts and CheckingAccounts in the code as well. If it is architecturally important to talk about the difference between the SavingsAccount in the 2010 release and the SavingsAccount after the new banking laws passed in 2011, then we can express that in the code too. To the degree that domain experts anticipate such changes, such changes can be modularized. In this case, maybe we can use class derivation to express all of these changes well.

There is a common misconception (based on a grain of truth) that commonality is the purview of data structure and of what-the-system-is, and that variation lives in the algorithms and functions of what-the-system-does. This would be literally true if the data were invisible to the market, and if all we visibly sold was function. How often were you told in your programming class that you should think of a Shape object in terms of its behaviors, and that the data structure was left to the choice of the implementer? And that the important attribute that changed from Shape to Shape was the methods (e.g. for rotation, which is different for a circle than for a rectangle)? If this were literally true, we could divide the design between these two worlds (as we already have in Section 5.2.1) and we'd be done with architecture.

It may be that data structures are more stable over time than algorithms, but data structures evolve as well. We probably use different internal representations for circles than for rectangles. Architectures should encapsulate both kinds changes in a way that preserves the overall form as much as possible. Most of what we discuss in this chapter aims toward that objective: allowing changes to what-the-system-is without upsetting the architectural form. You know this in several common guises: for example, class boundaries and inheritance can hide data changes from a user of the base class API.

5.3.3   Starting with Tacit Commonality and Variation

Pretend that we had a magic, universal paradigm, one that would allow us to create modules that would always encapsulate change as well as possible. What would that paradigm look like? It would capture the commonalities inside of a module and would allow the interface of the module to express the variations. Unfortunately, the world is a complex and sometimes messy place and we don't quite have such a single magic paradigm. The closest thing we have is classification by commonality and variation.

The good news is that we *can* tap into such a magic paradigm, albeit in an indirect way. When we look for the basic objects that users care about, we don't ask them to group things according to specific attributes of commonality and variation, but we follow business intuition. What drives this intuition is the way we think about associations between things in the world. Our brain is good at finding patterns (in the vernacular sense of the word, not the software design sense, though the two are related). A pattern in our mind captures common properties of a recurring thing along with some understanding of the variation within the recurrence. You know ice cream as ice cream because of its temperature and texture – that's what makes ice cream ice cream. However, chocolate and pistachio ice cream taste very much different, and our mind still classifies both of them as ice cream in spite of the fact that the primary end-user sense elicited by the eating-ice cream use case – that of taste – would cause us to classify them differently. Yet our mind captures the common pattern of ice cream being basically creamy and cold, and tucks away information that different kinds taste differently.

There is no universal, scientific approach to such partitioning. Classification is at least partially based in culture. David Snowden often tells the story about how people from different cultures classify cows, chickens, and grass. Westerners will put cows and chickens together as subjects of human consumption. Chinese will put cows and grass together in accordance with their natural link in agriculture. In the end, you want to do this partitioning on the basis of how the system will change over time. Often history is one of the best predictors of the future.

Perhaps the most creative part of software design is to partition the domain into units of decomposition that encapsulate change. These units of decomposition (and later, of composition) are called *modules*. This task requires a fine touch because this partitioning expresses so many important design desiderata at once. First, each module should correspond to the end users' cognitive model of their world. Second, each module should be as independent from the others as possible. Third, each module should be cohesive. Fourth, Conway's Law comes to bear: can you create modules so that each one encapsulates the domain expertise of a single team or a specific domain expert, so that it doesn't take a village to raise a module?

Because we can talk so explicitly about commonality and variation in the software world, it would be nice to use the same tools in the analysis world for the end user mental models. It would be nice to go to end users and ask, "What things in your cognitive model line up well along commonalities in data structure and have variation over time in the algorithms that implement the services you envision for those things?" If we can find consistent mappings from the end-user space to our software paradigms, then we'll get an architecture that works – that encapsulates change well. Of course it doesn't work that way. Ultimately we want to get to those commonalities and variations in our architecture, but we don't start there.

Fortunately, culture and human experience are often kind to us and provide a historic perspective on what works and what doesn't. This knowledge is in the heads of your subject matter experts, your *domain* experts.

> ### Technique 8
>
> Allow the module partitioning to follow domain knowledge. Think of domain knowledge as a timeless compression of the mental models of end users and other stakeholders – mental models whose patterns are tacitly driven by commonality and variation.

Experience shows that this partitioning best captures the invariant and stable parts of the system. This isn't something that formally can be proven. On the other hand, it almost stands as a tautology: to be a domain means to have the property of being invariant across your markets or stable over time. In the end, a good architecture doesn't reduce to computer science principles, but to your ability to connect to the human end of your system and to distill that knowledge as domain expertise.

Sometimes, you just can't get the domain knowledge. Maybe it's a green field domain, or maybe you have a novice team. It happens. In that case, we go back to the principles of Agile:

> ### Technique 9
>
> In the absence of domain knowledge, allow the module partitioning to follow the end user cognitive model of the domain. For every user "notion" create a corresponding architectural notion.

The end user's model of the moment, driven by current requirements, may be blind to the bigger picture. It's the nature of a modern project to want the software to work *now*. The question is: how long is *now*? If you don't have domain knowledge, you are stuck with the end users' sense of immediacy. Even though we have separated out the what-the-system-is part of the end user model from the domain model, the current feature still colors how the end user sees the domain. If we form the architecture around the end-user models of the moment, they are likely to change on the next release or even next week, leading to rework. Even the best user experience people can't compensate for this shortsightedness.

The compensation must come from a historical perspective. Domain knowledge integrates many past *nows* into a "long *now*" (Brand 1999). That's why it's better to form modules around domain knowledge than around the current end-user view. However, sometimes the end-user view is all you have. This is particularly common for new features. Use domain knowledge when you can get it, and the current end-user mental model when you can't.

History and context are also part of the "long now." You will buy some software instead of building it. You may build on top of an existing embedded base. These structures constrain the shape (the architecture) of what you can fit around them. Another key tip is:

Technique 10

Mind the embedded base and other system artifacts that are destined to be part of the end solution. Be mindful of how they might constrain the system structure or decisions about the system structure.

5.3.4 Commonality, Variation, and Scope

A software system may have hundreds of millions of entities. For example, a large business system may support tens of millions or hundreds of millions of accounts. (Think of your national tax system as an example.) Even though you may be a very productive programmer, you can't write that much code. So we use the commonality across these entities to *compress* the design.

We noted in the introduction that people find architecture daunting, partly because of such complexity. This complexity comes both from the *mass* of data that we have, and from the intricacies of *relationships* between the data. Architecture is about slicing away as much of the mass of data as we can while maintaining the relationships. While compressing down the mass of data, we want to retain its essence, or form.

There are two ways of extracting the essence of a thing or set of things. The first is *abstraction*, which means to put aside some attributes of some entity while retaining others. I can focus on the single most important attributes or features and put aside the rest. The essence of Cyrano de Bergerac is his nose (if we ignore his poetic talent). The essence of a savings account, to the end user, is to deposit, and withdraw and get interest (if we ignore how the actuaries view it).

The other alternative is to *generalize* the overall business characterization of the thing or set of things. Generalization always takes place with respect to some *context* – some set of shared assumptions. We get these shared assumptions from culture or from deep knowledge of our business: domain expertise. It is like abstraction because in fact I am throwing away information – if a general description is more compact than the original, something has to go! But what I remove from the description will be the tacit, non-distinguishing properties that anyone familiar with the domain would take for granted. So, for example, if I'm generalizing the concept of *bicycle* I don't need to explicitly mention the property of having two wheels. Such information is in fact encoded in the name itself: the prefix *bi-* implies "two." That is part of the business *context*, the assumptions its stakeholders presumably share.

Aha: this "presumably" is a tricky part. One benefit of the *everybody, all together, from early on* approach is that it encourages a culture to form. Words take on shared meaning. You can help this process with a Domain Dictionary, and we'll talk more about that at the end of the chapter in Section 5.4. The Domain Dictionary is a crutch: the desired end state is that team members, including end users, can share terms of the trade on a familiar basis.

Because the context lives on in domain knowledge, we lose little information in generalizing this way; we *do* lose information while abstracting. Too much computer science pedagogy these days emphasizes abstraction. Richard Gabriel admonishes us about the dangers of abstraction in his classic essay, *Abstraction Descant* (Gabriel 1998, pp. 17–32). He points out that the shared domain knowledge or cultural knowledge is a kind of "code," and that generalizing this way is a form of *compression* that uses the domain knowledge for the encoding and decoding. It is that compression, using tacit shared information, that makes it compact.

Technique 11

Capture your initial architecture at the most compressed level of expression that covers the scope of your business. Avoid abstracting or discarding any priceless information that may give insight on the form.

Let's look at a trivial example. Let us ask you to envision the interface `ComplexNumber` in your head. Now consider the complex numbers (1, -1) and (1, 1). Let's say that I created objects of those two complex numbers, gave them to you, and asked you to multiply one by the other to produce a third. What is the result? You knew the answer without having to look at the code of `ComplexNumber`, and without even having to know whether it used an internal representation of (r, θ) or *(real, imaginary)*. You probably used your cultural knowledge, particularly if you are an engineer, to recognize the shorthand form as indicating real and imaginary parts. And you used your cultural knowledge of what a complex number is to do the math.

Compression is Lean, in part because it reduces the waste of writing down information that is common knowledge to the business. Compression, again, ties closely to the role of domain expert. There is of course a great danger here: that you have team members who aren't on board to the domain yet. There are no quick fixes, but keep the domain experts handy, hiring expertise if necessary (see the pattern DOMAIN EXPERTISE IN ROLES, Coplien and Harrison 2004, pp. 150–151) and let them bring new hires up to speed (DAY CARE, Coplien and Harrison 2004, pp. 88–91), cross-train (DEVELOPING IN PAIRS, Coplien and Harrison 2004, pp. 165–167), and keep documentation on hand that teaches the core competencies of the business.

To compress effectively, you need a context, and the context is often delineated by a business scope. Who determines the scope? This is a business decision, and comes from the Business stakeholders (Section 3.2.2). Scope is tricky. For the banking account example: are both savings and checking accounts part of the same business? It depends how you view them: do you group them as having enough commonality that you view them as the same? Or do the variations over-power the commonalities so that they are different? These insights in fact can lead to an even higher-level partitioning:

Technique 12

In fact, the initial partitioning strives to create decoupled businesses whose concerns can be separated from each other.

These businesses can of course cooperate with each other, use each other's services, or share large amounts of common code. So-called infrastructure organizations can view other internal projects as end users, and can produce a software artifact that is shared across several organizations.

There are, however, serious challenges with internal infrastructure organizations that serve multiple internal customers. It is difficult for the internal vendor to make a product that is truly general and satisfies internal clients equally well, without giving into one of them at the expense of others. It is complicated enough if all the internal clients agree to a standard on a given date, but it is rare that such clients work together and rarer still if their release schedules align. Because each internal client wants minor changes timed to coincide with *their* release schedule, it complicates the situation beyond belief for the vendor. If the internal business interfaces are contractual rather than a multi-way Agile partnership, the enterprise runs the risk of a critical-path internal client (or an 800-pound gorilla external client) strong-arming the direction of the platform. If the gorilla wins, everybody else loses. Partnerships like this usually (but not always) rely on collocation of the vendor and consumer, so multi-site setups face a further liability.

Once you have done this high-level partitioning you can seek the top-level, most compressed level of expression within each partition. That's your top-level architecture. The fact is that we compress all the time: we don't take the design all the way to machine code, and register transfers, and bus design, and hardware architecture, and gate level design, and solid state design of the transistors, nor to the electrons and holes across a PN junction in a chip, nor down to the Fermi levels of the electrons in the silicon and isotope atoms of the devices. We cut it off at some level. You might argue that this is abstraction; fair enough, we won't take the word away from you. We don't view it as abstraction because, in fact, all that stuff is *there* already. We compress our understanding of something already built, something that exists, to use it: the dangers in doing so are minor. If arguments arise about a particular detail, the artifact itself is the oracle we can consult for resolution. Domain experts can help here, too. If we abstract our understanding of some domain and use the resulting information to build something that does not yet exist, we are likely to miss something important. That will hurt evolution. To embrace change requires the discipline of understanding what is likely to change, and what will likely remain stable.

In summary, we deal with complexity in three ways. We use partitioning to understand a complex system a piece at a time; partitioning groups things by their *common* attributes. We've already addressed partitioning in Section 5.2. We understand things that already exist by abstracting; we try to avoid that in architecture because the artifact doesn't exist yet. And last, we use compression to generalize complex systems under construction, building on *common* domain knowledge and on the *common* properties of the concept under discussion. This information in hand, we are one step closer to making it explicit in the code.

5.3.5 Making Commonalities and Variations Explicit

A user usually has more than one flavor of a concept in mind at once. A bank Account Holder may *talk* about accounts, but in fact might *think* concretely of savings and checking accounts. ElectroCard clients may think of printed-circuit cards, but in fact there are different kinds of cards: surface-mount technology, discrete components, and others. In all of these cases, the differences matter. However, the differences are qualitatively different than the differences between domains. The distinguishing factor is that these elements are bound by some invariance. Savings and checking accounts have remarkably similar places in the architecture and remarkably similar behaviors (reporting a balance, making a deposit, etc.) All printed circuit cards share basic principles of routing.

Each account, and each routing algorithm, is a module in its own right, yet these modules have a special relationship to each other: their commonalities. Programming languages are good at expressing invariants like these, as well as the variations.

To the end user with a long view, and also to the programmer, we can view change over time the same way. We have today's savings account with its relatively stable form, but we also have its evolution into tomorrow's savings account that reflects changes in the way we give interest to the customer. Eventually, we might have both in the system at once and give end user a selection of interest-bearing accounts. Over time we have a succession of modules that maintain a large degree of stability.

We use the term *commonality* both for the invariance across concurrent options and for stability over time. All of the variant modules are members of the same domain. So we can talk about a domain of accounts that includes savings and checking accounts – both today's and tomorrow's. We can talk about a domain of routing algorithms that includes Hightower routing and Lee routing – both for today's chip-based boards and tomorrow's surface-mount boards. These domains are the same whether they are driven by the end-user model or by domain expertise. It's just that we're broadening our scope a little bit.

The interesting question of what-the-system-is architecture is: *how* are these modules similar? Said another way: what is their commonality? We could answer the question in business terms, as we did in the preceding paragraph. Instead, we will start to think about how we will express these commonalities in code. This transformation from business conceptualization, to program conceptualization, might best be called *design*. It is a (probably tacit) activity you already do during design, whether using procedural design or object-oriented design or some other approach.

Commonality Categories

Before jumping to procedures and objects and templates and other paradigms, we're going to keep it simple at first. We also want to distance ourselves from programming language and other premature implementation biases. We look at the basic building blocks of form as computing has understood them for decades. We call them *commonality categories* (Coplien 1998). These building blocks are:

- Behaviors, often communicated as names (external behavior: e.g., to *rotate* (a name) or *move* (another name) a Shape)
- Algorithms (the sequence implementing the behavior: e.g., the algorithm for *moving* or *rotating* a shape)
- State

- Data structure
- Types (in the vernacular programming language sense)

That's just about it. These are the criteria that we seem to use when grouping software. We tend to look for the ways in which one of these properties stands out as a *common* feature across concepts in our mental models, and then form a partitioning or grouping around that commonality. We also look for how these same properties delineate individual concepts in our groupings.

This list is important because it seems to characterize the groupings that Von Neumann programming languages express. (By Von Neumann languages, we mean those that tend to express the form of software written in some Von Neumann computational model. This includes paradigms such as the procedural paradigm, the object paradigm, and modular programming, but is less applicable to rule-based programming, or the functional programming style of spreadsheets or of Scala's methods, for example.) Most popular programming languages of the past 50 years have drawn on this list for the kinds of commonality and variation that they express. It is a remarkably small list. In some sense, this list forms a simple, "universal paradigm" of design. If we can identify the commonalities and variations in the domain model and end-user model, we can use this list as a powerful tool for translation to the code.

Let's illustrate with some examples. Think again of savings and checking accounts. To the end user, they are all the same underneath – it's just money. The end user doesn't care very much about where the money is kept. The programmer using a `SavingsAccount` object or a `CheckingAccount` object doesn't care how the objects represent the money: whether they hold the amount as a data field or whether they partner with a set of transaction auditing objects to keep track of it. To the end user, it's an amount; to the programmer, this suggests a commonality in *data structure*. The *state* of that data structure varies over time. How do savings and checking accounts vary? What would make me choose one over the other is *behavior*. It is clumsier to *withdraw* (the name of a behavior) from a savings account than a checking account: there are different use cases, or algorithms, elicited in this same general behavior. Most savings accounts draw interest; many checking accounts don't. Most checking accounts have annual or per-use fees; savings accounts don't. Those are variations, and each one can be exemplified in a use case scenario. They are behaviors.

So you're in the banking business. You want to divide your business into autonomous segments. Do checking and savings have enough in common that they belong together in the same business? I compress checking and savings accounts into a notion called Consumer Account and conclude: yes, I want a line of business called Consumer Banking. Of course, I can't do this on the basis of two account types alone or even on the basis of accounts alone, but the concept generalizes. Alternatively, you can start by asserting that I have a line of business called Consumer Banking (a scope decision made by the business) and then ask the question of how to organize these account types into an architecture. The answer is: *according to some paradigm that can express commonality in structure and variation in state of the data and in the behaviors associated with the data.*

How about our guys at ElectroCard? They have two basic routing algorithms based on the classic Lee algorithm and the Hightower algorithm. These algorithms take a graph data structure as input and produce a multi-layer topology as output. (Think of the output as a geographic map of lands and seas that will be used to manufacture a circuit card. The lands (yes, they really use that term) will be manufactured in copper to connect electronic devices together, and the seas are a kind of plastic that separates the copper areas from each other.) The algorithms both have the same business *behavior*: they route lands on a circuit board. However, the Lee algorithm and Hightower *algorithms* are different. Furthermore, there are more refined differences pertaining to the differences in board technology (surface mount versus DIPs), but these are differences in *behavior*.

In both cases, we can use this knowledge to refine our understanding of partitioning and to choose suitable paradigms. We'll talk about that in the next two sections.

Next Steps

Sometimes, in a complex domain, even the domain experts may not agree on what the most fundamental organizing modules are! We talk a bit about that in Section 6.3 later on. But, first, let's get into more of the nitty-gritty of structuring.

5.3.6   The Most Common Style: Object Orientation

Object orientation has probably been the dominant design style (paradigm) on the planet for the past 15 or 20 years. That's a long time in Internet years. What makes it so enduring? Arguments abound. One of the often-heard arguments in the 1980s was that the object paradigm is "natural" for the way human beings think. A slightly more cynical view is that people associate computing with the Internet, the Internet with Java, and Java with object orientation. Another is that C++ rode the wave of the then-ubiquitous C language and for reasons of fashion led to the widespread use of the term "object-oriented."

Perhaps the most persuasive arguments come from the *direct manipulation metaphor*. The Smalltalk programming language was taking root at Xerox's Palo Alto Research Center (PARC) laboratory in the same era that interactive interfaces were coming into vogue there, and about the same time that Doug Englebart invented the mouse. Dahl and Nygaard, who invented object-oriented programming in their Simula 67 programming language, had the notion that objects should reflect the end user mental model. The object-oriented Smalltalk people wanted to extend that notion to the user interface in a way that the end user had the experience of directly manipulating the objects of their domain – objects that had a living representation or kind of proxy living in the memory of the machine. The end user should have the feeling of manipulating the objects directly. Brenda Laurel powerfully explores this metaphor in her book, _Computers as Theatre_ (Laurel 1993). The point is that there is a long tradition not only in object orientation, but also in interactive computing, of linking together the end user mental model with the structures in the software.

In the end, we don't care which of these rationales is the "right" one. They all ring true and, in any case, object orientation dominates contemporary interactive software. So much for the _why_ of object orientation. But next, ...

Just What is Object Orientation?

This has been a much-debated question with quite a few final answers. Object-oriented programming started with the Simula 67 programming language. Its inventors, Ole Dahl and Kristin Nygaard, viewed it as a way to capture the end user's mental model in the code. Such foundations are ideal for system simulations, which was what Simula was designed for. The vision of Dahl and Nygaard bridged the gap between the user world and the programmer world.

In 1987, one of main organs of object orientation – the ACM OOPSLA conference – published a "treaty" that unified competing definitions for object orientation at the time. The paper was called "The Treaty of Orlando" after the OOPSLA venue where the discussions behind the paper had taken place (Stein, Lieberman, and Ungar 1989). The paper defines object orientation mainly from the perspective of substitutability, which can be achieved using a number of programming mechanisms such as templates (the idea that a class keeps all of its objects consistent at some level) and empathy (which is more applicable to classless languages like **self**, where two objects share a relationship analogous to the subclass relationship of class-ful languages). There is an important concept lurking here, which is the introduction of the notion of class into the design space, which we'll revisit numerous times in this book. The object view is the Agile, end-user-centric view; often, the programmers have a class view of the same architecture.

If we view the current activity (of Section 5.3) as "technology selection," then we view object orientation as a "technology." We want to know when object-orientation is the right match for the domain model or end-user mental model. There should be a good match if both express the same commonality and variation. If the domain model visualizes market segment differentiation or variation over time as requiring changes to algorithms, without having to modify the existing data structures, then the object paradigm may be a good fit.

You know obvious examples from your basic education in object orientation. The perfunctory OO example of geometric shapes – circles, rectangles, and squares – is based on a set of variants that share common data members (such as their center and angle of rotation) and that vary in the algorithms that implement behaviors such as rotation, scaling, and area computation. It is unlikely that you thought of geometric shapes in terms of this derivation from commonality and variation. But the analysis works well.

More often than not, the modules in Agile programs end at the same place: object-oriented programming. In fact:

Technique 13

Most domains in simple, interactive applications lead to modules that are implemented using object-based or object-oriented programming. This is particularly true for entities that the program presents on an interactive interface for direct manipulation by users.

In a general sense the end user is himself or herself one of the objects in the system. We have yet to investigate other key architectural components that tie together the wetware of the end user with the software written by the designer. We'll do that with the interaction framework called Model-View-Controller-User (emphasizing that the User is also an object – in fact, the most important one). We implement Model-View-Controller-User with the familiar architectural pattern Model-View-Controller, or MVC for short. That leads us to another important technique:

Technique 14

The object structures in the what-the-system-is part of the architecture will become Models in a Model-View-Controller(-User) architecture.

We'll cover that idea more in Chapter 8 and Chapter 9.

As we hinted at the beginning of the chapter, it is important to distinguish between classes and objects. End users conceptualize the world in *objects*, whereas programmers are frequently stuck using programming constructs called *classes*. If we look solely at commonality and variation – and particularly the commonality of data structure and behavior and the variation of algorithm – the only difference between objects and classes is that groups of otherwise similar objects can vary in their state and identity. We'll see later that this simplistic model of object orientation doesn't fit the end user model of the world as well as it could because we're missing the notion of role: objects play roles according to what's going on at the time. This "going on at the time" necessarily evokes system dynamics, and we can't express anything that dynamic in anything as static as a class. However, that knowledge lives in the what-the-system-*does* part of the system, and classes serve us just fine to express what the system *is* (at least when domain analysis points us in the direction of the object paradigm).

So far we've focused only on what the system *is*; we also must accommodate what the system *does*, which will be the topic of Chapter 7, Chapter 8 and Chapter 9. Because of Technique 14, most the remaining material in this book will assume that the object paradigm drives the primary shape of the what-the-system-is architecture: that's where much of the leverage comes from in an Agile system.

In the mean time, you shouldn't take it for granted that everything will be object-oriented. Take our ElectroCard case as an example. In the next section we investigate the more general approach to selecting paradigms.

5.3.7 Other Styles within the Von Neumann World

As introduced in the previous section, object orientation is the prevalent paradigm in Agile projects. Even in Agile projects there is software that doesn't naturally align to the Agile values of frequent change or of close connection to the end user or customer, but you need it to support your business.

Because these bits of software are often out-of-sight and out-of-mind to the end user, you'll need to learn about them from your domain experts. The term "domain expert" usually conjures up an image of a businessperson or of a problem domain expert. Solution domain experts should be particularly high on your list both for their insight into the necessary supporting domains and for their knowledge of what design styles are most suitable for them. As is true of most software architecture (and of architecture in general), history, taste, and experience are excellent guides. Architecture is more art than science and it's important to defer to people and interactions over processes and tools in setting your architectural forms.

Nonetheless, knowledge of commonality and variation help shape the architecture. You can use them to justify the selection of a given paradigm or design style in your code commentary or architecture documentation. You can use them to guide your exploration of new domains or of the cost of bending an area of your architecture to fit a new market. Most important, the split between what is common and stable, and what is variable and changing, supports the central role of architecture in embracing change. Analyzing the commonalities and variations can help keep your team members collectively honest as they choose paradigms, design styles, tools and programming languages to achieve objects for maintainability.

Table 5-2 shows common configurations of commonality and variation that easily can be expressed in the C++ programming language. Note that in addition to the commonality categories (function, name, data structure, etc.) we also take binding time and instantiation into account. These indicators together suggest unique programming language features that are well suited to express the form of the business domain.

Note the very last row of the table: if we have commonality in related operations, and potentially in at least some of the data structure, with variation in algorithm and data structure (and of course in the state of the data) with run-time binding and possible instantiation, you use inheritance with virtual functions – the C++ way to implement object-oriented programming.

Table 5-3 shows the analogous relationships for C#. It isn't our goal here to help you *formalize* your architectural decision process. Perhaps these tables can support or inform your common sense. More importantly, we want to demonstrate that architectural decisions must take the solution domain into account. Just as a builder or architect takes building materials into account while building a house, so should software designers take paradigms into account when shaping the initial forms of a program.

These tables can help inform a process of domain analysis that establishes the key modules in a system, more or less according to these activities:

1. Group the entities of your problem space into sets of things that "belong together" from the perspective of form and which reflect a historically distinct area of the business. Each such grouping is a *domain*, and its members may form a *family*.

2. For each set, establish the main property that is common across its elements, and find the commonality category for that property.

3. Also establish the main way in which the members of each set vary and establish the commonality category for that variation.

4. Use the two commonality categories, together with a table such as in Table 5-1 or Table 5-2, to establish a candidate design paradigm for each set.

Table 5-2   Commonalities and variations for C++ language features.

Commonality	Variability	Binding Time	Instantiation	C++ Feature
Function Name and Semantics	Anything other than algorithm structure	Source	N/a	Template
	Fine algorithm	Compile	N/a	`#ifdef`
	Fine or gross algorithm	Compile	N/a	Overloading
Data Structure	Value of state	Run time	Yes	`struct`, simple types
	A small set of values	Run time	Yes	`enum`
	Types, values and state	Source	Yes	Templates
Related Operations and Some Structure	Value of state	Source	No	Module
	Value of state	Source	Yes	`struct`, `class` (object-based)
	Data structure and state	Compile	Optional	Inheritance
	Algorithm, data structure and state	Run	Optional	Inheritance with Virtual Functions (object-oriented)

Some sets won't naturally lead to the creation of families; use your experience and common sense. In fact, most of this process is common sense, and the above steps are just inspiration and encouragement. See Coplien (1998) for a more comprehensive description of this approach to domain analysis.

If we choose our paradigm carefully then it is easy to find where to make the kinds of changes that our analysis anticipated. In the object paradigm, this might mean changing the behavior of a method. The domain model is said to have *parameters of variation*, and by associating the right code (algorithm, class, value, etc.) with that parameter of variation we can generate different entities in the domain. Members of a domain are sometimes said to form a *family*, and the parameters of variation are like genes that we can turn on and off in the family's genetic code. Each complete set of parameters defines an individual *family member*. When we reduce the domain to code, the parameters of variation should be explicit.

Table 5-3   Commonalities and variations for C# language features.

Commonality	Variability	Binding Time	Instantiation	C# Feature
Function Name and Semantics (must be within a class scope)	Anything other than algorithm structure	Source	N/a	Generic
	Fine algorithm	Compile	N/a	Tag parameters
	Fine or gross algorithm	Compile	N/a	Overloading
Data Structure	Value of state	Run time	Yes	`struct`, simple types
	A small set of values	Run time	Yes	`enum`
	(class) Types, values and state	Source	Yes	Generic (but no operators)
Related Operations and Some Structure	Value of state	Source	No	Static class
	Value of state	Source	Yes	`struct, class`
	Data Structure and state	Compile	Optional	Inheritance
	Algorithm,data structure and state	Compile	Optional	Inheritance
	Run	Optional	Virtual functions

In the object paradigm, this might mean adding a derived class with a modified method. For generics or generative programming, it may mean changing a template parameter.

In this section we have overviewed domain analysis suitable to Lean architecture and Agile construction. Again, if you want to explore these ideas in more depth, see either Coplien (1998) or Evans (2003).

5.3.8   Domain-Specific Languages and Application Generators

So far we have discussed how to apply the results of commonality-and-variation-based domain analysis to a design using general-purpose languages. Some of the source code remains relatively stable, while the parameters of variation allow small changes, or provide well-defined hooks that connect with programmer-supplied customization code. Another approach to realizing a domain analysis is to create a first-class language that expresses the parameters of variation – not in some general-purpose syntax, but with the syntax and semantics of the business itself. Such a language is called an *application-oriented language* or *domain-specific language*.

One of the original goals of domain engineering was to provide domain-specific languages that perfectly capture business semantics. The term "domain-specific language" (DSL) in the 1980s and 1990s meant a language designed from the ground up to support programming in a fairly narrow domain. More recently, the term has been co-opted to mean any domain-focused programming effort embedded in a general-purpose language. It pays to survey this landscape a bit, and to consider the place of DSLs in your architecture.

The State of the Art in DSLs

It may be that the new association for the name is a reaction to the relative failure of the old one. True domain-specific languages are not very Agile because they encode commonalities and variations in a narrow, concrete expression of the business form. If the language is not perfectly designed, its lack of general-purpose programming features makes it difficult for the programmer to accommodate missing business concepts. Furthermore, if the domain evolves then the language must evolve with it – potentially leaving the previously written code base obsolete. There are a few efforts that have had the good fortune to succeed, but there have also been countless failures. The usual failure mode is that the language becomes brittle or awkward after a period of about five years. On the Øredev 2008 panel on domain-driven design, the panelists (Jim Coplien, Eric Evans, Kevlin Henney, and Randy Stafford) agreed that it is still premature to think of domain-specific languages as reliable production tools (Øredev 2008).

There are, however, notable broad successes. Parser generators like **yacc** and **bison** are good examples. There is promise in tools such as **antlr** (Parr 2007) to reduce a well-designed language to a development environment. However, the challenge of designing a good language remains large.

There are other techniques that are related to the modern definition of DSLs and which have had moderate success in niche areas. One of these is generative programming, which raised the bar for embedding domain semantics in a general-purpose language in 2000 (Eisenecker and Czarnecki 2000).

DSLs' Place in Architecture

A DSL smooths the interface between the programmer and the code that he or she is writing. Unless the DSL is specifically designed to tie together architectural components in a general way (such as CORBA'S Interface Definition Language) the DSL doesn't have much benefit for capturing the relationship of its domain to the rest of the software in the system. This latter concern is our dominant one in this chapter because we are concerned with managing the long-term interactions between domains, assuming that changes within a domain are encapsulated. A DSL provides the encapsulation (within the code provided by the domain engineering environment).

That means that for each DSL, you need to define an interface between the code produced by the domain engineering environment and the interfaces to the rest of the domains. The rest of the system should interface to the DSL through a single, relatively static interface instead of interfacing directly with the generated code – that's just basic attentiveness to coupling and cohesion.

Technique 15

Provide an API to the code generated from a DSL for use by the rest of the architecture.

Because you will not be managing the changes to the domain at that interface, the interface will probably not be built as the result of any long-term analysis of commonality and variation. Let common sense rule. If it makes sense for this interface to be a class, make it a class. If it makes sense for it to be a function, make it a function. Many DSL environments pre-define these interfaces: for example, **yacc** uses a combination of macros (for declaring the types of parse tree nodes and lexical tokens) and procedural interfaces APIs (for starting the parser and determining success or failure of the parse). Any other needed interface is up to the programmer.

5.3.9   Codified Forms: Pattern Languages

A pattern language is a collection of structures, called patterns, that includes rules for how they can be composed into a system. Individual patterns are elements of form that encapsulate *design* tradeoffs called forces, much as modules encapsulate the relationships between *implementation* procedures and data.

Patterns work best for incremental program design and construction with feedback. The designer applies one at a time according to need. However, the ordering is important. Patterns are collected together according to their precedence relationships in the design process. Each pattern makes sense only in a certain context, so a given pattern can be applied only if the patterns that were applied earlier create a context in which this one can be applied. This set of pattern linkages forms a grammar of sorts, with each pattern being a word in the grammar and the relationships between them guiding the productions. A collection of patterns related in this way is called a *pattern language*. A pattern language is in fact an architectural style for some domain. A pattern language offers the same level of freedom in detailed design as the programming paradigms we have discussed in this chapter, but it has the narrowness of application of a domain-specific language.

Pattern languages were popularized by an architect of the built world, Christopher Alexander, in work that has progressed from the late 1950s to the present time. The software community took notice of Alexander's work as early as 1968; one finds them mentioned at the first conference on software engineering (Naur and Randell 1968). But they didn't start gaining a real foothold in software until the pattern conferences called PLoPs (Pattern Languages of Programs) started taking place in 1994.

Most early patterns captured isolated structures of important but uncelebrated knowledge, a trend that in large part persists to this day. However, as parts of the community matured, pattern *languages* started to emerge. Today's noteworthy pattern languages of software architecture include:

- The POSA series (Buschmann et al 1996; Schmidt et al 2000; Kircher and Jain 2004; Buschmann, Henney, and Schmidt 2007a; Buschmann, Henney, and Schmidt 2007b);
- Fault-tolerant software patterns (Hanmer 2007);
- Model-View-Controller (Reenskaug 2003).

This list is meant to characterize some of the good available pattern languages but it is hardly complete.

Ideally, pattern languages are roadmaps for building entire systems or subsystems in some domain. They are an extremely Lean approach to development in that they build structure as the need for it arises. Patterns build on two fundamental approaches: local adaptation of form according to system needs, and incremental growth instead of lump-style development. Both of these are done in a way that preserves the form of the artifact as it has been developed so far, so a pattern is a form of *structure-preserving transformation*. Patterns differ from the domain analysis approach in that they capture the architectural form in documentation rather than in the code, and in that their purpose is to create structure according to a form rather than to guide the creation of form (architecture) for its own sake.

A few pattern languages exist that can guide you through evolutionary architecture development using local adaptation and piecemeal growth. So we add:

Technique 16

If you have a trustworthy pattern language for your domain, use it instead of domain analysis or end user input.

More realistically, patterns suggest architectural styles that can selectively guide the structure of your system. MVC is a good example: we'll talk a lot more about MVC in Chapter 8.

There are actually few mature pattern software languages in the public literature. Much of the use of pattern languages may lie within your own enterprise, growing over time as you use them to document architectural learning. Such documentation becomes a legacy (in the good sense of the word) for the next generation of product or product-builders. We'll discuss this issue more in the documentation section at the end of the chapter.

5.3.10   Third-Party Software and Other Paradigms

You might be asking: Where does my database management system fit? Good question! Software is complicated and often doesn't fit into a neat methodological framework. Software that you don't manage in-house, or which follows another design style, can lead to a mismatch in the interface between your software and the foreign software. Such software fits into two major categories: ones whose APIs are already determined by standards or by a vendor, and frameworks that you build in-house. Each of them is reminiscent of the situations we previously discussed with respect to DSLs.

First, let's consider third-party software and software whose form is dictated by standards. Too few companies consider software outside their own four walls, and end up re-inventing the wheel (and it's usually a much poorer wheel).[5] If you manage architectural variation well, procurement of external software or partnering with vendors can be a huge business win. Do a cost/benefit analysis before assuming that you should build it yourself.

---

[5] This is commonly called NIH, which stands for "Not IH" – "Not Invented Here" by default – but can, among other things, mean "Not In this Hallway."

Databases are a good example. Occasional rhetoric to the contrary not withstanding, database software development rarely falls within the Agile values. Databases are about processes and tools rather than people and interactions. Design methods (e.g., formal relational models), processes (e.g., normalization) and tools (e.g., commercial database servers) dominate database work, darkly overshadowing the Agile values. If end users must see SQL, they are really programmers who are working in the framework of a relational (or network, or hierarchical) model rather than their cognitive model of the business. Nonetheless, database approaches are a good match for many problems in the *solution* domain. Let common sense be your guide.

There are three considerations competing for your attention when evaluating third-party software: uniformity, autonomy, and suitability.

- *Uniformity*: You want to keep a small inventory of paradigms in your development shop. It's expensive to train everyone in multiple paradigms, to purchase (and maintain) the tool and language support for multiple paradigms, and so-forth. You can wrap a module in a paradigm suitable to the dominant project style: e.g., by using the ADAPTER and PROXY design patterns (Gamma et al 2005) to encapsulate the foreign software and its design style.

However, this approach has risks. Adding layers of transformation between the end user and the internal data model can lead to a mismatch between the end user's model of what is going on in the software and what *is* actually going on in the software. You can overcome that with an illusion, but illusions are difficult to sustain. Draw on deep domain knowledge grounded in experience, and otherwise view such encapsulation with skepticism.

The Lean ideal is to partner with your business suppliers to seek solutions that meet the needs of both partners. This is often a difficult ideal to sustain in the software world, but we have seen this approach succeed in some of our clients.

- *Autonomy*: If your vendor is remote, then it will be difficult to include their staff on a collocated cross-functional team. That implies that any changes to the semantics of architectural interfaces require coordination across organizational gulfs. That goes against the very purpose of architecture. You can address this using two techniques:

Technique 17

Leverage standards when dealing with third-party software.

---

and

Technique 18

Factor changes to third-party software into local parameters of variation or modules that are loosely coupled to the foreign software.

Standards are a staple of Lean. De facto standards are great; industry-wide standards are even better. The ideal interface between mutually foreign components should be a very thin pipe whose shape is dictated by the standard. By "thin," we mean that it doesn't know much about the business semantics. For example, XML supports thin pipes that are themselves ignorant of the business domain.

You can also reduce coordination between software vendors and clients by pushing all the changes to one side or another, and by decoupling the two sides through published parameters of variation. A simple example can be found in the setup software of your PC, which allows you to select a simple parameter of variation called "Language." Select Danish in that one place, and thousands of interfaces automatically adjust themselves accordingly. If you were to add a new language, like Swedish, you could accomplish most of the work on the platform side. The client needs only to know about a single new value that can be bound to one of the parameters of the system API. Analysis should establish a wide enough range in these parameters to anticipate the majority of variations that framework users will need.

As a further example, consider an organization where data designers and database users work together in a collocated setting. The database users make frequent SQL query changes, and the data designers make occasional changes to the schemata. You have the flexibility of organizing as a cross-functional team, and may need only minimal architectural expression of parameters of variation to the database schema. There may not be a need to administer those changes across an explicit architectural interface. In the mean time, standards keep the interface to the database server itself stable.

- *Suitability*: You want the architecture to fit both your domain model and the end user model. Maybe you're building a client-management system whose architecture revolves around domain concepts such as "client objects" and "market objects" defined during analysis. Your domain modeling results in an architecture where these become primary forms.

You can gain huge economies of scope by tapping into your clients' existing relational databases instead of re-inventing *that* wheel. So you have objects for clients and market concerns on one hand, and a database on the other hand. Which paradigm do you choose? There are no universal answers, but widespread experience offers hope that these paradigms can enjoy a happy marriage. If you can encapsulate the database-ness of the implementation inside the objects that come from your analysis, you get the best of both worlds. Again, this means that these objects must maintain a bit of illusion. Experienced programmers are up to the challenge, and you can use many of the same techniques mentioned under *Uniformity* just above.

If your software uses an Internet service or other remote API, you can treat it much the same as third-party software.

As for such software that you build in-house, it's more or less the same song, second verse. Leverage standards in the design of such software where possible. For example, it would be unwise to re-invent an SQL clone as an interface to a DBMS that you develop in-house. Keeping to standards affords you the option of migrating to a standard server should you need to do that for reasons of scaling, cost reduction, or some other business forcing function.

5.4   Documentation?

Many people will tell you that Agile means, "Don't do documentation," but they'd be wrong to claim that. You stop being Agile if you strive for *comprehensive* documentation. We want the documentation that packs the punch. Kevlin Henney notes that we should be able to reflect on our documentation and say, "That's the page I read that made the difference" (Coplien and Henney 2008). So the first rule of thumb for architecture documentation is: Don't sweat the small stuff. Focus on what matters.

Much of the documentation that "packs the punch" is that which describes relationships that you can't see in the code. In large building construction the real blueprints, called *as-builts*, aren't finalized until construction is complete. They show where every heating duct and ever water pipe lies within the walls, so the maintenance people can get at them should the need arise. You can't see them by just looking at the walls, so the knowledge ends up in a document. To assume exact locations for those artifacts before actually installing them would be guessing. These relationships shift around during design. So the second rule of thumb is: Think of your architectural documentation as an as-built more than as a forward engineering document. Use code as your forward engineering document. Notations and natural language descriptions are more likely to quickly become out of date during design because they are not directly in the value stream.

5.4.1   The Domain Dictionary

Words mean things – or, at least, they should. Just establishing a common project vocabulary can fend off misunderstandings and help the team come to a shared vision of scope and purpose. What is a customer? An account? A widget? The dictionary doesn't have to be large, and additions to it should be incremental. Make sure that they are reviewed and accepted by the stakeholders.

A nickname is a term defined in the data dictionary that becomes part of the use case vocabulary. Use of nicknames eliminates redundant clarification at each point the concept is invoked. For example, many use cases in a library system may deal with the concepts *title*, *author*, and *year of publication*. It is easier to refer to them collectively as *Book Publication Data* instead of recalling all three of these properties every time. Use your domain dictionary to record these nicknames. Alistair Cockburn calls them *information nicknames* and uses them for data concepts (Cockburn 2001, ff. 162) but you can apply them more broadly for what-the-system-is terminology. We will discuss a related concept called *habits* in Section 7.5.1. Habits are about what-the-system-does and usually do not belong in the domain dictionary.

Editing Language: the keystroke sequences and menus accessible to the user (vi, emacs…)
Text Buffer: manages the text in between its residence in a file
File: long-term storage for the text on a secondary storage device
Window: medium for displaying the edited text to the user for interactive editing
Input Device: keyboards, pointing devices, and other facilities for user input to the editor
Command: a human/machine interface gesture

Figure 5-2   A Domain Dictionary.

The domain dictionary (Figure 5-2) should be a key deliverable of the architecture effort. Developing this terminology during the analysis process is even better.

5.4.2   Architecture Carryover

Within a given product area, successive product generations share many common architectural elements. Basic domain concepts change slowly while the features and technology change more rapidly. This suggests that we might be able to re-use architecture. What might that mean?

The traditional view is that one can re-use platforms. However, success with such reuse has been slim at best, except in the case of generic software such as low-level libraries and operating systems, which have evolved to be domain-neutral. The pattern discipline evolved out of the beliefs that the best carry-over from the past is ideas and basic form, rather than code, and that such carry-over repeats often within well-delineated domains.

But what if the code *expressed* basic form instead of the structure of platforms? Some patterns might find representation in code. In this book we build repeatedly on the Model-View-Controller pattern, which we can describe as three roles with certain repeatable use cases that tie them together. You may have patterns from your domains that similarly can be expressed as abstract base classes. Patterns from the references of Section 5.3.9 may also have this property. If these patterns are documented (such as MVC and the patterns from Section 5.3.9), add them to your library of architectural documentation. Add these documents to new employees' reading lists. It is far more important, not to mention far more useful, to document these relationships of you core competencies than to document system APIs and algorithms. Let the APIs document themselves, using good identifier naming and other hallmarks of professional coding from *Clean Code* (Martin 2009).

5.5 History and Such

Domain analysis is a mature discipline with a history that goes back to its earliest apologist, Jim Neighbors in 1980 (Neighbors 1980). Domain analysis has shown up in many guises in the intervening 30 years. Jim Coplien worked with David Weiss and Robert Lai at Bell Laboratories as they rolled out their FAST system internal to the company (Weisss and Lai 1999). As is characteristic of the work of many domain engineering proponents, Weiss and Lai focused on producing domain-specific languages (DSLs). Coplien (1998) took a different tact, deciding instead to let general-purpose languages express the domain semantics directly. Avoiding DSLs leads to a less brittle programming environment over time, anticipating the Agile need to roll with change.

Eric Evans' *Domain-Driven Design* (2003) has become popular in recent years as interest in DSLs again rises. It has been one of the most successful works to popularize domain-driven approaches. However, today's DSLs are little more than languages embedded in other languages by convention, and Evans' book focuses more on analysis and design than on its reduction to a DSL. Nonetheless, the analysis behind these languages is a crucial activity to create resilient designs. Such designs can reduce cost and improve responsiveness over a product lifetime; see Knauber et al (2002) and Coplien, Hoffman and Weiss (1998).

What the System *Is*, Part 2: Coding It Up

It's *finally* time to write code. The Agile people out there have been screaming, "what's with all this documentation? We want some *code!*" The Agile people will have their revenge when we come to the what-the-system-does chapter; here we're endearing ourselves to the Lean perspective.

And, in fact, this section is a little anticlimactic. The code should be *really* lean. We'll start with the basics and then investigate add-ons little by little.

6.1   The Third Step: The Rough Framing of the Code

From a nerd-centric perspective, the following technique is perhaps one of the two most important statements in the book:

Technique 19

The essence of "Lean" in Lean architecture is to take careful, well-considered analysis and distill it into APIs written in everyday programming languages.

That means that the ElectroCard routing team (from Chapter 5) might produce these lines of code as one product of their architecture activity:

```
class CircuitGraph
end

def route(theCircuit)
end
```

or these lines if they are programming in C++:

```
#include "BoardLayout.h"
class CircuitGraph;
extern BoardLayout
route(const CircuitGraph theCircuit);
```

Remember these goals of Lean:

- To avoid producing artifacts without end-user value;
- To deliberate carefully before making a decision, and then to act decisively;
- To create processes and environments that reduce rework;
- To guide work according to overall consistency and harmony.

Lean architecture avoids producing wasteful artifacts simply by refusing to produce many historic artifacts of software architecture. In the simple version of `route` above, we don't produce a function body until it's needed. Algorithm isn't form; it's structure. Its details aren't fundamental to what the system *is*; they focus on what the system *does*.

But that doesn't mean that it is a casual declaration. In a way, we feel cheated after all that domain analysis. Many projects feel the need to show a mass of artifacts proportional to the work done. Here, the work isn't in the mass of the artifacts. The work is in dividing up the world and in carefully analyzing what the structure of the artifacts should be. It's a bit like Picasso, whom legend says charged $20,000 for a portrait he completed in ten minutes. The client was alarmed at the price, complaining, "But it took you only 10 minutes!" Picasso allegedly replied, "Ten minutes, and 40 years."

Last, we are building heavily on wisdom of the decades, if not the ages, by proactively standing on domain knowledge instead of hopping around in response to the learning of the moment. The learning of the moment is important, too, but it's not everything. The domain knowledge provides a context for such learning.

6.1.1 Abstract Base Classes

If most of the domains will be object-shaped – whether justified by domain knowledge, patterns, or input from the end user mental model – most of the architecture code will be abstract base classes. Each domain will be delivered as an abstract base class, perhaps together with a small set of declarations of supporting types, constants, or supporting procedures. In most systems, each domain will form a module (see Sections 5.3.1 and 5.3.3).

Abstract base classes (ABCs) represent an interesting paradox. They are real source code but generate no object code on their own. They guide system form but contribute nothing to the product footprint. Their main function is to guide programmers as they weave use case code into the product. It is instructive to think of ABCs as tools rather than as part of the product. One of the central concepts of Lean practice in Toyota today is something called *poka-yoke* (fool-proofing). Abstract base classes may not ensure that developers' code will work perfectly, but they do guide developers to write code that preserves the system form.

This might be an abstract base class for Accounts. Even in a scripting language like Ruby, it makes sense to concisely define the interface for clients of the Account class:

```
class Account

    def accountID
    end

    def balance
    end

    # Note that initialize from zero arguments is
    # illegal (enforced only at run time)

    initialize(accountID, initialBalance = 0)
    end

    :private initialize

end
```

Notice that we use an explicit method interface for `accountID`, rather than following the common Ruby convention of using `attr_reader`. The `attr_reader` directive telegraphs the implementation (for example, of the balance or account ID) as member data. That removes our freedom to change the way we generate these values: for example, from a database lookup. Good architecture hides these strategies as secrets of the concepts that contain them. We can express more insightful judgment and offer more refined names by writing explicit methods than automatically generated getters and setters can. Besides, getters and setters do not achieve encapsulation or information hiding: they are a language-legitimized way to violate them.

Here it is in C++:

```cpp
#include "AccountNumber.h"

class Account {
public:
    Account(AccountNumber accountID);
    virtual AccountNumber accountID(void) const = 0;
    virtual Currency balance(void) const = 0;
    .  .  .  .
private:
    Account(void);   // the interface documents that
                     // this is illegal, and the
                     // compiler enforces it
public:
    Account(AccountNumber, Currency initialBalance);
private:
    AccountNumber accountNumber_;
};
```

The whole purpose of an ABC is to keep us from having to understand all the variants beneath it in the inheritance hierarchy. For most clients of any of the types beneath the ABC, one size fits all. This works because all of the subtending types have the same behavior as published in the ABC's interface. It's about all of them sharing that commonality. Of course, each one implements selected behaviors differently by overriding them with unique algorithms. For most architectural purposes we want to encapsulate that variation, and the subtyping graph encapsulates it well.

Nonetheless, it can be good to articulate and publish key derived types that arise during analysis, and we can go one level deeper and include the base class for Savings Accounts in our architecture.

```
class SavingsAccount < Account

    # We will associate SavingsAccount with
    # TransferMoneySink at run time as needed
```

```ruby
    def initialize(accountID, initialBalance)
        super(accountID, initialBalance)
    end
    private :initialize

    def availableBalance; @balance; end
    def decreaseBalance(amount); @balance -= amount; end
    def increaseBalance(amount); @balance += amount; end
    def updateLog(message, time, amount)
        . . . .
    end

end
```

Or, in C++:

```cpp
class SavingsAccount:
        public Account,
        public TransferMoneySink<SavingsAccount> {
public:
    SavingsAccount(AccountNumber, Currency);
    Currency availableBalance(void);
    void decreaseBalance(Currency);
    void increaseBalance(Currency);
    void updateLog(string message, MyTime t, Currency);

private:
    // Model data
    Currency availableBalance_;
    AccountNumber accountNumber_;
};
```

These are in fact not ABCs, but concrete, fully fleshed-out system classes. (Here, we've put the method bodies aside for brevity.) You will have to make a project decision whether to defer such declarations as part of implementation or to consider them as part of architecture. One important guiding principle is: Abstraction is evil. To throw away this declaration in the interest of keeping the more general, pure Account declaration is to abstract, and to throw away information. What if your boss knew that you were throwing away business information? A reasonable compromise might be to separate the two administratively. But the architecture police won't come looking for you if you put it together with the Account declaration as a full first-class deliverable of the architecture effort.

Note – and this is a key consideration – that the `SavingsAccount` class is *dumb*. It doesn't even know how to do deposits or withdrawals. We're sure that your professor or object-oriented consultant told you that a good account class should be smart and should support such operations! The problem with that approach is that it fails to separate what the system *is* – which changes very slowly – from what the system *does*. We want the above class declaration to be rock-solid. Additions driven by use case scenarios need to go somewhere else. This leads to another key technique of Lean architecture:

Technique 20

Keep domain classes as dumb as possible so that their methods, which represent long-term stable domain properties, aren't mixed in with the more rapidly changing interfaces that support use cases.

What do we do with the methods that support use cases? We talk about that in Chapter 8 and a lot more in Chapter 9 but we can give a preview now. The C++ declaration above makes a curious use of the indirect template idiom (Coplien 1996):

```
public TransferMoneySink<SavingsAccount> {
```

Mechanically, what this line does in C++ is to compose the what-the-system-does code in `TransferMoneySink` with the what-the-system-is code in the `SavingsAccount` class. This line makes sure that objects of `SavingsAccount` support one of the many use case scenarios that a `SavingsAccount` object participates in: transferring money between accounts. In that use case scenario a Savings Account plays the role of a TransferMoneySink. This line is the connection from the what-the-system-is world up into the what-the-system-does world. There can, in general, be many more such derivation lines in the declaration.

In Ruby we do this gluing together at run time on an instance-by-instance basis. If we create a `SavingsAccount` instance,

```
thirdAccount = SavingsAccount.new(0991540, 10000)
```

it can only do the basic, dumb operations of a Savings Account: increasing, decreasing, and reporting its balance. What if we want to do something more exotic, like a withdrawal? A withdrawal is a much richer operation that may include transactions, report generation, and a host of other use case steps. We can bring those in from code explicitly designed for the situation, in a module called `MoneySource`:

```
module MoneySource
    . . . .
    def withdraw(amount)
        . . . .
    end
    . . . .
end


thirdAccount.extend MoneySource
thirdAccount.withdraw(5000)
```

Again, we cover these techniques more fully in Chapter 9.

Analogous to these class declarations for domains that are object-shaped, you'll also have:

- Procedure declarations (potentially overloaded) for procedural domains;
- Template or generic declarations for generative domains;
- Constant declarations for trivial parametric domains.

You get the idea. Keep name choices crisp and enlightening; see some good tips about this in the *Clean Code* book (Martin 2009). Remember that code is read 20 times for every time it is written. For architectural code the ratio is even more extreme.

Of course, system form evolves – albeit slowly. These declarations change over time. Good domain analysis, including careful engagement of all the stakeholders, helps to slow the rate of change to domain classes. That gives you a good architecture, a good foundation, to stand on as the project goes forward.

6.1.2   Pre-Conditions, Post-Conditions, and Assertions

Architecture provides great opportunities to support communication in a project. Alistair's diagram (Figure 1-1) gives a low score to written forms of documentation. However, he doesn't explicitly talk about code as a powerful medium of communication. Code is like documentation when people are sitting remote from each other; however, it can be more precise than natural language documentation. It is very powerful when combined with the other media in Alistair's diagram. More powerful than two people at a whiteboard is two people at a keyboard.

The ABC declarations look a bit too malnourished to communicate the intent of the API. We can say more, and still be Lean. In the interest of having *poka-yoke* (fool-proof) guidance for the programmer, we should capture information both about the class as a whole and about individual member function arguments and return values. These interfaces are a contract between the supplier and the user. Indeed, Bertrand Meyer has long used the term *design by contract* for interfaces like this, expressing the contracts as invariants (remember commonality from above?) that apply at the interfaces (Meyer 1994). In many programming languages, we can express such invariants as *assertions*. (These contracts exist as a basis for dialogue and mutual understanding, not as a way to hold a client to your way of doing things!)

Assertions were first popularized in the C programming language on the UNIX Operating System, and they have handily carried over to C++ and are found in many other languages including C# and Java. These assertions work at run time. If we are to use them, we have to run the code. That means that we can no longer use ABCs alone, but that we need to fill in the methods.

Ruby's open environment makes it trivial for anyone to add customized assertions. Here we add an assertion interface to `Object`:

```
class AssertionFailure < StandardError              # 1
    def initialize(message)                         # 2
        super message                               # 3
        puts 'Assertion failed: ' + message         # 4
        abort                                       # 5
    end                                             # 6
end                                                 # 7
                                                    # 8
class Object                                        # 9
    def assert(bool, message = 'assertion failure') # 10
        if $DEBUG                                    # 11
        raise AssertionFailure.new(message)         # 12
                                    unless bool     # 13
        end                                         # 14
    end                                             # 15
end                                                 # 16
```

The code in Ruby might look like this:

```
class SavingsAccount                                # 1
    def initialize(accountID, initialBalance)       # 2
        assert Numeric === initialBalance           # 3
```

```
    assert initialBalance >= 0                         #   4
    super accountID, initialBalance                    #   5
    assert                                             #   6
        availableBalance >= Euro.new(0.0).amount,      #   7
        'positive initial balance'                     #   8
    . . . .              # application code             #   9
    assert availableBalance == initialBalance          #  10
    assert SavingsAccount === self                     #  11
                                                       #  12
    assert true, 'reached end of initialize'           #  13
end                                                    #  14
                                                       #  15
def availableBalance                                   #  16
    assert SavingsAccount === self                     #  17
    @balance                                           #  18
end                                                    #  19
                                                       #  20
def decreaseBalance(amount)                            #  21
    assert SavingsAccount === self                     #  22
    assert Numeric === amount                          #  23
    assert amount <= availableBalance,                 #  24
        'cash on hand'                                 #  25
    @balance -= amount                                 #  26
    assert availableBalance >= 0,                      #  27
        'balance non-negative'                         #  28
end                                                    #  29
                                                       #  30
def increaseBalance(amount)                            #  31
    assert SavingsAccount === self                     #  32
    assert Numeric === amount                          #  33
    @balance += amount                                 #  34
    assert true 'reached end of increaseBalance'       #  35
end                                                    #  36
                                                       #  37
def updateLog(logMessage, timeOfTransaction,           #  38
                    amountForTransaction)              #  39
    assert SavingsAccount === self                     #  40
    assert Numeric === amountForTransaction            #  41
    assert logMessage.length > 0                       #  42
    assert logMessage.length < MAX_BUFFER_SIZE         #  43
    assert timeOfTransaction >                         #  44
            Time.local(1970, 1, 1, 0, 0, 0)            #  45
                                                       #  46
```

```
              .   .   .   .                            #  47
                                                       #  48
          assert true 'end of updateLog reached'      #  49
      end                                              #  50
  end                                                  #  51
```

The strange `assert true` clauses at lines 13 and 35 can be used with a debugger or code coverage tool that is integrated with assertions. You can change the implementation of `assert` to print its arguments even when the value of the boolean variable is true, and voila! You have a crude trace facility. The assertion also statically documents the programmer intent that the function have a single exit. It is imperative that the assertion be evaluated on each call of the function. Though it is more than a bit of a challenge to create an assertion that fires when it is *not* evaluated, its presence still communicates that intent.

In C++:

```
#include <assert>                                      //   1
                                                       //   2
SavingsAccount::SavingsAccount(                        //   3
                            AccountNumber id,          //   4
                            Currency amount):          //   5
                            accountNumber_(id),        //   6
              availableBalance_(Euro(amount)) {        //   7
    assert(this != NULL);                              //   8
    assert(availableBalance_ >= Euro(0.0));            //   9
                                                       //  10
    // application code will go here                   //  11
                                                       //  12
    assert(availableBalance_ == amount);               //  13
    assert(dynamic_cast<SavingsAccount*>(this)         //  14
                                != NULL);              //  15
    assert(true);                                      //  16
}                                                      //  17
                                                       //  18
Currency SavingsAccount::availableBalance(void) {      //  19
    assert(this != NULL);                              //  20
                                                       //  21
    // application code will go here                   //  22
                                                       //  23
    assert(true);                                      //  24
    return availableBalance_;                          //  25
}                                                      //  26
```

```
                                                            // 27
void SavingsAccount::decreaseBalance(Currency c) {          // 28
    assert(this != NULL);                                   // 29
    assert(c <= availableBalance_);                         // 30
                                                            // 31
      // application code will go here                      // 32
                                                            // 33
    assert(availableBalance_ >= Euro(0));                   // 34
    assert(true);                                           // 35
}                                                           // 36
                                                            // 37
void SavingsAccount::increaseBalance(Currency c) {          // 38
    assert(this != NULL);                                   // 39
                                                            // 40
    // application code will go here                        // 41
                                                            // 42
    assert(true);                                           // 43
}                                                           // 44
                                                            // 45
void SavingsAccount::updateLog(                             // 46
        std::string logMessage,                             // 47
        MyTime timeOfTransaction,                           // 48
        Currency amountForTransaction) {                    // 49
    assert(this != NULL);                                   // 50
    assert(logMessage.size() > 0);                          // 51
    assert(logMessage.size() < MAX_BUFFER_SIZE);            // 52
    assert(timeOfTransaction >                              // 53
                MyTime("00:00:00.00 1970/1/1"));            // 54
                                                            // 55
    . . . .                                                 // 56
                                                            // 57
    assert(true);                                           // 58
}                                                           // 59
```

Some of these assertions look trivial, but experience shows again and again that the "stupid mistakes" are common and that they can be the most difficult to track down. Furthermore, most "sophisticated mistakes" (if there is such a thing) usually propagate themselves through the system as stupid mistakes. So these assertions serve a secondary purpose of increasing the software quality right from the beginning. But their primary purpose is to convey information about the arguments – information that the types alone may not convey. For example, we see that there is an upper bound on the size of the log string to SavingsAccount::updateLog.

C# has an `Assert` feature as part of the `Debug` class. Like all `Debug` code, assertion calls are filtered out in release mode. C# `Assert` behaves much like C `assert`:

```
Debug.Assert(logMessage.size > 0,
        "Log messages cannot be the null string.");
```

If the assertion fires the programmer will be treated to a stack back trace. If you want only a single line of output before program termination, then use `WriteLineIf`:

```
Debug.WriteLineIf(logMessage.size > 0,
        "Log messages cannot be the null string.");
```

In general, we can assert the following:

Technique 21

Use assertions and contracts to embellish the program code to express interfaces between system modules.

Static Cling

These C-style assertions depend on information that is available only at run-time. For compiled languages like C++, we can also create assertions that the compiler evaluates at compile time using information that's available at compile time. That is more in the spirit of architecture as form. Such assertions have long been available in many programming languages using macros, templates and generics.

C++ now has a static assertion feature as part of the language. These assertions are most useful for compile-time bindings that are not direct source-time bindings. Such combinations often arise when using templates. Consider this example:

```
// Create compile-time "log" function                    //   1
                                                          //   2
template<int i> struct param {                            //   3
    enum{                                                 //   4
        isPowerOf2 = i&1? 0: param<i/2>::isPowerOf2       //   5
    };                                                    //   6
};                                                        //   7
```

```
                                                        //   8
template<> struct param<1> {                            //   9
    enum{ isPowerOf2 = 1 };                             //  10
};                                                      //  11
                                                        //  12
template <class T, int size>                            //  13
class BuddySystemBuffer                                 //  14
{                                                       //  15
    // Buddy system pools must be 2**n                  //  16
    static_assert(param<size>::isPowerOf2);             //  17
public:                                                 //  18
    . . . .                                             //  19
private:                                                //  20
    T pool[size];                                       //  21
};                                                      //  22
                                                        //  23
BuddySystemBuffer<double, 128> b1;   // o.k.            //  24
BuddySystemBuffer<double, 255> b2;   // error           //  25
```

The declaration at line 25 results in a compile-time error.

There are also simpler ways to capture static architecture relationships, which vary from programming language to programming language. For example a C++ base class may express a member function as a pure virtual function, as we have done with all of the member functions in the interfaces of MoneySource and MoneySink below:

```
class MoneySource {                                      #   1
public:                                                  #   2
    virtual void decreaseBalance(Currency amount) = 0;   #   3
    virtual void transferTo(Currency amount,             #   4
            MoneySink *recipient) = 0;                   #   5
};                                                       #   6
                                                         #   7
class MoneySink {                                        #   8
public:                                                  #   9
    virtual void increaseBalance(Currency amount) = 0;   #  10
    virtual void updateLog(string, MyTime,               #  11
            Currency)  = 0;                              #  12
    virtual void transferFrom(Currency amount,           #  13
            MoneySource *source) = 0;                    #  14
};                                                       #  15
```

These declarations remind programmers to create implementations of these functions in the derived classes. (In this case, we are using `MoneySource` and `MoneySink` as traits on other classes, and the pure virtual functions document what the traits expect of the objects into which they are injected.) We will discuss this technique more in Section 9.4.3.

Some languages such as Eiffel can check consistency between assertions at compile time. So, for example, you can define the contract terms for a base class method in the base class, and for the overridden method in the derived class. The Eiffel compiler ensures that the contracts obey the Liskov Substitutability Principle (LSP) (Liskov 1986), which is a classic formalization of proper object-oriented programming. Eiffel ensures that no derived class method expects any stronger guarantees (as a precondition) than the corresponding base class method, and that methods promise no less (as post-conditions) than their corresponding base class methods. This makes it possible for a designer to write code against the base class contract with full confidence that its provisions will still hold, even if a derived type object is substituted where the base class object is "expected."

We get to assert (for the final invocation of this pun) that:

Technique 22

If you face trading off between expressing an assertion in terms of static properties available at compile time, or dynamic properties available only at run time, be sure to include the static version. Also include the dynamic version if it adds value in validating the code.

6.1.3 Algorithmic Scaling: The Other Side of Static Assertions

Assertions are a stopgap measure to ensure at compile time, or at worst at run time, that the system doesn't violate architectural and engineering assumptions. Good code can make the assumptions true by construction. This is particularly true in programming languages with strong compile-time systems (like C++) and less so in dynamic languages (like Ruby).

ALGORITHMIC SCALING is a pattern described by Fred Keeve at AT&T in the 1990s (Adams et al 1998). The idea is that the entire system is parameterized with compile-time constant parameters at the "tops" of the architecture, such as the amount of total configured memory, the number of subscribers that the system should support, etc. These parameters can be combined in expressions that generate other parameters for use at lower levels in the architecture, which in turn propagate them to lower levels, and so forth. Such static parameters can be used to size data structures, for example.

For example, consider a video network based on a token-passing ring. The network acts like a ring of nodes. At any time there is only one token active on the ring. Tokens are passed from node to node around the ring. Anyone can read the token; whether a node can deposit something in the token is determined by the protocol.

The domain model includes network links, network nodes, and, at the top level, the ring itself. Consider that we use a class paradigm or object paradigm for each of these entities. (The ring may not be an object instance in any normal sense, but it is still part of some stakeholders' mental model of the system, and is therefore part of the domain model.) A network node may be declared as follows:

```
class NetworkNode {
public:
    static const TimeInterval MaxAllowableDelay =
        Milliseconds(30);
. . . .
```

The network link declaration may look like this:

```
class NetworkLink {
public:
    static const TimeInterval interNodeTime =
        Milliseconds(1);
    . . . .
};
```

The ring itself may be a template that allows the software to be configured for many different networks:

```
template<unsigned int numberOfNodes_>
class Ring {
public:
    static const numberOfNodes = numberOfNodes_;
. . . .
```

Given these declarations, we can generate a third constant, which is the maximum number of nodes on the network:

. . . .

```
static const unsigned MaxNumberOfNodes =
    NetworkNode::MaxAllowableDelay /
        NetworkLink::interNodeTime;
```

. . . .

Of course, this means that the declaration of `Ring` must have access to the declarations of both `NetworkNode` and `NetworkLink`.

These declarations not only establish and document pair-wise relationships between architectural modules, but also establish a thread of dependencies that ties parts together in a way reminiscent of aspects.

Of course, one can do something similar in Ruby or other scripting languages, but the values are evaluated at run time rather than at compile time (because there really isn't much of a distinction).

6.1.4   Form Versus Accessible Services

Architecture should capture the forms that you wager will remain stable over time. That such forms are stable doesn't mean that they are global or even that they are large. It doesn't imply that all of their APIs or attributes should be published to a client. We can separate each form's interface from the form itself.

It is useful to administratively separate the published interface of the form from the private interface. Abstract base classes are a natural way to express the public interface in most programming languages. In C++ abstract classes can also express the protected and private interface of a class. You can adopt or create conventions to capture such details in the syntax and semantics of other languages.

A closely related rule of thumb is that an architect shouldn't feign ignorance. Architects too often avoid writing down known details because they feel that larger concerns will later invalidate what they know. Sometimes, in fact, the details are more knowable in advance than are the larger or more exposed forms of a system. Assert and write down what you know. If the domain analysis finds a recurring, common, stable form, capture it somewhere, even if it supports only a single stakeholder. Great architecture is as much about detail as it is about the large structures. The architect Ludwig Mies van der Rohe is quoted as saying, "God is in the details," and he personally chose the doorknobs for the houses he designed. Like Mies van der Rohe:

Technique 23

Use the code to capture and assert what you know. Don't go looking for every detail during domain analysis, but if you uncover a detailed bit of knowledge, capture it in code so it doesn't get lost. Being a detail doesn't mean that it can't be common or stable.

6.1.5 Scaffolding

Just as scaffolding and ultimately plumbing and wiring must be part of a house design, so should software "scaffolding" figure into the design. This includes support for design styles that you know about early on and, like the other so-called details discussed in the previous section, are worth capturing in code.

Most of this "scaffolding" or "plumbing" is code that isn't part of a class interface but is just implementation. Simple constant declarations, static assertions, and other declarations are examples of such plumbing. Some scaffolding, however, does affect the interface. Here are some examples of scaffolding code:

- *Stubs for procedures and class methods that make it possible to generate, compose and run an otherwise partially complete system.* Because the architecture is pure form – just abstract base classes or APIs – it can't run. Stubs and mocks can fill in the cracks. It can give a project a tremendous sense of assurance if the entire system compiles and links with no undefined symbols. Going even further: if the system can be executed and can run even a simple "Hello World" application (or putting up the corporate logo on the screen) without crashing, and with all dynamically allocated memory deallocated or all resources freed before program exit, you have a strong assurance of some level of architectural soundness.

  Stubs and mocks might be implemented as simple assertions for code that should be unreachable. Consider a partially implemented domain class, designed to implement the interface of its abstract base class. Perhaps some of its methods are not yet implemented in the current release. Such methods should be stubbed with assertions or at least with code that takes reasonable action for error reporting or recovery. Going a step further, the presence of such classes suggests that the domain may not properly have been decomposed. Consider re-factoring the design (perhaps by splitting the class in two) so that every class implements the complete interface of its abstract base class.

- *Code for specific patterns that implement the architectural style.* Let's say that your architecture has an object that can change type at run time, but you want to hide that type change from the object clients. For example, a telephone may use an internal object for communicating with its voice network connection, and you may want that connection to transparently (to both the end user and to the internal software) change from the phone company's cellular interface to a public Ethernet interface whenever one is available. You want to use a combination of the FACADE and STATE patterns (Gamma et al 2005) to present a constant interface and identity to the client, while the FACADE maintains alternative implementations that can be swapped in and out of action at run time. These implementations probably share a common base class (`AudioNetworkInterface` in this example) that allows the FACADE to treat them generically. Such constructs are arguably the territory of architecture because they go to the foundation of the computational model and affect the form of the domain object.

  Another example of such an architectural style is to separate instantiation from initialization. This is important to implement mutually recursive data structures or to otherwise handle timing issues that require these two functions to be separated. Initialization is a business concern while instantiation can be viewed as a scaffolding issue. Specific architectural forms can handle these needs in an idiomatic way (Coplien 1992, 79–82).

  In general, there are many idioms and low-level so-called patterns that are important to capture in the architecture, even though they may not be present in the interface. Some of them, such as FACTORY METHOD (Gamma et al 2005), may affect the interface as well.

- *Programming language extension.* For example, Scala supports anonymous classes that nicely express role injection, which is something that we'll want to do in Chapter 9. C++ does not. If you want to inject just the bare minimum of roles at any given point in a C++ program, you need to simulate some of the Scala language. In this case, Scala provides anonymous classes while C++ does not. Therefore, the programmer must manually create an intermediate class that simulates what Scala does by composing a domain class with an injected class just long enough to make an object from it. In Scala, that class doesn't appear in the source code:

```
val source = new SavingsAccount with SourceAccount
```

In C++, it must:

```
class SavingsAccountWithSourceAccount:
    public SavingsAccount,
    public SourceAccount<SavingsAccount> {

        . . . .
};


SourceAccount<SavingsAccount> *source =
    new SavingsAccountWithSourceAccount;
```

- *Test points for use by system testers.* For example, system testers may want to run automatic tests that simulate GUI interactions; such an interface may double as a foundation for remote administration or trouble-shooting of the system. The system must provide a testing API that is accessible to such an external tool.

6.1.6   Testing the Architecture

Though this is not a book about testing, most testing books focus on the imperative and behavioral aspects of testing. It's important to bring out two more facets of testing more pertinent to this book: usability testing and architecture testing.

After you reach your first architecture deliverable, you can do both usability testing and architecture testing. In the spirit of Agile you can of course do partial testing along the way; don't leave it all until the end. And in the spirit of Scrum, you want your architecture work to be done-done-done before you start building on its foundations.

Usability Testing

A good program architecture complements the interactive interface of an Agile system, and vice versa. Usability testing can yield insights on architectural improvements. See Section 7.8 for a short discussion of this issue.

Architecture Testing

The goal of architecture testing is to find ways in which the architecture is either delivered broken, or in which it might "break" over time. What it means for an architecture to "break" is that changes in technology or customer needs become unreasonably costly.

Let's briefly consider what it means to review the ways in which an architecture is delivered broken. This is the classic approach in waterfall projects. In a classic architecture review, the heavyweight experts walk in the door long after the architects have finished their work, armed with expertise and insight. They bring a "dispassionate" external perspective to the project. Their scope is usually technical: Is this the best technology or framework for your business?

By all means, if a chance arises to snag an expert or consultant who happens to be passing by, you shouldn't pass it up. Common sense dictates that you seek insights wherever you can find them. However, it puts the project at risk to defer reflection on key decisions about system form, and reviewing an architecture whose form is already committed means that issues that arise in the architecture review will cause rework. The Lean philosophy is to pull such decisions forward. Instead of waiting until a review to bring in the big guns – who tell you all that is wrong with the system and saddle you with weeks of rework – you engage the big guns early.

The Agile way is to view domain experts as part of the team and to make sure they are there from the beginning. You want to apply domain experts' insights through forward engineering rather than using them to do a drive-by assessment late in the project. In the Scrum sense, they should be invested in the project like Scrum "pigs," rather than just contributing like "chickens."[1]

It is of course important to assess the appropriateness of a particular technology, or framework, or architectural form for a particular business need. In an Agile project, the team makes most of these decisions going forward instead of waiting for a third-party review. A third-party review can add value, but it's important to understand that outsiders bring their own perspective and agendas that are outside the team dialogue. They bring a fresh perspective, but they also lack the context of the complex interactions and perspectives of the stakeholders on the team. (If you have a stakeholder who isn't part of your extended team, ask yourself: could you improve things if they were?)

Many architectural drivers are non-technical. Though it may make no technical sense to use CORBA, the customer clientele may insist on it, and CORBA may end being the right choice for reasons of market acceptance. Like it or not, business stakeholders have their say in architecture reviews. So do the technical people, who can respond with their perspective on the

---

[1] These are common cultural terms in Scrum, where being a *pig* means to be materially involved in production, while being a *chicken* means to be supportively involved but not directly committed. The terms come from a joke about a pig and chicken starting a restaurant.

cost of such decisions. In the spirit of Agile, it takes a team with a high degree of trust to grapple with these issues and to drive to a bottom line such as return on investment.

Such traditional reviews, therefore, have a place. But the first order cost of architecture is its long-term cost. In the spirit of Lean, we're focused on the long term. Unexpected costs arise when developers have to make changes to parts of the system that were designed to be stable. If we can project such costs into the future, we can act on the architecture today to potentially lower the lifetime cost of software maintenance. "Maintenance" is where most software money goes (Boehm 1976; Lientz, Swanson and Tompkins 1978), so it pays to focus on it, rather than today's framework costs, in an architecture review.

As with any testing, there are three parts to architectural testing: creating the tests; applying the tests; and assessing the results. Creating the tests means creating business scenarios that foresee potential changes. Applying the tests means investigating how these changes deform the architecture. Assessing the results means evaluating the cost of accommodating such changes given the existing architecture.

Some of the best people to create future business scenarios are your sales and marketing people. They have their fingers on the pulse of the market, and possess knowledge of the market history and imagination for the market's future trends. As much as we are frustrated by their apparent unreasonableness when they come to us with new requirements, that is exactly the perspective you should be seeking in these reviews: to find the outlandish outliers in the market-scape. You can use standard risk analysis techniques to build a team consensus on the likelihood of each change and take that into account during cost assessment.

So start with your sales and marketing people – but don't stop there. Use your imagination to engage creative people in the review process. Don't forget changes in technology and standards. (Architects note that the nice things about standards are that there are so many of them, and that they can always be changed.) Use an open-ended brainstorming approach, and then revisit your findings to soberly assess the likelihood of each scenario. Your stakeholders may even be persuaded to view the activity as a way to generate new killer apps in the market!

For each scenario that your focus group creates, have your developers pretend that they are actually going to implement it. Convene a short design session to evaluate the cost of the change. Cost is roughly proportional to the number of architectural interfaces that have to change to accommodate the change in the market.

The business folks own the answer to the question: What does "unreasonably costly" mean? There is no free lunch, and no one should expect things always to be easy. Bertrand Meyer talks about his *law of continuity*, noting that good design should promise only that easy changes be inexpensive and that more fundamental changes be costly:

> Continuity is a crucial concern if we consider the real lifecycle of software systems, including not just the production of an acceptable initial version, but a system's long-term evolution. Most systems undergo numerous changes after their first delivery. Any model of software development that only considers the period leading to that delivery and ignores the subsequent era of change and revision is as remote from real life as those novels which end when the hero marries the heroine – the time which, as everyone knows, marks the beginning of the really interesting part. (Meyer 1994, p. 103)

Even the best design can't flatten the cost curve to a constant: there is always a price to pay for change. One good rule of thumb in answering the "unreasonably costly" question is to apply Meyer's model in a relative way. Assess the cost of a moderately complex change. If you can find a large set of changes that should be easier from a business context, or from the context of the end user mental model, and that are more expensive than the moderate change, your architecture may not be as good as it should be.

In doing this cost assessment, you should be careful to start by separating architectural costs from operational, training, customer retrofit, and other business costs that don't trace directly to the architecture. Evaluate the architecture for its own sake. In the end, everything matters, but you want to start by separating concerns; you'll find that helps clarify subsequent discussions of tradeoffs. Later, the business may recommend a sub-optimal architectural change (e.g., in the interest of embracing a standard that has gained market attention) because the overall business result will be better. Taking a cue from Lean, all decisions should focus on long-term results. Long-term arguments usually, but not always, work in the interest of an elegant architecture. Nerds: sometimes you'll lose these arguments, and you'll have to learn to take your medicine and buy into the bigger picture.

There is no good definition of architectural completeness (though we take a stab at it in Section 6.4). A good team is always refining the architecture as requirements become better understood and grow over the product lifetime. Architectures change, and minimizing their surprising costs reduces risk in the product's profitability. The team needs to agree what "done" means for "the architecture is done" at any given stage in the project.

See also Section 6.2.2, "Testing the relationships."

6.2 Relationships in Architecture

Object-oriented architecture doesn't just mean "a bag of objects." Just as in housing architecture, architecture is more than a parts inventory. It is about *relationships* between parts. We should communicate what we know about those relationships at design time – in the code.

6.2.1 Kinds of Relationship

Many of these relationships are dynamic and our treatment of them will come in Chapter 8 and Chapter 9. For example, the mapping of a role to the object playing the role is dynamic, and we capture the mapping in something called a Context object. (We will briefly say more about Context objects in the next section.) However, some of the relationships are static. Many such relationships are simple, well-known design relationships. Examples of these include:

- The use of one object type in the interface or implementation of another. The `#include` statements in C++ and `import` statements in Java and C# document (and enable) relationships between architectural entities.

- Static assertions, as described in Section 6.1.2.

- Algorithmic scaling as described in Section 6.1.3.

- Patterns, which are all about architectural relationships. While the patterns themselves deserve special treatment (see Section 5.4.2), actual instances of major patterns should be flagged in the code. Consider Model-View-Controller as an example. Use either of well-named classes (e.g., deriving from base classes called `Model`, `View` and `Controller` – a bit simplistic, but you get the idea) can help immensely. The code should speak for itself, but a crisp comment in the code is almost always better than a description in a separate document.

- Composition, particularly of classes. Object composition – the old HAS-A relationship of 1980s method notations – is often a low-level programming concern rather than an architectural concern. If composition has architectural overtones, then make such relationships visible. One place that they will become important in the DCI architecture of Chapter 9 is for the composition of the methodful roles that bear the logic for what-the-system-does, with the domain classes that bear the logic for what-the-system-is.

We can illustrate with an example. Consider a text editing application where one of the roles is a Selection. A Selection is a role that can be played by a line, a paragraph, a whole file, or maybe other things. One operation on a selection is to create a word iterator initialized to the beginning of the selection; the iterator can be advanced word by word to implement, for example, spell checking. We might find the code:

```
template <class ObjectPlayingSelector>
WordIterator
Selection<ObjectPlayingSelection>::newIterator(void) {
    . . . .
    unsigned nchars =
        dynamic_cast<ObjectPlayingSelection*>(this)->
            size();
    . . . .
}
```

In this context, `size` is a member function of the domain object into which the role has been injected. It may be that a `TextBuffer` object plays this role:

```
class TextBuffer: public Selection<TextBuffer>
{
public:
    unsigned size(void) {
        . . . .
    }
}
```

We want to document, and enforce at compile time, that any such compositions must contain at least the methods `newIterator` and `size`:

```
class SpellCheckSelectionBase {
public:
    virtual unsigned size(void) = 0;
    virtual WordIterator newIterator(void) = 0;
};
```

and then add code to enforce it:

```
template <class ObjectPlayingSelection>
class Selection:
```

```
    public SpellCheckSelectionBase {
public:
    WordIterator newIterator(void);

    . . . .

};
```

Because `TextBuffer` derives from the `Selection` template, all of the interfaces stipulated by the `SpellCheckSelectionBase` "compositor" are met.

6.2.2   Testing the Relationships

A crucial yet subjective measure of a good architecture is that its relationships tie modules together while sustaining maintenance autonomy for each one. How should you evaluate relationships?

First, each relationship should be self-evident to someone knowledgeable about the domains of application. "Sneak paths" violate our intuition about being able to make changes in relative isolation and lead to unpleasant surprises.

Second, the most important relationships are those between the code of geographically separated teams. Dependencies between code modules (classes, actual modules, functions, etc.) are probably the final (and sometimes least important) consideration.

Margaretha Price (Price and Demurjian 1997) has a simple rule of thumb for gauging relationships. Most simply expressed, general-purpose software should not depend on specific software, though specific software can of course depend on general-purpose software. One obvious example can be found in the relationship between a class and its base class: a class for a specific concept should never be the base class for the class for a more general concept. However, Price's relationships are more general, including, for example, the relationship between general-purpose platform APIs and feature-specific code. What constitutes *general-purpose* and *specific* is subjective but within the judgment of domain experts. Moving data, methods, etc. between architectural units can reduce these dependencies (but remember that relocating a function may reduce one set of dependencies while increasing others).

6.3   Not Your Old Professor's OO

Most Agile software is built from classes and objects, following a simple definition of object orientation based on commonality and variation, as in Table 5-1 and Table 5-2 (on page 98 and page 119, respectively: see the bottom right-hand cell in each of the tables). What, exactly, are the "building materials" we use for object orientation? Table 5-1 and Table 5-2 suggest that object orientation means that we take advantage of overridden functions in derived classes. But why should we talk about *classes* when it's called *object*-oriented programming? Classes are static, so a class architecture can capture only architectural statics. Agile is about embracing change – certainly in the classes, but how about in the run-time connection between objects? That's even more crucial to the concerns of usability and maintainability than the class structure is. We'll return to this question in detail in Chapter 9, but will explore the topic a bit here first.

Classes are the Lean part of Lean Architecture and Agile Software Development. Classes and their relationships may be complicated (in the Lean sense of the word) but are unlikely to be as complex (in the Agile sense of the word) as run-time object relationships are. One shortcoming of domain analysis techniques – including the object orientation of today's textbooks, which can be viewed as an advanced but constrained form of domain engineering – is that they are so static. We might expect an Agile world to be more dynamic.

History confuses the issue. Definitions of object-orientation abound, but one common lay definition of an object is a locus of related responsibilities. Responsibility-driven design is widely used and acknowledged as a well-grounded approach to object orientation. Most Smalltalk, Java, C#, and C++ programmers realized the responsibilities of analysis and CRC cards in *class* interfaces, and objects became invisible over time as design entities.

In this book we carefully distinguish three key building blocks of object-oriented design:

- *Objects*, which are the end users' conceptualization of things in their business world;
- *Classes*, which provide simple, encapsulated access to the data that represents business information;
- *Roles*, which interact in a use case to achieve some business goal.

Note that these are more or less design-time concepts. We want end user objects to correspond closely to programming objects, and there are few obstacles to achieving that ideal if you view the running system from the end user perspective. It's a bit different from the programmer perspective! Few programming languages allow us to actually program objects: we program classes. To complicate things even further, classes may serve other programming purposes. For example, we will see in Chapter 9 that classes (in the programming language sense) are one way to realize roles (in the design sense).

The data model shows up as classes in the code in most programming languages. If we are using old-fashioned object-oriented programming, these class interfaces will also publish methods that might directly appear in a use case. However, except in the very simplest case, these what-the-system-does methods tend to change at different rates, and in response to needs of different stakeholders, than the domain interfaces.

In Section 7.7 we will discuss two design alternatives for grouping the methods that come from behavioral requirements. In the first case, when it makes sense to use old-fashioned object oriented programming, these methods go together with the interface for the domain operations. In the second case when it makes better sense to disentangle the use case logic from the domain code, we put them in separate constructs called *roles*.

In the first case, domain methods and use case methods live together in the same class interface. These use case methods represent atomic events and operations on a single role rather than an interaction between roles. Code that uses this style exclusively, we will refer to as having an *Atomic Event architecture*. In the second case we will find a home for the use case logic in the code representing the roles involved in the use case. This is called the Data-Context-Interaction (DCI) architecture.

The C in DCI stands for *Context*. The Context object is a special kind of object that we will introduce in Chapter 9. Its job is to tie together the roles of the use case with the objects that will play those roles for the current use case. There is one class of Context object for each use case in the system. Context objects are another part of the "scaffolding" that supports the execution model.

But a Context object may in fact be more than that. Consider a Bank Account. Is it a domain data object? No: the real domain objects in a bank are transaction logs and audit trails. Yet a Bank Account looks like a domain object from the perspective of a withdrawal or deposit or money transfer. In fact, the best way to decouple concerns in a case like this is often to have a "traffic cop" object that implements the coordinating connections that make withdrawals and deposits and transfers possible. Context objects normally have no state other than the knowledge of the domain objects involved in the active use case that the Context represents. All domain information is represented by data in those domain objects. So what might look like a domain object early in analysis may end being a Context. And Context objects that are created just to support specific use cases may look a lot like domain objects.

What's nice about this is that, in all of these cases, the architecture can still be faithful to the end user model. That bodes well for good maintainability and usability. Furthermore, a programmer implementing use case scenarios such as withdraw, deposit and transfer may not need to know whether a Bank Account is a domain object or a Context: it just looks like a smart domain object. Programmers implementing use cases on the database can work directly in terms of transaction logs and audit trails, where the data actually lie.

Several such architectural styles may be combined within a given system. Such an architecture might have a hybrid layer of Context objects to bridge the two worlds of what-the-system-is and what-the-system-does (Figure 6-1). There can be arbitrarily many of these layers but humans have difficulty going beyond about five (the number of things that will fit in short-term memory).

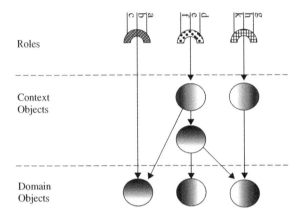

Figure 6-1   An Object-oriented Architecture.

Figure 6-1 shows the *object* relationships in a strongly object-oriented architecture that combines the Atomic Architecture and DCI approaches. The class relationships for such a system may be different, and depend on the programming language. In this chapter we have focused on the bottom layer – a layer that doesn't have to know much about its relationships to the items above it. It is a relatively static layer, and that suggests that even something as static as a class can capture most of its interesting semantics.

There are other objects and patterns of objects that are characteristic of object systems, in particular the Model-View-Controller architecture that provides the connection to the end user. Model, View and Controller are roles, and are often implemented as interfaces (as in Java or C#) or abstract base classes (as in C++). The Controller often has a close relationship to Context objects: Controllers often create Context objects. The domain objects often implement the Model role, though a Context object (like the Bank Accounts described above) can also play Model roles.

6.4   How much Architecture?

There are a few polarizing topics in software engineering discourse, and "how much architecture" is near the top of the list. Critics of the segregated up-front architecture efforts popular in large 1980s projects have even earned a disparaging acronym: *BUFD*, for "big up-front design." The same folks have come up with their own catchy acronym that tells us that up-front architecture is unnecessary work, saying: "You ain't gonna need it," or *YAGNI*.

6.4.1   Balancing BUFD and YAGNI

In fact, though there is an element of truth in each of their arguments, neither BUFD nor YAGNI get it entirely right. BUFD can't work because of emergent requirements. Even if there weren't emergent requirements, building too much up-front running code on speculation means the system has a lot of functionality that doesn't add immediate value in the market and which doesn't receive market feedback until long after it is delivered. (Think of how much code in your system has never been executed.) These aspects of software development are well known to most progressive software folks and have become part of the modern software engineering landscape. It's no longer cool to be BUFD.

The arguments against YAGNI are subtler, at least in light of prevailing software mores today. Many popular arguments in support of YAGNI are naïve: for example, that YAGNI is Lean because it avoids building something ahead of its need. The argument is naïve in the sense that it is also naïve to wait to build the basement or cellar of a house until you decide you want a basement recreation room or until the late fall harvest when you need a place for your potatoes. The basement is not only a functional *structure* that hosts a recreation room or your vegetables, but is also a *form* that supports and shapes the rest of the house. Furthermore, because of its position in the architecture, it's difficult to re-shape once it's in place. That suggests a process of up-front planning and thought.

The BUFD end of the spectrum is a caricature of Lean thinking (but lacking attention to the value stream and to constant, ongoing improvement) while the YAGNI end of the spectrum is a caricature of Agile thinking. You need both. Consider Figure 6-2, which presents a model of long-term cost as a function of the amount of effort put into architecture. The key is to find the minimum in the curve where you have enough architecture to

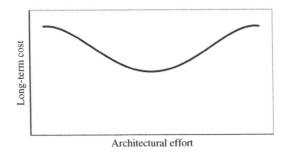

Figure 6-2   How much architecture?

enable development and to minimize rework, but not so much that you create unused artifacts or shelfware.

6.4.2   One Size Does Not Fit All

The answer to the question: "How much architecture should I do?" should vary from organization to organization based on need. What drives such a need? Boehm and Turner (Boehm and Turner 2003) argue that code mass and the degree of assurance about stability are two of the major drivers. Figure 6-3 shows Boehm's model of project cost as a function of architectural investment; it is a more elaborate version of the graph in Figure 6-2. The coordinate axis shows how much time needs to be added to the schedule for a given investment in architecture, while the ordinate access corresponds to the amount of architectural effort. Too little architecture leads to rework and added effort; too much architecture causes architecture work itself to dominate the schedule.

Of course, this figure is only a model. An Agile organization uses its own insight and experience to determine how deep to go into architecture. Also, the time expansion factor is heavily dependent on how much your organization can take advantage of the Lean Secret: to put everyone in one room at one time instead of drawing out architectural design over days or weeks of disconnected design activities, artifact creation, and reviews. Strive to bring all the information together at once so there are no delays in getting the information necessary to support an architectural decision.

6.4.3   When Are You Done?

How do you know when you're done with architecture? The following questions might help you decide:

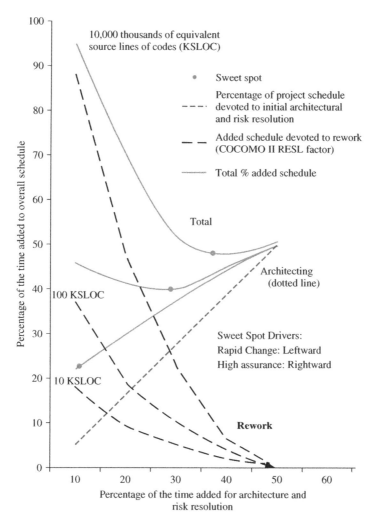

Figure 6-3 Effect of size on sweet spot. Source: Boehm and Turner, Balancing agility and discipline. Addison-Wesley Professional, 2003.

- Does the architecture contribute to solving the problem in the long-term problem definition (Chapter 4)? If not, consider why you built the architecture that you did.
- Can you test it (Section 6.1.6)? Stakeholders should develop the architecture to a point that they have confidence that it will support business goals in the future given the available sustaining investment.
- Are there readers for all of the documentation (Section 5.4)? Documentation can be minimal, in spite of our inclination that we need something other than abstract base classes to show for the work

we put into up-front design. Document architectural core competencies as patterns; otherwise, try to let the code speak for itself.

- Can you evolve it? Your architecture isn't done if you don't have a process to evolve it over time.
- Does it support your market? Ask whether it is easy to configure deliverables for different market segments. Assess whether the architecture supports convenient generation of product line members.
- Are architecture documents literate, and do they use consistent vocabulary (Section 5.4.1) and plain language so that stakeholders broadly can understand them?
- Last, does the team understand the architecture and the technology necessary to maintain it over time? The finest architecture created at the hands of an object wizard is useless if your team lacks object skills.

Your team will doubtless think of many more criteria to assess the architecture. Use your imagination, and challenge yourself.

And, of course, you are never really done with architecture. At any given time you need to trade off the business risk and return on investment against the architecture effort. Most of this is common sense. Revisit your architecture occasionally and assess the cost of augmenting or refining it, as well as the potential resulting payoff.

6.5   Documentation?

The code itself can be one of the most faithful forms of documentation and in any case is, and probably should be, the oracle for architectural insight. That is the first rule of thumb of architectural documentation. In a perfect world the code reveals the architecture and the designers' intent. Unfortunately, few programming languages are expressive enough to capture the nuances not only of the form of the data, but also the relationships between data, or between processes, while still capturing the essence of the system behaviors and the interactions between *them*. We usually need something else, and patterns are one of the best ways to capture the big picture. So the second rule of thumb for software architecture is to capture the big picture somewhere, and patterns are a powerful way to do that.

We're lucky if the source code gives us a clue about one or two of these properties, so we need supplementary documentation. Perhaps the main place of architecture documentation is to capture relationships that are not visible from the code itself. For example, we might have designed a given encryption algorithm to work particularly well with a separate compression algorithm. We wouldn't be able to find that in the code. Code commentary of course can help, but we should also capture such design decisions an architecture document at the level of the system partitions. So the third rule of thumb for architecture documentation is: Use structured prose to capture the major elements of form that are invisible in the source code.

Some of these invisible structures are so common that they become part of business core competency. They recur in your product. They may recur across multiple products. Such deep and often timeless forms should be captured as pattern languages. This leads us to our fourth rule of thumb: Documentation should focus on broad, lasting, and positive forms that capture core business competencies. Don't waste time creating redundant documentation for specific or fleeting forms; capture those in the code. To review our earlier discussion of patterns, see Section 5.4.2.

6.6   History and Such

To use the object-oriented programming concepts for design, and ultimately for architecture, can be traced back to Grady Booch's early work. He wrote his very first paper in 1984, called simply "Object Oriented Design." A growing number of methodologists, such as Peter Coad, explored this space throughout the 1980s, often in the context of OOPSLA, the annual ACM SIGPLAN conference on objects.

The object community split into two extremes during the 1980s. One half, typified by the Smalltalk community, focused on programming-in-the-small. They believed that proper focus on well-designed individual classes was enough to create good software because the system behavior arose through emergence from the interactions between objects. The other half remained steeped in the "big up-front design" traditions that predated object orientation, and turned to CASE tools and methodologies. Both schools grew during the 1980s, but neither was ever completely satisfying.

In May 1993 a group met at IBM in Thornwood, New York, to explore how to build a body of software design literature. In August of the same year, some of those people, together with a few new ones, met in Colorado and explored how the ideas of building architect Christopher Alexander might apply to software design. Patterns provided a breakthrough in thinking about design that was a relief from both extremes in the object-oriented community. The idea caught on quickly, but would focus largely on micro-architectures closely tied to the object-oriented model until some years later.

But also in the mid-1980s, Trygve Reenskaug was applying the concepts of roles in design using his OORAM methodology, and published a book about it in the mid-1990s (Reenskaug, Wold, and Lehne 1995). This work was one of the main foundations of DCI, which we present in Chapter 9.

What the System *Does*: System Functionality

One surprising by-product of the scenario-planning process is increased responsibility.

The Clock of the Long Now, p. 118.

Every system has two designs: the design of what it *does*, and the design of what it *is*. End users ultimately care about the services they receive from the software, and these almost always fall into the what-the-system-does category. However, the underlying domain model shows through the service interface. Recall how important the direct manipulation metaphor is to object-oriented programming. Also, for the sake of keeping down long-term cost (which customers and end users also appreciate) and of supporting change (which customers and most end users also appreciate) the vendor (that's you) also wants to start off with a good overall system form, and that form is grounded in what-the-system-is. At the beginning of a project you need to focus on both. This double-edged focus applies not only to good beginnings but is the heart of long-term product health.

It is crucial to always remember that the heart of what software delivers is a service, a service that is about action. Unlike buildings, computers have animation at human time scales, and this animation is key to their role in life. Luke Hohmann advises us that instead of architecture being the best metaphor we have for software system design, that we should look instead to another one of the arts: dance. Like architecture, dance is also about form, but it is alive and dynamic. Chapters 5 and 6 gave us our dance hall; now let's proceed to the dance.

Given that this is an Agile book, you might have expected the more user-facing what-the-system-does section to precede the architecture section. We would do that in an ideal world: we would drive design according to the pure desires of the end user and let nothing else distract us. We investigate the domain form a bit before discussing functionality in detail because it is more efficient that way. If the architecture terminology supports mutual understanding between the provider and user, we can move on to functionality with confidence – and improved long-term flexibility.

7.1   What the System *Does*

To decide what the system *does*, we first need to know *Who, What*, and *Why*. *Who* is going to use our software? *What* do they want to use it for? And *Why* should they use it? In Agile development the current popular form of *user stories* forms around this *Who-What-Why* mantra. "As an Account Holder (who), I want to transfer money between my accounts (what), so I can ensure that none of my accounts become overdrawn (why)."

7.1.1   User Stories: A Beginning

User stories are a good beginning, but probably not enough to ensure a good result. What do we actually know about the Account Holder? If I am the Account Holder I will use my online banking system to transfer the money. If the Account Holder is my 11-year-old son, he only has one account and will not need the functionality. If the Account Holder is my 85-year-old aunt, she will go to the bank and ask a bank employee to transfer the money for her. If the Account Holder cannot come to the bank, and doesn't have access to the Internet, a phone call to the bank would be the preferred solution. So we need to know more about the *Context*. Remember from Chapter 4 that we noted the importance of context in formulating the problem to be solved. Is the Account Holder an Internet user, who will do the transfer from home? Does the Account Holder use an intermediary in the bank to do the transfer? Does the bank want to offer this service from their ATMs?

A money transfer should be simple. The user chooses a source account, a destination account, and an amount. The system does a simple calculation and updates the balance on the two accounts. Two steps and we are done. Almost . . . we just need to know a *few* things more: Must both accounts be in the same bank? What are the consequences of transferring money from an account that will leave it with a negative balance? Should the transfer happen immediately? Can the user schedule the transfer to happen in the future? Can the future be in 10 years? What do we tell the Account Holder that only has one account, but attempts to transfer money? ("Error"?) Shall children have access to the feature? Can the user put in a recurrent transfer, for example once a month?

Maybe you know the answers to many of these questions if you have been working in a specific bank for years, and if you have deep domain knowledge. But bank policies are ephemeral and it can be hard to keep up to date with the current changes. If you are a designer, or even an architect, it's likely that someone else on the business side handles questions of scope. Maybe you think it should be possible to set up a recurring transfer, and it wouldn't take you long to code it. But it also needs to have a proper user interface. It has to be tested. It raises new questions like: How do you inform the Account Holder if there isn't enough money to do the transfer? So it is a business decision, and not a decision based on the developer's interpretation of the user story.

We could also explore the *why* perspective. Maybe the Account Holder transfers money because another account has a better interest rate, or because of the tax advantages that come from shifting the money into another account when going into a new year. Do these things matter? You don't really know until you have explored it. However, we do know that a designer's implicit assumptions have a huge impact on user interface design.

7.1.2   Enabling Specifications and Use Cases

These questions illustrate what has become a common experience within Agile development: *User stories are not enough*. Agile leaders have been augmenting use cases with test cases (Cohn 2004, p. 7) and constraints and business rules (Cohn 2004, p. 77). They even advocate the use of tools to overcome the text limitations of cards (Cohn 2004, p. 179). And the stories can be grouped into higher-level business areas, much as use cases collect scenarios (Patton 2009). As the Agile movement has learned from experience over the past ten years, the modern user story has in fact become a use case (Figure 7-1). Alistair Cockburn tells why he still uses use cases (Cockburn 2008):

> User stories and backlog items don't give the designers a *context* to work from ... don't give the project team any sense of "completeness" ... don't provide a good-enough mechanism for *looking ahead* at the difficulty of upcoming work
>
> ...
>
> Use cases are, indeed, heavier and more difficult than either user stories or backlog items, but they bring value for that extra weight. ... In particular, use cases fix those three problems.
>
> ...

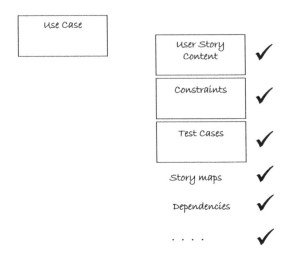

Figure 7-1   Use cases integrate many user story add-ons.

1. The list of goal names provides executives with the shortest summary of what the system will contribute to the business and the users. . . .

2. The main success scenario of each use case provides everyone involved with an agreement as to what the system will basically do, also, sometimes more importantly, what it *will not do* . . .

3. The extension conditions of each use case provide the requirements analysts a framework for investigating all the little, niggling things that somehow take up 80% of the development time and budget. . . .

4. The use case extension scenario fragments provide answers to the many detailed, often tricky business questions programmers ask . . . it is a thinking / documentation framework . . .

5. The full use case set shows that the investigators have thought through every user's needs, every goal they have with respect to the system, and every business variant involved . . .

But user stories are just "a promise for a future conversation," responds the Agilist. And it is true that it is important to talk about these things. The question is: What you do with the findings from the conversation? One output could be even more user stories:

"As an Account Holder I want to put in a recurrent monthly transfer so I can pay my bills from another account than where I receive my salary."

"As an Account Holder I want to transfer money to another Account
Holder so I can pay my rental skis."
"As an Account Holder I want to pay my bills over the Internet so
I don't have to go the post office".

We could also create user stories for other user roles such as bank
advisers, accountants, bookkeepers, and tax authorities. We could present
different motivations for the same feature and hope to be able to integrate
them together. If you put five domain experts in a room and brainstorm
user stories, you will get a lot of user stories very fast! That's a good way
to explore the requirements space. But how do you organize the 200 user
stories you created last week? You need to make a (hopefully ordered) list
based on the relationships between them, their cost, their business value,
and market timing, so that you can make sound business decisions about
when to initiate development on each of them.

Let's try to help the businesspeople out before things get too messy. And,
no, the help doesn't come from "sub-stories" (breaking down big stories
into smaller ones) or "epics" (collecting small stories into a bigger ones).
There is no reason to reinvent the wheel. The industry has been through
all of this before, and many of these proven practices honor both Lean
and Agile.

7.1.3 Helping Developers, Too

Much of the discussion about requirements focuses on keeping the business
people happy. We want them to feel they have given us something that
conveys their vision, and we want them to be able to do that without
having to know *too* much Ruby, C# or Java. It's easy to forget the customer
of these requirements: the development team.

A developer can in theory put on an analysis hat and get requirements
directly from the horse's mouth. Such an approach can perhaps work
in a small development project or in an informal business relationship.
Typically, though, developers lack the skills to do good analysis and lack
the business expertise necessary to take accountability for formulating the
requirements that will drive the business. However, we know – both in
Agile and non-Agile development – that the business too often hands off
work to the team prematurely. The team doesn't really know what the
business wants and sometimes lacks the wherewithal to gain valid clarification. Of course, it's impossible to create comprehensive requirements
(because of emergent requirements), so we'll always need *some* kind of
feedback loop that can keep the product on track after coding has started.

Even so, when a developer gets a requirement, it should be possible to
start development quickly. Requirements questions shouldn't arise from

the inadequacy of the spec, but rather should come as "surprises" that emerge during detailed design or coding. A good requirement should be *enabling* for the developer. Enabling specifications are not, however, a substitute for *everybody, all together, from early on*: rather, they are evidence that the Lean Secret is in fact in play.

The U.S. patent system uses the phrase *enabling specification* to describe a patent that is compelling enough to drive development without significant new research. In the same sense that a patent enables a craftsperson to re-create an invention, a requirement should enable a team member to reduce the need to practice, to the degree possible.

Jeff Sutherland has nurtured this concept of enabling specifications in Scrum (Sutherland 2009). Jeff says:

> It turns out that an enabling specification is exactly what is needed to maximize the process efficiency of executing a user story. The average process efficiency of teams executing user stories is about 20%. This means a story that takes one ideal day of work takes five calendar days to delivery. Systematic Software Engineering, a CMMI Maturity Level 5 company, has extensive data showing that teams that drive story process efficiency to over 50% will double their velocity systematically for every team.

7.1.4 Your Mileage may Vary

If you are a small project, then user stories may carry the day, together with test cases written on their reverse side, and with a story map adorning a team room wall (Patton 2009). In this chapter we will discuss many ways to focus on what-the-system-does: user stories, use cases, features, and even good old-fashioned requirements. As we have already done, we'll challenge a little bit of the conventional Agile wisdom along the way. But we won't give you a prescription.

Before we go further, we'd ask you to remember two things. The first is that the main purpose of any requirements formalism is just to provide a centerpiece for the face-to-face dialog that happens around it, and that such dialog is the best chance we have of building the shared perspective necessary to meet end user expectations. The second advice is that we provide no final answers, and that we encourage you to experiment to find what works for *you*. That may mean challenging yourself and trying out things you feel that you don't believe in. It may be worth it, but none of us can know in advance.

So let's revisit the *Who*, *What*, and *Why* questions in turn. Our goal is to go beyond the Agile Manifesto's "working software" to get *usable* software. We will add Lean practices to our agile approaches to reduce the waste of rework. *What-the-system-is* is the stable part of the architecture and *what-the-system-does* is the dynamic part. But even within *what-the-system-does* there is a part that we stabilize early – function has form, too – and a more dynamic part that lives out the "responding to change" part of the Agile Manifesto. We need both Lean *and* Agile.

7.2   Who is Going to Use Our Software?

In the beginning there were seldom any real users in Agile user stories (Jeffries, Anderson and Hendrickson 2001, pp. 25–28). For example:

> For each account, compute the balance by adding up all the deposits and subtracting all the deductions. (Jeffries, Anderson and Hendrickson 2001)

A lot of things called *user stories* still don't have a user. Many organizations have adopted the user story form "As a user . . . " but the user never gets to be anything . . . but a *user*. The user *role* was lost in translation. Is the user me? my child? my 85-year-old aunt? Good user stories clarify user roles that reflect the analyst's contemplation of the user's identity, bringing a crisp *user* back into the concept of user story. Agile user stories still don't have any story, but that's another story . . .

Before we go into the user roles, we point out that it is important to distinguish *user roles* from the roles in DCI. In DCI it is objects that can play different roles, so we can call them *object roles* to avoid confusion.

7.2.1   User Profiles

How do we define a user role? We first take cues from usability. Usability experts know how to research end user perspectives and how to consolidate these findings in *User Profiles*. A use case model represents end user interests in *Actors*. An Actor is a user role; therefore a User Profile can map directly to a use case Actor. The User Profile becomes the Actor description. User Profiles can of course also be used as the user roles in user stories.

If your organization doesn't have any usability specialists your team can still do some valuable user role modeling. Mike Cohn (Cohn 2004, chapter 3) has a nice four-step recipe of guidance.

7.2.2   Personas

For web applications it has become popular to create *Personas*. A Persona is an invented character with specific gender, age, family, profession, hobby, and everything else that you can imagine to know about the character. A persona "is someone you know so well as if you have slept with the person" is a popular saying within the Persona fad. A Persona can play many user roles in relation to your software – like a real person. A User Profile is not a specific person, but a user role based on facts about the real users. Personas have names like "Mary" or "John" while a User Profile has a user role name like "Database Administrator" or "Teenage Bank Customer."

7.2.3 User Profiles or Personas?

Personas can add value to organizations whose software is used by such a broad audience that it seems impossible to define a limited valuable set of user profiles – or where focus on users is a new thing for the organization. Instead of all stakeholders having their own private "Persona" in mind when they develop the software, they can now share a socialized, concrete description of a Persona. The risk is that you create software for that specific person instead of for a user role that many different persons can play.

In more mature organizations, where the team members have disciplined contact with end users, Personas come across as being unrealistic. They will be viewed as superficial and too different from the real users that the team members have encountered. In this kind of organization it is better to use *user profiles* than Personas. User profiles are empirically based characterizations of market segments, and particularly of those segments targeted by your product (Figure 7-2).

User Profile: Teenage user
Age: 13 to 17
Geographic region: U.S. and Australia
Internet use: School assignments, hobbies, entertainment, news, health issues they're too embarrassed to talk about, e-commerce.
Duty cycle: 85% use the web. Typical web time is 5 – 10 hours / week
Research abilities: Moderate to poor
Reading skills: Moderate to poor
Patience: Low, short attention span
Design considerations: Attracted to great graphics, but good clean page design

---

Figure 7-2   A User Profile. Adopted from Nielsen 2005.

Sometimes a Persona is too limiting, and the market too distant. You can use organizational patterns like Surrogate Customer (Coplien and Harrison 2004, pp. 116–117) to do your best to gain market insight in cases where you have limited contact with real customers. Constantine and Lockwood (Constantine and Lockwood 1999) also offer insight on how to develop reasonable requirements under such conditions. However, strive to be Agile and elicit ongoing feedback from your end user community.

7.2.4   User Roles and Terminology

Words mean things, and good descriptive names can help you converge on end user expectations. "Mary" and "John" don't carry much information as the name of a typical customer. The "Teenage User" (Figure 7-2) conveys much more information, and can be the basis for a "Teenage Bank Customer." Such terms are important not only in conversations between stakeholders, but also to keep the code readable and maintainable. Yes, you *do* use these agreed terms as names in your code! Traditional traceability that is formalized by tools is dead in Agile development (recall "individuals and interactions over processes and tools"). In Lean development we replace traceability with careful terminology work. A good user role name can convey a good understanding of the role. Go out and observe your users – and you don't have to sleep with them.

7.3   What do the Users Want to Use Our Software for?

This is the core of *what-the-system-does*. The *Who* and *Why* part help us get it right – they give us important *Context*.[1] *What-the-system-does* can be described in many ways: as requirements, as dataflow diagrams, as features, as actors and use cases, as user stories and acceptance tests, as personas and scenarios, as narratives, as story boards, as prototypes – and probably many more. When the system *does* something it implies *behavior*. The above techniques describe behavior more or less explicitly. A traditional requirement formulation could be: "The system shall transfer money from one account to another". Look familiar? It is not that different from our user story: "As an Account Holder, I want to transfer money between my accounts, so I can ensure that none of my accounts are overdrawn."

7.3.1   Feature Lists

Feature lists are yet another approach to capturing functionality. A feature description for the above requirement might say: "Transfer money from one account to another account". The word "transfer" indicates behavior but it is not explicitly described, which leads us to all the kind of questions we raised in the first part of this chapter.

The difference between a feature and a user story is subtle. In the beginning, when Kent Beck introduced user stories (Beck 2005), the only

---

[1] Here in Chapter 7 we use the term "context" more or less in its usual English language sense. The term has a more contextualized meaning in Chapter 9.

difference between a feature description and a user story was the fact that a user story was short and handwritten on a "story card." In the Agile world today most user stories are written in a computer tool like Excel or perhaps with a tool more explicitly tailored to that purpose. It is difficult to see the difference between a feature list and a list of user stories, except that the term *user story* is socially more acceptable in shops that view themselves as Agile.

7.3.2   Dataflow Diagrams

A dataflow diagram (DFD) – yet another alternative – would have a high level process called "Transfer money" with the data (e.g. amount and balance) flowing in and out from the process. The process is decomposed into sub-processes such as: "Define source and destination account", "Move money", and "Do accounting". The decomposition stops when the lowest level process can be called an "atomic" process (cannot be decomposed further). Dataflow diagrams can work well for a solo analyst, but they don't have a good track record to communicate knowledge between members of a development team. It's too easy to get lost in the many levels of decomposition.

7.3.3   Personas and Scenarios

Personas often go together with *scenarios*. A Persona scenario describes a specific scenario for that Persona. If the Persona is "Mary," and she is a 32-year-old single mom to 2-year-old Benjamin and 4-year-old Laura, working full time as a doctor's assistant – then the scenario can describe how Mary uses an ATM on her way home from work to transfer money from a savings account so she can pay a bill for a car repair. A Persona scenario focuses on what buttons Mary pushes and on what menu items she selects.

7.3.4   Narratives

A *narrative*[2] could use the same approach as for Personas but avoids creating a specific stereotype, instead developing a short story to explore system functionality. For example, we can invent a hypothetical person named Mary on the fly. She could be a trainer of police dogs. Her car is at the repair shop and she has her two police dogs in one hand and

---

[2] We use the term *narrative* so as not to confuse this kind of story with user stories. Alistair Cockburn uses the term *usage narratives* for stories that are reminiscent of the scenarios in a Persona and Scenarios approach. He avoids the term *story* in this context for the same reason: to avoid confusion with Extreme Programming user stories.

Benjamin on her arm. It is raining and there are 10 minutes until Laura's daycare closes. Here the story would be a vision of how the ATM could help Mary in this specific situation without focusing on the details of the user interface of the ATM. But the story can help us to be aware that there will be other requirements to the user interface than for the person doing bank transactions from the computer at home. The narrative focuses on the *context* (see Cockburn 2001, p. 18).

The narrative could have two parts: a *before* and *after*, that describe Mary's trouble before and after the bank gave her an easy way to transfer money. So we can have a *problem* narrative and a *vision* narrative that helps us understand the user's (or the business's) *motivation*. Using the combination of personas and scenarios clarifies the user's motivation, but it describes the user interface in kind of a convoluted, indirect way.

7.3.5   Behavior-Driven Development

User stories lack explicit behavior. A popular way to compensate is to add acceptance tests on the back of the user story card. It means that some of the questions we had in the beginning of the chapter will be answered as acceptance test criteria. For example "Test: if source account becomes negative after the transaction, the transfer will not be allowed." There will probably be more acceptance test criteria than there will be room for on the card, and they will be described somewhere else.

This shortcut approach suggests that we move the *what-the-system-does* insights into the test descriptions. That is exactly what Behavior Driven Development (BDD) (North 2006) is. In BDD, user stories are input to test scenarios that specify what the system does. The programmer codes the test scenarios directly in a test tool, and – voila! Now the programmer is in charge of the requirements. Maybe that is one step further than we want to go now. We don't want to lose our business domain experts and usability specialists in our eagerness to code. Code speaks very nicely to coders, but maybe not so well to the rest of the world.

7.3.6   Now that We're Warmed Up . . .

Let's back up a few steps and see where we're at. We have techniques to describe *what-the-system-does* that lack explicit behavior: traditional requirements, feature lists, and user stories (when used without acceptance tests). Then we have Personas and Scenarios that do have behavior, but which are limited to only a few specific examples. The rest of the behavior is left to the imagination of the programmer. Narratives are just stories that can give us a good shared understanding of the motivation. But you cannot test narratives, so they are a very incomplete statement of what the system does.

Prototypes

Maybe we should try simulating the situations in which these requirements arise. Prototypes are a great way to explore and test parts of what the system does. A prototype can test a user interface concept, parts of the functionality, or even performance or technical feasibility. An architectural prototype can also be very useful. Storyboards are a versatile usability technique. They were originally used to support design, but have also served well to validate the team's assumptions about the workflow for specific system functions. The team starts with storyboards that capture their vision of a user workflow and later proceed to validate their assumptions in a real environment.

Towards Foundations for Decisions

These are all good warm-up techniques: to begin the conversation, to brainstorm, to envision. Pick your favorite(s) and get on with it – until you are ready for consolidation. Architectural direction begs consolidated input. Consolidation ensures that the right people make the right decisions at the right time. Brainstorming and envisioning are both helpful and necessary, but they are *divergent* thinking techniques, and decisions should eventually precipitate from *convergent* thinking techniques. These are both business decisions and architectural decisions; the two go hand in hand.

Known and Unknown Unknowns

So what is our level of consolidation if we want to be both Lean and Agile? We don't want to do everything up front; that wouldn't be Agile. We don't want to defer decisions "to the last responsible moment;" that wouldn't be Lean. So we first of all need to know what decisions we must make to get the architecture right, and what decisions that we should defer. It would be useful to have a framework to organize those decisions. The first step is to separate the known knowns from the known unknowns, making the known unknowns as visible as possible. In the spirit of emergent requirements, we can't predict when the unknowns will become knowns, but we want to leave room for these realizations.

We also have to tuck away the fact in the back of our head that unknown unknowns lurk out there. Prototyping can help flesh these out by making them known unknowns or sometimes by eliminating the uncertainty altogether, as can the stakeholder dialog that comes with the "all hands on deck" mentality of Lean development. A sound domain architecture can reduce the cost of what-the-system-does requirement changes by limiting long-term rework to the overall form of the system. But before we deal with such surprises, it pays to have a framework that organizes what we *do* know.

Use Cases as a Decision Framework

Use cases are one example of such a framework. Use cases only make sense if your software supports a user's workflow. As a counter-example, it is hard to make use cases for a simple text editing system because you don't have consistent workflows. The same is true for systems without much user interaction, like industrial control systems and the embedded software in your car or clothes dryer. Maybe you have experiences with techniques that can help you to consolidate with these kinds of systems – perhaps using state machines, decision tables, and cause-effect charts. So which of these might you use instead of use cases? The answer is: It depends. We'll come back to this question in Section 7.7. For now we want to share our experiences with use cases as a Lean technique to consolidate what the system does.

Use cases get a bad rap. In spite of having a reputation of being heavyweight, use cases support Agile development very well. They are a powerful way to convey enabling specifications. Just think *increments* instead of up-front specification, and *collaborative game* (Cockburn 1999) instead of big up-front requirements analyst.

Let's investigate why the user wants to use our software before we go into consolidation.

7.4   Why Does the User Want to Use Our Software?

Before we answer this question it can be good to think about another question first:

Why does the business think the user wants to use our software?

Businesspeople deal with broad and diverse constituencies. In Scrum you have a product owner who balances all stakeholder interests in your software. End users are stakeholders, but for many businesspeople the customer – the paying stakeholder – is often more important than the end user. Even more important than the customer can be the enterprise itself – how does our company best thrive in the long term? The first step is to recognize these differences. It is amazing how many organizations lack a crisp picture of the difference between a customer and an end user (and it's furthermore stunning how many are completely out of touch with end users).

Narratives can be a good way to explore the interests of those we care about. In the example above with Mary as a single mom who wants to transfer money, the first focus is on helping Mary. But maybe Mary would prefer that the bank had open hours outside of her working hours, so she can go in and talk to a real person who could do the transfer for her (and another one who could hold the dogs and the kid) – of course without having to wait in line. So the motivation for the bank is maybe not so much to help Mary, but to avoid expanding the opening hours, or maybe to make more employees available to serve other customers in person. The bank wants to provide services to their customers in a way that saves them money and lets the customers do the work themselves – without losing business to their competitors. To motivate the bank customer to be loyal to the bank, it is a good idea to see them in context as end users. When we book airplane tickets we take the vendor who can both offer cheap tickets and provide us with an easy-to-use web site.

In the Scrum framework a good product owner will communicate the different stakeholders' motivation to the team. One way to do it is to tell or write narratives. Another is to give a stirring talk about the new product or service which, as one product owner told us, he found to be the most effective way to do it after twenty years of experimenting.

Use cases can be a concise, organized way to communicate these motivations. Each use case has a business motivation and a user motivation or intention as the introduction. A good old-fashioned stakeholder analysis works too. A lot of confusion and lack of motivation in development teams can be traced back to the fact that the team doesn't know *why* they have to do what they are doing. It also makes it difficult for team members to make informed decisions. And you cannot write everything down – that's one reason why Agile became popular. Let the people – and the code – talk.

7.5 Consolidation of What the System Does

So what criteria do we have for consolidation of *what-the-system-does*? Usable software is the key, and we need to know our users to build it. We collect data about our users and create User Profiles – or user role descriptions, or actor descriptions, or Personas – depending on your organization and culture. They tell us something about who the user *is*. But we also want to know what the user *does* – the user's behavior. Storyboards are a way to validate our assumptions about the user's behavior. The scenario part of personas and scenarios gives us an example of how we envision users using our system. The narrative gives us a vision of why we want the functionality. Dataflow diagrams can help us understand . . . the dataflow.

The part we want to focus on in relation to the user's behavior is the user's *workflow*, and how we want to support that workflow with our software: what the system does. In order to response to change we need to develop our software in small chunks such as iterations or Sprints. We incrementally build our software in a way that lets us adjust and respond to change between iterations. When we respond to change we want to know where we are, otherwise we are just *reacting*, not *responding*. We need a baseline. A baseline is coded and tested software that is ready for an internal or external release. *Test* is the keyword here. Teams should test the user workflow they want to support during each iteration. We want test as close to development as possible.

Requirements emerge – both externally and internally. The world and the business change, and because someone just changed their minds, requirements change. We learn more while we work with the domain and the system, and requirements change somewhat more. We work incrementally and come to new corners of the system. All this means that we take decisions about the functionality all the time. To avoid discussing the same issues over and over again we need to document our decisions about what the system does. We can of course change our decisions, but then we know from what and to what.

In the end many decisions will be documented in the code. That's fine. It might better be said that these decisions will be *encoded* in the code, and decoding is often no fun. One goal of the techniques in this book – particularly of domain-driven design and of the DCI architecture – serve the end of code intentionality: expressing the programmer intent in the code. It is important to have a shared language to document decisions, and that language rarely can be the programming language. After all, it is not all stakeholders that have programming languages as their primary language. And lots of meetings and meeting minutes aren't always the answer, either (who reads those any more?). So we need this framework that helps us navigate important decisions about functionality.

For now, we don't talk about decisions that the programmer can make; they are best documented as code. We talk about decisions that involve other stakeholders – especially the businesspeople such as Scrum's product owner.

Emergent requirements also call for decisions and we need a home for them as well. In traditional requirement specifications we don't really have room for emergent requirements – they are closed. User stories and features can in principle just grow for every new requirement, but that strategy causes you not to be able to see the forest for the trees. When do you have a duplicated user story? When is it just an overlap with another user story? How can you validate what you are missing? This approach works with very small and simple systems – for example, web pages where you can release a new version every day and get immediately feedback. Your decisions are documented on the web page, and your users test it. This is a nice, simple context.

The final thing you would like for *what-your-system-does* is that chunks of functionality be small enough to make release planning easy. What does release planning have to do with architecture? You want to know what functionality will challenge the architecture, and what functionality is just more of the same. One option at the disposal of the business is to pull architecturally risky functionality into an early iteration to avoid unpleasant surprises in a later iteration. This is one example of where you as an architect need to help the product owner to order the product backlog. You will be the one who knows if this risk reduction is necessary. It goes against the principle of naïve Agilists that the easiest things be tackled first, but that's a relatively minor issue relative to Agile's view of anything architecture-focused.

Our criteria for consolidation of *what-the-system-does* therefore has the following elements:

1. To support the user's workflow (usage scenarios);
2. To support test close to development (test scenarios);
3. To support efficient decision making about functionality (sunny day scenario (also known as the *main success scenario*) versus deviations);
4. To support emerging requirements (deviations);
5. To support release planning (use cases and deviations);
6. To support sufficient input to the architecture (terms and concepts from the scenarios);
7. To support the team's understanding of what to develop.

We have already revealed that use cases are one solution. But they aren't the only solution. Think about the above criteria. Do they fit your development context? What other techniques have you successfully used that served you well? Use your common sense!

We could have chosen to call it something else than use cases – maybe coining a fancy Japanese word – and could tell you that this is the new Lean requirement technique. It would probably have taken you some time before you recognized it as use cases. But we like transparency and will simply illustrate with an example. The goal is not to teach you to do use cases; the existing literature provides a bounty of good sources (Adolph et al 1998; Constantine and Lucy 1999; Cockburn 2001; Wirfs-Brock 1993). Our purpose is to show how the use case technique can help you in an Agile and Lean development environment, without having to reinvent techniques in order to call yourself *Agile* or *Lean*. We don't pretend to show you a perfect use case example. The process around the use case is more important than the use case itself.

7.5.1   The Helicopter View

Now you have warmed up and are ready for consolidation. Maybe you have a lot of user stories, and maybe some prototypes. Your businessperson has given her motivational talk, or your whole team has shared vivid narratives. You have a lot of input, and first you want to organize it and get an overview. What did our warm-up sessions teach us about the context?

Let us move away from the outdoor ATM and head indoors where it doesn't rain, and think of ourselves as citizens that want to do bank transactions from our home computers. The bank is not the evil moneymaker any more, but our partner in trying to make life easier for us. So what main services would we like the bank to offer us to do from home over the Internet? I'd like to be able to transfer money, view my latest transactions, add new regular payments, print account statements, and pay bills. A lot of other things came up during brainstorming, but these are the core services that the product manager thinks are important to start with. We could just call these "services", or "epics", or "overall requirements", or "features", but we prefer to call them use cases.

In order to call them *use cases* each of them should support a goal for the user, so we first of all need to define the user: in use case language this is the *actor*. During our brainstorming sessions we have explored the boundaries: Is age 11 too young? Is 85 years too old? Is it only private persons, or does it include professionals? Do we give access to a customer who has a loan, but no bank account in our bank? (do they exist?). We decide to call the actor "Private Account Holder." If we don't have a good description of that actor, we make it a high priority to develop one. We now have a simple overview:

Private Account Holder
- **View latest transactions**
- **Transfer money**
- **Print account statements**
- **Add regular payment**
- **Pay bill**

We want to make the first consolidation of the helicopter view. This will be the container within which most of our *what-the-system-does* decisions will belong, so we want to stabilize it as early as possible. One thing that we like early is a name for our system. Let us call it "Greenland Net Bank". Together with the actor description and the core use cases, it should give us a good picture of the overall context for the system.

While looking at the list of the use cases or maybe while thinking about how the first use case should begin, we notice that we need a login service. That is a classical discussion in use case land: Is "Log on" a use case? In most situations the answer is *no*. Remember we noted above that a use case has a goal in context. As a user I don't achieve anything by just logging on. I wouldn't be happy to tell my family about my day by saying "I really did something to day – I logged on to my bank ten times".

On one hand, logon is a necessary evil that is a precondition for something else. On the other hand, it's important to banking transactions. It is not only in the bank's interest that the access be secure, but it is also in my interest as an Account Holder. The logon procedure for banks can entail as many as four or five steps, so the system and the actor really have to do something. And we don't want to repeat these steps at the beginning of each use case. Can we defer the decision about how it should work? We could wait and take the decision later on, then our discussion can end, and we can move on. But why defer it? We will probably not get any more information that can help us. If we add services to an existing system, and logon functionality has already been established there, we are all set. Then we can just state: "the Account Holder is logged in" as a precondition in all use cases. If we have to change existing logon procedures, adding a new way of logging on, or don't have the functionality yet, *then* we have to do something. It is an important requirement. Use your common sense.

It could be a situation where common sense leads us to actually make the logon service a use case in itself. That's against good use case practice because logging on lacks a goal. Security must be a core business competency of "Greenland Net Bank." We need to bridge the shared concerns of the business and the programmer for good system security, and it can help to communicate the concerns in a use-case-like manner. It is not that important if we end up with a logon use case or not. What is important is that we have discussed it and built consensus about the decision, so we all know *why* we have a logon use case or not.

Habits: The Developer View and the User View

As developers we learn to avoid redundancy, because duplicated code is unmaintainable code. In analysis, it's a different story. Use cases focus on *context*, and if we repeat clarifying functionality in many use cases we don't care. When the repetition makes it too hard to keep updates consistent (because we have to edit the same content many times) then we have to do something. But we don't remove redundancy before we have to. Factoring out redundancy is a design activity and design is better expressed in other tools than use cases.

You are all working together with the business perspective on one hand and the developer interests on the other. Programmers and businesspeople view use cases differently. When a bank officer reviews a use case, he or she may want to see that all proper logon steps are there. It's important to authenticate the user with a password. It's important to see that this flow will allow the user to retrieve a password hint. It's important that we know the programmer will be led to the business rules about ensuring an adequately hard password. It doesn't matter whether these steps are consistently duplicated elsewhere: safety bears repeating. Besides, it would be difficult and even confusing to develop an authentication use case in isolation, because a good use case always plays out in the context of its goal. To talk about logging on in the absence of any goal leaves the business steps too context-free.

To the programmer, on the other hand, such repetition would, in the worst case, lead to unnecessary duplication of code. Computer science spent years developing formalisms called procedures just for the occasion, so a single closed copy of code can be "reused" at many points of invocation. But now the programmer bears the burden of comparing each new logon sequence with the old ones, line by line, to ensure that the same closed copy of the logon procedure applies in the new deviation as applied when the code was written. The contexts must be compatible, and questions of context require subtle clarification from the business when they arise. That's a waste of time.

It can be useful to compromise here and treat authentication as a use-case-like-thing, but one that is the purview of the programmer rather than that of the business folks. We call such a pseudo-use case a *habit*. We give it this name to distinguish from a use case. It is a developer tool to support design, and it lives largely in developer land. Habits are structures that help the team ask the right kinds of questions to make sure everyone is on the same page – the Lean goal of consistency. Remember, use cases (and habits as well) *represent* the requirement, but the answer of whether they actually *are* the requirement awaits end user feedback in the running system.

Habits help solve the long-running problem that use cases are often too detailed for the business and not detailed enough for the developers. That historically drives the business to user stories and the developers to test scripts. Rather than solving the problem, those fixes just widen the gap. Habits factor out recurring chunks of use case detail; that leaves more concise use cases for the business. Developers can take these repeatedly invoked chunks and use them to gain enough insight into the scenarios to conceive algorithms to implement them (Section 9.4.2). The algorithms need no intermediate representation: program code is fine. The business can continue to work at a higher level.

A habit isn't quite the same as the use case *includes* relationship because we don't want to destroy the understandability of the use case. Their primary purpose isn't to factor information from the use case to remove redundancy; instead, habits add detail in the same that business rules do. It's common to separate out business rules and other supporting details from use case descriptions. The use case is the information clearinghouse that points out other details you need, and the habit is one of these. Habits differ from nicknames (see Section 5.4.1) because their focus is more on activity than on data. Habits aren't quite algorithms because they can have a degree of non-determinism – sequencing decisions that don't matter, which as such are left to the programmer or the technology (just as can be true of use cases). Habits tend to be partial orderings of steps, and can represent business rules, algorithms, or steps in a use case.

In Figure 7-3 we show a scenario for Move Money and Do Accounting using a modified use case form that we'll call "habit form." The name, "Move money," reflects a level of detail. Contrast that name with "Transfer money," which implies a business transaction, whereas "Move money" is more mechanical. The habit lacks an intent and a motivation; we can get those from each enclosing use case. (The intent and motivation can differ across the use cases that invoke Move Money and Do Accounting!)

Habit Name: Move Money and Do Accounting

Preconditions: A valid Source Account and Destination Account have been identified, and the amount to be transferred is known

Sequence:
1.   Greenland Net Bank verifies funds available
2.   Greenland Net Bankupdates the accounts
3.   Greenland Net Bankupdates statement info

Post-conditions:
✓   The periodic statements reflect the exact intent of the transaction (a transfer is a transfer — not a pair of a withdrawal and a deposit)

Figure 7-3   Move Money and Do Accounting Habit.

Though Figure 7-3 communicates important requirements, it satisfies no business goal in itself. The developer cares about it because it is a recurring common block of logic, so it is good a foundation for the DCI structures that implement what-the-system-does. Though the habit has no business goal it is an important collection of detail that may recur in multiple use case scenarios. Making this fragment into a habit satisfies both constituencies' needs for a single closed copy.

Habits should not have variations. First, it is difficult to conceptualize how a variation at this level generalizes across all the use cases employing the habit. Second, it can too easily lead to replicated and potentially conflicting descriptions of the variation in the use case and the habit. Keep variations in the use cases.

The pre- and post-conditions for a habit tend to be written at a low level. They can drive a design by contract approach (Section 6.1.2) in the code.

They are specific to the code and can drive unit tests for that code. Take care not to add preconditions or post-conditions that would be invalid for any use case using the habit. Also, keep the business-oriented pre- and post-conditions in the use case: duplicating them can lead to redundancy and inconsistency.

Trimming the Scope

How about printing statements? Does the Account Holder really need to be able to print account statements? That is the businesspeoples' call. The development team can perhaps convince the business about the benefits of delaying this service until Greenland Net Bank faces the broader issues of document handling. Now we have an updated list:

Private Account Holder {
Log on
View latest transactions
Transfer money
Add regular payment
Pay bill

"This is too simple", you may think. "Five use cases and I have the overview? The system I am working on is much more complicated." But this is actually realistic. The complexity lies in the variations within use cases, so is not reflected in the total number of use cases. If a single team has more than 15 use cases in its helicopter view, something is wrong! You are probably also in trouble if the product has to manage more than 240 use cases at once (Cockburn 2008).

If you have more use cases than that, then maybe you have an unrealistically long release plan (like, a year to the first release?). Or maybe you have defined your use cases at an overly detailed level. Or maybe you have included use cases that only have other systems as actors, and not user roles representing real human beings (there are better notations than use cases to that end). Most projects balance about eight use cases well. Choose actor names as well as use case names with care; you have to live with them for many months or years.

Involve all key stakeholders when creating and refining use cases. Remember the Lean Secret. You want to involve the whole team including both developers and testers – because they are going to have to understand the context and detail well enough to implement and test them. You want the business, represented by a product owner, product manager, or the like. You want the architect and the usability specialist (if you have any). And you want domain experts, no matter what they are called in your organization. The consolidation of the helicopter view can be done in a couple of hours – if you are already warmed up. That's Lean.

7.5.2   Setting the Stage

There can be other actors you want to add to the stage, such as the existing bank software that Greenland Net Bank depends on. Dig a bit into this. If you haven't done it already, you should identify the *people* you have to work with who represent these systems. Add these *system* actors to your helicopter view if it improves your overview.

It is time to consolidate the business motivation and the user intention. This is done on a per-use-case basis. Let's take the *Transfer money* use case as example:

> Business motivation: "As a part of our strategy *Empower customers to do their banking business from home* we see money transfer as an important service. The Account Holder can keep an eye on their accounts, and can transfer money to an account that is getting low, or that the Account Holder knows will get low soon. It can save us (the bank) time we use on sending letters when an account is overdrawn, and it can also save us closing (and later re-opening) accounts. As an expanded service we would also like the Account Holder to be able to transfer money to other Account Holders' accounts – both within our bank and to and from other banks. Our competitors already provide that service, and we cannot wait too long to offer it as well."

Maybe your team and the rest of the stakeholders only need the first sentence written down because you already know the business motivation well, and you just need a hint. It is not so much how you document it. It is to make sure that all stakeholders know the business motivation. Use common sense.

> User intention: "As an Account Holder, I want to transfer money between my accounts, so I can ensure that none of my accounts become overdrawn and my debit card is closed".

Yes, you can put in a user story here – or several user stories – or something else. Use your imagination. You are in good shape when the business motivation and the user intention point in the same direction and aren't in conflict.

To set the stage it's important to *scope* the use cases in relation to each other. You want to know what conditions surround a use case scenario when it starts up, and what conditions you can expect at the end. Often a post-condition of one use case is the precondition of another. Scoping therefore also helps to validate your helicopter view. It also provides a foundation for the first business scoping that you need for a rough release plan. We do this by adding a *precondition* and a *post-condition* to each use case. Continuing our Transfer Money example:

> Precondition: "The private Account Holder is logged on to Greenland Net Bank, and an overview of the Account Holders accounts is present on the screen."
> Post-condition: "The amount that the private Account Holder entered is moved from source account to destination account. The two accounts balance, and the transaction logs are updated".

In the first part of the consolidation phase we are in "sunny day scenario" mode. We focus on how things happen when they go well. We can later carry these pre- and post-conditions in to the code, as we discussed in Section 6.1.2.

Your product owner is now ready for the first raw release plan:

Release 1: Log on and View latest transactions

Release 2: Transfer money

Release 3: Add regular payment

Release 4: Pay bill

We can of course not put dates on yet, but it is a good beginning, and it implies an ordering of work. The stage is set, but nothing is moving yet. Let's play.

7.5.3   Play the Sunny Day Scenario

Remember? Good use cases are about *increments* and *collaborative games*. We don't want to specify everything at once, but embrace the Lean principles of just-in-time work. And we don't want analysts writing use cases at their desk, but want them to become the centerpiece of a focused conversation. Begin with the sunny day scenarios for the use cases of the first release. The first release in our example contains the "Log on" and the "View latest transactions" use cases. Both "Log on" and "View" use cases can be problematic in an ideal use case world because the user goals are not obvious, but we sometimes allow them for reasons we described earlier. We won't detail the description of the release 1 use cases here. Instead we will continue our example with the sunny day scenario of the "Transfer money" use case of release 2.

When it comes to define the steps of a sunny day use case scenario many Agile people give up and call use cases too heavy, but it is a crucial and worthwhile investment. It requires thinking, discipline, and decisions to ensure progress. Thinking, conversation and discipline just provide the basis for decisions. The use case scenarios help us to know what decisions we need to take. Think about who will take the decisions, and when, if we don't take them now.

When you are inclined to postpone a decision, ask yourself: "Is this a decision that the programmer can make while coding?" If the answer is yes, it is fine; then leave the decision to the programmer. If the answer is no, ask yourself if you can take the decision now or if you need more information first. If you need more information make sure to get it in a timely fashion. Early decisions are the Lean approach while late decisions are the Agile approach. Structured use case descriptions developed incrementally can help us to know the right time for a decision.

A structured use case description begins with:

- a table[3] with one column for step numbers, one for the use case actor, and one for the system responsibility:

Step	Actor intention (Constantine and Lucy 1999)	System responsibility (Wirfs-Brock 1993)
1.		

- the actor name or system name at the beginning of every step:

Step	Actor intention	System responsibility
1.	*The Account Holder* selects a source account and chooses to transfer money.	*The Greenland Net Bank* shows source account, provides a list of destination accounts, and a field to enter the amount.

- terminology that is carefully and consistently thought out and written down:

Step	Actor intention	System responsibility
1.	The Account Holder selects a *source account* and chooses to transfer money.	The Greenland Net Bank shows source account, provides a list of destination accounts, and a field to enter the amount.
2.	The Account Holder selects a *destination account*, enters the amount, and accepts.	The Greenland Net Bank moves money, does *accounting*, and shows the Account Holder a *receipt* for the *transaction*.

---

[3] The table's two-column format is inspired by Rebecca Wirfs-Brock. She introduced the idea of *conversation* into use cases by having the user's action in the left column and the systems reaction in the right column. The names of the columns are taken from Constantine and Lockwood (1999) and their idea of *essential use cases* where you ensure to leave UI design details to the UI designer, and system design details to the system designer. UI design and system design are expressed much better in tools other than use cases.

Stop! This is important:

> The terms and concepts you choose to use in the use case scenarios are input to the architecture.

This isn't just the find-the-nouns exercise we did to find classes in the old days. Remember, this is input to *what the system does* (see how it works in Chapter 8 and Chapter 9). Good names keep the connections to end users and other human beings alive.

A step is not a step before the system has reacted on the actor's action.[4] Think as a user: do you feel that a system has done anything, if you don't get any sign of activity from the system? Or think as a tester: does it make sense to test the actor's selection of a destination account before the actor has entered the amount and accepted the transaction? The tester maybe wants to test that the system shows a valuable list of destination accounts, and that can be done after step 1. Whether it makes sense to make a separate test scenario for step 1 or to make a test for the whole "sunny day scenario" is at the tester's discretion. But the structure is provided now, and the tester can begin to script test scenarios at the same time as the developer begins to design and code. This parallelism reduces your development latency.

Two steps, and we are done with a sunny day scenario for one use case. Is it that hard? The hard part is not so much the format – the team can learn that. It is more the discipline of thinking and of decision-making. We have to decide what terminology we want to use. To document these decisions we may need a glossary. A domain can gain a lot from not only having a glossary per team, but to have a shared online terminology document. A glossary for here and now could be seen as an Agile approach, while the online terminology document would be the Lean approach; we wouldn't have to discuss the meaning of the same terms over and over again.

Other key decisions remain. Should the Account Holder choose to do the transfer action before choosing the source account – or the other way around? Who takes that decision and when? This should be the decision of a UI designer. In the collaborative game you have that person on board to help you take these kinds of decisions. All right, maybe not . . . Then keep the wording so flexible as possible with respect to the order in which things happen.

For example, in step 1 we don't tell if the actual implementation will be noun-verb or verb-noun. The action and account are both accounted in the same step and the specific order really doesn't matter from a use case point

---

[4] There can be some exceptions where we can play with an empty step for the user intention: for example to indicate when the user has to wait for the system to do its part.

of view, because the *business* doesn't care about the order. In the use case we focus on the overall workflow, the back-and-forth from actor action to system reaction, from a business perspective. If the actor has to enter and/or select a lot of information in the same window, we still consider it one use case step. The UI designer has to design the window in a way that makes is most usable for the actor. And the user interface should fit the user's mental model as closely as possible. You build and test-drive prototypes of the user interface to ensure that. These prototypes work well as a parallel activity to the use case definitions.

If you haven't got lost in UI details now, you maybe pondering other questions: Does this sunny day scenario include transfers to accounts other than those belonging to the Account Holder? Does "other accounts" mean other accounts in this bank, or in all banks? Does "all banks" mean banks in this country, or in all countries? Please call your product owner! Oh, your product owner is already here. Good! Then we can move on. First of all you want to track the status of your decisions. We do that by adding a comment or question column to the use case step (Table 7-1).

Table 7-1   Scenario with commentary.

Step	Actor Intention	System Responsibility	Comment
1.	The Account Holder selects a *source account* and chooses to transfer money.	The Greenland Net Bank shows *source account*, provides a list of *destination accounts*, and a field to enter the amount.	Should the Account Holder choose to transfer money first and then the account – or the other way around?
2.	The Account Holder selects a *destination account*, enters the *amount*, and accepts.	The Greenland Net Bank moves money, does accounting, and shows the Account Holder a *receipt* for the *transaction*.	What are the rules for destination account? (own account, other accounts, other banks?) Is receipt the right term? Do we need a receipt if it is among Account Holder's own accounts? Does the Account Holder need to be able to print the receipt?

Note that use cases are a tool to support the playing of the collaborative game. It is not a one-man show to write a specification. We want everyone to be a part of asking the questions and to help take the decisions. Then we all know the reasoning behind the decisions, and we can move much faster during implementation. Everybody, all together, from early on.

The big questions like the "other account" question should not only be hidden in a column like this. The business owns this decision, and it is closely related to release planning – and architecture. What does release 2 – Transfer money – entail? Does it transfer money only to and from the Account Holder's own accounts? And if we expand to other accounts will it still be the same use case? Here we have to go back to investigate the end user mental model. Does the Account Holder care about the differences between "other" accounts?

The authors' bank doesn't think that we as Account Holders have a different model for our own accounts, other accounts in the same bank, and accounts in other banks. They all show up on the same list of "destination" accounts as soon as we have entered an account number and have given it a name. So that's the model we as users carry with us. If it is our bank that has been teaching us to have that model in mind, or if we had it before is hard to tell. But it seemed natural to do it like this, so maybe it was right from the beginning.

Things might get complicated only when we want to transfer money to a bank in another country. It's not that different for us as Account Holders, but clearly very different for the bank as business. Again we need both usability specialists and business domain experts to develop the *expectation*. From the usability point-of-view we can investigate the user's mental model in relation to accounts. Is a "destination" account just another account, no matter who owns it in what country? Maybe that's the conclusion. Then the business domain expert can say that its underlying business processes and business rules differ so radically from the domestic case that it could be an impediment in design and implementation to include it in the same use case. Use common sense. A likely outcome could be that all domestic account transfers for private Account Holders will be in the use case Transfer money, and another use case, Transfer money to international bank account, will take care of the transactions to other countries. If we overlook the usability issue in this decision we risk a user interface as in our bank that doesn't make it obvious where to go to transfer money to another country.

Business Rules

Did we hear someone ask about business rules? That is a big part of the banking business, as well as many others. Do we express business rules in use cases? Banks classify customers according to business criteria such as credit history, debt, and net worth, and apply different rules to different classes of customers. How much can your account be overdrawn before the bank reacts? How long will the bank go to inform you before they close your credit card? Will the bank automatically transfer money from another account of yours if there is money on it?

These are all business rules. A use case shouldn't invoke customer categories every time you touch a service that differs according to customer type. You might start by defining common terms (ones that you hopefully already use in the business) such as "customer type." Then you can create a place where you can look up what customer types you have in the business. Whether it is part of your glossary, your data dictionary, or your description of business rules depends on what makes (common) sense in your organization.

Business rules can be named and referenced from a use case as well. We can for example name a business rule *Overdrawn*. Then you can have a business rule dictionary that tells what *Overdrawn* means for each customer type. Changes in business rules are a common source of emerging requirements, and business rules are another example of knowledge that typically is documented outside the programming language.

Maybe your domain is more technical and business rules are not a big deal. Maybe you have complicated algorithms instead. The same principle applies here: name the algorithms and document them somewhere else where you can find them and easily update them.

Algorithms, business rules, data dictionary, UI design, glossary … it doesn't sound very Agile? Well, if you can do fine without – and still develop usable software that survives the competition, then good for you. Our experience is that you risk discussing the same things over and over again and/or you leave important business and usability decisions to the developers alone at their keyboards. It's risky to leave business decisions to developers working in isolation – not to mention the amount of rework this will cause. Such rework maybe feels Agile, but certainly isn't Lean.

We haven't forgotten: during our work with the sunny day scenario we adjusted our helicopter view:

Private Account Holder $\left\{ \begin{array}{l} \text{Log on} \\ \text{View latest transactions} \\ \text{Transfer money to domestic bank account} \\ \text{Add regular payment} \\ \text{Pay bill} \\ \text{Transfer money to international bank account} \\ \text{Print account statement} \end{array} \right.$

We added the new use case for international money transfer. And then the Print account statement use case came back? Why? During the discussion about the transfer use case it became clear that these kinds of decisions were important for the architecture (Section 5.2.2), which is something we didn't realize before. So though these use cases won't all make it into the first four releases they *still* can have an impact on architecture, so we don't want to hide them. Key use cases can inform the form even of what-the-system-*is*. The product owner's updated release plan could look like this:

Release 1: <u>Log on and View latest transactions</u>

Release 2: <u>Transfer money to account in our bank</u>

Release 3: <u>Add regular payment</u>

Release 4: <u>Pay bill</u>

Release 5: <u>Transfer money to other domestic bank</u>

Release *n*: <u>Print account statement</u>

Release *n+1*: <u>Transfer money to international bank account</u>

Now Release 2 is easier to predict and handle than it was before. But we still have a ways to go before we can put dates on the release plan. And why do we talk so much about the user's workflow? Two steps – not a lot of workflow to me! Just wait, because we've covered only the simple foundations so far. The really interesting stuff is about to come in the next section.

7.5.4   Add the Interesting Stuff

The main reason to consolidate the sunny day scenario early is to establish a structure for deviations. Everything that deviates from the sunny day scenario is a new use case scenario within the use case. When we have added two new deviations, we have added two new scenarios – at least. When we begin to combine several deviations together with the sunny day scenario it can blossom into many scenarios. But, what is a deviation? It is all the things that we have discussed and decided weren't part of the sunny day scenario. It includes all the things that we haven't thought about yet – the unknown unknowns. And it is a lot of our emerging requirements.

So let's move back into brainstorm mode for a while. Our use case is now named <u>Transfer money to domestic bank account</u>, and we want to list everything we can think about that will deviate from the sunny day scenario. That means that we have to decide what our default assumption is for the destination account list in the sunny day scenario. What kind of transfer will we see most, or as a bank business will we support most often? Let us say that the priority is to transfer money between the Account Holder's own accounts. The business makes some decisions, informed by the developers, and we can update our sunny day scenario (Table 7-2).

The only changes are in the comment column, because that feels like the obvious place to document our decision, or that part of the decision. The decision about creating a new use case for international money transfer is documented in the fact that the new use case exists at all. The rest of the decision – other domestic accounts – is partly documented in the extended

Table 7-2   Transfer money: the sunny day scenario.

Step	Actor Intention	System Responsibility	Comment
1.	The Account Holder selects a *source account* and chooses to transfer money.	The Greenland Net Bank shows *source account*, provides a list of *destination accounts*, and a field to enter the *amount*.	Should the Account Holder choose to transfer money first and then the account, or the other way around? *By default the Greenland Net Bank shows a list of Account Holder's own accounts (except for the source account).*
2.	The Account Holder selects a *destination account*, enters the amount, and accepts.	The Greenland Net Bank moves money, does accounting, and shows the Account Holder a receipt for the transaction.	Is *receipt* the right term? Do we need a receipt if it is among Account Holder's own accounts? Does the Account Holder need to be able to print the receipt?

name of the use case, and will be further documented in the deviations of the use case Transfer money to a domestic bank account. Let's brainstorm some deviations:

- Transfer money to domestic account other than own account (does it matter what bank?)
- Save information about other bank account and add it to the destination list
- Check if there is enough money to transfer (what message if not?)
- Print receipt (open issue)
- Ask for password before transaction (mandatory?)
- Account Holder only has one account (message?)
- Amount is too small (any rule?)
- Amount is too big (any rule?)
- Schedule the transfer at a later date
- Remove added destination accounts
- If transaction lasts longer than 15 seconds?
- If transaction fails? (for what reasons?)

With businesspeople, testers, developers, usability specialists, and domain experts around the table, this list can grow fast (Table 7.3)! There are ever-new questions to ponder. If we need a password to accept the transaction, is that yet another step in the sunny day scenario? What are the rules for valid amounts? There are countless things to clarify, and

Table 7-3   Transfer Money use case deviations.

Ref. Step No.	Action Causing Branching	Comment
1a.	The Account Holder wants to transfer to another Account Holder's account.	The Account Holder needs to enter a registration number and account number.
1b.	The Account Holder wants to add another Account Holder's account to the destination list.	The Account Holder can name the account (mandatory?)
2a.	There is not enough money on the source account to do the transfer.	Give an error message, and forego the transaction. (Who is in charge of messages to Account Holder?)
2b.	The Account Holder accepts transfer to another Account Holder's account.	The Greenland Net bank asks for password before accepting the transfer.
2c.	The amount doesn't pass the validation rules.	Validation rules?
2d.	The Account Holder enters a later date for the transfer.	The Greenland Net Bank provides an option to enter a later date. The transfer will happen at that day according to *bank days*. (How long into the future can the date be set?)
2e.	The transaction takes longer than the accepted minimum time.	Reasons for while it take longer? Actions when it does? Accepted minimum time?
2f.	The transaction fails.	Reasons for failure? Actions to recover? Appropriate messages?

countless decisions. And then again: there is much consolidation. Some of us love tables (Table 7-4).

Every time we consolidate, we answer some questions and take some decisions. And we ask new questions, and we get more to decide. That's the nature of progress in software development. Most deviations belong to a specific step in the sunny day scenario. We refer to that step in the first column. What is the difference between this list of deviations and a list of requirements, or features, or user stories? Not a lot when we look at them one by one. We could formulate each of them as user stories, if that would make us feel more Agile. "As an Account Holder I want to be stopped if I transfer more money than I have on my account so I don't overdraw my account".

Well, maybe it's not the best user story in the world. The user story form could help us to see who the real stakeholder is here: "As a bank I want

Table 7-4   Adding room for emergent requirements.

Ref. Step No.	Action Causing Branching	Comment
1a.	The Account Holder wants to transfer to another client's account.	The Account Holder needs to enter registration number and account number.
1b.	The Account Holder wants to add another account holder's account to the destination list.	The Account Holder can name the account (mandatory?)
1c.	*Emergent requirement . . .*	
1d.	*Emergent requirement . . .*	
2a.	There is not enough money on the source account to do the transfer.	Give an error message, and forego transaction. (Who is in charge of messages to Account Holder?)
2b.	The Account Holder accepts transfer to another Account Holder's account.	The Greenland Net bank requests a password before accepting the transfer.
2c.	The amount doesn't pass the validation rules.	Validation rules?
2d.	The Account Holder enters a later date for the transfer.	The Greenland Net Bank provides an option to schedule a transfer some number of *banking days* in the future. (How far into the future can the date be set?)
2e.	The transaction takes longer than the accepted minimum time.	Reasons for while it take longer? Actions when it does? Accepted minimum time?
2f.	The transaction fails.	Reasons for fail? Actions to recover? Appropriate messages?
2g.	*Emergent requirement . . .*	
2h.	*Emergent requirement . . .*	

to stop my customers from transferring money that they don't have so I can stay in business". No, that doesn't really work either. Use common sense. You are also welcome to handwrite the deviations on index cards, and put them on the wall (or in a box) – then you can call it a user story in its original meaning.

For now we will continue to call such situations *deviations* from the sunny day scenario. And what we really get from linking the deviations with the sunny day scenario is *structure*. We can now discuss a step in a sunny day scenario. We can even focus on the system part of a step in a sunny day scenario where we anticipate architectural challenges. Or we can discuss a deviation and its consequences. It provides focus to discussions towards good *decisions*. And it gives our businessperson some structured input to the release plan. To plan Release 2 in better detail, the businessperson can now examine the deviation list and decide which deviations must be in Release 2, and which deviations can wait.

As soon as we have stabilized a sunny day scenario, the team can estimate it. And after that can the deviations be estimated when they are stabilized. The use cases will grow. It's not so much that we add more use cases – that will be the exception. And it's not because we add to the sunny day scenario – that is also rare. Use cases grow because we keep on adding deviations.

Here is a key point: *We can add deviations incrementally!* These deviations are our real scope: extensions, exceptions, alternatives, variations, error handling, and nonfunctional requirements. This is where much of the revenue-generating work comes. Can they all be one-liners? Maybe. Our experience is: most of the time. That's why most product developments more or less get by with user stories, except they too often lose track of the relationships between them. Other than that, keeping things small and simple is how we keep it Agile. Use common sense.

If we can add use case scenarios incrementally, then we can introduce them into releases incrementally, and we can code them up incrementally and deliver them *just in time*. This incremental approach supports a key Lean tenet. And it goes without saying that it supports the Agile agenda of responding to change.

How about our emerging requirements? See Table 7-4. The empty rows await emerging requirements. Most emerging requirements come in the guise of deviations to a sunny day flow. Once in a great while we get an entirely new use case. Knowing the scope of the change helps us know the order of magnitude we have to deal with. Most of the time when we add or remove a whole use case, it is caused by growing knowledge about the nature of our use cases or even about the domain. Sometimes a new use case emerges from an existing use case, as we saw when the use case <u>Transfer money</u> gave birth to a new use case <u>Transfer money to international account</u>. Sometimes we merge two use cases because we realize that they are not different – maybe one of them is just an extension (deviation) of the other one.

At this point it is prudent to relate a warning:

Warning! If you are inclined to divide a use case such as "Transfer money" into three use cases: "Select accounts", "Transfer money",

> and "Do accounting" you are decomposing and are better served using decomposition tools such as dataflow diagrams.

Wait a minute! Our security specialist looks over my shoulder: "The Account Holder has to enter password only when accepting a transfer to another account? Isn't it part of the sunny day scenario? It should be!" Why? Does it make sense to ask for password when you transfer money between your own accounts? "It is our policy. We should always ask for password before a transaction."

How does that fit our user's mental model? We ask the usability specialist. "There is another principle going on here: consistency" our usability specialist says "So we can probably introduce passwords for all transfers without disturbing the user's mental model. Especially if we do it from the first release before end users have formed habits." Our sunny day scenario got a step more (Table 7-5).

It's good that we realized early that we need this extra step! We want our sunny day scenario to be as stable as possible. Otherwise it is hard to handle the deviations – which we now must revisit in light of this latest change. Our deviation (2b) where the system asks for password before transfer to another account goes away. Do we delete the row and renumber the rest of the deviations? Do we mark the deviation as deleted or moved to sunny day scenario, but keep the row? Use common sense. The decision is documented anyhow. You create supplementary documentation only if you want a record of why the decision was made, by whom, and maybe when. We have to renumber the deviations anyhow. Have fun identifying how many changes we have made to our deviation list (Table 7-6).

Remember: the richness of use cases comes in the deviations, and they come freely and frequently. They are where the variation happens. We consolidated the sunny day scenario early to establish a structure for deviations: that's the commonality. The main success scenario of a use case is its stable business characterization and changes rarely if ever. It provides an anchor for the deviations, and the deviations are what give us growth in functionality.

You can also have fun finding five faults (like the children's game of finding differences between two pictures). It requires many eyes – and at least one tester – to keep the use case descriptions consistent.

But we would rather let you use time on another exercise:

> Identify all terms and concepts from the sunny day scenario and the deviations that you think will affect the architecture.

Table 7-5 Adding the password step.

Step	Actor Intention	System Responsibility	Comment
1.	The Account Holder selects a *source account* and chooses to transfer money.	The Greenland Net Bank displays the *source account*, provides a list of *destination account*s, and a field to enter the *amount*.	Should the Account Holder choose to transfer money first and then the account, or the other way around? *As default the Greenland Net Bank shows a list of Account Holder's own accounts (except for the source account). When Account Holder adds other accounts they will show up on the default list for that specific Account Holder.*
2.	The Account Holder selects a *destination account*, enters the amount, and accepts.	The Greenland Net Bank shows the transfer information (*source account*, *destination account*, date, amount) and requests a password to approve the transfer.	The default date is the current date.
3.	The Account Holder enters the password and accepts the transfer.	The Greenland Net Bank transfers the money, updates the accounts, the statement info and the transaction log. The Greenland Net Bank issues a receipt for the transaction.	Habit: <u>Move money and do accounting.</u> The Greenland Net Bank verifies funds available, updates the accounts, and updates the statement info. (Defines *transfer* and *accounting*.) Is *receipt* the right term? Do we need a receipt for the Account Holder's own accounts? Does the Account Holder need to be able to print the receipt?

And what about the product backlog if you are using Scrum? A deviation is usually a nice-sized product backlog item. A sunny day scenario should only be one product backlog item in itself. A half-sunny day scenario doesn't add a lot of business value. If a sunny day scenario is more than one person can do in a half Sprint, then you can divide the sunny day scenario into steps, but you don't deliver any business value before all the steps are implemented.

Table 7-6   The deviations updated.

Ref. Step No.	Action Causing Branching	Comment
1a.	The Account Holder adds a text to the transaction on the source account.	Shouldn't this be a part of the sunny day scenario? What is the default text if the Account Holder doesn't add a text?
1b.	The Account Holder wants to transfer to another Account Holder's account.	The Account Holder needs to enter registration number and account number.
1c.	The Account Holder wants to add another Account Holder's account to the destination list.	The Account Holder can name the account (mandatory?)
2a.	There is not enough money on the source account to do the transfer.	Give an error message, and forego the transaction. (Who is in charge of messages to Account Holder? Define *minimum account balance*?)
2b.	The Account Holder adds a text to the transaction on the destination account.	Isn't this in the sunny day scenario? What is the default text if the Account Holder enters none?
2c.	The amount doesn't pass the validation rules.	Validation rules?
2d.	The Account Holder enters a later date for the transfer.	The Greenland Net Bank provides an option for enter a later date. The transfer will happen at that day according to *bank days*. (How long into the future can the date be set?)
3a.	Password fails.	Standard procedure?
3b.	The transaction takes longer than the accepted minimum time.	Reasons for while it take longer? Actions when it does? Accepted minimum time?
3c.	The transaction fails.	Reasons for failure? Actions to recover? Appropriate messages?
All	The Account Holder looks for online help.	Who is responsible for online help?

7.5.5   Use Cases to Roles

Businesspeople, usability specialists, testers and developers work on use cases together. Developers can't really develop an implementation only through documents and handoffs. In particular, it's important to give developers the opportunity to exercise feedback both to clarify their understanding of the end user motivation and need, and to relate their expertise about implementation constraints. Together, the expectations of both sides may evolve.

What are often just clarifying definitions to the business are software artifacts to the developer. We want to establish a path from the former to the latter. Use cases encourage good terminology that provides the traceability, and the DCI architecture provides a place to express this terminology in code.

Roles from the Use Case

Look again at Table 7-5 above (page 199). We find step descriptions such as:

1.	The Greenland Net Bank displays the *source account*, provides a list of *destination account*s, and a field to enter the *amount*	Should the Account Holder choose to transfer money first and then the account, or the other way around?

Notice that we have italicized *source account*, *destination account* and *amount*. From a pure use case perspective the italics might designate a definition in the domain dictionary, and that helps the business clarify its needs to itself. But to the developer, these terms provide strong implementation hints. DCI strives to capture such concepts directly in the code. In the implementation we call them *object roles* to distinguish them from use case actors.

The use case helps us understand the responsibilities of these roles. For example, we can deduce from above that *source account* should provide information that can identify itself to the Account Holder. That becomes a responsibility of the *source account* object role. As we go deeper into the use case and its transfer of money we will find more responsibilities for the *source account*, *destination account*, and other object roles. Exploring these responsibilities may cause us to expand or refine the use case.

This is a simple example with only "Greenland Net Bank" as the name of the system. More commonly, more systems will be named in the system column (and of course there may be more actors in the actor problem). Each of these systems has responsibilities with respect to the use case. In many cases these system names will also become object roles.

For example, consider a new service that allows an Account Holder to take a loan from the bank over the net or at an automated teller machine. The use case involves the Loan Department as a system that must approve the loan request (perhaps automatically in real time). From the point of view of the main use case, whose discussions are primarily between the Account Holder and Greenland Net Bank, the Loan Department is just another role. The software folks will want to view it that way, too. It will become an object role in DCI.

Does the team define these roles as part of analysis or part of design? Does this discussion belong here in Chapter 7 or in Chapter 9? Ah, such are the deep questions of life. And we don't care. Remember: the whole team works as one so that the business can inform the developer and the developer can inform the business. Everybody, all together, from early on. Experience will teach you the details of this process.

Bridging the Gap between the Business and the Programmer

In Figure 7-3 above, we introduced the concept of a habit, which captures a recurring use case fragment in closed form. In classic use case style, the software-side responsibilities accrue to "the system," or, if we are more selective in our terminology, "the bank." These terms convey little new insight either to the business people or the developers. Rather than resorting to general-purpose business-speak, and to avoid resorting to terminology like *abstract base classes* or *database transaction logs*, we can use better metaphors to describe these concepts. In particular, we can communicate many of these metaphors as object roles. Object roles are programmer constructs in the DCI architecture that reflect parts of the end user mental model.

In Figure 7-3 above, we use the rather sterile term "Greenland Net Bank"("the system") for everything the software does. This leaves the end user without much insight into what is going on, and leaves the programmer with an overly broad and nebulous notion of the context. Consider this alternative representation of the sequence:

1. **SourceAccount** verifies funds available.
2. **SourceAccount** and **DestinationAccount** update their balances.
3. **SourceAccount** updates the statement info.

This model makes metaphorical sense to the end user. Further, it helps the programmer close the feedback loop to ensure that he or she shares the end user's mental model. Here, the new concepts **SourceAccount** and **DestinationAccount** are not use case actors, but are actor-like agents inside the Greenland Net Bank system – object roles. They will become software concepts in the implementation, represented by abstract base classes or other interfaces. What do they interface to? Objects. Just as a use case actor is a role perspective on some human being, so an object role is a behavioral slice of a software object. We'll explore object roles in depth in Chapter 9.

Use this approach selectively, remembering that all analogies (and metaphors) break down somewhere. Don't force a metaphor unless the team seems to need a concept to latch onto, or a vision that will move dialog and understanding forward.

7.6   Recap

Did we achieve our criteria for consolidation? Let us recap. Our goal was:

1. To support the user's workflow (usage scenarios);
2. To support test close to development (test scenarios);
3. To support efficient decision making about functionality (sunny day scenario versus deviations);
4. To support emerging requirements (deviations);
5. To support release planning (use cases and deviations);
6. To support sufficient input to the architecture (terms and concepts from the scenarios);
7. To support the team's understanding of what to develop.

7.6.1   Support the User's Workflow

We have stabilized the sunny day scenario and decided on the three steps – and their order – that the user and the system have to perform together to get the desired result. The deviations that we have defined so far belong to a specific step in the sunny day scenario. When the use case grows incrementally through the deviations, we have to decide where each one belongs in the flow. It keeps us conscious about the workflow we support. Do we know if the system will support the best workflow for the user? Ask your usability specialist – or do what he or she would have done, and carry out a usability test.

7.6.2   Support Testing Close to Development

As soon as we have stabilized the sunny day scenario the tester (or system engineer (Section 3.2.1)) can begin to define test scenarios. If the tester feels comfortable enough to begin to write or script test scenarios you know your use case is in pretty good shape. The tester's activity will add many valuable deviations to the use case. The structure of the test scenarios is already given by the relationship between the sunny day scenario and the deviations. Now it is just up to the tester to define which of the scenarios, and especially, combination of scenarios, that makes most sense to test. That decision is a core competence of testing. You don't risk that requirements support one structure, design and code another, and test a third. The solutions to this dilemma has historically fallen into two categories:

1. The classical solution is to have test wait doing the test scenarios until usage scenarios have been coded. Result: delays in development and test as an afterthought (I think most of us have been there).

2. The "Agile" solution where tests are written before the code. Result: a) Requirements are expressed in test scripts and we loose business, usability, and other stakeholders that don't talk in code. b) We dig into details too early. c) We will lack the tester's competence of what is important to test, and just do a "test all" thing and risk getting a false sense of security.

The use case scenarios help ensure that we are all on the same page before we code and test the scenarios. The system design and test design can happen in parallel, and we are ready to test as soon as a scenario is coded.

7.6.3   Support Efficient Decision-Making about Functionality

The examples in the text support this and hopefully convince you that we have the support we need for decision-making. The current status of the sunny day scenario, the deviations, the wording of each scenario, and the comments and questions, all reflect the current status of the decisions you have made about what the system does. When you need to take a new decision you know the exact context: the right use case, whether it is a sunny day scenario or deviation, which step in sunny day scenario, or which deviation. That supports efficient decision making immensely!

7.6.4   Support Emerging Requirements

A use case can emerge or be merged with another. When it merges it is because we realize that two use cases are basically the same. If you experience that often, it is a red flag: your use cases are too detailed from the beginning. A more organic way to work with use cases is to let them emerge: one use case can grow out of another use case. Be careful not to let it happen prematurely – then you risk the merge problem later. You'll get a sense that it is premature because the emergent use case will seem immature. But the most common emergence will happen on the deviation level. We add and sometimes remove deviations along the way. The deviations will be implemented in different iterations depending on the product owners' ordering of the product backlog (if we are in Scrum land). In other words: the deviations are the nicely sliced units that we can use to make our release plans realistic.

7.6.5   Support Release Planning

When we have identified our maximum of more or less 15 use cases, we are ready for the first raw release plan. After we have consolidated the sunny day scenario and brainstormed the deviations we can make a bit more detailed release plan. The release plan is ready for dates when the sunny day scenarios and the most important deviations are estimated.

Once the release dates have been fixed, it is a question of working on the most important items for each release. By nature the sunny day scenario is the most important of any use case. To implement a deviation before the sunny day scenario is not common sense. After that it is a business call to decide which of the deviations are required before a release. *What makes use cases long is the list of deviations*, not the sunny day scenario – it shouldn't be more than 7 steps long, and is shorter most of the time. But we can easily get 30 to 50 deviations per use case (just think error handling), and the number of scenarios can grow exponentially with every deviation added. So the real complexity and scope hides in the deviations. We rise to the occasion with our flexibility and ability to be Agile. The deviations are the units we can play with when we make changes in priority and order, when we handle emerging requirements, and when we take care of the consequences for our release planning.

7.6.6   Support Sufficient Input to the Architecture

The use case descriptions help us to be conscious about concepts and terminology. To be conscious about concepts and terms require *understanding*. To do a good architecture we need to understand our system. We extract the terms and concepts from the use cases and use the words *consistently* in our architecture and code. It helps us to get *readable* code, as we will see that the use cases drive the code form when using the DCI architecture (Chapter 9). Readable code is *maintainable* code. Maintainable code helps the architecture to last longer. Good architecture that last longer, makes developers more happy and business more valuable. We love happy endings.

7.6.7   Support the Team's Understanding of What to Develop

A few more details are required to ensure a happy ending. To understand, the team must be involved. You can have the best use cases in the world written by the best analyst in the world. If the team hasn't been a part of the process, the use cases are useless. The team has to start all over again in order to understand. It is not because your team is stupid. It is because 90% of the knowledge is now in the analyst's head, and the rest is maybe in the use cases. If user stories are a "Promise for a future conversation," use cases are "Reminders for discussions and decisions" about what the system does. The good thing is that they are *structured* reminders!

So when Kent Beck (Beck 1999, p. 90) says "Business writes a story" and Scrum emphasize that the product owner is responsible for the product backlog, please don't read this as saying that the business writes user stories in isolation and the product owner creates the product backlog without involving the team. All that does is to re-introduce the "throw it over the wall" specifications to Agile and Lean development. "Throw it over the wall" is the main reason why waterfall development has so bad a reputation today. Lean is about not having stovepipes, or walls over which things are thrown. Agile is about individuals and interactions. Let's be in the spirit of Agile and Lean: *everybody, all at once, from early on.*

7.7 "It Depends": When Use Cases are a Bad Fit

A use case captures a sequence of events – a collection of related scenarios – that take the end user toward some goal in some context. What if you have difficulty expressing a user interaction in that form? Sometimes, use cases are a bad fit. If you look at a scenario and you can't answer the contextual questions, "Why is the user doing this?" and "What is his or her motivation in context?" then use cases are probably a bad fit for your domain (or you aren't well-enough connected to your users!) If it's the former, you should seriously explore alternative formalisms to capture requirements.

What alternatives, you ask? *It depends* is the answer. Some designs in fact are dominated by such operations. Think of a graphical shapes editor that features "use cases" such as rotating, re-coloring, re-sizing, creating and deleting objects. From a use case perspective, these are atomic operations. Though each of these operations may require multiple end-user gestures, each is still a single step in a use case. The number of gestures or mouse clicks required to achieve a goal is a user interface design issue, not a requirement issue. Moving an object, or re-coloring it, is not an algorithm in the mathematical or even vernacular sense of the word; it is atomic. If there is no business need to group such operations together, then each is a command in its own right and we really don't need use cases. The user is not working with *a sequence of tasks to reach some goal in a context.* Each command reduces to a primitive operation on the domain object itself, and MVC alone with its direct manipulation metaphor is enough to get the job done If you choose use cases to capture the input to a system dominated by atomic operations, you'll end up with hundreds of use cases that belabor the obvious.

7.7.1 Classic OO: Atomic Event Architectures

One way to explain the success of object-oriented programming is that it rode the coattails of graphical user interfaces and mice. These human interaction styles captured our imagination and led to computing as a companion thinker rather than as a distant subcontractor. The human satisfaction with immediate feedback, the speed (or at least the illusion of speed) with which one could drive to a solution, and the human-like behaviors of these interfaces at Xerox PARC paved a path for Smalltalk's influence on the world.

The link between this user engagement and Smalltalk in particular, or object orientation in general, is more than incidental. There is a continuum of representation from the end user's mental model of the world, to the graphical interface, to the structure of the objects beneath the interface. The idea is that the user manipulates interface elements in a way that fools his or her mind into thinking that they are manipulating the objects in the program – or, better, the real world objects that those programmatic objects represent. To place an item in one's shopping cart in an online bookstore gives the end user, at least metaphorically, the feeling of actually shopping with a shopping cart. This is sometimes called the direct-manipulation metaphor (Laurel 1993). We'll later talk about the Model-View-Controller-User architecture (Section 8.1) as the most common way to create the illusions that support this metaphor.

To get something done on a direct manipulation GUI, you first choose an object (like a book) and then "manipulate" it (put it in your shopping cart). It feels awkward to instead first say, "I'm going to buy a book" and then select the book. This is because we are *thinking* about the book before the actual *doing* of deciding to purchase. We probably wouldn't have come to the website if we had to dwell on the question of whether we wanted to buy a book. This is called *a noun-verb interaction style*: we choose the noun (the book) first, and the action (to buy) second.

Notice the close correspondence to our architecture, which has a what-the-system-is part (the books) and what-the-system-does parts (the use cases such as: buying a book, finding earlier editions of the book, and retrieving reviews of the book).

The noun-verb metaphor leads to interfaces that take us through a sequence of screens or contexts. When we select the book, we are in the context of thinking about that book. The book has a physical representation on the screen (as a picture of the book, as its ISBN, or its title and author) that fills our conscious mind. The conscious processes of our mind focus on that object. There are many things we can do with that object, and our thinking process leads us to where we want to be. Only then will we "execute a command." The "command" is something like "put this book in my shopping cart" and on most graphical interfaces we would enact the scenario by pushing a button labeled "Add to shopping cart."

This means that the object on the screen (the book) is like the object in the program, and from the screen we can see how to manipulate that object in the ways that make business sense (put it in the cart, retrieve reviews, etc.) Those are, in effect, the member functions on that object. The customer works, and invokes commands, in a very focused context: that of the object. The object becomes the command interpreter – one primitive operation at a time.

This style of interaction in turn leads to the architectural style that we call *atomic event architectures* in this book. Such a style focuses on the objects and what we can do with them, rather than on the "scenarios" that exist in retrospect as the collection of these events and commands. We can take the context for granted. More precisely, we focus on the roles that the objects can play in the current context (though a book can play the role of a doorstop, we focus on a different role when purchasing a book online). We give users choices, allowing them to interact with programs in an Agile way: one choice at a time. If we focused on the scenario instead, we'd have a master plan that would preclude choosing different books in a different order, and which would remove the user's option to change course at any time (to just forget the current book and go onto another, or to take a book back out of the shopping cart).

7.8   Usability Testing

Usability testing focuses on the interaction between the end user and the system, ensuring that typical end users who fit within the user profiles can accomplish what they need to accomplish. Good usability testing requires the skills of specially trained and experienced testers. User experience people perform such tests by giving end users sample exercises or tasks to do, and they monitor the interactions between the end user and the envisioned system. They note carefully what screens are involved in the use case, and what interactions transpire between the user and the system. What this testing does for the architecture is to validate whether we've captured the end user mental model.

Product organizations too often defer usability testing until after the software is done, treating it like an acceptance test. By then, it's too late. If a fundamental change to the interface is needed, it signals a lapse in properly capturing the end user mental model. That can mean that the architecture is built on the wrong concepts. If the conceptual underpinnings are wrong, it will take more than refactoring to recover. That may mean delaying the current release or postponing the fix to a later release. Too often the necessary changes affect the basic form of the architecture so much that the cost is prohibitive, and the end users must live with the problems in perpetuity.

Instead, usability testing should be used as a forward-engineering technique. Use the insights that usability testing gives you into the interface models to fine-tune your architecture. This can be difficult in traditional organizations because there is often a wide gap between architects, implementers, and user experience people. But if you're a Lean team – everybody, all together, from early on – you have the organizational foundations for this feedback loop.

You can go one step further by combining usability testing with dynamic architecture testing, using CRC (Candidate object, Responsibilities, and Collaborators) cards (Beck 1991). Bring together your team and have each team member play the role of one or more objects in the system. Each team member holds an index card representing either a system domain object, or a system role or object role as we introduced in Section 7.5.5. The facilitator asks the end user to run through a use case scenario. As the user tells of performing some gesture (pushing a button on the screen or pulling down the menu) the appropriate role or object rises to the occasion by providing the necessary service. These responses are the responsibilities of the object or role's public interface; the team member writes these down on the left column of the card as they arise. If a role or object requires the cooperation of another role or object to further the transaction, then the corresponding team member is asked to carry on the "execution" and to write the appropriate responsibility on his or her card. When the first team member hands off control to the second, he or she writes down the role or object of the second in the right-hand column of the card. It is useful to use a talking stick or cat toy or other "sacred artifact" as the program counter in this exercise.

When you're done, compare what's on the cards with what's in the architecture.

7.9   Documentation?

The first thing to remember is that your main goal should be that the team is talking together. Everybody has some set of insights, and everybody needs the insights of others. Traditional organizations make it difficult to build the network of connections that allow all the right insights to find their proper homes. User stories are a kind of cultural artifact that teams can use as focal points for the discussions that lead to a shared vision of the job to be done. As Mike Cohn says, user stories *represent* the requirement rather than *being* the requirement. Use cases are the same to a degree, but also provide a structure for requirements and a record of how that structure, and its requirements, came into being. The written literature of a culture provides foundations that an oral culture cannot, and much of the value of use cases is to concretize decisions, in particular decisions about the *why* of design.

Given that context, the use cases themselves are important Agile documents. Remember that documents serve two purposes: communication in the now, and corporate memory in the future. Use cases as a form help structure thinking in the now. They provide a place to track dependencies between yet-to-be-implemented items on the product backlog and for work in progress on the Sprint backlog in Scrum. That's part of being an enabling specification.

Whether use cases should be maintained as historic documents is a matter for individual projects to decide. You want to keep use cases if they codify important learnings to which the team may want to return in the future. Sometimes you want to remember why you did something a certain way when the reasoning may not be obvious from the code itself. A good example is code that deals with a side effect from an interaction between two use cases. Perhaps keeping use cases around will save rework in development, to re-inventing the reasoning and mechanisms that were understood when design decisions were made in the past. Therefore, throwing away the use case wouldn't be Lean. So if you have a need for such history, and if you have a way easily to recover such documents on demand, you might consider keeping them.

Keep a little data on how often you go back to old use cases. Once in a while, both of us authors go through our closets at home and are astonished at how many of our clothes we haven't worn in one or two years. It's always a hard decision to take them to charity because we want to save them for sentimental reasons. But we have limited closet space. And it costs your project time to keep use cases around and to keep them current. If you find that archived use cases haven't seen the light of day in a few months, stop keeping them. Clean your closet. It's part of the Lean principle of keeping your workplace clean.

One alternative to keeping use cases in the long term is the idea of "disposable analysis,"[5] where the use case serves the communication function without the overhead associated with its role as an archival artifact. If that's the case, throw the use case away after it's coded up. To keep it around isn't Lean.

Even end user documentation has value. When you walk up to an iPod, you don't yet have a mental model of what it is. It's an MP3 player, it's an iTunes interface. If a new customer comes to the iPod from a different MP3 player it's important to establish iTunes as the place where you do configuration and management, and that the iPod may be much simpler than your old MP3 player. That's a paradigm shift for the end

---

[5] Thanks to Paul S. R. Chisholm for this delightful term.

user – a shift that they may be unable to make by themselves. Lightweight tutorials and examples can help establish the metaphors that support good user experiences. Of course, deeper interaction models (up means louder and down means softer) should be built-in and should not depend on documentation to be useful.

7.10   History and Such

Ivar Jacobsson pioneered use cases in 1992 (Jacobsson 1992) and tried to offer them to the market through his methodology, Objectory.

Rebecca Wirfs-Brock was one of the first who moved beyond high-level graphical conceptualizations of use cases to describing what actually goes on inside of a use case. She later pioneered the two-column description of conversations in terms of actors and actions (Wirfs-Brock 1993). Rebecca's format has been adopted neither by RUP nor by Alistair Cockburn, but has been embraced in the usability world (e.g. Constantine and Lockwood 1999). It is used in practice in many organizations and is our preferred form in this book.

Use cases have been a part of UML from about 1995 – from the very earliest days.

Alistair Cockburn re-interpreted use cases and started to bring his vision into the software world through his book _Writing Effective Use Cases_ (Cockburn 2001). Cockburn's vision is completely in harmony with the Agile vision he nurtured as one of the organizers behind and signers of the Agile Manifesto. Rebecca's interpretation of use cases is also completely compatible with Agile.

The XP community (whose origins date from around 1997) viewed the UML-based history of use cases in the 1990s as something to be avoided, and supplanted them with user stories. User stories worked together with other XP principles and practices such as on-site customer and test-driven development to support rapid development of small systems. However, user stories as self-contained minimalist units had problems scaling to systems thinking. In complex systems, the relationships between stories were as important as the stories themselves. Methodologists gradually started adding features to user stories to accommodate some of these concerns: for example, Mike Cohn recommends adding information for the testers. At this writing these individual variations have caused the definition of "user story" to diverge broadly and there is no single accepted definition of the term.

Coding It Up: Basic Assembly

Your architecture is ready, and a new feature request has made it to the top of your work queue or your Sprint backlog. Or maybe a user is banging on your door or burning your ear on the phone begging for new functionality. It's time for the rubber to meet the road. If you're a coder, this is the fun stuff. Let's sling some code.

But wait – as we sling code, we don't want to bury our heads inside of our screens and ascend to nerd heaven. It's important to honor the original goals of object orientation and be ever attentive to the end users' world models. That's why we've taken you through the preceding chapters. The Agile nerds will tell you that the code is the design. The Agile businesspeople will tell you that the design should be outwardly focused. We'll show you that they both can be right.

Before we jump right into the code, we'll spend a little bit of time introducing MVC and a set of concepts that are broadly associated with it. Most Agile architectures arise from an MVC framework, so we will discuss MVC as a foundation for the details that ensue. We'll then describe two architectural approaches: one that supports short, snappy event-driven computation, and the other that supports goal-oriented task sequences that the user wants to complete. In this chapter, we will discuss classical object-oriented architecture, where we distribute use case responsibilities directly into domain classes. We'll leave the incorporation of full use case requirements to Chapter 9. We end up the chapter with guidelines for updating domain classes to support the new functionality.

8.1   The Big Picture: Model-View-Controller-User

MVC is a time-honored (since 1978) architecture framework that separates information representation from user interaction. Calling it MVC-U emphasizes the most important object in the framework: the user. It is the user's system interaction model that gives rise to the rest of the MVC structure. We'll use the terms interchangeably in this book, adding the *U* particularly when we want to emphasize the user engagement.

We are right at home with MVC-U in separating what the system *is* from what the system *does*. It's not a coincidence. The early vision of object-orientation was to capture the end user's mental model in the code. This dichotomy, of thinking and doing, is a widely embraced model of the end user's mental organization, and has found some kind of home in almost every paradigm in Western history. Computing has not escaped that dichotomy, and objects are no exception to the rule.

8.1.1   What is a Program?

Let's talk video games for a second. If you're playing an interplanetary war video game, you feel that you really *are* in that fighter ship, piloting it – if it's a good game. The computer or gaming system disappears and you are absorbed in total engagement. Brenda Laurel describes this experience of engagement in her insightful book, *Computers as Theatre* (Laurel 1993).

The goal of a program is to create a reality that you can experience as such. For most of you reading this book, these realities are often modeled after your business world. When I use a program to logically retrieve an item from a warehouse, I am not literally touching the crates. The program may enact robots or may print out an instruction for a warehouse worker to fetch an item, but the end result is as if I had done it myself. Therefore, the program creates an illusion: *I* didn't really move the item. At some level, all of programming is about creating illusions. Good illusions are contrived to fit the models that lie latent in the end user's brain.

MVC-U helps the programmer create such illusions. The first step is to bridge the gap between the end user's mental model in his or her brain, and the computer data in the program (Figure 8-1). That measure alone works well for simple models, as one might find in a graphical shapes editor. More often than not, things are more complex than that. My old friend Dennis DeBruler used to say that complexity is proportional to the number of distinct, meaningful ways you can look at a thing. MVC-U allows multiple views of the same data – for example, a pie chart and a bar graph view of simple data, or a floor plan view and front elevation view of a house in a CAD program. We need a tool to coordinate the views, if

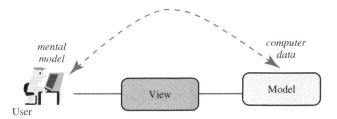

Figure 8-1   The view bridges the gap between brain and model.

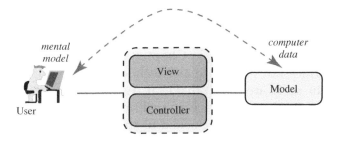

Figure 8-2   The Model-View-Controller paradigm.

multiple views are in play concurrently. The coordination itself is done by a part of the tool called the Controller (Figure 8-2).

8.1.2   What is an Agile Program?

Interactive programs live close to human beings. We can in fact think of them as an extension of human reasoning and mental processing, much as Alan Kay envisioned the DynaBook (Kay 1972) as a lifelong companion computer that extends human brainpower. Humans live and react in human time scale and their mental activities face an ever-changing world. If the software doesn't keep up with that change, it leaves the human mentally behind their world's pace. As Agile is about responding to change, it is instructive to consider how an Agile mindset can help the world of interactive computing.

Contrast the interactive world with a batch-processing world. Human users don't interact with batch programs, at least not while the programs run. Users may type the data that is fed to the program and they may read the printout from the program, but only long (by machine time scales) after the program execution has been extinguished. Such programs tend to structure themselves around relatively stable business processes. In fact, over time these programs tend to become constrained by other programs and processes in the batch stream. This isn't always true: for example, all the popular search engine sites depend on long-running batches to keep the search data fresh, but those kinds of systems tend to be the exception rather than the rule.

We can also contrast interactive code with embedded code. Embedded code is often fast running and often must meet real-time deadlines, such as one might expect from the firmware controlling the fuel injection in your car. But that software is *embedded* in the hardware it controls and is often quite distant from any direct user interface. It is usually constrained by the industrial processes for the hardware in which it is embedded, so its rate of change is usually low.

Most of the time, Agile code has an interactive user interface, and that interface usually gives the user a feeling of engagement with a real world where change is the name of the game. That includes the programming styles discussed both here and in Chapter 9. Such an interface is often a graphical interface but it can use any technology that helps the end user engage with the software. What makes it Agile? This level of engagement pushes change into the user's face, in real time: Agile responds to change. In the same sense that teams are asked to engage their customers in Agile development, so an end user engages Agile *software* after the shrink-wrap comes off. It's about individuals and interactions – not only with other people, but also with the software, and one doesn't find as much of this kind of interaction in batch or embedded systems.

If one looks at the foundation of object-orientation, it comes back to capturing the end user's mental model of the world in the code. If that world is a dynamic world, then we're likely talking Agile software – embracing change along with collaboration between the end user (beyond-the-customer) and the code. How do we manage interaction between the end user and the software? The Model-View-Controller-User framework has become a de facto standard for such systems. *There exists a fundamental, deep and incestuous relationship between Agile, object orientation, and Model-View-Controller-User.*

Before we elaborate on MVC in the next section, it's probably important to answer the question: "How do I apply Agile development techniques to my embedded platform code?" Similar questions arise for batch code. While there is no universal answer, there is a strong tendency for the techniques of Agile software development to serve interactive applications, and to be less useful or relevant in batch and embedded applications. But the exceptions are too numerous to ignore. The rule of thumb is to use common sense. As Grandpa Harry said: If the shoe fits, wear it. If you know your requirements, and know that they won't change, then maybe Agile is overkill for you and waterfall is just fine. There, we said it. It's just that it's very rare that we find real projects with the luxury of being in that position. If you are, be conscious of the gift that fate has given you and take advantage of it!

So much for Agile: how about Lean? While Lean development's benefits really shine in an environment where user needs evolve or vary widely, they even add value to stable systems that have little direct user interaction. It is always a good idea to reduce waste and inventory, and to continuously and passionately strive towards process improvement. Many of this book's techniques therefore apply beyond so-called Agile projects. So, which of the book's practices are Lean and which are Agile? We'll leave that to your reasoning; the answer may not even be the same all the time. We hope that the book provides enough background and context that you can use your common sense to judge the answer.

O.K., now let's move into the nerdy stuff.

8.1.3 MVC in More Detail

Model-View-Controller (without the *U*) has found expression in countless articles and books as a framework with a familiar set of APIs. We won't repeat them here. Unfortunately, while many of these descriptions satisfy MVC-U's goal to separate the interface logic from the business logic, they miss the other goals of direct manipulation, of supporting multiple business domains, of supporting Conway's Law, of supporting the DynaBook metaphor or the Tools and Materials metaphor (Riehle and Züllighoven 1995). For a deeper understanding of MVC, you can read a bit about its history from the perspective of its creator (Reenskaug 2003). For those who want a reminder of MVC responsibilities, see Table 8-1.

Table 8-1   MVC APIs.

Model	View	Controller
▪ Updates its data at the request of commands from the Controller ▪ Notifies appropriate views when its state changes ▪ Can be asked to register/de-register Views	▪ Presents a particular representation of the data to the user ▪ Can ask Model for the current value of data it presents to users ▪ Can handle its own input ▪ Together with the Controller, handles selection	▪ Creates and manages Views ▪ Handles selection across Views ▪ Passes commands to the Model ▪ Handles commands that apply to the entire window

8.1.4 MVC-U: Not the End of the Story

While MVC does a good job of helping end users (and programmers, too, of course) interpret the data in the program, and start to make sense out of how an interesting algorithm might interact with those data, it doesn't capture anything about the algorithms themselves, of what they do, or of how they work. That may or may not be important. In "classical object-oriented programming," the algorithms are trivial relative to the structure of the data, and we turn our attention to the data. But sometimes it matters.

A Short History of Computer Science

We can characterize many object-oriented systems as having relatively simple external behaviors that operate on richer and more interesting data structures inside the software. These simple or "atomic" exchanges between people and software have dominated object orientation since its earliest support of graphical user interfaces. To appreciate the broader landscape of software architecture a bit more, we whimsically look back in history.

Computers were a wonderful invention. They allowed people to describe a repetitive task once, such as tabulating the tax on each of 10,000 payroll records, so that untiring machine could apply that task to each of those records. The job of the computer was to compute; data were the subject of those computations. Early programs were collections of these mundane algorithms linked together into increasingly complex computations.

The focus was on the structure of the computations, because that's where the business intelligence lay. All the algorithms for a given "job," which was usually a batch of computations thrown together, were loaded into memory. Then, one by one, data records were fed to the program through the card reader or were consumed from a disk file. The data throughput was massive: a card reader could read 1000 cards a minute, and each card bore 960 bits. Each data record had a short lifetime. However, the organization of the data was uninteresting except for its layout on the punch card or paper tape: one had to know which data appeared in which columns, but little more than that. The representation of data inside the computer program followed the organization of the procedures. The data were passed from procedure to procedure as arguments. Copies of (or references to) the data lived on the activation records of the procedures as local variables. Users never interacted *with* the program; they interacted with the IBM 026 cardpunch machines to prepare the data *for* the program, and they interacted with the 132-column printout produced *by* the program.

Fast forward about thirty years through many interesting intermediate developments such as block worlds and SHRDLU (Shrdlu 2009) and databases, and we come to the era of three interesting machines at Xerox PARC: the Dove, the Dorado, and the Dolphin. Though graphical screens had been around for a while, these machines took the interactive interface to new limits. There was no card reader; you interacted with the machine through the GUI and a strange device created by

Doug Englebart called the *mouse*. Each mouse click caused the machine to do something – instantaneously. Each function (or method) was small, designed to respond in human time scales to human interactions. There was no massive data input: the mouse and keyboard were typically 8-bit devices that could operate roughly at human typing speed, about 1000 times slower than a card reader. Now, the data lived *in* the program instead of living on the cards. The world had been turned inside out. These new machines would be the birthplace of a new style of programming called object-oriented programming.

Atzmon Hen-tov notes a parallel development on the programming side that explains the rise of Agile approaches in a simpler way:

> In the old days, computing was very expensive, so only critical stuff was computerized. As a result, (since the cost of a mistake was high), rigid disciplines ruled. Today, costs are low and everything is computerized. Most systems today are not critical and have low price for mistakes. The high overheads of the rigid disciplines don't suit such systems and hence agile evolved. (Hen-tov 2009)

We present this little history to illustrate a key principle that has dominated object-oriented programming for years: the methods are small in relation to the data, and the overall method structuring is relatively unimportant with respect to the overall data structuring. This balance between a dominating data structure and a repressed method structure characterizes many interactive programs. Consider the graphical shapes editor again. We don't think of the operations on shapes as being algorithms. Such operations are usually encapsulated in a single shape and are tightly tied to the shape-ness of the shape: recolor, move, and resize. The same is true for the primitive operations of a text editor: inserting and deleting characters.

Atomic Event Architectures

Consider a shape-editing program (again). You might need a degree in geometry to understand the polytetrahedra and the data structures used to represent them, but the operations on them are simple: move this shape to here, recolor that shape to be this color. Even the most advanced operations, such as graphical rotation, are still atomic algorithms without much rich structure (Table 8-2).

In good object-oriented programs of the 1980s, methods were very small – in Smalltalk programs, they were commonly two or three lines long. We were encouraged to think of a method on an object the same way that we think of an arithmetic operator like + on an integer: simple, atomic, and precise. In the parts of your program that have that nature

Table 8-2   Two Agile architecture styles.

Concern	Atomic Event Architecture	DCI Architecture
User goal	Direct manipulation of a domain object to ask it to do something	A sequence of tasks toward a goal in some context
Requirements Formalism	According to need: state machine, custom formalism: it depends	Use cases
Technology	Good old-fashioned object-oriented programming	Multi-paradigm design (procedures and objects); DCI
Design focus	Form of the data	Form of the algorithm
Scope	Single primary object or a small number of statically connected objects	Multiple objects that dynamically associate according to the request
Interaction Style	Noun-verb: select an object first to define a context, and then select the operation	Sometimes verb-noun: select the use case scenario first, then the objects
Example	Text editor: delete character Bank system: print account balance	Text editor: spell-check Bank system: money transfer

the algorithms aren't terribly important (at least to the system form, to the architecture) and we shouldn't fret about how they mirror the user mental model. We discuss that style of architecture, a so-called atomic event architecture, here in this chapter.

DCI Architectures

On the other hand, algorithms are, or should be, first-class citizens in most programs. Consider a text editor, which you may right now think of as a simple program with primitive operations such as inserting or deleting a character. But how about spell checking? Or global search-and-replace? These are *algorithms*. We could make them into methods, but the question is: methods of *what*? I can spell-check a file, or a buffer, or perhaps just the current selected text. This isn't just a matter of adding a spell-check method to some object: spell checking is an important concept in its own right. For such cases – and they are many – we need MVC's complement: the Data, Context and Interaction (DCI) architecture (Table 8-2). We cover DCI in Chapter 9.

8.2   The Form and Architecture of Atomic Event Systems

Atomic event systems have very little concern with the user model of how he or she organizes sequences of work. In Chapter 7, we discussed use case as a way to capture what the system does *when it is important to understand a sequence of work towards a goal in a context*. We'll talk more about those kinds of systems, called task-oriented systems, in Chapter 9. But what about the rest – those "it depends" systems from Section 7.7?

In fact, most interactive systems today are dominated by atomic event semantics. Every keystroke that you enter in a text editor, forms editor, or web page is of that nature. Most mouse-click operations are of that nature. What characterizes these interactions is that they are difficult to describe in terms of any algorithm that is of significance to the user. Because it is implemented on a Von Neumann machine, such functionality is of course an algorithm in the end, and we can of course find its code in the program. But we won't find it in the end user's head. What we instead find in the end users' head is a data model – a model of the data or form of their world, where each piece of data is "smart" and knows how to do its domain duty in a way that appears trivial and atomic to them. Perhaps computers augment end user's information *processing* power in a domain (if they even do that), but it is more that they help the end user master and organize data. Deleting a shape in a shape-drawing program is an example: it doesn't take many MIPs, but the program organizes everything in a way that affords end users conveniences.

8.2.1   Domain Objects

O.K., let's see what the architecture of an atomic event system looks like. Let's start with the end user mental model. What is the user thinking? The user's worldview is dominated by the data structure at this point. In our shape editor, it's the shapes. In a text editor, it's the text. These are our good friends the domain objects from Chapter 5, and they will always be with us (the objects at the bottom of Figure 8-1). What else?

8.2.2   Object Roles, Interfaces, and the Model

Consider the shapes editor again. What domain object should support the **delete** function? Maybe it is an operation on a shape that removes it from the screen. But what if several shapes are highlighted, and the user presses delete? Now it is an operation on a collection. Collections of objects live in the domain model; groups of graphical objects are a common structure in shape programs. We could replicate the operation and add a lot of context-sensitive complexity – but, instead, we return to the user mental model. To the user, the deleted "things" are both special cases of *selections*. When one deletes something, what one deletes is the current *selection*. Now, a **selection** isn't a class in the Shape hierarchy; it's a *role*. (More precisely, we call it an *object role* to distinguish it from the concept of *user* *role* introduced in Chapter 7). A Shape can play the object role of **selection**. So can a **collection** of shapes.

Assume that we've already captured the selection object role during our analysis of what-the-system-does. These object roles appear as part of the atomic system architecture as ordinary Java interfaces, C# interfaces, or C++ abstract base classes (on the right of Figure 8-3). Each interface is designed as a partial wrapper onto an existing domain object. In other words, the class for the corresponding object should implement the corresponding interface. The mapping of interfaces to domain classes is many to many.

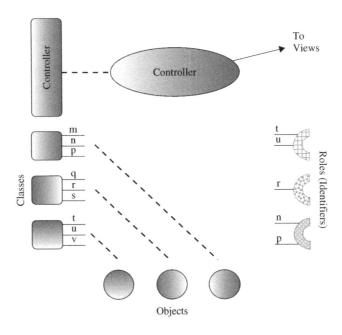

Figure 8-3   Basic atomic event architecture.

Object roles are a crucial part of the end user mental model. When users think about what they're operating on or playing with, they think objects. When they think about what those objects are going to do or how they are going to do it, they usually think in terms of the roles those objects play. This will become more important when we use the DCI architecture to start supporting a user mental model that operates on several object roles together, but it's true even for simple operations. When I ask the ATM to print the balance for the account currently on the screen, I momentarily forget exactly what kind of account it is. I think of it in its object role as a printable account, not as a savings account or checking account. That class distinction is irrelevant to the action of printing.

The Controller declares identifiers in terms of these interface types. It will either instantiate the appropriate domain object in response to a user command, or will otherwise bind its object role identifier to a suitable domain object (one that implements that object role) when an atomic command is invoked. The Controller then carries out its duties in terms of the interfaces on the object roles, and the actual work gets done down in the domain objects (Figure 8-3).

Within the MVC framework, these object roles become interfaces to the Model objects. The object roles and interfaces capture the user notion of what-the-system-does, and the domain objects (and classes) capture the user's mental model of what-the-system-is. We are simply interpreting MVC as an architectural framework that stores and organizes the results of our domain design and use case analysis.

Example

Let's look at our simple financial system as an example. Our Account Holder wants to print the balance on the account currently displayed on the screen. How did it get there? Right now, we don't care. The analysts know that there are use case scenarios that bring us to this point, and that we want to give the user the ability to print the balance on that account.

The term "account" here refers an instance of one of any number of account types. When in a situation where it can be printed, it plays a specific object role that is characterized in part by its ability to print its balance. What do we call that object role? We could very simply call it **AccountWithPrintableBalance**. The object role obviously supports the responsibility of printing the balance but it could in theory support other responsibilities. And an account in this state is likely to take on other object roles at the same time, such as having the ability to disburse or receive funds.

The design is simple. The logic in the Controller will be written in terms of identifiers that represent object roles; in most programming languages, these will reduce to declarations in terms of interfaces (or abstract base classes in C++). The APIs of those interfaces express the business functions that map from the end user's mental model of the task being accomplished.

At some time during the program execution those identifiers will become bound or re-bound to objects. Those objects are instantiated from classes whose member functions implement the method declarations in the interfaces. When implementing a new use case, it is up to the designer to create and fill in such methods.

The Ruby code for the object role could be as simple as this:

```
class AccountWithPrintableBalance
    def printBalance(outputDevice)
```

```
    end
end
```

Or, in C++:

```
class AccountWithPrintableBalance {
public:
    virtual void printBalance(OutputDevice) = 0;
};
```

This type is used to declare one of the methodless object roles on the right of Figure 8-4 and it is called a *methodless object role type*. The Controller is likely to have a method that responds to a print command, and within the scopes accessible to that method we'll find the actual methodless object role identifier declared. This identifier is the programmer's "handle" to the role. The logic in the Controller binds this identifier to the account object of interest, and uses it to invoke the `printBalance` method.

We'll get to the domain classes soon – Section 8.3.

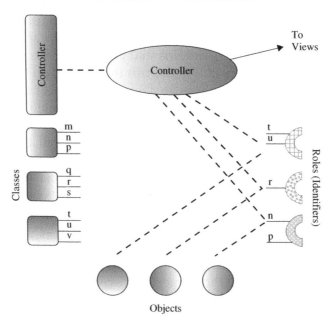

Figure 8-4   Linking up the domain objects with the Controller.

8.2.3   Reflection: Use Cases, Atomic Event Architectures, and Algorithms

In general, analysis starts with user stories, becomes a bit more disciplined in use cases, from which we can extract scenarios, and is carried into design as algorithms. There is an important shift between use case scenarios and algorithms. Scenarios are about *what*; algorithms are about *how*. In general, design isn't so simple that we can simply write down use case scenarios in the code. For example, we always write code sequentially, and if there are two steps in an algorithm, we can say which will precede the other. Such steps may correspond to end user activities and the end user may not care about the order in which they are executed.

While developers view redundancy as a liability in code, analysts view redundancy as an asset in requirements. Any single use case step alone lacks the context of the other steps. This context is crucial during analysis. Each use case therefore usually provides the full context of all of the steps leading up to the realization of a user goal. Use of "includes" relationships in use cases to pull out common steps that provide context from the steps that remain in the use case de-contextualizes that step. However, in code, it is different: we want one, single, closed copy of the code. We seek out steps that recur across multiple use cases as we go through the transition from use cases to algorithms, and capture them as use case *habits*. These map naturally onto Context objects in DCI.

As a specific example, to deposit to your checking account the system must know both the amount you are depositing and the account to which it is being deposited. The requirements may, in general, not say anything about which of these two is done first. The end user mental model (for example, based on habit or expectations) may provide hints for this. However, because the code implements concrete decisions, it may impose an ordering constraint on the scenario that is not present in the requirements. The algorithm may also implement nonfunctional requirements that are stated separately as rules in the requirements. Use cases have a place both for such essential system behaviors and for such rules.

However, in atomic event systems, the individual behaviors are usually simple enough that there is very little sequencing. We will return to this issue in Section 9.5.1.

8.2.4 A Special Case: One-to-Many Mapping of Object Roles to Objects

Sometimes an end user envisions an object role whose responsibilities actually belong together as an object role, but which for technical, historical or other reasons, map onto multiple objects. For example, an end user may view an audio headset as a single device playing a single object role, whereas the hardware actually has a driver object each for the microphone and the earphone. In this case:

1. Keep the AudioHeadset object role, implementing it as an interface or abstract base class;

2. Create a new AudioHeadsetAggregate class. This class will coordinate the Microphone and Earphone objects through a HAS-A relationship

3. Create an instance of AudioHeadsetAggregate and bind it to an identifier declared in terms of AudioHeadset

It's a quick and dirty solution, but it works. The opposite case (which is more obvious, perhaps: the user thinks of the microphone and earphone as being separate object roles with separate muting and volume controls, though those functions are controlled by methods on a single driver object) can also be easily handled: both an Earphone and Microphone object role can be bound to the same driver object.

8.3   Updating the Domain Logic: Method Elaboration, Factoring, and Re-factoring

Now we have enough context to update the architecture!

For there to be domain objects, there must be domain classes (unless you are programming in a classless language such as **self**). The actual workhorses of an atomic event system, the domain classes, live behind the abstract base classes produced in our what-the-system-is activities of Chapter 5.

The central guiding Lean principle at work in the domain architecture is *poka-yoke*: enabling constraints. As programmers rush to get a feature to market they are likely to be less attentive to the gross system structure and form than to the correctness of the business logic. The domain architecture encodes soberly considered form that can guide development in the excitement of new feature development. It is like I am building a house. The architect and carpenters leave space for the stove and oven in the kitchen, but the owners will choose and install the stove only later. When the gasman or electrician arrives to install the stove, they don't have to decide where to put it: it fits in one place. They can install it without disrupting the structural integrity of the carpenter's work, or the aesthetics or kitchen workflow vision of the architect. Those parts of the domain architecture that the project imports from the market or from other projects reflect another Lean principle: leveraging standards – the real-world analogies to the stove being standard stove widths and standard fittings for electrical and gas connections.

Do I sometimes need to trim or cut the cabinets a bit, or add gas or electrical adaptors when installing a stove? Of course. Architecture isn't meant to be cast in stone, but to be an overall guiding light that makes it difficult to create errors of form. Software architecture sometimes needs minor adaptation to accommodate unforeseen needs of a use case scenario. The larger such accommodations are, the more the need for an "all hands on deck" session to assess the extent of the adjustment on all parts of the system.

8.3.1 Creating New Classes and Filling in Existing Function Placeholders

We fill in class member functions or create domain classes as needed, as new use case scenarios call on us to implement their logic. These classes follow many of the common practices you know from good object-oriented design. The designer can organize these classes into class hierarchies to express knowledge about the organization of domain entities or simply to gain the common benefits of inheritance, such as code reuse.

One can argue whether the derived classes – or for that matter, whether any of the classes – should formally be thought of as part of the architecture. After all, architecture is about form, and classes are about structure. However, this is a rather unhelpful argument to have or to resolve, and it's one of those wonderful decisions about which you can let the manager flip a coin. Of course, in the end everything matters; what you call things is a matter of what elicits the best communication in your culture. We can't tell you that.

In the atomic event architecture, user actions are simple and usually correspond to short, simple (hence the word "atomic") operations. Such operations correspond closely to ordinary object methods. One of the easiest, Agile ways to add atomic event functionality is to embed the user-focused feature code in the domain objects (Figure 8-5). This is a particularly relevant technique for small-team projects, such as one might find working on a real-time device controller.

Filling in the domain member functions is straightforward, guided by domain experts' insight and programmers' familiarity with the business. Requirements from the use cases can guide the implementer, but the implementer should not focus too closely on any single use case, keeping the broad domain needs in mind. On the other hand, later re-factoring (re-arranging the code without changing functionality) can evolve today's version of the method (written for this use case) into a more general method. Because domain design drove the structure of the class API, such re-factoring doesn't erode the architectural integrity of the interface.

Domain Analysis

↓

```
class SavingsAccount <
            AccountWithPrintableBalance
        def initialize(balance)        . . . . end
        def availableBalance           . . . . end
        def decreaseBalance(amount) . . . . end
        def increaseBalance(amount) . . . . end
        . . . .
```

Added from use case → *def printBalance(output_device)*

```
        . . . .
    end
        . . . .
end
```

Figure 8-5   Atomic member functions.

Example

Continuing our example from Section 8.2.2, let's look at what the class declaration would look like. Consider an account SavingsAccount that we want to code so it can play the object role of **AccountWithPrintableBalance**. The code could look as simple as this:

```
class SavingsAccount < AccountWithPrintableBalance
    def printBalance(output_device)
        . . . .              # do the actual printing
    end
    . . . .
end
```

Or, in C++:

```
class SavingsAccount:
    public AccountWithPrintableBalance
{
public:
    void printBalance(OutputDevice);
```

```
    . . . .
};


    . . . .


void SavingsAccount::printBalance(OutputDevice printer)
{
    // do the actual printing on the printing device
    . . . .
}
```

Up until this time, `SavingsAccount::printBalance` may have been just a stub that fired an assertion or threw an exception – an architectural placeholder that anticipated the arrival of this use case scenario. But now the time has come to code it up – just in time, in line with Lean principles. We will do the same for all other account types that must support the **AccountWithPrintableBalance** object role.

8.3.2 Back to the Future: This is Just Good Old-Fashioned OO

Such an architectural style evolves to organize "smart" objects: objects that can do more than lie around like dumb data. They can serve user requests. Take care to honor good cohesion within objects and de-coupling between objects; the "smart-ness" of an object shouldn't be an excuse to give it dominion over a host of other objects that it controls or coordinates.

We will later contrast this approach with the DCI approach, which teases all the what-the-system-does functionality out of the dumb domain objects, leaving them dumb. That localizes the more rapidly changing functional logic elsewhere, where its maintenance doesn't become entangled with the domain code. In fact, the atomic event architecture has a liability in that it fattens the interfaces of the domain classes and makes them less "domain-y" – they become hybrid homes for what-the-system-does-and-is alike.

8.3.3 Analysis and Design Tools

Agile is skeptical of tools ("individuals and interactions over processes and tools"), but a tool can be a good thing if it diminishes the tyranny of a process and encourages interactions between individuals. CRC cards (Beck 1991) are one such tool. CRC stands for *C*andidate Object, *R*esponsibilities and *C*ollaborators, and a CRC card is a simple office note card or recipe card with these three fields. We talked a bit about using them to test the architecture in Section 6.1.6 but they are more commonly used as a design tool.

Figure 8-6 shows an example CRC card. A group sits together to read through use case scenarios in turn to create CRC cards whose responsibilities reflect the work to be done. During these scenarios it is usually best to think of the cards as objects (or sometimes as object roles, as described below), rather than as classes. You should strive to gather closely related responsibilities together in each object interface. That will raise the chances that the code for the object – usually coded as a programming language class – will be cohesive.

```
Picture

Rotate                          Canvas
Width                           ColorMap
Height
Location
Move
```

Figure 8-6   A CRC card.

People commonly think of CRC cards as a way of allocating responsibilities to objects: dividing up the work of reaching the goal of a scenario, so that all the necessary responsibilities are accounted for in all the scenarios. Once the object responsibilities have been identified, it is straightforward to code up the classes. In an atomic event architecture each card has a mixture of domain responsibilities and responsibilities that tie directly to a use case.

CRC cards can be used to envision and evolve other artifacts than system objects. A small stockpile of CRC cards can represent the domain classes of a system. Domain class responsibilities come from domain experts rather than from scenarios. Again, in an atomic event architecture, this difference between object and class is largely unimportant.

In Chapter 9 we will cover the DCI architecture. At run time, objects support both the responsibilities that support the use cases and the responsibilities of the deeper domain logic. However, we want the design expressed in source code that separates these two kinds of responsibilities. First we create CRC cards for the domain classes, based on domain expertise as above. We can use CRC cards a second time to distribute use case responsibilities across *object roles*. An object role becomes a use case interface to an object, leaving the general domain operations in the classes. The DCI architecture combines object roles and classes in run-time objects that have all the necessary functionality to actually run, while decoupling the what-the-system-does code from the what-the-system-is code.

A team using CRC cards can be attentive to the specific coupling and cohesion goals of the project as we discussed in Sections 5.2 and 5.3. For example, it may be a goal to keep together all the code that reflects the skill set of a particular geographic location. CRC cards have no built-in coupling and cohesion metric. Use common sense, taste, experience, and insight.

8.3.4   Factoring

Factoring is a simple technique that helps grow the architecture over time. You may notice after a while that methodful object role after methodful object role contains the same logic, and that the logic is independent of the type of the class into which it is injected. That logic can be factored into a base class.

8.3.5   A Caution about Re-Factoring

Re-factoring is a time-honored and effective technique to keep code clean locally. Try to develop a habit of leaving the code cleaner than when you found it; you'll thank yourself later. Robert Martin's book *Clean Code* relates good tips not only about re-factoring, but also about coding conventions that reflect key lean principles (Martin 2009).

Re-factoring is relatively ineffective at fixing architectural problems that span architectural units. Re-factoring should leave code functionality provably invariant, or at least arguably invariant, while improving its structure or expressiveness. It's easy to make such arguments within class scope, particularly if you have a good re-factoring browser that avoids accidentally causing an identifier reference to become bound to a declaration in a different scope than intended. But it is almost impossible to reason about functional invariance when you start moving definitions and declarations across class boundaries.

Will you have to bite the bullet and make such adjustments to your code? They're hard to avoid completely. But a good up-front architecture can reduce them. To argue that you should start with a casually or briefly considered design and then let re-factoring bring you to good code structure recalls an old adage from Grandpa Harry: Hope is not a plan.

8.4   Documentation?

We already have user requirements captured in use cases (Chapter 7), and now have their realization as algorithms captured in the code itself.

Additional documentation is unlikely to add more value – but, as they say in Scrum: inspect and adapt.

It's important to keep use cases and code up to date with each other if you keep use cases around (presumably, you do keep the code around). Nothing is worse than misleading documentation. Consider investing in literate programming and tools like **doxygen** and **Javadoc**, though real-world success with them has been mixed.

Some organizations (especially small teams) keep their CRC cards handy, and turn to them if they need to evaluate emergent scenarios. Alternatively, CRC cards can be created again from scratch on an as-needed basis.

8.5   Why All These Artifacts?

If you're a good old-fashioned object-oriented programmer who has learned to live lean with just objects and classes, all these additional artifacts may look superfluous (and it's going to get even just a little bit worse in Chapter 9). Why do we introduce object roles?

One reason is that object roles usually figure important in the end user's mental model, as described in even some of the trivial examples in this section. Another reason is that as we start to handle more exotic end-user operations when we discuss task-oriented styles, the object roles become an important locus of form that is crucial from a user's perspective: an encapsulation of what the system *does* in a particular use case. For the sake of uniformity, most of the time we use object roles and interfaces even for the simple case.

Another reason for object roles is that we want to explicitly express the form (which is what architecture is all about) separately from the implementation. It can become difficult or impossible to reason about the fundamental form of the system if the code obscures or obfuscates it. Being able to tease out abstract base classes and object roles separate from their derived classes allows us to reason about form. This is important for anyone trying to understand the big picture in a large system – and that implies most of us. Seeing the whole is a key Lean principle.

Software interfaces are a time-honored architectural practice to help decouple parts of the system from each other as well. Such decoupling is a central admonition of the "Gang of Four" (GOF) book (Gamma et al 2005, p. 18) but it has appeared earlier in dozens of texts.

Because we often want to separate the behavioral code from the basic platform code, it is sometimes a good idea to use the DCI architecture even when dealing with requirements that look like atomic events. It's your choice. We talk about DCI in the next chapter. Right after the history lesson.

8.6 History and Such

Object-orientation of course has been around since Simula 67 in 1967. Ole-Johan Dahl and Kristin Nygaard received funding to create an Algol compiler in the early 1960s, and they created the language as an extension of that project. The language was first introduced at a conference in Hamburg in September, 1965 (Dahl and Nygaard 1966).

Trygve Reenskaug invented the Model-View-Controller architecture at Xerox PARC in 1978. Its goal was "to support the user's mental model of the relevant information space and to enable the user to inspect and edit this information" (Reenskaug 2003).

Later Reenskaug would act on his feeling that object-oriented programming languages had lost too much of the notion of object and had started focusing too much on classes. Object-oriented design was missing the concept of object role. Reenskaug would publish his OORAM book that featured object roles as first-class entities of the object model in 1995 (Reenskaug, Wold, and Lehne 1995).

CRC cards came out of the work by Ward Cunningham and Kent Beck (Ward was at Tektronix, and Kent was at Apple) as a way to teach object-oriented thinking. Rebecca Wirfs-Brock, who also worked at Tektronix, popularized CRC cards through her book on responsibility-driven design. However, the first C in CRC never really stood for *class*. The concept had been used in Tektronix for other concepts including abstract classes and subsystems. When Rebecca started working on her second book (Wirfs-Brock and McKean 2003), she really wanted to rename the cards to RRC (carefully note the title of the book that would result), but the stickiness of the name CRC led them to leave it alone – even as she got comments from reviewers.

So "CRC cards" had become a legacy name, in spite of the fact that they could be used for roles (or interfaces, classes, and other abstractions). Rebecca allowed the acronym to persist – but only because she made the C stand for *Candidate* (a concept that would become permanent only when it became proven in the design) instead of for *class*. So today "CRC" stands for *Candidate Objects, Responsibilities, and Collaborations*.

Trygve Reenskaug recalls a conversation with Rebecca Wirfs-Brock at the WOOD conference in Norway in May of 1998. They were discussing responsibility-based design. Trygve suggested that it's not classes that have responsibilities: it's their roles, and he reports that Rebecca concurred.

Coding it Up: The DCI
Architecture

Chapter 8 described an architecture for the relatively simple case where activities in the functional requirements correspond closely to member functions on domain classes. In this chapter we describe how the architecture can encapsulate and express functional requirements that come from true use cases: more elaborate sequences of tasks carried out to accomplish some goal in a context.

9.1   Sometimes, Smart Objects Just Aren't Enough

At the beginning of Chapter 8 we described the kinds of programming structures well suited to a Model-View-Controller architecture, such as the common primitive operations of a graphical shapes editor. In operations such as moving or re-coloring a shape, the algorithmic structure is trivial relative to the program data structure. The Controller can catch the menu selection or mouse button push that indicates a certain command given the context where the gesture occurred, and it can directly dispatch a request to the right model (domain) object to handle that request. Clever designers that we are, we will have enhanced the API of the domain object so that it supports such requests in addition to the "dumb data" operations we take for granted in domain objects.

But computers help us do more than just store data; sometimes, they can tackle complex tasks that actually make the computer seem pretty smart. In most of these cases the end user is thinking of some goal they want to attain through a short sequence of tasks. (It's still a *short* sequence: if the sequence starts verging into coffee-break-duration territory, we don't have an Agile interactive program on our hands any more, but a batch program in disguise.) *The sequence of tasks achieves some goal in a context.* Now, we are firmly in use case land: it is exactly these kinds of tasks that use cases capture. In this space, we are operating at human scales of time and scope.

Both MVC and DCI are about people and their interactions with machines, and that puts us squarely in Agile space. While MVC "separates the parts of a program that are responsible for representing the information in the system and the parts that are responsible for interaction with the user," DCI "minimize[s] any gap that might exist between the programmer's mental model of her program and the program that is actually stored and executed in the computer. In particular, it concretizes how the system realizes system operations as networks of communicating objects" (Reenskaug 2008).

9.2   DCI in a Nutshell

Trygve Reenskaug's DCI system offers an exciting alternative to good old-fashioned object-oriented programming so we can encapsulate the what-the-system-does code on a per-scenario basis. Ordinary object-oriented programming lumps what-the-system-is and what-the-system-does interfaces together. However, these two interfaces change at different rates and are often managed by different groups of people. We want the domain logic (what the system is) to be cohesive; we want the code of each feature to be cohesive; we want good de-coupling between the domain logic and feature logic; and we want to capitalize on Conway's Law. The DCI architecture addresses each of these needs.

To grossly simplify DCI, it separates the architecture into a *d*ata part (the domain part, or what the system *is*, as in Chapter 5) and an *i*nteraction, or feature part (what the system *does*) (Figure 9-1). The interaction part

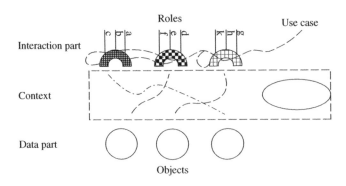

Figure 9-1   DCI in a Nutshell.

becomes connected to the data part on an event-by-event basis by an object called the Context. The architecture can be viewed as Data and Interaction code dynamically connected together by a Context: hence the name Data, Context, and Interaction, or DCI.

The data part comprises the basic, rather dumb domain entities that come from the end user mental model. Data object interfaces are simple and minimal: just enough to capture the domain properties, but without operations that are unique to any particular scenario.

The interaction part expresses a use case, replete with its sunny day scenario and all of its deviations (shown in Figure 9-1 as the multiple potential paths of execution through the roles). We can conceptualize a use case as a single graph of partially ordered steps. However, most use cases express scenarios in terms of interactions between the user roles and the *object roles* involved. So we take the monolithic partial ordering of steps and divide it at object role boundaries. The code captures the use case in terms of object roles instead of being a monolithic procedural structure.

We try a poor metaphor here to illustrate. Think of a central hub for trains. The trains go out from the hub in the morning and eventually come home to roost at night. Each one visits many train stations along the way. Each train station can play the role of a stop for that train; its responsibilities are to discharge passengers and take on new ones, as well as perhaps to take on food, fuel, or a new driver. That train's route is a use case scenario. We could present it as one long track, but the station boundaries are interesting demarcations of the train's journey. The collections of all the train routes (deviations) together are analogous to a use case: a collection of potential scenarios between a user (or *actor*, which here is a train) and the system (the collection of stations). The DCI analogy extends further here because each station is an object that can play many object roles, each object role corresponding to a train stopping at the station.

Object roles are collections of related responsibilities that accomplish their work through each other's responsibilities. We can talk about how waiter and chef roles complete the tasks of a restaurant through their responsibilities without talking in detail about individual waiters or chefs. Some of these responsibilities are just humble services of the domain object that plays the object role during a specific use case enactment. For example, that a chef turns on the gas on the stove or looks up a recipe is unimportant to everyone except the chef: that is likely part of the chef's domain makeup, rather than a use case responsibility.

When a system event occurs, code in the *environment* (often in the MVC Controller object) finds a Context object that understands the object-role-to-object mapping for the use case that corresponds to the event. (We'll discuss later how it finds that Context object.) That allows each domain object to play an object role. The Controller passes control to the Context object, which "wires up" the object roles to the objects, and then kicks off the execution by invoking the object role method that initiates the use case; this is called the *trigger*. In general each object may play several object roles, and a given object role may be played by a combination of several objects together.

9.3   Overview of DCI

The goal of DCI is to separate the code that represents the system state from the code that represents system behavior. This separation is related to but different from MVC's split between data representation and user interaction (Figure 9-2).

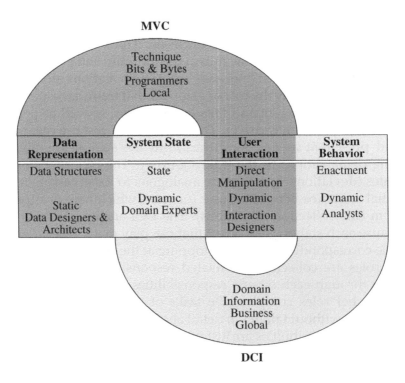

Figure 9-2   Relationship between MVC and DCI.

MVC and DCI are designed to work together as a way for the programmer to reason about the end user's mental models and to capture those models in the code.

9.3.1   Parts of the User Mental Model We've Forgotten

Think of it this way: every piece of software has several structures inspired by real-world, business, and customer concerns and perspectives. Each domain model we built in Chapter 5 is an example of such a model, one that captures the underlying essence of the business structure. The object roles we developed in Section 7.5.5 reflect the end user model of how the program works. Both of these are rather static structures.

In the days of procedural programming, procedures were a natural mechanism to describe program enactment – what the program does. Object-orientation has all but outlawed them. This unnecessary taboo has quashed the expressiveness of object-oriented designers for thirty years. Curiously, the techniques that have recently evolved around object orientation have slowly brought us back to where we can again capture algorithms in an object-oriented framework.

You'll remember our simple picture from earlier in the book (Figure 2-1 on page 28) that splits the design world into what the system is and what the system does. Figure 9-3 is a re-take of that picture. In the what-the-system-is part we have our familiar friends, the classes and the objects (and especially the objects), from Chapter 5. On the other side of the line,

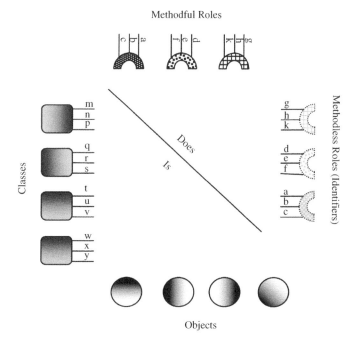

Figure 9-3   Basic DCI architecture.

we find artifacts called *methodless object roles* and *methodful object roles*. The methodless object roles are also old friends: they come from the object roles we created in Section 7.5.5 to capture the end user's cognitive model of the action. Those object roles came directly from the use case (specifically, from a habit).

We represent these roles as identifiers in the programming language, and we refer to the role in the code by referring to its identifier. The identifiers may just be pointers that address the object to which the role is bound, or they may be macros that evaluate to an object pointer, or they may be function invocations, or something else. The goal is to give the programmer the impression that these interactions take place via methods on roles.

These identifiers can be typed, and we refer to their types as *methodless object role types*. These types present the interface to the role: its collected responsibilities. In Java and C#, these types are expressed as interfaces; in C++, we cheat a bit and use abstract base classes. Together these object roles and types are part of the *functional architecture* of the system. They document and codify the contracts between system parts by which they interact to do the end user's bidding. They are form, not structure: the form of enactment.

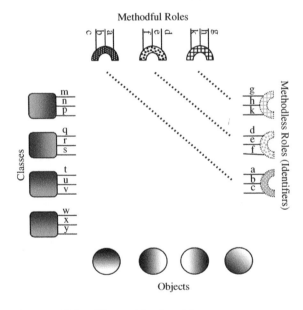

Figure 9-4 Association of identifiers with algorithms.

9.3.2 Enter Methodful Object Roles

The methodful object roles are new animals here. From the outside, they look much like the methodless object roles, that is, like Java or C# interfaces or abstract base classes. But unlike methodless object roles, their methods are filled in with code. These object roles carry the real knowledge of what the system *does*. The use cases and habits live in these methodful object roles. Whereas methodless object roles are *form*, methodful object roles are *structure*.

The system behavior lies distributed throughout the domain objects in classic object orientation. The *behavior* becomes arbitrarily fragmented according to the *domain* partitioning. Because these are two, sometimes orthogonal views, and because domain partitioning is usually the dominant structure in object orientation, we lose the ability to reason cleanly about use case scenarios. The methods may still be atomic and polymorphic and a lot of other things that sound good, but which make any given use case scenario devilishly hard to understand. By contrast, methodful object roles bring the fragments of the algorithm together in one place that corresponds to one concept of the end user world model. (We call this model the *volitive* world model: the end user's model of the form of the action rather than the form of the domain or of the data.)

We still need artifacts that represent the form of the functional architecture apart from its structure, and that capture the interface of the object roles apart from the implementations of their algorithms. Those are the methodless role types, and they often act as the base type for the methodful roles. We desire these methodless object role types because these interfaces change less often than the methods themselves. We want to capture the two different rates of change in two different artifacts. Agile is about managing change, and the interfaces have a different rate of change than the methods. We might have architects oversee the interfaces, and application programmers take care of the methods. In the ideal case, user interaction code (often in the Controller) will usually talk to a methodful object role through an identifier declared as a methodless object role, typed as an interface (Figure 7-1). The real benefit comes in programming languages with compile-time typing because they enforce compliance between the methodless role type interface and the methodful role.

Because methodful object roles have implemented methods and member functions, they can't be Java or C# interfaces. We're not in Kansas any more. Our programming languages are missing a feature to express these concepts. We'll get to that in a second.

These object roles capture what the objects *do*. Well, *what* objects? Ultimately, it's the domain objects. We create domain objects that lack methods to specifically support the what-the-system-does architecture, because domain objects are there to capture the domain (what-the-system-is) structure only. We need to somehow combine the domain objects' code with the code that runs the scenarios. To do that, we will *inject* the scenario code into the classes from which those objects were created.

Where does that code come from? We can count on there being a single, closed, maintainable copy of that code in the methodful object role. We can inject that code into each class whose objects must take on the corresponding object role at some point during their lifetime (Figure 9-5).

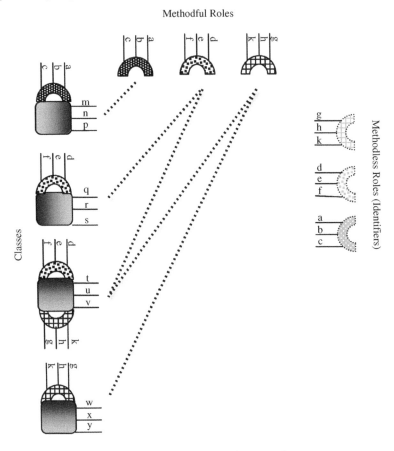

Figure 9-5   Using traits to inject algorithms into domain classes.

9.3.3 Tricks with Traits

How do we do that? We can use a programming approach called *traits* (Schärli et al 2003). A trait is a holder of stateless methods. If you don't know traits, you can think of them as a little like mix-ins. Traits use language tricks (different tricks in different languages and environments) to effectively compose *classes* together. We treat one class as though it is an object role, while the other class is a domain class, and we inject the logic of the former into the latter. We can make a methodful object role a trait of a class to inject its functionality into that class. This leaves methodful object roles generic, decoupled from the class into which they are injected. The word "generic" rings true here in several implementations of traits, as we'll often turn to a programming language feature of the same name to implement them. Methods of the object role can invoke methods of the domain class into which they are injected. We'll show you details in the next section.

Now we can finally get back to objects. The objects come and go in the system as initialization and business scenarios create and destroy them. Each object can take on all the object roles for all the scenarios we have designed it to support. Of course, multiple objects will often (in fact, usually) work together to support any single given scenario. When there is work to be done, where do we go to get it done? How does that object know of the other objects with which it is supposed to collaborate during an enactment?

9.3.4   Context Classes: One Per Use Case

We define a Context class for each use case and for each habit (page 277). A Context knows the object roles that are involved in any given use case, and its implementation holds the methodless object role identifiers declared in terms of their methodless object role types (interfaces or abstract base classes: Figure 9-6). For any given invocation of a use case scenario, those

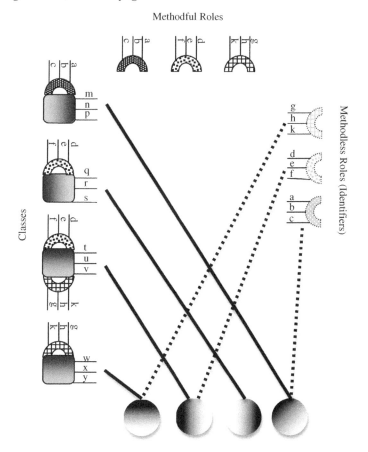

Figure 9-6   DCI object instantiation and identifier bindings.

object roles must be bound to objects. Those bindings can be externally retrieved through public methods of the respective Context object.

There is one Context object per use case, *not* per use case scenario. The Context is able to set up the object role-to-instance mappings under all the possible starting conditions for a given use case, and then start off the use case. Even though the Context may always start the use case with the same method on the same role, the use case may follow millions of different paths depending on the argument values and states of the domain objects. The code in the methodful roles should capture the logic not only for the sunny day scenario but also for the deviations. Each use case may have dozens of such deviations.

To start up a use case we instantiate its Context object. The Context object can use any means available to bind its object role identifiers to any objects that exist in the system. Of course, it uses contextual knowledge to ensure that a given object role is bound only to an object that supports that object role's interface. Programming languages with static type checking can help enforce this assumption and can produce compile-time errors if the designer tries to create the wrong associations.

And then the Context object just invokes the first method of the first object role. An object plays that role, and the method starts executing for the object into which the role is injected. If that object needs to communicate with another, it does so in terms of its role identity rather than its object identity because we describe the use case in terms of roles rather than objects. Where is its role identity? A methodless object role identifier serves as the name of the role. Any role can interact with any other by invoking a suitable method on that role's methodless object role identifier.

The DCI architecture wires up that role to the object for which its methods are invoked on a use case-by-use case basis. Invoking a role method causes code to be executed that retrieves the identity of the object currently playing that role from the Context object. The designer provides the code that maps roles to instances on a per-use-case basis.

This may sound a bit contrived, but let's look at some of the design tradeoffs here:

1. Polymorphism: At the level of programming-in-the-large, it's gone. Actually, we have moved it to the Context object, which dynamically and explicitly chooses a group of objects to take a given set of behaviors (method invocations) instead of deferring the method choice to the last microsecond of invocation. So we remove much of the uncertainty of the where-will-this-polymorphic-dispatch-end-up problem. There is still a degree of uncertainty because of the dynamic binding of Context object role identifiers. However, the binding is under explicit control of the business logic in Context, so we can reason about the dispatching in business terms. Besides, the scenario logic is all in the methodful object roles – for any given

object role and method, there is just one implementation. The polymorphism plays out only in the methodful object roles' invocation of methods on `self`, methods that are deferred to the domain object. Trygve Reenskaug, the inventor of the DCI approach, says: "We solve the problem by suspending polymorphism for the methods that are essential for the integrity of the solution." Of course, you can still use good old-fashioned polymorphism in the domain classes – a powerful way to organize the software families that come out of domain-driven design.

2. There is a nice degree of compression going on here. All objects that play a given object role process the same interaction messages with the same methods. That's Lean.

3. Code readability: Algorithms now read like algorithms. You can look at the code of a methodful object role and reason about it, analyze it, maybe even stub it off and unit test it.

4. The rapidly evolving what-the-system-does code can evolve independently of the (hopefully more stable) what-the-system-is code. The domain structure no longer defines nor constrains the run-time structure. Early in system development you'll be filling in methods of both kinds of classes together, but the domain-driven design will help the domain class methods become stable over time.

5. We now have a place to reason about system state and behavior, not just object state and behavior.

6. Though not simplistic, DCI is simple. It is as simple as it can be, if our goal is to capture the end user's mental models in the code – end user engagement is crucial to success in Agile. That's usually a good thing, because it helps contain evolution well and helps us understand and communicate requirements better. In addition, it was the whole goal of object-orientation in the first place. Consider these four concepts: having a usability focus in design, object orientation, Agile software development, and the DCI paradigm – they are all just different ways to express the same deep fundamentals.

7. We make the code more failure-proof by keeping the domain interfaces minimal and separate from the feature logic. They are no longer polluted with the role operations as in the atomic event architecture. The domain classes provide simpler, clearer design constraints than in ordinary object-oriented programming.

What we have done here is to tease out a different kind of commonality than we talked about in Chapter 5. The object roles and Context objects define a recurring commonality of *behavior* or *algorithm* that is independent of the objects that carry out those algorithms, and also of the classes of the objects that carry out the algorithm. Those commonalities relate closely to the end-user mental model (volitive model) of system behavior. What varies is the set of objects into which those behaviors' roles are injected, enactment by enactment.

Context objects can themselves play object roles that come from the end user mental model! Consider the public interface of a Context object: it provides the API by which we enact individual use cases. Let's say that we group related use case scenarios ("related" in the sense that they work with the same object role combinations and that they use similar strategies to map object roles to objects) together in one Context object. That object now represents a collection of related responsibilities. That's an object in the end user mental model, or more precisely, the object role played by some object. We'll explore this concept further in Section 9.6.

In the following sections, we illustrate how to use DCI with the simple banking funds transfer example from Section 7.5.3.

9.4   DCI by Example

We kick off a DCI design when the business decides that the software needs to offer a new service that can be expressed in terms of scenarios. DCI is optimized for designs where the form of the scenario is as important as the form of the underlying data model. We think of a banking transfer (primarily) as an algorithm that operates on two or more financial instruments (which are the secondary focus – we are concerned about their details only with respect to their object roles in the transfer).

9.4.1   The Inputs to the Design

DCI starts with two major inputs that together capture the end user mental model of their world. The first input is the domain model, which we reduced to code in Section 6.1. In addition to the code, we have the domain documentation that was also developed in Chapter 5, and may also have some domain-level patterns that describe high-level system form. For example, a banking system may include financial instruments, transactions, audit trails, and other actuarial artifacts that capture the current state of holdings and investments.

The second input is the role model, which we developed in Section 7.5.5. The role model conveys the user's understanding of system dynamics. For example, a funds transfer in a bank would involve financial instruments as object roles called source account and destination account.

In addition to these two inputs, we also need the use case scenario that we are implementing. The use case will become an algorithm that

Use case name: Transfer Money
User intent: To transfer money between his or her own accounts.
Motivation: The Account Holder has an upcoming payment that must be made from an account that has insufficient funds
Preconditions: The Account Holder has identified himself or herself to the system
Happy day scenario:

Step	Actor Intention	System Responsibility
1.	Account Holder enters a source account and requests an account transfer	System displays the source account, provides a list of valid destination accounts, and a field to enter the amount
2.	Account Holder selects a destination account, enters the amount, and accepts	System displays transfer information and requests a password
3.	Account Holder enters the password and accepts the transfer	System moves <u>money and does accounting</u>

Variations:
1a. Account Holder has only one account: tell the Account Holder that this cannot be done
2a. The accounts do not exist or are invalid…
Post-conditions:
✓ The money is moved
✓ The accounts balance
✓ The log reflects the exact intent of the transaction (a transfer is a transfer, not a withdrawal and a deposit)

Figure 9-7 Transfer money use case (evolved from Table 7-5).

we reduce to code for the new business service. We use the use case of Figure 9-7.

9.4.2 Use Cases to Algorithms

In Section 7.5.5 we discussed the design path that takes us from user stories to use cases to algorithms. Use cases are overkill for atomic event architectures, but they capture important scenarios and variations for more complex requirements. It's important to realize that a use case is not an algorithm, and that the algorithm in the code may reflect sequencing decisions, implementation of business rules, and other details that aren't explicit in any single use case scenario.

Let's start with the use case for transferring money between two accounts in Chapter 7, which we introduced in Section 7.5.1. This is a classic use case that captures the users' (Account Holders') intent, the responsibilities they must fulfill to carry out that intent, and the system responsibilities that support the Account Holders in achieving their goal. This use case builds on a use case habit that does the actual money transfer (<u>Move Money and Do Accounting</u>).

We will examine the <u>Move Money and Do Accounting</u> habit (use case fragment) in more detail below. How will that use case habit know which accounts to use? The <u>Transfer Money</u> use case must be stateful: that is, it must remember the decision made in step 3 for use in step 6. Here are three possible approaches to passing this information:

1. The methodful object role for the <u>Transfer Money</u> use case remembers the accounts and uses them when it sets up the Context object for the <u>Move Money and Do Accounting</u> habit. We talk more about this approach in Section 9.4.5.

2. The Controller takes on this responsibility somewhere over in MVC. However, the Controller is architecturally quite a bit distant from this use case logic, and that implies bad coupling. It may mean that programmers will need to make coordinated updates if there is a change in the kinds of accounts supported by the bank.

3. The <u>Transfer Money</u> use case stores the information in the Model. If the Model contains a transaction object that scopes the account selection and transfer, this could work out well. However, it may require some ingenuity on the part of the developer if this transaction time is overly long. It also greatly complicates things if multiple applications simultaneously use the same Model object.

In Figure 9-8, we recall the <u>Move Money and Do Accounting</u> habit from Section 7.5.1. The habit captures what the system does after the Account Holder or some other actor initiates a money transfer. We'll use it as our coding example, showing how to capture those business interactions in code. Before coding, we have to translate the use case or habit *sequence* into an *algorithm* that a computer can execute. In general, use case scenarios also must be translated to algorithms.

Habit Name: Move Money and Do Accounting

Preconditions: A valid Source Account and Destination Account have been identified, and the amount to be transferred is known

Sequence:

1. SourceAccount object verifies funds available
2. SourceAccount and DestinationAccount update their balances
3. SourceAccount updates statement info

Post-conditions:
   ✓ The periodic statements reflect the exact intent of the transaction (a transfer is a transfer–not a pair of a withdrawal and a deposit)

Figure 9-8 Move Money and Do Accounting habit (updated from Figure 7-3).

We describe the algorithm in terms of the object roles (as discussed in the next section) from the previous step. The focus moves from actors in the real world to the software artifacts in the program. This is where the transition happens that makes object-oriented programming what it is: a way to capture the end user conceptual model in the program form. We'll formalize this transition in the next step when we choose a concrete expression for object roles that captures the actor semantics, but we try to look ahead a bit here already.

The habit in Figure 9-8 presents the perspective of a single stakeholder, which may be the Account Holder. Yet the code must run for all stakeholders. While there is no concept of a transaction in the mental model of the Account Holder, there is such a concept in the mental model of the Actuary. Such complications make the code a bit more involved than we can deduce from any single scenario alone. This is one weakness of DCI. One rarely will be able to find the main success scenario in the code, but instead will find it woven together with the decision points associated with its deviations. It would take strong measures to circumvent this problem, and would probably require moving outside Von Neumann paradigms to express this behavior branching in a radically different way. Rule-based and dataflow approaches might apply here, but the solution is outside the scope of our discussion here.

The actual algorithm may look like this; it is one of several possible viable implementations:

1. Source account begins transaction
2. Source account verifies funds available (notice that this must be done inside the transaction to avoid an intervening withdrawal! This step reflects deviation 2a from Table 7-4.)
3. Source account reduces its own balance
4. Source account requests that Destination Account increase its balance
5. Source Account updates its log to note that this was a transfer (and not, for example, simply a withdrawal)
6. Source account requests that Destination Account update its log
7. Source account ends transaction
8. Source account informs the Teller Object that the transfer has succeeded

We map the use case steps into an algorithm (Table 9-1) that the computer can execute in a deterministic way. It becomes ordinary procedural code. We will implement the code by linking together small, individually understandable operations on roles. The algorithm also captures business needs that come from other requirements, such as the need to not lose any

Table 9-1 Scenario-to-algorithm mapping.

1. **Source Account** verifies funds available (deviation 2a in Table 7-4)	1. **Source Account** begins transaction.
	2. **Source Account** verifies that its current balance is greater than the *minimum account balance* plus the withdrawal *amount*, and throws an exception if not
2. **Source Account** and **Destination Account** update their balances	3. **Source Account** reduces its own balance by the *amount*
	4. **Source Account** requests that **Destination Account** increase its balance
3. **Source Account** updates statement information	5. **Source Account** updates its log to note that this was a transfer
	6. **Source Account** requests that **Destination Account** update its log
	7. **Source Account** ends transaction
	8. **Source Account** returns status that the transfer has succeeded

The algorithm captures deviations for situations such as negative account balances, which is not in the sunny day scenario

money in the process (implemented as transactions) and the deviation for a potentially negative balance (the conditional test in step 2).

9.4.3 Methodless Object Roles: The Framework for Identifiers

Each scenario is expressed in terms of responsibilities of object roles that originate in the mind of the end user. We want these roles also to find their way into the mind of the programmer and into the code itself. What are called *actors* in the requirements domain sometimes become object roles in the coding domain; however, it is more common that actors remain to be human beings outside the system, and object roles represent the concepts inside the system – though those concepts are mirrored in those humans' minds.

We represent methodless object roles just as identifiers, and they are usually declared within the scope of their Context object (Figure 9-9). Each methodless role has its own type when implemented in a language with compile-time typing. We call these types simply *methodless object role types*, and they correspond to the way we classify object roles in a use case. They are to the what-the-system-does architecture as abstract base classes are to

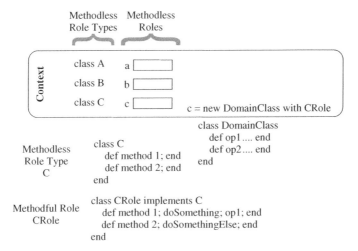

Figure 9-9 Object roles.

the what-the-system-is architecture. The translation from use case concepts to object role types and object roles is straightforward (see Section 7.5.5).

In C++, we code up methodless object role types as abstract base classes; in C#, they are interfaces. Because Smalltalk and Ruby lack compile-time typing there is neither a need nor a place for a methodless object role type. In these more dynamic languages, object roles can be of type `Object`.

There is often just one just identifier within each Context for each methodless role type. In languages with stronger compile-time typing, the abstract base class hides the implementation of the methodful object roles from the object role's clients (which in turn are usually other object roles). As we'll see later, methodful object roles are often coded in a generic way using techniques like templates, and we don't want the role-level system interactions to be dependent on domain object details that show up in the template parameter of the methodful object role.

There is no need to separate the type of the declared methodless role identifier from the type of the methodful role in Ruby, Objective-C and Smalltalk. We may still want to use abstract base classes as the interfaces to roles, for parallelism with the use of abstract base classes in the what-the-system-is architecture described above. So we can still declare methodless role types that have neither algorithm code nor data structure. They are pure protocol. The implementation will come later in the methodful object roles that are sub-classed from the methodless object role types. This separation gives us the flexibility to define a role-based architecture up front, building on deep domain knowledge that incorporates foresight from previously built systems, without investing too deeply in implementation.

```
module MoneySource                                        #   1
    def decreaseBalance(amount); end                      #   2
    def transferTo(amount, recipient); end                #   3
end                                                       #   4
                                                          #   5
module MoneySink                                          #   6
    def increaseBalance(amount); end                      #   7
    def updateLog(message, time, amount); end             #   8
    def transferFrom(amount, moneySource); end            #   9
end                                                       #  10
```

In C++:

```
class MoneySource {                                       //   1
public:                                                   //   2
    virtual void decreaseBalance(Currency amount) = 0;    //   3
    virtual void transferTo(Currency amount,              //   4
            MoneySink *recipient) = 0;                    //   5
};                                                        //   6
                                                          //   7
class MoneySink {                                         //   8
public:                                                   //   9
    virtual void increaseBalance(Currency amount)         //  10
                = 0;                                      //  11
    virtual void updateLog(string, MyTime,                //  12
            Currency) = 0;                                //  13
    virtual void transferFrom(Currency amount,            //  14
            MoneySource *source) = 0;                     //  15
};                                                        //  16
```

The **MoneySource** object role member functions are virtual. In theory, we could bind all the member function invocations at run time by putting all the type information into the templates that implement the traits. However, that would complicate the C++ code and make it less readable. Instead, we use the common C++ approach that abstract base classes define the protocol / interface to a group of classes whose objects will play that role.

The virtualness of the functions makes it possible for Context objects and other citizens of the program, such as MVC objects, to access **MoneySource** and **MoneySink** accounts generically. They also document and enforce the domain contract for the objects that will play these object roles. For example, all MoneySource objects must have a decreaseBalance method, and all MoneySink objects must have an increaseBalance method. These are dumb, simple domain methods that methodful object roles expect to be present in the objects for which they execute. Placing these pure virtual functions in these base class interfaces provides a compile-time guarantee that the derived classes will meet the expectations of the methodful object roles.

9.4.4 Partitioning the Algorithms Across Methodful Object Roles

Now it's time to capture the use case requirements as algorithms in the methodful object roles. This is the heart of DCI's key benefits to the system stakeholders: that the original requirements are clear from the code itself.

Traits as a Building Block

Before discussing methodful object roles in the next section, we take a quick diversion here to describe traits in a bit more detail. Our goal in DCI is to separate the use case knowledge in one place from the domain knowledge in another. We want to separate system state from system behavior. Both the behavior knowledge and the domain knowledge have the outward appearance of being collections of behaviors. We think of such a collection as being an object when representing the form of the domain, and as being an object role when representing the end user's model of system behavior.

What we want to do in DCI is to compose an object role and its algorithms together with an object and its domain logic. However, few programming languages support object roles with methods and few programming languages let us program objects. Instead, the main building blocks are classes. To a first approximation, what we want to do is to glue two classes together. More specifically, the class representing the object roles is a collection of stateless, generic methods. They must be able to work with a somewhat anonymously typed notion of `this` or `self`, because the class with which the object role is composed determines the type of the object. The class representing the domain logic is, well, just a class. How do we compose these two? That's what traits do for us.

In Smalltalk

Schärli did his original implementation of traits in Smalltalk. Each class gets an additional field that implicates the traits with which it is composed, together with other properties of traits that we don't need for DCI. Furthermore, in DCI, we block the possibility of trait overrides in the class. This traits field is used during method lookup if the desired method selector isn't found in the methods of the class itself: the method dictionaries of the injected object roles (classes) are checked if the class search fails. We will return to the Smalltalk implementation in more detail in Section 9.8.5 below.

In C++

In C++, it's a bit more straightforward. Consider a trait T that contains algorithms t1 and t2:

```
template <class derived> class T                          // 1
{                                                         // 2
public:                                                   // 3
    virtual void derivedClassFunction(int, int) = 0;      // 4
    void t1(void) {                                       // 5
        derivedClassFunction(1, 2);                       // 6
        . . . .                                           // 7
    }                                                     // 8
    void t2(void) {                                       // 9
        . . . .                                           // 10
    }                                                     // 11
};                                                        // 12
```

This trait represents the object role T, a role characterized by its methods t1 and t2. Note that T presumes on the class into which it will be injected to support the method void derivedClassFunction(int,int) (line 4). Of course, an object role doesn't have to depend on the presence of a function in its target class, but it's a common situation that we want to support.

We include the type parameter derived for the common case that the trait wants to express business logic in terms of the type of the actual object involved in the use case. Making it a parameter leaves the trait generic so that it is possible to decouple its maintenance from that of any domain class in particular. A common use of this parameter is to provide access to SELF, which is the (typed) object currently playing the object role:

```
template <class ConcreteDerived>
class TransferMoneySource: public MoneySource
{
protected:
    ConcreteDerived *SELF(void) const {
        return dynamic_cast<ConcreteDerived*>(this);
    }
```

This construct makes it possible for the object role member functions to directly invoke operations in the interface of the class whose object currently is playing the object role. It is a more general way to achieve the same

effect as the pure virtual function at line 4 of the declaration of `template`
`T` above. Consider such a member function of the `TransferMoneySource`
object role template, which decreases the balance in its object through the
class interface of, for example, a `SavingsAccount` class into which it has
been injected:

```
void withdraw(Currency amount) {
    SELF()->decreaseBalance(amount);
    . . . .
}
```

We want to inject this object role into classes of all objects that play this
role at some time or another so the class gives those objects the appearance
of supporting `t1` and `t2` in their public interface. Let's assume that one
of those objects is an object of class `D`. We inject the object role when we
declare `D`:

```
class D: public T<D>
{
public:
    void derivedClassFunction(int a, int b) {
        . . . .
    }
    . . . .
};
```

Now all instances of `D` will have the appearance of supporting methods `t1`
and `t2` in their public interface. We can inject additional object roles into
`D` using multiple inheritance. It's safe to do this because traits contain no
data. Of course, it's important to resolve name collisions between object
roles (the C++ compiler will tell you if there is any ambiguity and if you
need to do so). It should also be obvious that the trait `T` can be injected into
other classes as well, while remaining the single, closed definition of the
algorithms `t1` and `t2`. So, to introduce what the declaration looks like for
the account example,

```
class SavingsAccount:
    public TransferMoneySource<SavingsAccount>
{
public:
    void decreaseBalance(Currency amount) {
        . . . .
    }
};
```

In Ruby

Ruby is even more elegant. Here is the role, **TransferMoneySource**, declared as a Ruby module that will be used as a trait. In Ruby we don't need the extra level of the methodless object role types because the interesting typing happens at run time, so it doesn't cause type dependency problems at compile time. However, we can include the MoneySource methodless object role type as documentation, and for parallelism with the class hierarchy in the domain architecture:

```ruby
module TransferMoneySource
    # A methodful object role
    include MoneySource, ContextAccessor

    def transferTo
      . . . .
      self.decreaseBalance context.amount
      . . . .
    end
end
```

(The ContextAccessor module gives us access to the run-time Context; we'll be talking about Contexts in more detail later.) We also have an ordinary domain class, like a SavingsAccount, into which we want to inject this trait:

```ruby
class SavingsAccount
    . . . .
    def decreaseBalance(amount)
      . . . .
    end
end
```

At some point in the execution we may instantiate a SavingsAccount object, and shortly thereafter we may decide that we want it to participate in a money transfer use case in which it will play the object role of a **TransferMoneySource**. In Ruby, we make this association at run time:

```ruby
sourceAccountForTransfer = SavingsAccount.new(account)
sourceAccountForTransfer.extend TransferMoneySource
context.setAmount amountToBeTransferred
sourceAccountForTransfer.transferTo
```

The `extend` directive dynamically injects the methods of `Transfer-MoneySource` into the account object at run time.

Some languages support traits even more directly. Scala (Odersky et al 2008) is one such language; we will discuss its implementation of traits and DCI in Section 9.8.1.

With traits and object role injection in hand, let's go on to defining methodful object roles!

Coding it Up: C++

Here we apply the approach of Section 9.2 to this example. This is a boring algorithm to the extent that most of the processing takes place inside one object role: the Source Account (`TransferMoneySource`). The Destination Account (`TransferMoneySink`) contains a little logic to receive the funds.

Let's write the C++ code first. (If you find C++ unfriendly, just skim this section and focus on the Ruby example below.) First we define some macros as a convenient way to look up the current object bindings for the object roles involved in the use case. We need to look up two object roles: the object currently playing the current object role (self), and the recipient of the transfer. We define macros as follows:

```
#define SELF \                                               // 1
        static_cast<const ConcreteDerived*>(this)      // 2
                                                             // 3
#define RECIPIENT ((MoneySink*) \                       // 4
    (static_cast<TransferMoneyContext*> \               // 5
    (Context::currentContext_)->destinationAccount())))  // 6
```

The SELF macro evaluates to point to *whatever object is playing the current object role*. It is used by code within an object role to invoke member functions of the object role self, or `this`. As we shall see shortly, this allows the code in the object role to "down-call" to methods of the derived class into which the trait is injected.

Using macros makes it possible to use object role names directly in the code. So we can say something like:

```
RECIPIENT->increaseBalance(amount)                        // 7
```

and that will find whatever object is currently playing the object role of the recipient, and will apply the `increaseBalance` method to it. We could also do this with inline member functions `self()` and `recipient()`, but the function syntax is slightly distracting. Use the member functions if that is your taste.

Next, we create a template that implements the trait for the object role.

```
template <class ConcreteDerived>              //   8
class TransferMoneySource: public MoneySource //   9
{                                             //  10
```

Now we come to the interesting parts: the object role behaviors. We can start with a single, simple behavior that implements the transfer of money from the current object role (**TransferMoneySource**) to the object role **TransferMoneySink**.

```
public:                                        //  11
                                               //  12
  // Object role behaviors                     //  13
  void transferTo(Currency amount) {           //  14
      // This code is reviewable and           //  15
      // meaningfully testable with stubs!     //  16
      beginTransaction();                      //  17
      if (SELF->availableBalance() < amount) { //  18
          endTransaction();                    //  19
          throw InsufficientFunds();           //  20
      } else {                                 //  21
          SELF->decreaseBalance(amount);       //  22
          RECIPIENT->transferFrom(amount);     //  23
          SELF->updateLog("Transfer Out", DateTime(), //  24
                              amount);         //  25
      }                                        //  26
      gui->displayScreen(SUCCESS_DEPOSIT_SCREEN); //  27
      endTransaction();                        //  28
  }                                            //  29
```

The code also accesses the macro RECIPIENT, which returns the object playing the object role of the **TransferMoneySink**. We'll talk about that member function later.

Here is the analogous code for the other trait, representing the **TransferMoneySink** object role.

```
template <class ConcreteDerived>           //   1
class TransferMoneySink: public MoneySink  //   2
{                                          //   3
public:                                    //   4
```

```
    void transferFrom(Currency amount) {              //  5
        SELF->increaseBalance(amount);                //  6
        SELF->updateLog("Transfer in",                //  7
                        DateTime(), amount);          //  8
    }                                                 //  9
};                                                    // 10
```

The classes `TransferMoneySource` and `TransferMoneySink` together capture the algorithm for transferring money from a source account to a destination (sink) account – independent of whether it is a savings or investment account. (We'll look at savings and investments accounts below.) The algorithm is a top-down composition of two sub-algorithms: an outer `transferTo` algorithm that invokes in an inner `transferFrom` algorithm. We associate those algorithms with the object roles to which they are most tightly coupled. Other than that, they behave just as procedures in a simple procedural design.

Each of these methodful object roles captures its part of the algorithm of transferring money from one account to another. Each method is a reasonably sized mental chunk of the overall algorithm. This chunking helps us understand the overall transfer in terms of its pieces, instead of overwhelming the reader with a single procedure that captures all the steps of the transfer. Yes, we use procedural decomposition here – or is it just a method invocation? The point is that the right logic is in the right place with respect to the roles that come from the end user mental model. The transfer logic doesn't belong to any single account class.

Coding Up DCI in Ruby

The Ruby code is in fact a little less impressive because so many of the type relationships are hidden until run time. That's probably a good thing: there are no points for impressive code. The whole point of DCI to the programmer is that the code be more readable, and we'll take language support where we can get it.

The C++ version uses macros to clean up the syntax; there is a DCI aesthetic that an object role should look like an identifier, and not like a function call as it would in C++ if we lacked macros. Ruby's syntax doesn't unnecessarily distinguish between identifiers and functions. In C++ we do method injection using templates; in Ruby, we'll use run-time reflection.

We can add convenience for the programmer working on the methodful roles with a little architectural expressiveness in the methodless role. Consider the methodless role **MoneySource**, which we introduced above as an interface to the simple operations that make a **MoneySource** a money source. We can add methods that provide access to other roles used by the methods of the methodful roles that extend **MoneySource**:

```
module MoneySource                                        #   1
    def decreaseBalance(amount); end                      #   2
    def transferTo(amount, recipient); end                #   3
    # Role aliases for use by the methodful role          #   4
    def destination_account                               #   5
       context.destination_account                        #   6
    end                                                   #   7
    def creditors; context.creditors end                  #   8
    def amount; context.amount end                        #   9
end                                                       #  10
```

Now, if there is code inside a methodful role like **TransferMoneySource** that wants to access the **DestinationAccount** role, it can simply invoke des-tination_account. We'll see that in the code of the `TransferMoneySource` module below.

Let's start with the `TransferMoneySource` trait. In Ruby it is a `Module`. `Module` is the superclass of `Class` in Ruby. Modules can be used as mixins in another class. Mixins achieve our goal of composing two different "classes" into one object. That gives the end user an integrated view of a single object that combines domain functionality and business behavior, while allowing the programmer to treat these two facets separately.

```
module TransferMoneySource                                 #   1
   include MoneySource, ContextAccessor                    #   2
                                                           #   3
   # Object role behaviors                                 #   4
                                                           #   5
   def transferTo                                          #   6
     beginTransaction                                      #   7
     raise "Insufficient funds" if balance < amount        #   8
     self.decreaseBalance amount                           #   9
     destination_account.transferFrom amount               #  10
     self.updateLog "Transfer Out", Time.now, amount        #  11
     gui.displayScreen SUCCESS_DEPOSIT_SCREEN               #  12
     endTransaction                                         #  13
   end                                                      #  14
 end                                                        #  15
```

The `include` directive on line 2 brings the Context object into the picture. We'll talk about Contexts in the next section. They're the place where object roles become connected to their objects. If the method in one methodful object role operates on another object role in the current use case, it has to have a handle to the object currently playing that object role so it can make it the target of the appropriate method invocation. So if `MoneySource` wants to deposit money in the `MoneySink`, it looks up the `MoneySink` object `destination_account` in the Context as in line 10 in the above code.

Note that because this module invokes methods like `decreaseBalance` at line 9 and `updateLog` at line 11, it is defined as an abstract base class in Ruby. The domain object must provide the `updateLog` function. The Context will glue together this object role with the domain object. We'll discuss this below.

Other than that, the `transferTo` method simply captures the responsibilities it has as an object role in the money transfer use case.

Here is the analogous code for the TransferMoneySink object role.

```
module TransferMoneySink                            #  1
    include MoneySink, ContextAccessor              #  2
                                                    #  3
    # Object role behaviors                         #  4
                                                    #  5
    def transferFrom                                #  6
        self.increaseBalance amount                 #  7
        self.updateLog 'Transfer in', Time.now,     #  8
                context.amount                      #  9
    end                                             # 10
end                                                 # 11
```

Again, these two modules implement object roles that together define what it means to transfer funds between two accounts.

9.4.5 The Context Framework

We need a Context class for each use case. The Context brings together the elements of the end user's mental models for a use case.

Consider our end user Marion who wants to do a funds transfer. One part of Marion's brain has the concepts MoneySource and MoneySink in mind when enacting this use case; those are the roles of what-the-system-does. Another part of Marion's brain has reasoned about the transfer in terms of an amount, in terms of Marion's InvestmentAccount and in terms of Marion's SavingsAccount: these are the things of what-the-system-is.

The main job of the Context is to manage the mapping between these two perspectives.

In more detail, the job of the Context object for a given use case is:

1. To look up the actual objects that should participate in this particular use case invocation. This is like a "database lookup," using knowledge at hand to find the actual domain objects that represent the data of interest in this "transaction;"

2. To associate these objects with the object roles they play in the current use case of this type;

3. To start enactment of the use case when its trigger method is called;

4. To publish the interface bindings for use by the methodful object roles that participate in this use case.

Think of the associations between the object roles and objects as being like a simple table that the Context object builds inside of itself (Figure 9-10). A fresh Context object and a fresh set of associations between object roles and instances come together for each use case enactment. The Context

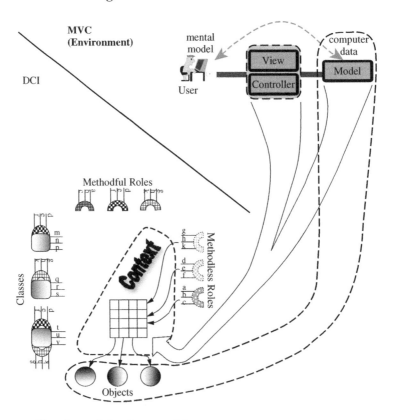

Figure 9-10   The place of the Context object.

builds the table using data in the *environment* (mainly in the data and the Controller of the MVC code) together with its knowledge of how the use case pieces (algorithms, object roles and objects) fit together.

The Ruby Code

Since this scenario accomplishes a money transfer, let's name the Context class `TransferMoneyContext`. The `TransferMoneyContext` class doesn't encapsulate the scenario per se, but encapsulates knowledge of what actors to bring to the stage for a given scene of the play. It might look like this:

```
class TransferMoneyContext                              #  1
    attr_reader :source_account,                        #  2
            :destination_account, :amount               #  3
```

The Context provides APIs that clients can use to map a role onto the object currently playing the role. These APIs can be used by code within one role that wants to invoke a method on another role. The methods `attr_reader`, `source_account` and `destination_account` are readers for the methodless object roles held within the body of the context object. They are set up when the Context is initialized (below, at lines 12 and 15 of the code). In fact, to the programmer, these accessors themselves behave as the methodless object roles: they are the symbols used by one object role to access another.

The code continues:

```
    include ContextAccessor                             #  4
                                                        #  5
    def self.execute(amt, sourceID, sinkID)             #  6
        TransferMoneyContext.new(amt, sourceID,         #  7
                sinkID).execute                         #  8
end                                                     #  9
                                                        # 10
```

We need to include a `ContextAccessor` (the code follows below). The `include` statement makes the accessor a mixin of the Context. The definition of the class method `self.execute` – the *trigger method* – at line 6 shows how he Context starts execution of a use case. This Context, called `TransferMoneyContext`, is designed to start up the <u>Transfer Money</u> use case. The static method creates an instance of the Context object, passing on the execution arguments to its `initialize` method (also coming below). Once the Context is set up, at line 8 this *class* execute method calls the *instance* execute method (line 19, below) to actually run the use case.

The `initialize` method is straightforward. It retrieves the objects that will enact the use case, injects object role methods into those objects as necessary, and leaves a Context object ready to execute:

```
def initialize(amt, sourceID, sinkID)              # 11
    @source_account = Account.find(sourceID)       # 12
    @source_account.extend TransferMoneySource     # 13
                                                   # 14
    @destination_account = Account.find(destID)    # 15
    @destination_account.extend TransferMoneySink  # 16
    @amount = amt                                  # 17
end                                                # 18
                                                   # 19
```

The Context object comes into being at the beginning of the use case enactment. It has to go through memory and find the objects (the actors) for this act in the play. It then has to cast them (in the theatrical sense) into the object roles they will play. The `Account.find` invocations at lines 12 and 15 round up the actors, perhaps going into some database and finding them on the basis of some criteria (here, hopefully, on the basis of having the right account number).

The magic occurs at line 13. The `extend` method invocation causes the methods of `TransferMoneySource` to be injected into the `source_account` object. In Ruby, we can do this without regard to the class of the `source_account` object.

The final bit of the Context object is the instance execution method. The `execute` method (the trigger method) simply transfers control to the method of the first methodful object role to receive control in the use case (line 21). The `execute_in_context` method comes from the `ContextAccessor` mixin and is used to stack contexts (as when invoking the code of a habit from within another use case: habits are like use cases and also have their own Contexts).

```
def execute                                # 19
    execute_in_context do                  # 20
        source_account.transferTo          # 21
    end                                    # 22
end                                        # 23
```

Each Context object uses a `ContextAccessor`:

```
def ContextAccessor                        #  1
    def context                            #  2
        Thread.current[:context]           #  3
```

```
    end                                              #   4
                                                     #   5
    def context=(ctx)                                #   6
        Thread.current[:context] = ctx               #   7
    end                                              #   8
                                                     #   9
    def execute_in_context                           #  10
        old_context = self.context                   #  11
        self.context = self                          #  12
        yield                                        #  13
        self.context = old_context                   #  14
    end                                              #  15
end                                                  #  16
```

This module is included in each of the methodful object roles. That is a more static way of doing the same thing as the extend directive, bringing in the accessor as a mixin in each of the methodful object roles. The main job of the ContextAccessor is to stack execution contexts. Here, in Steen Lehmann's Ruby implementation, the Thread contexts serve as a place to store variables that are local to currently executing thread, so they become an ancillary part of the context stacking arrangement. The code creates no actual threads.

The C++ Code

Here is the analogous code in C++:

```
class TransferMoneyContext                           //   1
{                                                    //   2
public:                                              //   3
    TransferMoneyContext(void);                      //   4
    void doit(void);                                 //   5
    MoneySource *sourceAccount(void) const;          //   6
    MoneySink *destinationAccount(void) const;       //   7
    Currency amount(void) const;                     //   8
private:                                             //   9
    void lookupBindings(void);                       //  10
    MoneySource *sourceAccount_;                     //  11
    MoneySink *destinationAccount_;                  //  12
    Currency amount_;                                //  13
};                                                   //  14
```

The private data sourceAccount_ and destinationAccount_ (lines 11 and 12) are the methodless object roles. They are declared in terms of the methodless object role types `MoneySource` and `MoneySink`, respectively. The Context object holds a reference to an object that captures the transfer amount as well, which was likely established during a previous use case. During any single use case enactment, these members hold the binding of methodless object roles to the domain objects into which the methodful object roles have been injected. Each use case is like a performance of a play, and we cast (in the theatrical sense) an actor to play each of the given object roles. Here, the object roles are represented by the member data of `TransferMoneyContext`, and the domain objects represent the actors. Each actor has memorized his or her script or scripts: that is, we have injected the methodful object roles into each domain object according to the object roles it may be called to play. It soon will be time to call them on stage. Lights, camera – and when we instantiate the Context object, we get action.

The `TransferMoneyContext` object is constructed from within an *environment*, which is the term we use in DCI to describe the code that initiates the enactment of the use case. An environment starts up a system operation. In most applications, the environment is usually a Model-View-Controller instance responding to a gesture from an end user. The actual invocation may come either from the Controller or from the simple methods of MVC's domain models.

When we create an instance of the `TransferMoneyContext` class, it finds the three objects it will be working with: the object representing the source account, the one representing the destination account, and the one representing the amount of the transfer. If the Controller orchestrated the earlier use cases that established the source account, destination account, and transfer amount, then it can remember those selections, and the Controller and Context can agree on how to share that remembered information. Alternatively, the system data can remember them. The system data are part of the model information in the MVC framework (Figure 9-10). The Controller can retrieve those data from the model and supply them to a new `TransferMoneyContext` class constructor when it is created:

```
TransferMoneyContext(Currency amount,
                     MoneySource *src,
                     MoneySink *destination);
```

Alternatively, the `TransferMoneyContext` object can do a "database lookup" in the system domain objects, relying on identifiers declared globally or elsewhere in the environment (e.g., in the Controller). We assume the latter for the time being, but we'll consider other options later.

`TransferMoneyContext` needs very little code to set up and execute the use case for transferring money:

```
TransferMoneyContext::TransferMoneyContext(void)           // 1
{                                                          // 2
    lookupBindings();                                     // 3
}                                                          // 4
                                                          // 5
TransferMoneyContext::TransferMoneyContext(                // 6
    Currency amount,                                      // 7
    MoneySource *source,                                  // 8
    MoneySink *destination):                              // 9
    Context()                                             // 10
{                                                          // 11
    // Copy the rest of the stuff                         // 12
    sourceAccount_ = source;                              // 13
    destinationAccount_ = destination;                    // 14
    amount_ = amount;                                     // 15
}                                                          // 16
                                                          // 17
TransferMoneyContext::doit(void)                           // 18
{                                                          // 19
    sourceAccount()->transferTo(amount());               // 20
}                                                          // 21
                                                          // 22
void                                                       // 23
TransferMoneyContext::lookupBindings(void)                 // 24
{                                                          // 25
    sourceAccount_ = databaseLookup();  // maybe an      // 26
                                 //    Investment         // 27
    destinationAccount_ = . . . .;      // maybe Savings // 28
    amount_ = . . . . ;                 // chosen amount // 29
}                                                          // 30
```

Notice that the `doit` member function (the trigger member function) retrieves the identity of the accounts from its own local member functions. Remember that the `SavingsAccount` is also participating in the use case, playing the object role of the `MoneySink`. How does it get access to the Context, so that it can find the objects playing the roles with which it needs to interact?

Making Contexts Work

The notion of Contexts is fundamental to the end user's concept of what's going on at the business level. It deserves the same stature at the design level as the concepts of `this` and `self` do at the programming level.

General-purpose programming language constructs help us reason about and express the behavior of local objects, but not the behavior of the system as a system (recall Figure 9-2 on page 238). It would be nice if programming languages arranged for each object role method to have access to a Context object pointer in the same way that they provide `self` or `this`. Maybe DCI will someday lead language designers down that path. Already, Trygve Reenskaug's Baby UML environment does this (Reenskaug 2007), and the Qi4j project at Jayway in Sweden is exploring this area as well.

One downside of DCI is that programmers must do some housekeeping to keep things working. Most of this housekeeping can be captured in a few simple practices and rules. Remember these rules when creating a Context object:

1. Create a new Context class for each distinct use case so there can be a new Context instance for each use case enactment. With cleverness and experience, you can start to build class hierarchies of Context objects that reflect some of Ivar Jacobsson's original vision of a type theory for use cases.

2. Each Context object should have a default constructor (one with no arguments) that the environment (e.g., a domain data object or a MVC controller) can conveniently instantiate and turn loose to do what it needs to do. You might add specialized constructors that take arguments such as references to participants in the use case.

3. Each Context object should have a separate `doit` (or `enact` or `run` or other suitably named) method that runs the use case scenario. Alternatively, you can adopt a convention that the Context constructor itself will trigger the use case scenario implicitly.

4. Its interface should publish pointers (identifiers) for all object roles involved in the corresponding use case. The Context object is the oracle for the mapping from the methodless object role identifiers to the objects bearing the methodful object role logic. Every object role involved in the use case should be able to find any other object role involved in the use case – and the Context object is the source.

5. The identifiers for these object roles should be typed in terms of the methodless object role types rather than the methodful object role declarations. This ensures that the APIs between methodful object roles don't depend directly on each other. This is particularly important in languages like C++ with strong compile-time type systems because it limits the compile-time coupling between methodful object roles.

Our goal is to code the methods of methodful object roles so they directly reflect the algorithm we derive from the use case. We don't want to clutter the code with explicit logic to map object roles to objects. Ideally, we refer to an object that plays a given object role knowing only the name of the object role it plays. We assume that the system has taken care of the rest. These object role names are exactly the bindings made available in the interface of the Context object. For example, in the money transfer example, the `TransferMoneyContext` member functions `sourceAccount` and `destinationAccount` name the object roles with which we are concerned. So if we make the Context object available, it is only one step away to access the object role handles. In our Ruby example, the methodful object role programmer has access to the methodless object role identifiers through getter methods on the Context object (see page 259).

Here, we propose four ways to pass a suitably typed Context reference to the places it is needed in the code. Most of the advice is relevant to C++. Ruby programmers can read it for inspiration, but option 4 works well enough for all cases in Ruby that the other alternatives probably are distractions for Ruby programmers. We can take advantage of Ruby's cultural conventions; C++ is used in enough different cultures that one size does not fit all. The fourth and last proposed alternative is the recommended way even for C++ programmers, but your programming culture or application may suggest that one of the other three is better for you.

1. *The simple case where object role bindings are already arguments to the methods in the methodful object roles.* The Context object itself passes the individual methodless object role identifiers as arguments to the methodful object roles that need them:

```
TransferMoneyContext::doit(void)
{
    sourceAccount()->transferTo(amount(),
                                destinationAccount());
}
```

This gives the methodful object roles (such as `sourceAccount()` here) access to all other objects with which they communicate, through their role interfaces, to carry out the entire use case scenario.

2. *Pass the Context to the methodful object role interface of each domain object when the Context object maps the methodless object roles to the domain object at the beginning of the use case.* This approach simulates the approach used by the original BabyUML implementation of DCI. Consider the original code from our simple funds transfer example above:

```
void                                            //   1
TransferMoneyContext::lookupBindings(void)      //   2
{                                               //   3
    sourceAccount_ = databaseLookup();          //   4
    destinationAccount_ = . . .                 //   5
    amount_ = . . . .                           //   6
}                                               //   7
```

We can add APIs to object role interfaces that take a Context object
as an argument. We must augment the interfaces of the methodless
object role types to support the invocation of setContext from the
Context objects as in lines 9–12 and 24–27:

```
class MoneySource {                             //   1
public:                                         //   2
    virtual void transferTo(double amount) = 0; //   3
    virtual void decreaseBalance(double amount) //   4
                                          = 0;  //   5
    virtual void payBills(void) = 0;            //   6
                                                //   7
    // Context Stuff                            //   8
    virtual void setContext(                    //   9
                  PayBillsContext*) = 0;        //  10
    virtual void setContext(                    //  11
              TransferMoneyContext*)= 0;        //  12
};                                              //  13
                                                //  14
class MoneySink {                               //  15
public:                                         //  16
    virtual void increaseBalance(               //  17
                  Currency amount) = 0;         //  18
    virtual void updateLog(string,              //  19
                  Time,                         //  20
                  Currency)= 0;                 //  21
                                                //  22
    // Context stuff:                           //  23
    virtual void setContext(                    //  24
                  PayBillsContext*) = 0;        //  25
    virtual void setContext(                    //  26
              TransferMoneyContext*) = 0;       //  27
};                                              //  28
```

These APIs cache the information locally for later use, but we will implement the APIs in the methodful object roles that implement the MoneySource and MoneySink interfaces (i.e., in TransferMoneySink and TransferMoneySource). Now we can invoke these setContext APIs from within the Context objects. This is the Context object's way of broadcasting, to all the objects involved in a given use case, the handles to the other methodless object roles involved in the use case. Each object can cache away the object role handle information it feels it needs for the use case. Here is what the TransferMoneyContext code might look like:

```
void                                                       //  1
TransferMoneyContext::setContexts(void) {                  //  2
    sourceAccount()->setContext(this);                     //  2
    destinationAccount()->setContext(this);                //  3
    amount()->setContext(this);                            //  4
}                                                          //  5
                                                           //  6
TransferMoneyContext::TransferMoneyContext(void)           //  7
{                                                          //  8
    lookupBindings();                                      //  9
    setContexts();                                         // 10
}                                                          // 11
                                                           // 12
void                                                       // 13
TransferMoneyContext::lookupBindings(void)                 // 14
{                                                          // 15
    sourceAccount_ = databaseLookup();                     // 16
    destinationAccount_ = . . .                            // 17
    amount_ = . . . .                                      // 18
}                                                          // 19
```

We use the simple helper methods that live in the protected interface of the methodful object role class to act as local handles to the other object roles in the use case scenario:

```
MoneySource* template<class ConcreteDerived>               //  1
class MoneySink::recipient(void) {                         //  2
        return                                             //  3
            TransferMoneyContext_->                        //  4
                destinationAccount();                      //  5
    }                                                      //  6
```

If we also have a <u>Pay Bills</u> use case with its own Context, then the **MoneySink** object role should also support access to the object playing the object role of the **Creditors**:

```
std::list<Creditor*> creditors(void) const {      //   7
    return payBillsContext_->creditors();         //   8
}                                                 //   9
```

For the <u>Pay Bills</u> scenario, we also need a `PayBillsContext` object analogous to the `TransferMoneyContext` object:

```
void                                              //   1
PayBillsContext::setContexts(void)                //   2
{                                                 //   3
    sourceAccount()->setContext(this);            //   4
}                                                 //   5
                                                  //   6
PayBillsContext::PayBillsContext(void)            //   7
{                                                 //   8
    lookupBindings();                             //   9
    setContexts();                                //  10
}                                                 //  11
                                                  //  12
void                                              //  13
PayBillsContext::lookupBindings(void)             //  14
{                                                 //  15
    // These are like database selects / lookups  //  16
    sourceAccount_ = . . .                        //  17
    creditors_ = . . . .                          //  18
}                                                 //  19
```

In this C++ implementation, the `setContext` member function is overloaded within each methodful object role. The Context type is the basis for the overloading: there is a separate `setContext` for every type of use case scenario in which the methodful object role participates. This of course has the strong liability of needing to add APIs to many methodful object roles every time a use case is added. The implementations of these methods in the derived classes cache away just those methodless object role identifiers from the Context interface that it needs for the use case. Alternatively, each one could cache a pointer to the Context object, which is guaranteed to persist for the duration of the use case.

We also add code in the trait to remember the Context when it identifies itself to all the objects involved in its collaboration. Here we show two `setContext` setters, one for each of two different Context objects. Because only one Context runs at a time, we can save a bit of space by sharing the two Context pointers in a single union:

```
public:                                                  //   1
    // Context stuff                                      //   2
    void setContext(TransferMoneyContext *c) {           //   3
        TransferMoneyContext_ = c;                       //   4
    }                                                    //   5
    void setContext(PayBillsContext *c) {                //   6
        payBillsContext_ = c;                            //   7
    }                                                    //   8
public:                                                  //   9
    TransferMoneySource(void):                           //  10
        TransferMoneyContext_(0) {                        //  11
    }                                                    //  12
private:                                                 //  13
    union {                                              //  14
     TransferMoneyContext *TransferMoneyContext_;        //  15
     PayBillsContext    *payBillsContext_;               //  16
    };                                                   //  17
```

With the Context information safely cached inside the trait, the trait can now map any object role name to the object currently playing that object role in the existing enactment. In C++ each trait should provide a member function named after the object role, and each such member function should return a pointer to the object playing that object role in the existing use case. These functions are of protected access so they are accessible only to the object role (trait) itself and potentially to the domain object which we anticipate might have knowledge of this object role in unusual circumstances (though that wouldn't be recommended practice):

```
protected:                                               //  18
    MoneySink *recipient(void) {                         //  19
        return                                           //  20
                TransferMoneyContext_->                   //  21
                    destinationAccount();                //  22
    }                                                    //  23
```

Let's say that we have a `SavingsAccount` with `PayBillsContext` injected into it. We augment it only to inject the **TransferMoneySink** object role into it. We do this by inheriting the parameterized class:

```
class SavingsAccount:                                    //  1
        public Account,                                  //  2
        public TransferMoneySink<SavingsAccount> {//  3
public:                                                  //  4
    SavingsAccount(void);                                //  5
    virtual Currency availableBalance(void);             //  6
    virtual void decreaseBalance(Currency);              //  7
    virtual void increaseBalance(Currency);              //  8
    virtual void updateLog(string, MyTime,               //  9
                    Currency);                           // 10
                                                         // 11
private:                                                 // 12
    // Model data                                        // 13
    Currency availableBalance_;                          // 14
};                                                       // 15
```

`CheckingAccount` is similar:

```
class CheckingAccount:                                   //  1
        public Account,                                  //  2
        public TransferMoneySink<CheckingAccount> {//  3
public:                                                  //  4
    CheckingAccount(void);                               //  5
    virtual Currency availableBalance(void);             //  6
    virtual void decreaseBalance(Currency);              //  7
    virtual void increaseBalance(Currency);              //  8
    virtual void updateLog(string, MyTime,               //  9
                    Currency);                           // 10
                                                         // 11
private:                                                 // 12
    // The data for the model                            // 13
    Currency availableBalance_;                          // 14
};                                                       // 15
```

`InvestmentAccount` may again be similar, and so forth.

For Context objects used in this style, we can add guidelines to those started back on page 268:

A. Inside the constructor of each Context object, invoke the `setContext` method of each object role that is involved in the use case scenario, passing in the Context object itself as an argument. This allows each object to cache references to its collaborators in the scenario.

B. Add an API that can be used to bind to the objects attached to each of the object roles involved in the Context's use case scenario.

3. *Pass the Context object as an argument to all methods of methodful object roles.* Think of the Context as being a super object that contains, in a very strong sense, all objects that will be involved in a given use case scenario. In the same sense that an object method passes the `self` or `this` identifier to the methods it calls, so we can envision each and every of the methods in a methodful object role receiving a reference to their shared Context. No programming language provides such an argument automatically as most of them do for `this` and `self`, so we can provide it explicitly.

This approach is clumsy to the extent that each method is cluttered with an additional argument. The Smalltalk implementation of DCI in BabyUML avoided this clumsiness by changing the Smalltalk compiler to look up contexts automatically, but here we try to avoid any solution that could not easily be ported from one installation to another. Though the approach is clumsy, it avoids the administrative boilerplate of the previous approach above.

4. (Recommended) Let each methodful object role access a global Context object through macros or functions whose syntax distinguishes such access as object role access. Object roles interact with each other to realize a use case scenario. The source code can be written in terms of object role references rather than object references to better match the end user mental model of the object role interaction. Macros make it possible to use a syntax that hides the "active" nature of an object role name invocation: that it actually resolves to an object pointer according to the object-role-to-object mapping in the Context object.

At any given time, the code is executing only within a single Context. The code within one Context may create another and, as described earlier, Context objects can stack. However, the fact that there is only one Context executing at a time makes it possible to maintain a single, "global" Context object pointer. Furthermore, the fact that the type of that context can be inferred by knowing what function is executing (since that Context is what started it off), we can safely use static casting to restore full Context type information to a generic pointer that stands in for all Context types. In C++, the pointer access can be buried inside of a macro that also does the necessary down-casting to the appropriate derived Context class. That derived class provides interfaces to retrieve the object pointers for the object roles that they represent. In Ruby, the code is straightforward, and is how we presented the example above (see page 260):

```
def execute                               # 19
    execute_in_context do                 # 20
        source_account.transferTo         # 21
    end                                   # 22
end                                       # 23
```

The `transferTo` method goes to the Context object to retrieve the object role bindings it needs to continue its work.

So let's again look at our banking example, which has the object role **TransferMoneySource** for financial transfers. It participates in a use case together with another object role, which we'll call the **RECIPIENT**. Together with the code for the `TransferMoneySource` trait, we include the macro:

```
#define RECIPIENT \
    ((static_cast<TransferMoneyContext*>    \
    (Context::currentContext_)->destinationAccount()))
```

If you want a higher degree of paranoia in the code, you can change the `static_cast` to a `dynamic_cast` and check for a null result:

```
#define RECIPIENT \
    (((dynamic_cast<TransferMoneyContext*>(              \
                        Context::currentContext_)?  \
            dynamic_cast<TransferMoneyContext*>(     \
                        Context::currentContext_):   \
            (throw("dynamic cast failed"),           \
                static_cast<TransferMoneyContext*>(0)) \
        )->destinationAccount()))
```

Now we can define the `transferTo` method for the **Transfer Money Source** object role in terms of the object roles, like **RECIPIENT**, with which it interacts:

```
if (SELF->availableBalance() < amount) {      //  1
    endTransaction();                         //  2
    throw InsufficientFunds();                 //  3
} else {                                      //  4
```

```
        SELF->decreaseBalance(amount);                    //  5
        RECIPIENT->transferFrom(amount);                  //  6
        RECIPIENT->updateLog(                             //  7
                        "Transfer In",                    //  8
                        DateTime(),                       //  9
                        amount);                          // 10
}                                                         // 11
```

Note the use of the special object role **SELF** at lines 1, 5 and 7, which designates the object for which the object role is currently executing. Its macro is simply:

```
#define SELF \
        static_cast<const ConcreteDerived*>(this)
```

The `ConcreteDerived` parameter will be bound to the appropriate template argument in the template for the **TransferMoneySource** object role:

```
template<classConcreteDerived>
class TransferMoneySource: public MoneySource
{
```

Your innovativeness may discover other approaches that are even better for your own situation. Be Agile: inspect and adapt.

Habits: Nested Contexts in Methodful Object Roles

It's common practice to compose "re-usable" use case scenarios into higher-level scenarios. Ivar Jacobsson's original vision of use cases provided for an *includes* relation between a high level use case and a "smaller" use case on which it depended to complete interactions with the end user. However, this might weaken fundamental properties of use cases, such as being oriented toward a business goal, or reinforcing redundancy between use cases. Here, we demote these use case fragments from the stature of being full use cases and instead call them *habits*. A habit captures a set of use case steps that recur across multiple use cases, but which in themselves may not meet the criteria of being a use case. They just convey a step in achieving a user goal. They are tools principally for the developer.

As discussed earlier, it is a good idea if each use case captures the entire context of the relationships between the steps. This clarifies analysis of user needs and provides context for the designer. Splitting use cases using the *includes* approach breaks down this continuity during analysis. However, if we are dutiful in maintaining this continuity during analysis – even at the expense of duplicated steps between alternate or otherwise related scenarios – then we can factor out the common parts during design. This is just another kind of commonality analysis. We call one of these common fragments a habit. We represent habits in the code, but we keep them intact with their associated non-habitual steps in their original scenarios.

Let's use our banking software as an example. We already have a use case for transferring money (Figure 9-7 on page 247). Let's say that we also want a use case for paying bills automatically from our account. Our new use case can use the money transfer habit to make the actual transfers, letting it take care of the logging and transactions and other "details." We can see the new use case in Figure 9-11. Note the invocation of Move Money and Do Accounting – the fact that it is underlined is a cue that it is another habit, which for all intents and purposes behaves like a use case at the coding level.

Use Case Name: Pay Bills from Selected Account

User Intent: To use money from one of my accounts to pay an equal amount to each of my creditors

Motivation: To be able to let the bank automatically pay my bills monthly, or for me to be able to pay all bills on demand with a minimum of effort

Preconditions: The Account has a list of known creditors. The Account Holder has identified the Source Account and a default amount to pay to each creditor

Basic Scenario:

Step	User Intent	System Responsibility
1.	Homeowner selects account list and requests to pay all bills	Greenland Net bank Moves Money and Does Accounting for each account in the list

Post-conditions:
   ✓ All post-conditions of Transfer Money hold

Figure 9-11   Pay bills use case.

Note that there are two ways of thinking about paying bills. One approach gives the responsibility of identifying creditors to the bank; another approach gives that responsibility to the **AccountHolder**. In the former approach, any creditor who can legitimize their claim against the **AccountHolder** is allowed by the bank to queue for payment. In the latter case, the **AccountHolder** must remember (with the help of my software) both to whom I owe money, and to add to or remove creditors from such a list based on my discretion. These two modes of bill paying lead to two different designs because they distribute responsibility differently. It is the same responsibilities distributed differently across objects. What makes the difference? The difference comes from how the responsibilities aggregate together into different object roles. These are two different designs – and two different use cases. Here, the **AccountHolder** chooses to trust the bank to screen his or her creditors, and is happy to pay whoever the bank believes is owed money by him or her.

The Pay Bills use case starts off knowing the **SourceAccount** (a role) from which the bills will be paid, and an amount to be applied to the account for each creditor. The Context for the Pay Bills use case will be given those or can find them when it is created. We create a **SourceAccount** role that is specifically suited to this use case because it offers a `payBills` method, and it appears in the code as `TransferMoneySource`. We can frame out the code (really only pseudo-code at this point) like this:

```
def payBills                                        #  1
    # Assume that we can round up the creditors      #  2
    creditors.each do |creditor|                     #  3
        # transfer the funds here                    #  4
end                                                  #  5
```

In C++:

```
void payBills(void) {                               // 1
    // Assume that we can round up the creditors    // 2
    for (; iter != creditors.end(); iter++ ) {      // 3
        try {                                        // 4
            // transfer the funds here               // 5
        } catch (InsufficientFunds) {                // 6
            throw;                                   // 7
        }                                            // 8
    }                                                // 9
}                                                    // 10
```

If we wish, we later can come back and change the algorithm to sort the creditors by amount owed, by how long it has been since we last paid them, or whatever else we choose to do. Those are all possible use case deviations. For now, let's keep it simple.

We must solve two problems here. The first is to retrieve a stable set of creditors that will remain constant across the iterations of the `for` loop. Remember that DCI is designed to support the rapidly changing relationships between objects that one finds in a real-world system, and that we don't want new creditors coming into the picture after we've decided to pay the bills (no more than creditors want to potentially be dropped from the list of remunerated candidates should conditions change). We retrieve the list of creditors from the context and store it locally to solve that problem:

```
.  .  .  .
creditors = context.creditors.dup
creditors.each do |creditor|
    TransferMoneyContext.execute(creditor.amount_owed,
            account_id,
            creditor.account.account_id)
.  .  .  .
```

Also, in C++:

```
.  .  .  .
list<Creditor*> creditors = CREDITORS;
    list<Creditor*>::iterator i = creditors.begin();
        for (; i != creditors.end(); i++ ) {
.  .  .  .
```

The second problem is: How do we "invoke" the <u>Move Money and Do Accounting</u> habit from within the new code for paying bills? It is usually the environment – a Controller or a domain object – that sets up the Context object and invokes its `doit` (trigger) operation. Here, flow of control into the code for the habit doesn't come directly from an end user gesture, but from another use case (which itself was probably started by an interaction on the GUI). That means that the enclosing use case for paying bills must set up the context for the funds transfer habit. It as if <u>Pay Bills</u> reaches outside the program and presses the <u>Transfer Money</u> button on the screen.

As it stands, the `TransferMoneyContext` object makes that difficult to do because it is in charge of mapping the use case scenario object roles to their objects, using context from the Controller or from hints left in the model objects. We fix this by adding a new constructor for the `TransferMoneyContext` object that allows the bill payment use case code to override the usual database select operation or other lookup used by the Context object to associate object roles with objects:

```
TransferMoneyContext::TransferMoneyContext(          // 1
    Currency amount,                                 // 2
    MoneySource *source,                             // 3
```

```
                MoneySink *destination)                    //   4
{                                                          //   5
    // Copy the rest of the stuff                          //   6
    sourceAccount_ = source;                               //   7
    destinationAccount_ = destination;                     //   8
    amount_ = amount;                                      //   9
    setContexts();  // if using style 3 from p.275         //  10
}                                                          //  11
                                                           //  12
// We need this function only if using                     //  13
// style 3 from page 275:                                  //  14
                                                           //  15
void                                                       //  16
TransferMoneyContext::setContexts(void) {                  //  17
    sourceAccount()->setContext(this);                     //  18
    destinationAccount()->setContext(this);                //  19
}                                                          //  20
```

The new, complete codified use case scenario looks like this:

```
template <class ConcreteDerived>                           //   1
class TransferMoneySource: public MoneySource {            //   2
  . . . .                                                  //   3
  // Object role behaviors                                 //   4
  void payBills(void) {                                    //   5
      // While object contexts are changing, we            //   6
      // don't want to have an open iterator on an         //   7
      // external object. Make a local copy.               //   8
      std::list<Creditor*> creditors = CREDITORS;          //   9
      std::list<Creditor*>::iterator iter =                //  10
                                 creditors.begin();        //  11
      for (; iter != creditors.end(); iter++ ) {           //  12
          try {                                            //  13
              // Note that here we invoke another           //  14
              // use case habit                             //  15
              TransferMoneyContext transferTheFunds(       //  16
                          (*iter)->amountOwed(),           //  17
                          SELF,                            //  18
                          (*iter)->account());             //  19
              transferTheFunds.doit();                     //  20
          } catch (InsufficientFunds) {                    //  21
              throw;                                       //  22
          }                                                //  23
```

```
        }                                               // 24
      }                                                 // 25
      . . . .                                           // 26
   };                                                   // 27
```

In Ruby, it looks like this:

```
module TransferMoneySource                              #  1
include MoneySource, ContextAccessor                    #  2
    .   .   .                                            #  3
def transfer_out                                        #  4
    raise "Insufficient funds" if balance < amount      #  5
    self.decreaseBalance amount                         #  6
    destination_account.transfer_in amount              #  7
    self.update_log "Transfer Out",                     #  8
            Time.now,                                   #  9
            amount                                      # 10
  end                                                   # 11
                                                        # 12
  def pay_bills                                         # 13
    creditors = context.creditors.dup                   # 14
    creditors.each do |creditor|                        # 15
      TransferMoneyContext.execute(                     # 16
              creditor.amount_owed,                     # 17
              account_id,                               # 18
              creditor.account.account_id)              # 19
    end                                                 # 20
  end                                                   # 21
end                                                     # 22
```

When the `TransferMoneyContext` object comes into being, it becomes the current context, replacing the global context pointer `Context::current-Context`. That allows the methods of the methodful object roles inside the **Transfer Money** use case to resolve to the correct objects. Notice that the Context object lifetime is limited to the scope of the `try` block: there is no reason to keep it around longer. At the end of the scope its destructor is called, and it restores `Context::currentContext` to its previous value. Therefore, Contexts implement a simple stack that the Context base class can represent as a linked list:

```
class Context {                                     //   1
public:                                             //   2
    Context(void) {                                 //   3
        parentContext_ = currentContext_;           //   4
        currentContext_ = this;                     //   5
    }                                               //   6
    virtual ~Context() {                            //   7
        currentContext_ = parentContext_;           //   8
    }                                               //   9
public:                                             //  10
    static Context *currentContext_;                //  11
private:                                            //  12
    Context *parentContext_;                        //  13
};                                                  //  14
```

9.4.6   Variants and Tricks in DCI

You can use DCI to express subtle but important relationships in architecture. Here we introduce a few of them. Use your ingenuity to explore further refinements and variants on DCI. In particular, your programming language may offer forms of expression well suited to DCI.

Context Layering

All along we've been telling you that SavingsAccount is a domain class. We lied. The real domain classes in banking are transaction logs and audit trails. A SavingsAccount is simply a special kind of context object that happens to correspond to the end user mental model.

We'll cover context layering more in-depth in Section 9.6; it is a central notion of DCI and deserves its own section. However, it is an advanced technique, so we leave it until last.

Information Hiding

One can argue that only the methods of methodful object roles should ever call domain member functions. In Smalltalk, of course, any of the domain or object role methods can be invoked through any identifier bound to the object. Ruby allows us to restrict access to symbols, but not selectively – only on a wholesale basis. In C++ it is possible to limit these invocations to the code for the object roles that objects of that class are allowed to play. We can do that simply by making the domain class interface `private`, and by extending a friendship relationship to the chosen object roles:

```
class SavingsAccount:                              //   1
        public Account,                            //   2
        public TransferMoneySink<SavingsAccount> { //   3
friend class TransferMoneySink<SavingsAccount>;    //   4
public:                                            //   5
    SavingsAccount(void);                          //   6
private:                                           //   7
    Currency availableBalance(void);               //   8
    void decreaseBalance(Currency);                //   9
    . . . .                                        //  10
private:                                           //  11
    // The data for the model                      //  12
    Currency availableBalance_;                    //  13
};                                                 //  14
```

Selective Object Role Injection

The above presentation of DCI in C++ is based on injecting object roles at compile time. That means that any possible injection that might be needed at run time must be set up beforehand. As a consequence, every class is decorated with every possible object role that it might play. It might be better if we could do injection in a more just-in-time, minimal, incremental way. One might even call it lean injection.

Lean injection is natural to Scala. When we instantiate an object from a class we inject all the object roles it will take on during its lifetime. Different objects of the same class may have different object role interfaces. A `Sav-ingsAccount` class might be instantiated as an object with `SourceAccount` behavior in one use case, while another `SavingsAccount` instantiation might be injected only with the `DestinationAccount` behavior.

```
val source = new SavingsAccount with SourceAccount
```

Of course, one can do the same thing with `extend` in Ruby. We can do injection completely independent of instantiation, so we can inject the object role right up until the last microsecond before its functionality is needed:

```
@source_account = SavingsAccount.new
@source_account.extend SourceAccount
```

The `extend` directive causes the methods of (the module) `SourceAccount` to also become methods of the (object) `source_account` (originally of class `SavingsAccount`). These newly injected methods are called *singleton methods* because they belong singly to this object and have nothing to do with the class. This is unlike the C++ solution (below), which employs explicit class composition and traits as a way to achieve its goal. It is more like the Scala solution, except technically there is no new class here – not even an anonymous one. The injected methods belong to the object.

We can implement analogous functionality in C++ though the syntax is considerably messier. What Scala does in the above example is to create a new, anonymous class composed from `SavingsAccount` with a `SourceAccount` trait. C++ does not support anonymous classes, so we must do the work that the compiler would do for us if we were programming in Scala.

```
class SavingsAccountWithSourceAccount:
    class SavingsAccount,
    class SourceAccount<SavingsAccountWithSourceAccount>
{
public:
    . . . .
};


. . . .


Account *source = new SavingsAccountWithSourceAccount;
```

Unfortunately, this can lead to an explosion in the number of scaffolding classes that the programmer needs to write with very little software engineering benefit.

9.5   Updating the Domain Logic

In the atomic event architectural style, we have two coding tasks after the interfaces and abstract base classes are framed out: to write the functional business logic, and to flesh out the domain logic in the Model of MVC. The same is true here. Nevertheless, in the atomic event style these two kinds of code co-exist in the domain classes. Here, we have already separated out the functional business logic into the object role classes. Let's step back and again compare the DCI approach to domain class evolution with what we already presented in Chapter 8.

9.5.1 Contrasting DCI with the Atomic Event Style

There are two basic ways to add what-the-system-does functionality to an object-oriented system: to add short, atomic operations directly to the domain objects, or to use the DCI architecture. DCI applies only when we have use cases that describe a sequence of tasks that are directed to some end-user goal. If the "use case" is a simple, atomic action, then use cases are the methodological equivalent of shooting a fly with an elephant gun.

Most object-oriented architectures over the years have been created as though they were atomic event architectures, which meant that they failed to separate the volatile what-the-system-does logic from the more stable domain model. We described some examples in Section 8.2. Those implementations usually correspond to highly visual or physical end-user interactions.

It has been a long time now that objects have established a beachhead in the traditionally algorithmic areas of business, finance, and numeric computation. All of these areas, perhaps former strongholds of FORTRAN, RPG, and COBOL, have traditionally embraced algorithms as a primary organizing principle. These algorithms have multiple steps, each one of which corresponds to some user intention. In an Agile world, which is usually interactive, each user intention is taken in by the system and fed back to the user in discrete acknowledgments of completion. We want those sequences captured in the code – at least as well as we used to in FORTRAN, RPG, and COBOL. This notion of relating to increments of user intent comes from Constantine and Lockwood's essential use cases (Constantine and Lockwood 1999).

Any given system will usually have a combination of these two architectural styles. We recommend the following approach as rules of thumb – but *only* as rules of thumb.

- If a system or subsystem has a critical mass of scenarios and use cases that reflect sequences of conscious user intents, then design that entire subsystem using the DCI architecture. Make even the atomic operations part of the object role interfaces and keep the domain interfaces clean. Sometimes this means duplicating the object role interface in the domain object (because that's the right way to elicit the domain behavior), and it's likely that the methodful object role will only forward its request to the domain object. *Example*: Work items in a work ordering system participate in many algorithms. There are many dependencies between work items and scheduling deadlines, and the algorithms are exposed to these dependencies. Most operations on work items are really operations on object roles (Item Being Worked On, Next Item To Be Worked, Successor Item, Last Item, Dependent Item, etc.)

- If a system or subsystem is dominated by atomic operations, and has only a few true use cases, then use plain old object-oriented programming. All of the system work is done by methods on the domain objects. This may slightly erode the cohesion of the domain objects (because the actions on them require a bit of help from other objects) but the overall architecture will be simpler and easier to understand. *Example*: A simple shape editor that is part of a document processing application is based largely on atomic operations (resize, move, change color). Even some operations that look like use cases, such as evenly distributing objects along a horizontal range, can be thought of as atomic operations on a higher order concept such as a selection. Treat use cases as an exception.

- If neither the use case semantics nor the atomic semantics dominate, use a hybrid. Atomic operations can go direct to the domain objects, while methodful object roles can be used to package up the use cases. *Example*: The `TextBuffer` class whose instances hold the text in a text editing application supports atomic operations such as inserting and deleting characters, but it might also play an object role in a spell-checking or global-search-and-replace scenario.

Take two pragmatic considerations into account when making these selections. The first is that there is no need to choose one style over the other. Choosing a style is a matter of meeting programmer and designer expectations, to avoid surprises. There is no technical reason that the two cannot co-exist. The second point, which bears additional consideration, is that the above decisions should reflect organizational and business concerns. A large, complex organization sometimes works more smoothly if the code providing end-user functionality can more fully be separated from the code that captures domain logic.

9.5.2   Special Considerations for Domain Logic in DCI

We have created the methodful object roles that are carefully translated from the end-user use case scenarios. In an ideal world, we would do this translation without regard to the established APIs in the domain classes or, alternatively, we would take the domain class APIs as givens. Being more pragmatic, we realize that the domain classes and methodful object roles have insights to offer to each other. Just as in the atomic event architectural style, the interface between the methodful object roles and the domain classes evolves in three major ways: domain class method elaboration, factoring, and re-factoring.

In Section 8.3 we described how to update domain logic for the atomic event architecture case. In contrast with the atomic event approach, the

DCI approach leaves the domain classes untouched and pure. What does "pure" mean? It means *dumb*. The domain classes represent system data and the most basic functionality necessary to retrieve and modify it. These classes have no direct knowledge of user tasks or actions: they sustain the relatively staid state changes local to an individual object without worrying too much about the coordinated object dynamics at the system level.

This has distinct advantages for the architect and long-term benefits to the end user. The Model of MVC-U stays cleanly a model, rather than a mixture of several user mental models. Instead of mixing the what-the-system-does logic in with the what-the-system-is logic as we did in the atomic event architectural style, here we keep it separate. Separation of validly separate concerns is always a good architectural practice.

When we start work on a new use case scenario, the logic in the methodful object roles usually depends on services from the domain objects. The classes for these objects may or may not exist yet, even though the APIs exist as coded interfaces in the architecture. Remember, the domain class API is simply an abstract base class, and there may or may not be a class behind it to support any given interface. The time has now come to create those classes.

Just as in the non-DCI case, filling in the domain member functions is straightforward. The DCI approach to actually writing domain class member functions is the same as for writing the general domain member functions to support the atomic event architectural style. See Section 8.3.

This leads us to a key Lean property of DCI: it leads to just-in-time delivery of code. As each new use case scenario (or atomic action) comes in from the market, we can encode it as a methodful role. We don't need to do any specific preparation ahead of time. We do, of course, need to undertake the general preparation of a good domain analysis and the building of the domain framework for the architecture. But that framework consists largely of domain declarations and needs very few method bodies to get started. After we create the methodful role increment, we can now go into the domain classes and implement the dumb domain methods declared in the domain framework's abstract base classes. But we need to implement only those methods necessary to support the new use case (Figure 9-12). So even the domain classes can evolve incrementally – just-in-time. This limits speculative development and the waste of rework. We don't defer decisions (thinking) until the last responsible moment to make work for more immediate needs. Instead, we think more and do less up front, and defer the implementation to the last responsible moment.

Member functions are one problem; bringing in the object role traits is another. In C++, we use the Curiously Recurring Template Idiom (Coplien 1996) to mix in the object role logic (line 3):

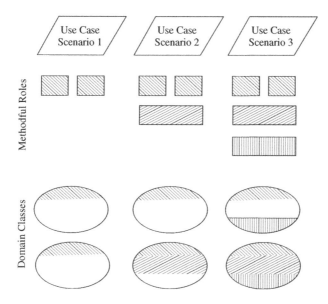

Figure 9-12 Just-in-time code delivery.

```
class SavingsAccount:                                  //  1
      public Account,                                  //  2
      public TransferMoneySink<SavingsAccount> {       //  3
public:                                                //  4
   Currency availableBalance(void);                    //  5
                                                       //  6
   // These functions can be virtual if there are      //  7
   // specializations of SavingsAccount                //  8
   void decreaseBalance(Currency);                     //  9
   void updateLog(string, MyTime, Currency);           // 10
   void increaseBalance(Currency);                     // 11
};                                                     // 12
                                                       // 13
class InvestmentAccount:                               // 14
   public Account,                                     // 15
   public TransferMoneySource<InvestmentAccount> {     // 16
public:                                                // 17
   Currency availableBalance(void);                    // 18
   void decreaseBalance(Currency);                     // 19
   void updateLog(string, MyTime, Currency);           // 20
};                                                     // 21
```

It's as simple as that. In Ruby, it's even simpler: the Context object mixes in the appropriate methodful role to the domain object right before enacting the Use Case. C++ sets up the arrangements at compile time; Ruby, at run time (line 4):

```
sourceAccount = InvestmentAccount.new(account)      # 1
sourceAccount.extend TransferMoneySource            # 2
destinationAccount = SavingsAccount.new(account2)   # 3
destinationAccount.extend TransferMoneySink         # 4
sourceAccount.transferTo                            # 5
```

9.6 Context Objects in the User Mental Model: Solution to an Age-Old Problem

In the old days we used to say that classes should reflect real-world concepts, but the question arises: How real is real? Consider a SavingsAccount, for example, as discussed throughout this chapter. Is it real? The fact is that if you go into a bank, you can't walk into the safe and find a bag of money on a shelf somewhere with your account number on it.

Your SavingsAccount isn't real, but it is part of your conceptual world model. That leaves us with a bit of a conundrum if we want to split the world into the domain part that reflects the actual form of the domain, and the behavior part that corresponds to your anticipated use of the domain model. What, exactly, *is* a SavingsAccount?

Before completely answering that question, it's useful to look at what the domain classes really are in a banking system. Banks are complex accounting entities with money flowing in dozens of different directions all the time, all with the goal of optimizing the bank's margins. Your SavingsAccount money isn't in a bag somewhere, but is more likely lent out to other clients so they can buy houses, or it's invested in pork bellies in Chicago or in gold in New York. It's complicated, and it's really hard to track down exactly where your money went and when it went there.

Complicated – but not impossible. If banks are anything, they are both accurate and precise regarding these transactions. Every transfer takes place as a transaction that's guaranteed not to lose any money along the way, even if a server or a network link goes down. These transactions are supported by database technology. As a further hedge against failure, there are transaction logs that can be used to recreate the sequences of events that led to your money being invested in those pork bellies. And there are audit trails over these transaction logs that have to reconcile with each other, further reducing the margin of error to the point of being almost negligible.

This has several implications. Your SavingsAccount balance at any given time isn't sitting in an object somewhere, nor is it even spinning on a disk as a value. It is dynamically calculated by spanning the audit trails, adding up any deposits (either that you made to the account, or that the bank made in terms of an interest accrual) and subtracting any withdrawals (including your own disbursements as well as any fees charged by the bank). As such, the SavingsAccount isn't a piece of "smart data," but is a collection of algorithms! It is a collection of related algorithms that implement a collection of related use cases that work in terms of object roles such as **SourceAccounts** and **DestinationAccounts** and **ATMs**, such that those object roles are bound to the transactions and audit trails related to *your* account.

We've seen this concept before. It's called a Context. It's just a collection of related scenarios (withdrawals, deposits, and balance inquiries) toward their respective goals, each one in some context. A Savings Account may now look like this:

```
class SavingsAccount                                      #  1
  attr_reader :account_id                                 #  2
  include ContextAccessor                                 #  3
                                                          #  4
  def initialize(account_id,                              #  5
        credentialsA,                                     #  6
        credentialsB)                                     #  7
  @account_id = account_id                                #  8
  @dbh = DBI.connect(                                     #  9
        "DBI:Mysql:retail:accounthost",                   # 10
        credentialsA, credentialsB)                       # 11
  end                                                     # 12
```

We start off the account with a getter to retrieve the account ID. We can think of the Savings Account in fact of just being a wrapper for an account ID with a bunch of fancy methods for operating on it. That's really what your Savings Account is: just an account ID. Because it is a special kind of Context (a collection of related scenarios) we include the `ContextAccessor` module.

To initialize a `SavingsAccount` object we remember its account ID and create a connection to the database. As a client of the Savings Account, wanting to use it as a money source in a financial transfer, we would say:

```
myMoneySource = SavingsAccount.new("0991540",
            "dbadmin", getpass).extend MoneySource
```

This is complicated. The resulting object is a `SavingsAccount` domain object, implemented as a Context object, able to play the role of a **MoneySource** role!

What does the rest of the code look like? We can go on with a definition of the `withdraw` method:

```
def withdraw(amount)                                        # 14
    execute_in_context do                                   # 15
        raise "Bad argument to withdraw" if amount < 0      # 16
        @dbh['AutoCommit'] = false                          # 17
        begin                                               # 18
            raise "Inadequate funds" if balance < amount    # 19
            @dbh.do("INSERT INTO debits (amount, time) \    # 20
                    VALUES(?, ?)",                          # 21
                    amount, Time.now)                       # 22
            @dbh.commit                                     # 23
        rescue                                              # 24
            raise "Withdrawal transaction failed"           # 25
            @dbh.rollback                                   # 26
        end                                                 # 27
    end                                                     # 28
end                                                         # 29
```

The `execute_in_context` clause allows us to stack Context objects. We then go into the scenario between the banking software and the database server that accomplishes the withdrawal. Note that it raises an exception if the `balance` is less than the amount to be withdrawn. How is `balance` calculated? As mentioned before, it is not a number sitting inside of an object or spinning on a disk, but is dynamically calculated. It might look something like this:

```
def balance                                                 # 31
    return_value = 0.0                                      # 32
    execute_in_context do                                   # 33
        begin                                               # 34
            credits = @dbh.prepare("SELECT * \              # 35
                FROM credits WHERE account_id = ?")         # 36
            credits.execute(@account_id)                    # 37
            credits.fetch do |row|                          # 38
                return_value += row[1]                      # 39
            end                                             # 40
                                                            # 41
            debits = @dbh.prepare("SELECT * \               # 42
```

```
            FROM debits WHERE account_id = ?")        # 43
        debits.execute(@account_id)                   # 44
        debits.fetch do |row|                         # 45
            return_value -= row[1]                     # 46
        end                                            # 47
    rescue                                             # 48
        raise "Balance transaction failed"             # 49
        @dbh.rollback                                  # 50
        return_value = 0.0                             # 51
    ensure                                             # 52
        credits.finish                                 # 53
        debits.finish                                  # 54
    end                                                # 55
    return_value                                       # 56
    end                                                # 57
end                                                    # 58
```

An account balance by definition is the sum over all credits less the sum of all the debits. If we add a new initialize function,

```
def Account.find(account_id, dbName, dbPass)           # 60
    SavingsAccount new(account_id, dbName, dbPass)     # 61
end                                                    # 62
```

then the rest of the code can treat SavingsAccount instances as ordinary domain objects, even though the class is implemented as a Context.

This DCI architecture allows us to separate the atomic concerns at the level of databases, debits and credits from the end-user concepts of deposits, withdrawals and accounts. Most important, it allows us to represent a Savings Account for what it is. It doesn't belong in the Data part of DCI because it has no data (other than an account ID). We could conceive of it as a role, a role played by the database or by the database constituent parts, but that's not very satisfying. What it is, in fact, is a collection of habits that tie together a different set of data objects (the database objects) every time we instantiate a new one. That fits perfectly into the DCI architecture as a Context.

Though SavingsAccount is a Context, it occupies much the same space in the end user's mind as domain objects do. That means that it can play roles such as **SourceAccount** and **DestinationAccount**. To the banker, it is just a home for what they view as business use cases. Everybody wins.

We find hybrid Context-Domain objects in many domains. Consider a telephone office: is a Phone Call an object? Very few telecommunications systems have a Phone Call object, analogous to the fact that few banking systems have Account objects. (Some systems have a notion called a

Half Call that represents the connection interests of a single terminal device.) Phone Call could also be a Context that manages object roles such as **CallingParty** and **CalledParty** (pronounced "call Ed party"). The Context could associate these roles with the appropriate domain objects (crosspoints, time slots, ports, conference bridges) according to the needs of the call and the active feature set.

It is tempting to go too far in this thinking. If you bring all the Context objects together with Domain objects, you again have mixed the what-the-system-is methods and what-the-system-does methods together in the same interface, and we're back to the original problems of classic object-oriented programming. Use your common sense. Let the stakeholder mental models be your guide. Keep concepts separate if they have different rates of change, if the concepts are maintained by separate groups of people, or if they have low mutual coupling. (You can review these techniques in Chapter 5.)

9.7 Why All These Artifacts?

You're probably thinking: "We got by with just classes all of these years (and sometimes with a little thinking about objects even at design time). Why, all of a sudden, do we need all of this complexity?" With the more complete DCI model in hand, we can give a better rationale than we did in Section 8.4.

The simple answer (if you like simple answers) is that all of this is essential complexity. Too much object-oriented design over the past twenty years is rooted in abstraction: the conscious discarding of information to help emphasize information of current interest. The problem with abstraction is that the decision about what to throw away is made at one point in time and its repercussions are often invisible until later. In software development, such decisions are usually committed during analysis and design before the realities of implementation hit. That's too early to understand what should be kept around and what should be discarded. A better position is to ground the design in long-term domain invariants, and to keep those around. That's what Chapter 5 was about.

A related reason is that this is the stuff floating around in the head of the end user. The artifacts that we have focused on in this chapter come from the end users' model of system behavior in the same sense that Chapter 5 is rooted in their notions of program form. To the degree the software captures the end user's world model, it's a good thing:

- Directly, it helps developers communicate with users in terms of their mental models of the world instead of computer-ese – along the lines of the Agile value of individuals and interactions over processes and tools.

- It provides a short path from user mental models to the code, which makes it possible to use tight feedback loops so the code converges on user expectations – along the lines of the Agile value of customer collaboration.

- It makes it easier for us to reason about forms that are important to the user, such as the form of the sequencing of events toward a goal in a context, and to raise our confidence that the code does what we (and ultimately, the end user) want it to – along the lines of the Agile value of working software.

- It catches change were it happens and encapsulates it, rather than spreading it across the architecture (as would be the case if we distributed parts of the algorithm across existing classes) – along the lines of the Agile value of responding to change.

No, we didn't just come along and add this list as an afterthought or as an opportunistic way to shoehorn these ideas into buzzword-dom. The techniques have come out of a conscious effort to strive towards the values that underlie Agile.

But let's get out of the clouds and get into the nitty-gritty.

Why not Use Classes Instead of "Methodful Object Roles"?

In most contemporary programming languages we actually do use classes as a way to implement methodful object roles. Scala properly has traits, which are in effect just methodful object roles. We foresee the need for a new programming language feature, which is a kind of generic collection of stateless algorithms that can be mixed into existing classes without having to resort to a "trick" like traits. Traits are a convenient and adequately expressive way of expressing these semantics in the mean time. It's unlikely that such a language feature would make or break a project; it would only relieve temporary confusion or perhaps help new project members come on board a bit more quickly.

Why not Put the Entire Algorithm Inside of the Class with which it is Most Closely Coupled?

Even if one believed that one could identify this class, it wouldn't be the only one. There is another problem of essential complexity: the class structure is not the behavior structure. There is a many-to-many mapping between these use cases and the classes of the objects that they orchestrate. If one class "owns" the algorithm, what do we do for other classes that want to play the same use case? That would mean duplicating the code manually, and that would be error-prone for all the reasons that we hate code duplication. Therefore, we "re-use" it, semi-automatically, using traits or another suitable method.

Then Why not Localize the Algorithm to a Class and Tie it to Domain Objects as Needed?

That's essentially what we do, and essentially what traits are.

Why not Put the Algorithm into a Procedure, and Combine the Procedural Paradigm with the Object Paradigm in a Single Program?

This is the old C++ approach and in fact is the approach advocated in *Multi-paradigm design for C++* (Coplien 1998). The main problem with this approach is that it doesn't express relationships between related algorithms, or between related algorithm fragments, that exist in the end user's head. It obfuscates the role structure. These algorithms are not single closed copies of procedural code, but they play out through object roles.

A scenario that runs through objects frequently needs intimate knowledge about those objects. A closed procedure can access the internals of an object only through its public interface. If we put the use case scenarios in closed procedures, it would cause the interfaces of the objects to bloat to support this close relationship between the use case and the objects. By instead injecting the procedure (bit by bit) into the objects, we allow the code of the algorithms to gain access to object internals (such as domain object private methods) if needed. We need to add new interfaces to domain objects only for business-level functionality that is germane to the use case, rather than adding low-level access methods needed by the use case.

Does this mean that procedural design is completely dead? Of course not. There are still algorithms that are just algorithms (Freud's "sometimes a cigar is just a cigar"). We can encapsulate algorithms in the private implementation of classes using procedural decomposition. There's nothing wrong with that. However, those concerns are rarely architectural concerns; we leave those to the cleverness of designers and architects as they come to low-level design and the craftsmanship of implementation.

If I Collect Together the Algorithm Code for a Use Case in One Class, Including the Code for All of its Deviations, Doesn't the Context Become Very Large?

Yes, it can be large. However, this code actually does belong together in a single administrative entity. Further, each Context encodes information about roles that are absent from old-fashioned object-oriented programs, so there is useful information in that extra code. The Context's role mapping makes it possible to leave domain classes dumb, which makes them easier to understand. And it makes it possible to separate out the use case code, which not only makes it easier to understand, but which simplifies maintenance as well. We encourage you to experiment with further partitioning of the Context code according to the broad architectural principles of Chapter 5, using your common sense, taste, insight, and experience.

So, What do DCI and Lean Architecture Give Me?

We claim that this style of development:

- Modularizes use case scenarios and algorithms in the software so you can reason about, unit test, and formally analyze the code with respect to functional requirements.

- Maps the architecture onto a domain model that reduces the time and expense of determining where new functionality should be added.

- Produces an architecture that can support a GUI or command set with few surprises for the user – because it is based on the end user mental model.

- Gives you all the flexibility of MVC in separating the data model of the program from the user interface.

- Leads to a design that encourages the capture and expression of essential complexity, which means that when you need to express essential complexity, you don't need to go in with dynamite and jack hammers to make changes: the right structure is already there.

- Allows you to introduce functionality just in time, whether the code is in the traditional platform code or in the application code.

And Remember . . .

This is an Agile book, and you are (at least sometimes) an Agile programmer. We encourage you to think (oh, yeah, it's a Lean book, too), to plan a bit, and to not just take our word for how to do things. We provide you examples to stimulate your thinking; these *concepts* in hand, you can tune the code to your own local needs. There are a million ways to map object roles to objects, to inject methods into classes, and to make the context available to the methodful object roles. Here, we have focused on Ruby and C++ implementations. The idioms and approaches you use in Java, C# and Objective C will be different. Use your ingenuity. And read on for a few more hints.

9.8   Beyond C++: DCI in Other Languages

We've illustrated DCI in Ruby here for two reasons. First, the Ruby implementation of DCI is relatively straightforward and clean. Second, we wanted to communicate DCI concepts clearly, and anyone who reads Ruby code thinks that they understand it. And we've illustrated DCI in

C++ here for two reasons. First, the DCI implementation is statically typed and is based on templates; we wanted to show that DCI works even under these restrictions. The second reason is the relative breadth-of-use of C++ in real-time and complex problems that have the most need for such expressiveness.

However, DCI is hardly a Ruby or C++ phenomenon. It is broadly based on the notion of injecting collections of methods into a class. C++ and most other classful languages tend to use classes as their building blocks for this injection, so it reduces to class composition – Schärli's original notion of traits. Other languages cannot only support DCI well but in many instances can do so better than C++ because their type systems are varyingly more dynamic.

9.8.1 Scala

Scala is one such language. In September of 2008, Bill Venners (Odersky et al 2008) demonstrated the first application of DCI in that language. Scala is interesting because it has traits as full first-class language citizens; it looks almost like it was made for DCI.

What's more, Scala has one significant advantage over C++. C++ forces us to do the object role injection (class composition using templates) in the declaration of the domain class at compile time. That suggests that the addition of any object role to a domain will require the recompilation of all code in that domain. (As is true in almost all languages, the domain code must actually be changed only if the new injection creates name collisions.) In Scala, the injection is done at the point of object instantiation:

```
. . . .
trait TransferMoneySource extends MoneySource {
  this: Account =>
  // This code is reviewable and testable!
  def transferTo(amount: Long, recipient: MoneySink) {
    beginTransaction()
    if (availableBalance < amount) {
      . . . .
}
. . . .
val source = new SavingsAccount with TransferMoneySource
val sink = new CheckingAccount with TransferMoneySink
. . . .
```

Bill Venners has contributed a Scala variant of our running Accounts example in Appendix A.

9.8.2 Python

Serge Beaumont and David Byers have contributed a rendition of the Accounts example in Python that dates from October 2008. The Python code is quite faithful to the DCI paradigm. It is a fascinating implementation that binds object role methods to the domain objects in a fully dynamic way: the object role methods are injected into the domain objects only for the duration of the use case scenario for which they are needed! Contrast this with the C++ implementation that pre-loads the object role methods into the classes at compile time and the Scala implementation that loads the object role methods into the object at instantiation time. You can find the Python implementation in Appendix B.

9.8.3 C#

Christian Horsdal Gammelgaard has provided an early version of DCI in C#, and it is shown in Appendix C. The code features the way that C# handles traits using extension methods. Extension methods are methods that can statically be bound to a class at run time. They take explicit object pointer arguments rather than using a transparent `self` argument to give the illusion of being inside of the object. With that minor concession the illusion is good enough: collections of methods can be added to a class at run time to give the illusion of class composition.

9.8.4 . . . and Even Java

To date, native Java solutions are less satisfying than those offered by the older C++ language and the newer Ruby, Python and Scala solutions. These modern languages seem to offer a good point of compromise – and perhaps a near-ideal solution – for expressiveness and performance. The C++ solution shines in expressiveness and performance but suffers accidental coupling that has high configuration management costs. It is difficult to balance expressiveness (e.g., to avoid self schizophrenia) and performance (avoiding multiple levels of function calls) in Java.

The Qi4j framework (Qi4j 2006) from Rickard Öberg and Niclas Hedhman provides an environment that enhances Java to the point where it supports DCI well. A Qi4j programmer decorates Java code with annotations used by the framework to arrange the right role-to-object bindings at run time. Qi4j is no longer pure Java, but a bit of syntactic saccharin on top of Java that removes the problems of self-schizophrenia and run-time overhead that plague most Java attempts at implementing DCI. Fine-tuning on Qi4j continues and a release of the Qi4j platform is anticipated before the scheduled publication of this book. It is the best option today for Java programmers to use DCI.

9.8.5 The Account Example in Smalltalk

DCI grew out of the Smalltalk culture, and most of the early work on DCI was done in Squeak. Appendix F offers a tour through the account example that Trygve Reenskaug developed as a concept demo in his DCI-based IDE, BabyUML (Reenskaug 2007).

9.9 Documentation?

A good architecture reduces the need for additional explicit documentation. In DCI, the code is the documentation of the algorithm! Abstract base classes for the domain classes are themselves a treasure of information about the partitioning of the system into domains and about the general facilities of each domain. A major theme of Agile communities is code-as-documentation, and it's a great common-sense approach that makes life easier for everyone who interacts with the code.

Programming language designers spend a lot of effort making languages expressive: in fact, such expressiveness is exactly what distinguishes programming languages. From the perspective of computational complexity, all common programming languages are equally powerful. The evidence for any programming language offering any significant productivity improvement is slim. Nevertheless, they express things differently. Smalltalk emphasizes minimalism; C++, richness of features and static typing; Java, a degree of cultural compatibility with C++ but with some Smalltalk semantics; and so forth. Given all this expressiveness, your coding language is a pretty good language for describing what the code does.

Given that, here are some good tips for supporting your documentation efforts – or, more precisely, for going beyond brute-force textual descriptions of the program design.

- *Choose the right language, and let the code do the talking.* If you're using use cases and DCI, what language best expresses your scenarios? If you're using an atomic event style, what language best expresses the semantics of the system events? Experiment with generally available languages to see which one best fits your need. Create your own domain-specific languages only with extreme caution; the cost in creating and sustaining the environment and infrastructure for a language is high, and it's difficult enough to express yourself in an existing language, let alone create the language in which you then must learn to express yourself (Section 5.3.8).

- *Keep it short.* While the abstract base classes for the domain design should cover the scope of the business, don't load up the interfaces with gratuitous hooks and embellishments.

- *Choose good identifier names.* This may seem like a strange item to include in this list, but don't underestimate its value. Lovingly name each identifier with the same care as for a first-born child. You'll be using these names a lot as you pair program or otherwise discuss the code with your colleagues. Many identifiers at the architectural level will rise to the level of the vernacular that you share with your customers. Strive to make them feel included by using their names for things, rather than yours.

- *Document architectural intent with pre- and post-conditions.* Just delimiting the range of values of a scalar argument speaks volumes about a piece of code. Such documentation evolves along with the code (unlike external text documents which are too often forgotten), can boost visibility of the alignment of the business structure with the code, and can give programmers constraints that focus and guide their work. This is Lean's notion of failure-proof (*poka-yoke*) in the small.

- *Use block comments.* Let the code speak for itself on a line-by-line basis, but use explicit comments only as the introduction to a major opus of code (such as a class or package) or where the code is particularly tricky. If the block is longer than 3 lines, a lot fewer people will read it, and the chances of it being out-of-date will increase faster over time than if it were shorter.

In general, some of the best work you can do to support the architects in their goal to reduce discovery costs is to keep the code clean. You'll find your own practices and ceremonies for doing this, but take some cues from the experts in Uncle Bob's *Clean Code* book (Martin 2009).

9.10 History and Such

The ideas behind DCI first started coming together in about 2005. By late 2006, Trygve was casting DCI (only to be so named much later) as a technique suitable to a Theory Y management style in opposed to a Theory X style. Theory Y aligns with many of the stereotypes of Agile, while Theory X aligns with many of the stereotypes of the industrial age. By August 2008 the BabyUML project had reached its goal, and DCI was a reality. By mid-2009 implementations were being traded around the DCI community in many programming languages.

9.10.1 DCI and Aspect-Oriented Programming

DCI arose as a conscious attempt to capture the end user's model of the algorithm in the code rather than as a solution to an engineering problem. Aspect-Oriented Programming, by contrast, can be viewed as an engineering solution to an architectural problem. Most implementations of AOP (most notably AspectJ (Ramnivas 2003)) make it almost impossible to reason about the functionality of aspectualized code without global knowledge of the program.

The origins of AOP are more profound than meets the eye. Gregor Kiczales created them in part as a path to bring the power of reflection to everyday programmers in familiar packaging. Reflection is a keystone of software evolution but has been unable to capture the imagination of the programming public. DCI is also a form of reflection, and of explicitly manipulating the object model at run time: run-time association from object roles to objects as the primary form of polymorphism is one example. In this sense AOP and DCI have common goals and common roots, but the mechanisms, syntax, and semantics have little in common.

Jim Coplien first presented DCI as an alternative to AOP at the European Science Foundation Workshop on Correlation Theory Vielsalm, Belgium in August 2008. DCI brings together logic that is "tangled" into domain classes the same way that particle states are entangled in quantum computing.

9.10.2 Other Approaches

DCI is reminiscent of many other programming techniques and platforms: of dependency injection, of Spring (Mak 2008), of the capability-based architecture of the IBM System 38, of mixins (Moon 1986), as well as AOP as mentioned above. DCI is in fact a way of implementing a regularized reflection layer in the architecture. These other related technologies all have elements of reflection, and many of them can be used as techniques to implement DCI.

We usually think of reflection as a way of treating classes like objects; in DCI, we use reflection to treat objects like roles. DCI in fact can build on mixins: a trait is really a mechanism to implement mixins, and mixins are a mechanism to keep business and domain logic separate in their own classes while combining their behaviors into a single object. To that, DCI adds the source language notion of being able to think and program in roles. It also presumes an environment (often provided by the programmer) that orchestrates the role-to-object mapping on a per-use-case-scenario basis.

Other approaches have existed in the past to separate features from the business logic. Most of these, such as multi-paradigm design (Coplien 1998) were conceptually nice but created poor patterns of coupling and cohesion in the architecture.

# CHAPTER 10

As for computer professionals routinely thinking and acting with long-term responsibility, that may come gradually as a by-product of the Year 2000 comeuppance, or life extension, of environmental lessons, and of globalization (island Earth).

The Clock of the Long Now, p. 86.

The computer code we are offhandedly writing today could become the deeply embedded standards for centuries to come. Any programmer or system designer who takes that realization on and feels the full karmic burden, gets vertigo.

Jaron Lanier quoted in *The Clock of the Long Now*, p. 120.

Christopher Alexander, an urban planner and architect of the built world, talks about great architecture as being the result of millions of selfless acts of individuals. He, too, understood the Lean Secret of a whole team:

> It is essential only that the people of a society, together, all the millions of them, not just professional architects, design all the millions of places. There is no other way that human variety, and the reality of specific human lives, can find their way into the structure of the places. (Alexander 1979, p. 164)

This quote, together with the quotes that open this chapter and dozens more like them, underscore the weightiness of software architecture in the future of humanity. In his address at OOPSLA 1996, Alexander charged the software discipline with the future of beauty and morality in our world – goals that come through our own architectural strivings.

As regards building architecture, Alexander (Alexander 1974, preface), Darke (1979) and others note that no method will get you there. It is larger than the tradition of software architects alone, but is the purview of entire teams building software. It comes down to the individual, humble acts of a few individuals. When Grandpa Harry built his cozy, functional house or his warm cabin in the woods, he used no method. A tightrope walker performs largely out of instinct. Both create beauty that is more firmly grounded in practice or experience than in any notation or any sense of scientific grounding. Alexander's whole quest for beauty in patterns also traces back to this grounding in experience, exercised through trial and error in the present. All of these processes fundamentally depend on feedback, and feedback depends on a good dose of humility towards the incertitude of the future.

Computing is still young; domain analysis goes back only to 1980 or so, and DCI came together only in 2009. We look to readers of this book to carry both into the future. The final chapter is yours. You're Lean, and you're Agile, so you'll fare well.

Scala Implementation of the DCI Account Example

```scala
import java.util.Date

// Account is just a base class for the domain
// objects, that are different kinds of accounts
// (e.g. SavingsAccount, CheckingAccount...)

trait Account {
  private var balance: Long = 0
  def availableBalance: Long = balance
  def decreaseBalance(amount: Long) {
    if (amount < 0)
      throw new InsufficientFundsException
    balance -= amount
  }
  def increaseBalance(amount: Long) {
    balance += amount
  }
  def updateLog(msg: String, date: Date,
                amount: Long) {
    println("Account: " + toString + ", " + msg + ", "
      + date.toString + ", " + amount)
  }
}
```

```
// MoneySource is a methodless role type that captures
// the form (interface) of part of the
// Transfer behavior

trait MoneySource {
  def transferTo(amount: Long, recipient: MoneySink)
}


// MoneySink is a methodless role type that captures
// the form (interface) of the other part of the
// Transfer behavior

trait MoneySink {
  def increaseBalance(amount: Long)
  def updateLog(msg: String, date: Date, amount: Long)
}


// TransferMoneySink is the methodful role for the
// recipient in a money transfer

trait TransferMoneySink extends MoneySink {
 this: Account =>
 def transferFrom(amount: Long, src: MoneySource) {
   increaseBalance(amount)
   updateLog("Transfer in", new Date, amount)
 }
}

class InsufficientFundsException
    extends RuntimeException


// This is the methodful role for the source account
// for the money transfer

trait TransferMoneySource extends MoneySource {

  this: Account =>

  // This code is reviewable and testable!
```

```scala
  def transferTo(amount: Long, recipient: MoneySink) {

    beginTransaction()

    if (availableBalance < amount) {
      endTransaction()
      throw new InsufficientFundsException
    }
    else {
      decreaseBalance(amount)
      recipient.increaseBalance(amount)
      updateLog("Transfer Out", new Date, amount)

        // recipient is the role on the other
        // side of the transfer
      recipient.updateLog("Transfer In",
              new Date, amount)
    }

    gui.displayScreen(SUCCESS_DEPOSIT_SCREEN)
    endTransaction()
  }
}


// SavingsAccount is the class of domain objects
// representing the concept of Savings Accounts,
// CheckingAccount is analogous for checking

class SavingsAccount extends Account {
  override def toString = "Savings"
}

class CheckingAccount extends Account {
  override def toString = "Checking"
}

// This is just the test driver.

object App extends Application {
  val source =
        new SavingsAccount with TransferMoneySource
  val sink = new CheckingAccount with TransferMoneySink
```

```
    source.increaseBalance(100000)
    source.transferTo(200, sink)
    println(source.availableBalance + ", " +
        sink.availableBalance)
}
```

Account Example in Python

```
"""
DCI proof of concept
Context is a separate object to the Collaboration (again for
exploration of alternatives). Made a class for it, but a
Dictionary is also possible.

Author: David Byers, Serge Beaumont
7 October 2008
"""

import new

class Role(object):
    """A Role is a special class that never gets
    instantiated directly. Instead, when the user wants
    to create a new role instance, we create a new class
    that has the role and another object's class
    as its superclasses, then create an instance of that
    class, and link the new object's dict to the original
    object's dict."""
        def __new__(cls, ob):
            members = dict(__ob__ = ob)
            if hasattr(ob.__class__, '__slots__'):
              members['__setattr__'] = Role.__setattr
```

```
            members['__getattr__'] = Role.__getattr
            members['__delattr__'] = Role.__delattr

        c = new.classobj("%s as %s.%s" %
            (ob.__class__.__name__,
            cls.__module__, cls.__name__),
            (cls, ob.__class__), members)
        i = object.__new__(c)
        if hasattr(ob, '__dict__'):
            i.__dict__ = ob.__dict__

        return i

    def __init__(self, ob):
        """Do not call the superclass __init__. If we
        did, then we would call the __init__ function in
        the real class hierarchy too (i.e. Account, in
        this example)"""
        pass

    def __getattr(self, attr):
        """Proxy to object"""
        return getattr(self.__ob__, attr)

    def __setattr(self, attr, val):
        """Proxy to object"""
        setattr(self.__ob__, attr, val)

    def __delattr(self, attr):
        """Proxy to object"""
        delattr(self.__ob__, attr)

class MoneySource(Role):
    def transfer_to(self, ctx, amount):
        if self.balance >= amount:
            self.decreaseBalance(amount)
            ctx.sink.receive(ctx, amount)

class MoneySink(Role):
    """The receiving part of the transfer behavior"""
    def receive(self, ctx, amount):
        self.increaseBalance(amount)
```

```python
class Account(object):
  """The class for the domain object"""
    def __init__(self, amount):
        print "Creating a new account with balance of " +
            str(amount)
        self.balance = amount
        super(Account, self).__init__()

    def decreaseBalance(self, amount):
        print "Withdraw " + str(amount) + " from " +
            str(self)
        self.balance -= amount

    def increaseBalance(self, amount):
        print "Deposit " + str(amount) + " in " +
            str(self)
        self.balance += amount

class Context(object):
    """Holds Context state."""
    pass

class TransferMoney(object):
  """This is the environment, like the controller,
  that builds the Context and offers an interface
  to trigger the Context to run"""
    def __init__(self, source, sink):
        self.context = Context()
        self.context.source = MoneySource(source)
        self.context.sink = MoneySink(sink)

    def __call__(self, amount):
        self.context.source.transfer_to(
            self.context, amount)

if __name__ == '__main__':
    src = Account(1000)
    dst = Account(0)

    t = TransferMoney(src, dst)
    t(100)

    print src.balance
    print dst.balance
```

Account Example in C#

Christian Horsdal Gammelgaard provides the following code in C#, using the extension method facility as a way to demonstrate injection of role functionality into a domain class.

```csharp
using System;

namespace DCI
{
    // Methodless role types
    public interface TransferMoneySink
    {
    }

    // Methodful roles
    public interface TransferMoneySource
    {
    }

    public static class TransferMoneySourceTraits
    {
        public static void TransferFrom(
                this TransferMoneySource self,
                TransferMoneySink recipient, double amount)
        {
            // This methodful role can only
            // be mixed into Account object (and subtypes)
```

```
        Account self_ = self as Account;
        Account recipient_ = recipient as Account;

        // Self-contained readable and testable
        //   algorithm

        if (self_ != null && recipient_ != null)
        {
            self_.DecreaseBalance(amount);
            self_.Log("Withdrawing " + amount);
            recipient_.IncreaseBalance(amount);
            recipient_.Log("Depositing " + amount);
        }
    }
}


// Context object
public class TransferMoneyContext
{
    // Properties for accessing the concrete objects
    // relevant in this context through their
    // methodless roles
    public TransferMoneySource Source {
        get; private set;
    }

    public TransferMoneySink Sink {
        get;
        private set;
    }

    public double Amount {
        get; private set;
    }

    public TransferMoneyContext()
    {
        // logic for retrieving source and sink accounts
    }

    public TransferMoneyContext(
                TransferMoneySource source,
```

```
                        TransferMoneySink sink,
                        double amount)
    {
        Source = source;
        Sink = sink;
        Amount = amount;
    }

    public void Doit()
    {
        Source.TransferFrom(Sink, Amount);

        // Alternatively the context could be passed
        // to the source and sink object.
    }
}


/////////////// Model ////////////////

// Abstract domain object
public abstract class Account
{
    public abstract void DecreaseBalance(
                    double amount);
    public abstract void IncreaseBalance(
                    double amount);
    public abstract void Log(string message);
}


// Concrete domain object
public class SavingsAccount :
    Account,
    TransferMoneySource,
    TransferMoneySink
{
    private double balance;

    public SavingsAccount()
    {
        balance = 10000;
    }
```

```csharp
    public override void DecreaseBalance(
                                    double amount)
    {
        balance -= amount;
    }

    public override void IncreaseBalance(
                                    double amount)
    {
        balance += amount;
    }

    public override void Log(string message)
    {
        Console.WriteLine(message);
    }

    public override string ToString()
    {
        return "Balance " + balance;
    }

}


/////////// Controller ////////////////

// Test controller

public class App
{
    public static void Main(string[] args)
    {
        SavingsAccount src = new SavingsAccount();
        SavingsAccount snk = new SavingsAccount();

        Console.WriteLine("Before:");
        Console.WriteLine("Src:" + src);
        Console.WriteLine("Snk:" + snk);

        Console.WriteLine("Run transfer:");
```

```
            new TransferMoneyContext(src, snk, 1000).Doit();

            Console.WriteLine("After:");
            Console.WriteLine("Src:" + src);
            Console.WriteLine("Snk:" + snk);

            Console.ReadLine();
        }
    }
}
```

Account Example in Ruby

This rendition comes from Steen Lehmann.

```ruby
require 'osx/cocoa'

#!/usr/bin/env ruby
# Lean Architecture example in Ruby -
#  with ContextAccessor

# Module that can be mixed in to any class
# that needs access to the current context. It is
# implemented as a thread-local variable.

module ContextAccessor
  def context
    Thread.current[:context]
  end

  def context=(ctx)
    Thread.current[:context] = ctx
  end

  def execute_in_context
    old_context = self.context
    self.context = self
    yield
    self.context = old_context
  end
end
```

```ruby
#
# This is the base class (common code) for all
# Account domain classes.
#

class Account
  attr_reader :account_id, :balance

  def initialize(account_id)
    @account_id = account_id
    @balance = 0
  end

  def decreaseBalance(amount)
    raise "Bad argument to withdraw" if amount < 0
    raise "Insufficient funds" if amount > balance
    @balance -= amount
  end

  def increaseBalance(amount)
    @balance += amount
  end

  def update_log(msg, date, amount)
    puts "Account: #{inspect}, #{msg}, #{date.to_s}, \
        #{amount}"
  end

  def self.find(account_id)
    @@store ||= Hash.new
    return @@store[account_id] if @@store.has_key?
        account_id

    if :savings == account_id
      account = SavingsAccount.new(account_id)
      account.increaseBalance(100000)
    elsif :checking == account_id
      account = CheckingAccount.new(account_id)
    else
      account = Account.new(account_id)
    end
    @@store[account_id] = account
    account
  end
end
```

```ruby
# This module is the methodless role type. Since
# we don't really use types to declare identifiers,
# it's kind of a hobby horse. We preserve those APIs
# for consistency with the other languages. This also
# provides a single common place to create aliases
# for the role bindings

module MethodlessMoneySource # the API only
  def transfer_out; end
  def pay_bills; end

  # Role aliases for use by the methodful role
  def destination_account; context.destination_account end
  def creditors; context.creditors end
  def amount; context.amount end
end

module MethodlessMoneySink # the API only
  def transfer_in; end
  def amount; context.amount end
end

# Here are the real methodful roles

module MoneySink
  include MethodlessMoneySink, ContextAccessor

  def transfer_in
   self.increaseBalance amount
   self.update_log "Transfer In", Time.now, amount
  end
end

module MoneySource
  include MethodlessMoneySource, ContextAccessor

  def transfer_out
    raise "Insufficient funds" if balance < amount
    self.decreaseBalance amount
    destination_account.transfer_in
    self.update_log "Transfer Out", Time.now, amount
  end

  def pay_bills
    creditors = context.creditors.dup
    creditors.each do |creditor|
```

```
      TransferMoneyContext.execute(
        creditor.amount_owed,
        account_id,
        creditor.account.account_id)
    end
  end
end

#
# Creditor is an actor in the use case, and is
# represented by an object of this class
#

class Creditor
  attr_accessor :amount_owed, :account

  #
  # The "find" method is set up just for demonstration
  # purposes. A real one would search a database for a
  # particular creditor, based on more meaningful
  # search criteria
  #

  def self.find(name)
    @@store ||= Hash.new
    return @@store[name] if @@store.has_key? name

    if :baker == name
      creditor = Creditor.new
      creditor.amount_owed = 50
      creditor.account = Account.find(:baker_account)
    elsif :butcher == name
      creditor = Creditor.new
      creditor.amount_owed = 90
      creditor.account = Account.find(:butcher_account)
    end
    creditor
  end
end

# Implementation of Transfer Money use case

class TransferMoneyContext
  attr_reader :source_account, :destination_account, :amount
  include ContextAccessor
```

```ruby
  def self.execute(amt,
                   source_account_id,
                   destination_account_id)
    TransferMoneyContext.new(amt,
      source_account_id,
      destination_account_id).execute
  end

  def initialize(amt,
                 source_account_id,
                 destination_account_id)
    @source_account = Account.find(source_account_id)
    @source_account.extend MoneySource

    @destination_account =Account.find(destination_
        account_id)
    @destination_account.extend MoneySink
    @amount = amt
  end

  def execute
    execute_in_context do
      source_account.transfer_out
    end
  end

end

#
# This is the Context for the PayBills use case
#

class PayBillsContext
  attr_reader :source_account, :creditors
  include ContextAccessor

  # This is the class method which sets up to
  # execute the instance method. For more details,
  # see the text of CHAPTER 9 (page 342)
  def self.execute(source_account_id,creditor_names)
    PayBillsContext.new(source_account_id,creditor_names).
                                                  execute
  end

  def initialize(source_account_id, creditor_names)
```

```ruby
      @source_account = Account.find(source_account_id)
      @creditors = creditor_names.map do |name|
        Creditor.find(name)
      end
    end

    def execute
      execute_in_context do
        source_account.pay_bills
      end
    end
  end

end

#
# The accounts are pretty stupid, with most of
# the logic in the base class
#

class SavingsAccount < Account
  include MoneySink
end

class CheckingAccount < Account
  include MoneySink
end

#
# Test drivers. First, transfer some money
#

TransferMoneyContext.execute(300, :savings, :checking)
TransferMoneyContext.execute(100, :checking, :savings)

puts "Savings: #{Account.find(:savings).balance},
Checking: #{Account.find(:checking).balance}"

# Now pay some bills
PayBillsContext.execute(:checking, [ :baker, :butcher])

puts "After paying bills, checking has: " \
  "#{Account.find(:checking).balance}"
puts "Baker and butcher have " \
  "#{Account.find(:baker_account).balance}," \
  "#{Account.find(:butcher_account).balance}"
```

Qi4j (Qi4j 2006) is a Java framework that support class composition to achieve a DCI-like architecture. The implementation relies heavily on annotations. You can read more about the annotations and the framework in the reference. This code comes from Steen Lehmann.

```java
@Concerns({PurchaseLimitConcern.class,
                  InventoryConcern.class})
public interface OrderComposite
    extends Order, HasLineItems, Composite
{
}

public abstract class InventoryConcern
    extends ConcernOf<Invoice>
    implements Invoice
{
    @Service InventoryService inventory;

    public void addLineItem( LineItem item )
    {
        String productCode = item.getProductCode();
        int quantity = item.getQuantity();
        inventory.remove( productCode, quantity );
        next.addLineItem( item );
    }
}
```

```java
    public void removeLineItem( LineItem item )
    {
        String productCode = item.getProductCode();
        int quantity = item.getQuantity();
        inventory.add( productCode, quantity );
        next.removeLineItem( item );
    }
}

@Concerns({PurchaseLimitConcern.class,
        InventoryConcern.class})
public interface OrderComposite
    extends Order, HasLineItems, EntityComposite
{
}

@SideEffects( MailNotifySideEffect.class )
@Concerns({PurchaseLimitConcern.class,
        InventoryConcern.class})
public interface OrderComposite
    extends Order, HasLineItem, EntityComposite
{
}

public abstract class MailNotifySideEffect
    extends SideEffectOf<Order>
    implements Order
{
    @Service MailService mailer;
    @This HasLineItems hasItems;
    @This Order order;

    public void confirmOrder()
    {
        List<LineItem> items = hasItems.getLineItems();

        StringBuilder builder = new StringBuilder();
        builder.append( "An Order has been made.\n");
        builder.append( "\n\n");
        builder.append( "Total amount:" );
        builder.append( order.getOrderAmount() );
        builder.append( "\n\nItems ordered:\n" );
        for( LineItem item : items )
```

```
        {
            builder.append( item.getName() );
            builder.append( " : " );
            builder.append( item.getQuantity() );
            builder.append( "\n" );
        }
        mailer.send( "sales@mycompany.com",
                     builder.toString() );
    }
}
```

Account Example in Squeak

This is a fileout of Trygve Reenskaug's Squeak implementation of the BankTransfer example. The standard Squeak text format is somewhat unreadable, so the file has been hand edited to simplify reading. (Actual program statements are numbered, all other lines are comments.)

The appendix is broken up into sections that correspond to the views of the program supported.

A method in one object is triggered by a message that is sent from a method in the same or another object. The Squeak syntax is simple, if unusual. *In each example below, a corresponding Java-like expression is added below it.*

Assignment to a variable is done with :=

```
foo := 6.
foo = 6;
```

Comments are enclosed in double quotes: *"This is a comment"*

There are three kinds of messages: Unary, binary, and keyword. Unary messages are executed first, then binary, and finally keyword messages.

Unary message:

```
account balance
account.balance()
```

Binary message:

```
a + b
```

Here, a is an object, + is a message selector, b is an argument. In Java we would just say a+b.

Keyword message:

```
ctx transfer: 500 fromAccount: 1111 toAccount: 2222
ctx.transfer:fromAccount:toAccount:
  (500, 1111, 2222).
```

Colon is a permissible character in message selectors (method names). A class is created by sending a message to its superclass:

```
Object subclass: #BB5Testing
    instanceVariableNames: ' '
    category: 'BB5Bank-Testing'
```

All methods return a value. The default is `self` if nothing else is specified:

```
^ returnValue
return returnValue
```

Statements are separated by a point (.). Cascaded messages to the same receiver are separated by semicolons (;). So:

```
self
        fromAccountNumber: from;
        toAccountNumber: to;
        executeInContext: [self transferAmount: amount].
```

is equivalent to:

```
self fromAccountNumber: from.
self toAccountNumber: to.
self executeInContext: [self transferAmount: amount].
```

An expression in square brackets ([]) is a *block object*. It can be saved in instance variables, passed around in arguments. It is evaluated by sending it a suitable messages such as `value`, `value:`, `value:value:` depending on the number of arguments. It is most commonly used in a test expression such as:

```
balance < amount ifTrue:
  [self notify: 'Insufficient funds'. ^self].
if (balance < amount) {
    self.notify: ('Insufficient funds'); return self}
```

A DCI example:

```
self executeInContext: [self transferAmount: amount]
```

F.1   Testing Perspective

```
Object subclass: #BB5Testing
    instanceVariableNames: ' '
    category: 'BB5Bank-Testing'
```

```
"Tests (static methods)"
```
BB5Testing class>>test1
```
    " START HERE to perform test.No visible result if
            test OK."
    | bank ctx |
    bank := BB5Bank new.
    (bank addCheckingAccountNumbered: 1111) increase: 2000.
    bank addSavingsAccountNumbered: 2222.
    self assert:
            [(bank findAccount: 1111) balance = 2000.
            (bank findAccount: 2222) balance = 0].
    ctx := BB5MoneyTransferContext new.
    ctx bank: bank.
    ctx transfer: 500 fromAccount: 1111 toAccount: 2222.
    self assert:
            [(bank findAccount: 1111) balance = 1500.
            (bank findAccount: 2222) balance = 500].
```

F.2   Data Perspective

Note: The two account classes are identical. They are kept separate for illustrative purposes.

F.2.1   BB5Bank

```
Object subclass: #BB5Bank
    instanceVariableNames: 'accounts'
```

```
        category: 'BB5Bank-Data'
```

```
"private methods"
BB5Bank>>initialize
    super initialize.
    accounts := Dictionary new.
```

```
"access methods"
BB5Bank>>addCheckingAccountNumbered: aNumber
    ^accounts at: aNumber put:  BB5CheckingAccount new.
BB5Bank>>addSavingsAccountNumbered: aNumber
    ^accounts  at: aNumber put:  BB5SavingsAccount new.
BB5Bank>>findAccount: accountNumber
    ^accounts at: accountNumber ifAbsent: [nil]
```

F.2.2   BB5SavingsAccount

```
Object subclass: #BB5SavingsAccount
    uses: BB5MoneyTransferContextTransferMoneySink
    instanceVariableNames: 'balance'
    category: 'BB5Bank-Data'
```

```
"private methods"
BB5SavingsAccount>>initialize
    super initialize.
    balance := 0
```

```
"access methods"
BB5SavingsAccount>>balance
    ^balance
BB5SavingsAccount>>decrease: amount
    balance := balance - amount.
BB5SavingsAccount>>increase: amount
    balance := balance + amount.
```

F.2.3   BB5CheckingAccount

```
Object subclass: #BB5CheckingAccount
    uses: BB5MoneyTransferContextTransferMoneySource
```

```
    instanceVariableNames: 'balance'
    category: 'BB5Bank-Data'
```

"private methods"
BB5CheckingAccount>>initialize
```
    super initialize.
    balance := 0.
```

"access methods"
BB5CheckingAccount>>balance
```
    ^balance
```
BB5CheckingAccount>>decrease: amount
```
    balance := balance - amount.
```
BB5CheckingAccount>>increase: amount
```
    balance := balance + amount.
```

F.3 Context Perspective

Note: All context classes are subclass of BB1Context.

F.3.1 BB5MoneyTransferContext

```
BB1Context subclass: #BB5MoneyTransferContext
    uses: BB5MoneyTransferContextMyContext
    instanceVariableNames:
     'bank fromAccountNumber toAccountNumber'
    category: 'BB5Bank-Context'
```

"role binding methods"
BB5MoneyTransferContext>>MyContext
```
    ^self
```
BB5MoneyTransferContext>>TransferMoneySink
```
    ^bank findAccount: toAccountNumber
```
BB5MoneyTransferContext>>TransferMoneySource
```
    ^bank findAccount: fromAccountNumber
```

"access methods"
BB5MoneyTransferContext>>bank: bnk
```
    bank := bnk.
```

```
BB5MoneyTransferContext>>fromAccountNumber: aFromNumber
    fromAccountNumber := aFromNumber.
BB5MoneyTransferContext>>toAccountNumber: aToNumber
    toAccountNumber :=  aToNumber.


"trigger methods"
BB5MoneyTransferContext>>transfer: amount
          fromAccount: from toAccount: to
    self
        fromAccountNumber: from;
        toAccountNumber: to;
        executeInContext: [self transferAmount: amount].
            "Dive into role interaction, start in"
            "role 'MyContext' which is identical to self"


"role structure methods"
BB5MoneyTransferContext class>>roleStructure
    ^IdentityDictionary new
        at: #TransferMoneySource put: #(#TransferMoneySink );
        at: #TransferMoneySink put: #();
        at: #MyContext put: #(#TransferMoneySource );
        yourself.
BB5MoneyTransferContext class>>roleNames
    ^ self roleStructure keys
```

F.4   Interaction (RoleTrait) Perspective

Note: Traits are named by concatenating the Context name with the Role name.

F.4.1   BB5MoneyTransferContextTransferMoneySource

```
BB1RoleTrait named: #BB5MoneyTransferContextTransfer
MoneySource
    roleContextClassName: #BB5MoneyTransferContext
    category: 'BB5Bank-Traits'


BB5MoneyTransferContextTransferMoneySource>>transfer: amount
    self withdraw: amount.
    (BB5MoneyTransferContext playerForRole:
```

```
                   #TransferMoneySink) deposit: amount.


BB5MoneyTransferContextTransferMoneySource>>
    withdraw: amount
    self balance < amount ifTrue:
        [self notify: 'Insufficient funds'. ^self].
    self decrease: amount.
```

F.4.2 BB5MoneyTransferContextMyContext

```
BB1RoleTrait named: #BB5MoneyTransferContextMyContext
    roleContextClassName: #BB5MoneyTransferContext
    category: 'BB5Bank-Traits'


"role methods"
BB5MoneyTransferContextMyContext>>transferAmount: amount
    (BB5MoneyTransferContext playerForRole:
         #TransferMoneySource) transfer: amount
```

F.4.3 BB5MoneyTransferContextTransferMoneySink

```
BB1RoleTrait named: #BB5MoneyTransferContextTransfer
MoneySink
    roleContextClassName: #BB5MoneyTransferContext
    category: 'BB5Bank-Traits'


"MoneySink role methods"
BB5MoneyTransferContextTransferMoneySink>>deposit: amount
    self increase: amount.
```

F.5 Support Perspective (Infrastructure Classes)

F.5.1 BB1Context (common superclass for all contexts)

```
Object subclass: #BB1Context
    instanceVariableNames: 'data roleMap mergedContext'
```

```
        category: 'BB1IDE-Support'


"execution methods"
BB1Context>>executeInContext: aBlock
    " Put this context on the execution stack. "
    self reselectObjectsForRoles.
    ^ aBlock
        on: self
        do: [:ex | ex]


"data manipulation methods"
BB1Context>>reselectObjectsForRoles
    | messName mCtx mRoleMap |
    roleMap := IdentityDictionary new.
    self class roleNames
        do: [:roleName |
            self roleMap
                at: roleName
                put: (self
                    perform: roleName
                    ifNotUnderstood: [nil])]


"runtime services (static methods)"
BB1Context class>>currentContexts
    | myInstances ctx |
    myInstances := OrderedCollection new.
    ctx := thisContext." Squeak context, not DCI context!! "
    " move down the stack "
    [ctx := ctx findNextHandlerContextStarting.
    (ctx notNil and: [(ctx tempAt: 1) class == self])
        ifTrue: [myInstances addLast: (ctx tempAt: 1)].
    ctx notNil]
        whileTrue: [ctx := ctx sender].
    ^ myInstances


BB1Context class>>playerForRole: roleName
    self currentContexts
        do: [:contextb |
            (contextb includesKey: roleName)
                ifTrue: [^ contextb at: roleName].
            nil].
    self error: 'role named: #' , roleName , ' not found'.
    ^ nil
```

F.5.2 BB1RoleTrait (all RoleTraits are instances of this class)

This class is part of the DCI infrastructure for compiling RoleMethods etc. The name of a Role Trait is the concatenation: **ContextName, RoleName**

```
Trait subclass: #BB1RoleTrait
    instanceVariableNames: 'roleContextClassName'
    category: 'BB1IDE-Support'
```

BB1RoledTrait methods, including a spacial compiler for Role Methods, are not shown here.

Bibliography

(Adams et al 1998) Adams, Michael, James Coplien, Robert Gamoke, Robert Hanmer, Fred Keeve, and Keith Nicodemus. Fault-tolerant telecommunication system patterns. In Linda Rising, ed., The Patterns Handbook: Techniques, Strategies, and Applications. Cambridge University Press, January 1998, 189–202.

(Adolph et al 2002) Adolph, Steve, Paul Bramble, Alistair Cockburn, and Andy Pols. Patterns for effective use cases. Reading, MA: Addison-Wesley, 2002.

(Alexander 1974) Alexander, Christopher. Notes on the Synthesis of Form. Oxford University Press, paperback edition, 1974.

(Alexander 1979) Alexander, Christopher. The Timeless Way of Building. Oxford: Oxford University Press, 1979.

(Allen and Henn 2006) Allen, Thomas J., and Gunter Henn. The organization and architecture of innovation: Managing the flow of technology. Oxford: Butterworth-Heinemann, 2006.

(Auer and Miller 2002) Auer, Ken, and Roy Miller. Extreme programming applied: playing to win. Pearson Education, 2002.

(Austin et al 1998) Austin, S., Baldwin, A., Li, B., and Waskett, P. Analytical Design Planning Technique (ADePT): a dependency structure matrix tool to schedule the building design process. Construction Management and Economics, December 1999.

(Ballard 2000) Ballard, Glenn. Positive vs. negative iteration in design. From URL www.leanconstruction.org/pdf/05.pdf, accessed 18 July 2008.

(Beck 1991) Beck, Kent. Think like an object. In UNIX Review, September 1991, ff. 41.

(Beck 1994) Beck, Kent. Simple Smalltalk testing: with patterns. Smalltalk Report 4, October 1994.

(Beck 1999) Beck, Kent. Extreme programming explained: Embrace change. Reading, MA: Addison-Wesley, 1999.

(Beck et al 2001) Beck, Kent, et al. The Agile Manifesto. `www.agilemanifesto.org`, February 2001, accessed 15 November 2008.

(Beck 2002) Beck, Kent. Test-driven development by example. Addison-Wesley, 2002.

(Beck 2005) Beck, Kent. Extreme programming explained, 2nd edition. Pearson Publications, 2005.

(Beck and Gamma 1998) Beck, Kent, and Eric Gamma. Test infected: Programmers love writing tests. Java Report, July 1998.

(Beyer and Holtzblatt 1998) Beyer, Hugh, and Karen Holtzblatt. Contextual design. San Francisco: Morgan Kauffman, 1998.

(Bjørnvig 2003) Bjørnvig, Gertrud. Patterns for the role of use cases. Proceedings of EuroPLoP '03, p. 890.

(Boehm 1976) Boehm, B.W. Software engineering. IEEE Trans. Computers. C-25 (Dec. 1976), 1226–1241.

(Boehm 1981) Boehm, Barry W. Software engineering economics. Englewood Cliffs, NJ: Prentice-Hall, 1981.

(Boehm 2009) Boehm, Barry. Balancing agility and architecture. Keynote at JaOO 2009. Aalborg, Denmark, 5 October, 2009.

(Boehm and Turner 2003) Boehm, Barry, and Richard Turner. Balancing agility and discipline: A guide for the perplexed. Addison-Wesley Professional, 2003.

(Booch 2006) Booch, Grady. Patterns, Patterns and more Patterns. 2 March, 2006. URL `www.handbookofsoftwarearchitecture.com/index.jsp?page=Blog&part=2006`, accessed 13 November 2009.

(Brand 1999) Brand, Stewart. The Clock of the Long Now. New York: Basic Books, 1999.

(Brandt 1995) Brandt, Stewart. How buildings learn: what happens to them after they're built. New York: Penguin, 1995.

(Buschmann et al 1996) Pattern-oriented software architecture volume 1: a system of patterns. Wiley, 1996.

(Buschmann, Henney and Schmidt 2007a) Buschmann, Frank, Kevlin Henney and Douglas C. Schmidt. Pattern-oriented software architecture volume 4: a pattern language for distributed computing. Wiley, 2007.

(Buschmann, Henney and Schmidt 2007b) Buschmann, Frank, Kevlin Henney and Douglas C. Schmidt. Pattern-oriented software architecture volume 5: on patterns and pattern languages. Wiley, 2007.

(Buxton and Randell 1969) Buxton, J. N., and Randell, B., eds. Software engineering techniques: Report of a conference sponsored by the NATO Science Committee, Rome, Italy, 27–31 Oct. 1969. Brussels: NATO, Scientific Affairs Division.

(Byers 2008a) Byers, David. Personal E-mail correspondence, 7 October 2008.

(Chelimsky et al 2010) Chelimsky, David, et al. The RSpec book: Behaviour driven development with Rspec, Cucumber, and friends. Pragmatic Bookshelf, 2010.

(Cockburn 1999) Cockburn, Alistair. Software development as a cooperative game. Talk at 1999 ObjectActive conference, MidRange, South Africa, 1999. URL http://alistair.cockburn.us/Software+development +as+a+cooperative+game, accessed 7 November 2009.

(Cockburn 2001) Cockburn, Alistair. Writing effective use cases. Reading, MA: Addison-Wesley, 2001.

(Cockburn 2007) Cockburn, Alistair. Agile software development: The cooperative game, 2nd ed. Reading, MA: Addison-Wesley 2007.

(Cockburn 2008) Cockburn, Alistair. Why I still use use cases. 9 January, 2009. URL http://alistair.cockburn.us/Why+I+still+use+use+ cases, accessed 18 November 2009.

(Cohn 2004) Cohn, Mike. User stories applied: For agile software development. Reading MA: Addison Wesley, 2004.

(Cohn 2010) Cohn, Mike. Succeeding with Agile: Software Development using Scrum. Reading, MA: Addison-Wesley, © 2010.

(Constantine and Lockwood 1999) Constantine, Larry, and Lucy A. D. Lockwood. Software for use: a practical guide to models and methods of usage-centered design. Reading, MA: Addison-Wesley, 1999.

(Coplien and Devos 2000) Coplien, James, and Martine Devos. Architecture as metaphor. Proceedings of the World Multiconference on Systemics, Cybernetics and Informatics, Orlando, Florida, Institute of Informatics and Systemics, pp. 737–742., July 24, 2000.

(Coplien and Erickson 1994) Coplien, James O., and Jon Erickson. Examining the software development process. Dr. Dobbs Journal of Software 19(11), October 1994, pp. 88–95.

(Coplien and Henney 2008) Coplien, James, and Kevlin Henney. Agile architecture is not fragile architecture. Presentation at QCon 2008, 10 June, 2008, London. www.infoq.com/presentations/Agile- Architecture-Is-Not-Fragile-Architecture-James-Coplien- Kevlin-Henney, accessed 23 August 2009.

(Coplien, Hofmann and Weiss 1998) James Coplien, Daniel Hoffman, David Weiss. Commonality and variability in software engineering. IEEE Software 15(6), November/December 1998, p. 40.

(Conway 1986) Conway, Melvin E. How do committees invent? Datamation 14(4), April, 1968.

(Coplien 1992) Coplien, James O. Advanced C++ programming styles and idioms. Reading MA: Addison-Wesley, 1992.

(Coplien 1996) Coplien, James O. A curiously recurring template pattern. In Stanley B. Lippman, editor, C++ Gems, 135–144. Cambridge University Press, New York, 1996.

(Coplien 1998) Coplien, James O. Multi-paradigm design for C++ Reading, MA: Addison-Wesley, 1998.

(Coplien and Harrison 2004) Coplien, James, and Neil Harrison. Organizational patterns of agile software development. Upper Saddle River, NJ: Prentice-Hall/Pearson, July 2004.

(Coplien and Sutherland 2009) Coplien, James and Jeff Sutherland. Scrum sensibilities. Scrum Gathering, Orlando, Florida, 16 March 2009. URL `www.scrumalliance.org/resources/618`, accessed 13 November 2009.

(Coplien et al 1998) Coplien, James O., Daniel M. Hoffman and David M. Weiss. Commonality and variability in software engineering. IEEE Software, 15(6), November/December 1998, pp. 37–45.

(Cross 1984) Cross, Nigel, ed. Developments in design methodology. Chichester, UK: Wiley, 1984.

(Dahl and Nygaard 1966) Dahl, Ole-Johan, and Kristen Dahl and Nygaard. SIMULA – an Algol-based simulation language. In D. E. Knuth, ed. Communications of the ACM 9(9), August/September 1966.

(Darke 1979) Darke, J. The primary generator and the design process. Design Studies, 1(1):36–44., 1979.

(Davidson 1999) Davidson, E.J. Joint application design (JAD) in practice. Journal of Systems & Software, 45(3), 1999, 215–223.

(DuBois 2006) DuBois, Paul. Using the Ruby DBI module. URL `www.kitebird.com/articles/ruby-dbi.html`, 28 November 2006, accessed 27 December 2009.

(Eisenecker and Czarnecki 2000) Eisenecker, Ulrich, and Krysztof Czarnecki. Generative programming: Methods, techniques and applications. Reading, MA: Addison-Wesley, 2000.

(Evans 2003) Evans, Eric. Domain-driven design: tackling complexity in the heart of software. Addison-Wesley: 2003.

(Fowler 2006) Fowler, Martin. Using an agile software process with offshore development. Web site. `http://martinfowler.com/articles/agileOffshore.html` July 2006, accessed 26 September 2009.

(Fuhrer 2008) Fuhrer, Phillip. Personal E-mail conversation of 17 October 2008.

(Fraser et al 2003) Fraser, Steven, Kent Beck, Bill Caputo, Tim Mackinnon, James Newkirk and Charlie Pool. Test driven development (TDD). In M. Marchesi and G. Succi, eds., XP 2003, LNCS 2675, pp. 459–462., 2003. © Springer-Verlag, Berlin and Heidelberg, 2003.

(Gabriel 1998) Gabriel, Richard P. Patterns of software: Tales from the software community. New York: Oxford University Press, 1998.

(Gamma et al 2005) Gamma, Eric, et al. Design patterns: elements of re-usable object-oriented software. Reading, Ma: Addison-Wesley, © 2005.

(Glass 2006) Glass, Robert L. The Standish Report: Does it really describe a software crisis? CACM 49(8), August 2006, pp. 15–16.

(Graham 2003) Graham, Ian. A pattern language for web usability. Reading, MA: Addison-Wesley, © 2003.

(Greening 2010) Greening, Dan. Enterprise Scrum: Scaling Scrum to the executive level. Kauai, Hawaii: HICSS 2010, January 2010.

(Hanmer 2007) Hanmer, Robert S. Patterns for fault tolerant software. John Wiley, 2007.

(Henning and Vinovski 1999) Henning, Michi, and Steve Vinoski. Advanced CORBA® programming with C++. Reading, MA: Addison-Wesley, © 1999.

(Hen-tov 2009) Hen-tov, Atzmon. E-mail correspondence of 12 November 2009.

(IEEE1471 2000) IEEE recommended practice for architectural description of software-intensive systems. ANSI/IEEE 1471-2007, ISO/IEC 42010: 2007.

(Jacobsson 1992) Jacobsson, Ivar. Object-oriented software engineering: A use-case driven approach. Reading, MA: Addison-Wesley, 1992.

(Janis 1971) Janis, Irving L. Groupthink. Psychology Today, November 1971, 43–46, 74–76.

(Janzen and Saledian 2008) Janzen and Saledian, Does test-driven development really improve software design quality? IEEE Software 25(2), March/April 2008, pp. 77–84.

(Jeffries, Anderson and Hendrickson 2001) Jeffries, Ron, Ann Anderson and Chet Hendrickson. Extreme programming installed. Reading, MA: Addison-Wesley, 2001.

(Kay 1972) Kay, Alan. A personal computer for children of all ages. Xerox Palo Alto Research Center, 1972.

(Kerth 2001) Kerth, Norman L. Project retrospectives: A handbook for team reviews. Dorset House Publishing Company, 2001.

(Kircher and Jain 2004) Kircher, Michael, and Prashant Jain. Pattern-oriented software architecture volume 3: patterns for resource management. Wiley, 2004.

(Knauber et al 2002) Knauber et al. Quantifying product line benefits. In F. van der Linden, ed., Lecture Notes on Computer Science 2290, PFE-4 2001. Springer-Verlag, 2002, p. 16.1.

(Kruchten 1999)   Kruchten, Philippe. The Software architect, and the software architecture team. In P. Donohue, ed., Software Architecture. Boston: Kluwer Academic Publishers, pp. 565–583.

(Kruchten, Capilla and Dueñas 2009) Kruchten, Philippe, Rafael Capilla, Juan Carlos Dueñas, The decision view's role in software architecture Practice. *IEEE Software* 26(2), Mar./Apr. 2009, pp. 36–42.

(Laurel 1993)   Laurel, Brenda. Computers as theatre. Reading, MA: Addison-Wesley, 1993.

(Lieberherr 1996)   Lieberherr, Karl J. Adaptive object-oriented software: The Demeter method with propagation patterns. PWS Publishing Company, Boston, 1996. ISBN 0-534-94602-X, available at `www.ccs.neu.edu/research/demeter`.

(Lientz, Swanson and Tompkins 1978) Lientz, B.P., E.B. Swanson and G.E. Tompkins. Characteristics of application software maintenance. Communications of the ACM 21(6), 1978, pp. 466–471.

(Liker 2004) Liker, Jeffrey K. The Toyota Way. McGraw-Hill, 2004.

(Liskov 1986) Liskov, Barbara. Data abstraction and hierarchy. SIGPLAN Notices 23(5), May 1986.

(Martin, Biddle, and Noble 2004) Martin, Angela, Robert Biddle and James Noble. The XP customer role in practice: Three case studies. Proceedings of the Second Annual Agile Development Conference, 2004.

(Mak 2008) Mak, Gary. Spring recipes: A problem-solution approach. New York: Apress (Springer-Verlag), 2008.

(Martin 2004)   Martin, Angela. Exploring the XP customer role, part II. Proceedings of the 5th annual conference on Extreme Programming and Agile Processes in Software Engineering, Jutta Eckstein and Hubert Baumeister, eds.

(Martin 2009) Martin, Robert C., et al. Clean code: A handbook of agile software craftsmanship. Reading, MA: Pearson, © 2009.

(Meyer 1994)   Meyer, Bertrand. Object-oriented software construction (second edition). Prentice-Hall, 1994.

(Moo 1986) Moon, David A. Object-oriented programming with Flavors. Proceedings of OOPSLA 1986. ACM Software, 1986.

(Moore 2001) Moore, Thomas. Original Self. New York: Perennial, 2001.

(Nani 2006) Nani, Christel. Sacred Choices: Thinking outside the tribe to heal your spirit. Harmony, 2006.

(Naur and Randell 1968) Naur, Peter and B. Randell, eds. Proceedings of the NATO conference on software engineering. Nato Science Committee, October 1968.

(Neighbors 1980) Neighbors, J. M. Software construction using components. Tech Report 160. Department of Information and Computer Sciences, University of California. Irvine, CA. 1980.

(Neighbours 1989) Neighbors, J. M. Draco: A method for engineering reusable software systems. In Biggerstaff, T. J. and A. J. Perlis, eds., Software Reusability, Vol. 1: Concepts and Models.ACM Frontier Series. Reading, AM: Addison-Wesley, 1989, Ch. 12, pp. 295–319.

(Nielsen 2005) Nielsen, Jakob. Usability of web sites for teenagers. Alertbox. URL `www.useit.com/alertbox/teenagers.html`,31 January 2005, accessed 10 January 2010.

(NOAD 2007) New Oxford American Dictionary, 2007.

(North 2006) North, Dan. Introducing BDD. Better Software, March 2006.

(Noble and Weir 2000) Noble, James, and Charles Weir. Small memory software: patterns for systems with limited memory. Reading, MA: Addison-Wesley, 2000.

(Odersky et al 2008) Odersky, Martin, Lex Spoon and Bill Venners. Programming in Scala: A comprehensive step-by-step guide. Artima, 2008, `www.artima.com/shop/programming_in_scala`, accessed 4 October 2008.

(Olesen 1998) Olesen, Dan R. Developing user interfaces. San Francisco: Morgan Kaufmann, 1998.

(Parnas 1978) Parnas, David. Designing software for ease of extension and contraction. Proceedings of the 3rd International Conference on Software Engineering. Atlanta, GA., May 1978, pp. 264–277.

(Parr 2007) Parr, Terrence. The definitive Antlr reference: building domain-specific languages. Pragmatic Bookshelf, 2007.

(Patton 2009) Patton, Jeff. Telling better user stories: Mapping the path to success. Better Software 11(7), November/December 2009, pp 24–29. URL `www.nxtbook.com/nxtbooks/sqe/bettersoftware_1109/index.php?startid=24`, accessed 12 November 2009.

(Petroski 1992) Petroski, Henry. Form follows failure. Technology Magazine 8(2), Fall 1992.

(Poppendieck and Poppendieck 2006) Poppendieck, Mary and Tom Poppendieck. Implementing lean software development: From concept to cash. Reading, MA: Addison-Wesley, 2006.

(Price and Demurjian 1997) Price, Margaretha W., and Steven A. Demurjian. Analyzing and measuring reusability in object-oriented design. OOPSLA '97 Proceedings, pp. 22–23.

(Qi4j 2006) Qi4j in 10 Minutes. `www.Qi4j.org/163.html`, accessed 2 October 2008.

(Ramnivas 2003) Laddad, Ramnivas. AspectJ in action. Manning Publications, 2003.

(Raskin 2000)   Raskin, Jeff. The humane interface: New directions for designing interactive systems. Reading, MA: Addison-Wesley, 2000.

(Reenskaug, Wold, and Lehne 1996) Reenskaug, Trygve, P. Wold and O. A. Lehne. Working with objects: The OOram software engineering method. Greenwich: Manning Publications, 1995.

(Reenskaug 2003)   Reenskaug, Trygve. The Model-View-Controller (MVC): Its past and present. From `http://heim.ifi.uio.no/trygver/ 2003/javazone-jaoo/MVC_pattern.pdf`, accessed 10 October 2008. August 2003.

(Reenskaug 2007)   Reenskaug, Trygve. BabyUML: A laboratory for exploring a new discipline of programming. 2007. URL `http://heim. ifi.uio.no/~trygver/themes/babyuml/babyuml-index.html`, accessed 14 November 2009.

(Reenskaug 2008)   Reenskaug, Trygve. The common sense of object-oriented programming. URL `http://heim.ifi.uio.no/~trygver/ 2008/commonsense.pdf`, September 2008, accessed 3 January 2010.

(Reeves 2005)   Reeves, Jack W. What is software design – 13 years later. In developer.* Magazine, 23 February 2005. URL `www. developerdotstar.com/mag/articles/reeves_13yearslater.html`, accessed 12 November 2009.

(Riehle and Züllighoven 1995)   Riehle, Dirk, and Heinz Züllighoven. A pattern language for tool construction, integration based on the tools, materials metaphor. In Pattern Languages of Program Design.Edited by James O. Coplien, Douglas C. Schmidt. Addison-Wesley, 1995. Chapter 2, pages 9–42.

(Rybczynski 1987) Rybczynski, Witold. Home: A short history of an idea. New York: Penguin, 1987.

(Rybczynski 1989) Rybczynski, Witold. The most beautiful house in the world. New York: Penguin, 1989.

(Schärli et al 2003) Schärli, Nathanael, Stéphane Ducasse, Oscar Nierstrasz and Andrew Black. Traits: Composable units of behavior. Proceedings of European Conference on Object-Oriented Programming (ECOOP'03), LNCS, vol. 2743, Springer Verlag, July 2003, pp. 248–274.

(Schmidt et al 2000) Schmidt, Douglas, Michael Stal, Hans Rohnert, and Frank Buschmann. Pattern-oriented software architecture volume 2: patterns for concurrent and distributed objects. Wiley, 2000.

(Shalloway, Beaver and Trott 2009) Shalloway, Alan, Guy Beaver, and James R. Trott. Lean-Agile software development: achieving enterprise agility. Reading, MA: Addison-Wesley Professional, 2009.

(Shrdlu 2009) SHRDLU. Wikipedia. URL `http://en.wikipedia.org/wiki/SHRDLU`, 10 June 2009, accessed 7 November 2009.

(Siniaalto and Abrahamsson 2007a) Siniaalto, Maria, and Pekka Abrahamsson. Comparative study on the effect of test-driven development on program design and test coverage. ESEM 2007. First international conference on empirical software engineering and measurement, 20-21 September 2007, pp. 275–284.

(Siniaalto and Abrahamsson 2007b) Siniaalto, Maria, and Pekka Abrahamsson. Does test-driven development improve the program code? Alarming results from a comparative case study. Proceedings of Cee-Set 2007, 10–12 October 2007, Poznan, Poland.

(Smiles 1860) Smiles, Samuel. Self-help: with illustrations of character, conduct and perseverance. New York: Harper & Brothers, 1860. Published as Self-Help (Peter W. Sinnema, ed.) New York: Oxford University Press, 2002.

(Snowden 2009) Snowden, Dave. Leadership, self-organization and metaphor. Scan-Agile Conference, Helsinki, Finland, 15 October 2009.

(Snowden and Boone 2007) Snowden and Boone. A Leader's framework for decision making. Harvard Business Review, Nov. 2007.

(Standish Group 1995) The Standish Group report: Chaos. T23E-T10E Standish Group Report, © 1995, `http://www.scs.carleton.ca/~beau/PM/Standish-Report.html`. `http://www.cs.nmt.edu/~cs328/reading/Standish.pdf`, accessed 31 October 2009.

(Stein, Lieberman, and Ungar 1989) Stein, Lynn Andrea, Henry Lieberman and David Ungar. A shared view of sharing: The Treaty of Orlando. Addendum to the OOPSLA '87 Conference Proceedings, ACM Press, 1989, 43–44.

(Stevens, Myers and Constantine 1974) Stevens, W. P., Myers, G. J., and Constantine, L. L. Structured design. IBM Systems Journal 13(2), 1974, pp. 115–139.

(Sutherland 2003) Sutherland, Jeff, SCRUM: Another way to think about scaling a project. 11 March 2003, accessed 28 November 2007. URL `http://jeffsutherland.org/scrum/2003_03_01_archive.html`.

(Sutherland 2007) Sutherland, Jeff. Origins of Scrum. July 2007, accessed 20 July 2008, `http://jeffsutherland.com/scrum/2007/07/origins-of-scrum.html`.

(Sutherland 2008) Sutherland, Jeff. The First Scrum: Was it Scrum or lean? URL `http://jeffsutherland.com/scrum/2007/11/is-it-scrum-or-lean.html`, August 10, 2008, accessed 10 December, 2008.

(Sutherland 2009) Sutherland, Jeff. Enabling specifications: The key to building Agile systems. URL `http://jeffsutherland.com/scrum/2009/11/enabling-specifications-key-to-building.html`, 25 November 2009, accessed 17 December 2009.

(Swieringa and Wierdsma 1992) Swieringa, Joop, and Andre Wierdsma. Becoming a learning Organization: Beyond the learning curve. Reading, MA: Addison-Wesley, 1992.

(Takeuchi and Nonaka 1986) Takeuchi, Hirotaka, and Ikujiro Nonaka. The New new product development game. Harvard Business Review, Reprint 86116, January-February 1986.

(Tuckman 1965) Tuckman, Bruce W. Developmental sequence in small groups, Psychological Bulletin 63. Washington, D.C.: American Psychological Association, 1965, pp. 384–399.

(Weinberg 1999) Personal interview with Jerry Weinberg, 31 May, 1999.

(Wikipedia 2009) Wikipedia. "Autopoiesis." `http://en.wikipedia.org/wiki/Autopoiesis`. 6 March 2009, accessed 29 March 2009.

(Weiss and Lai 1999) Weiss, David M., and Robert Chi-Tau Lai. Software product-line engineering: A family-based software development process. Addison-Wesley, 1999.

(Wirfs-Brock 1993) Wirfs-Brock, Rebecca. Designing scenarios. Smalltalk Report 3(3), November/December 1993.

(Wirfs-Brock and McKean 2003) Wirfs-Brock, Rebecca, and Alan McKean. Object design: Roles, responsibilities and collaborations. Reading, MA: Addison-Wesley, 2003.

(Womack et al 1991) Womack, James P., Daniel T. Jones, and Daniel Roos. The machine that changed the world: The story of lean production. New York: Harper Perennial, 1991.

(Wu and Wen 2006) Wu, Cheng-Wen, and Xiaoquing Wen. VLSI test principles and architectures: Design for testability. Morgan Kaufmann, 2006.

(Yourdon and Constantine 1975) Yourdon, E., and Constantine, L. L. Structured design. Englewood Cliffs, NJ: Prentice-Hall, 1979; Yourdon Press, 1975.

(Øredev 2008) Panel on domain-driven design. Øredev 2008, Malmø, Sweden, 19 November 2008.

(Østergaard 2008) Østergaard, Jens. Personal E-mail exchange, 8 October, 2008.

Index

abstract base classes (ABCs) 133–7, 146, 202
abstraction 81, 108
AccountHolders 59
ACM OOPSLA conference 115
actors 171, 181, 237
ADAPTER design pattern 125
advocate 54
Agile Manifesto 4, 7, 23
Agile Systems
  principles 3–4
  scope of 8–9
  production 7–10
Algol 233
algorithm 220, 245
algorithmic scaling 144–6
antlr 121
AOP (Aspect-Oriented Programming) 99, 302
APIs 21, 40, 99
application generators 120–2
application-oriented language 121
architect role 42
architectural completeness 152
architectural effort 160
ARCHITECTURE ALSO IMPLEMENTS pattern 53
architecture carryover 128–9
ARCHITECTURE CONTROLS PRODUCT pattern 53
architecture testing 149–52

artifacts 294–7
as-builts 127
'ask five times' exercise 64
Aspect-Oriented Programming (AOP) 99, 302
assertions 137–44
assessment of architecture 160–2
Atomic Event architecture 157, 158, 206–8
  domain objects 221
  form and architecture of 220–6
  object roles, interfaces and the model 221–4
  one-to many mapping of object roles to objects 225–6
  use cases, atomic event architectures and algorithms 224–5
  vs DCI 286–7
autonomy 91
  of third-party software 125–6
autopoietic systems 68

BabyUML environment 268, 269, 275
BabyUML project 301
base class object 104
baseline 179
behavior 45, 245
Behavior Driven Development (BDD) 46, 57, 175
behavior modeling 46
Bell laboratories 88

Printed and bound by CPI Group (UK) Ltd, Croydon, CR0 4YY

27/10/2024

14580378-0002